GOOD THINKING

An Introduction to Logic

GOOD THINKING
▬▬An Introduction to Logic▬▬

Third Edition

GERALD RUNKLE
Southern Illinois University at Edwardsville

Holt, Rinehart and Winston, Inc.

Fort Worth   Chicago   San Francisco   Philadelphia
Montreal   Toronto   London   Sydney   Tokyo

Publisher Ted Buchholz
Acquisitions Editor Jo-Anne Weaver
Project Editor Michele Tomiak/Steve Welch
Production Manager Ken Dunaway
Design Supervisor Vicki McAlindon Horton
Copyeditor Sandra M. Colby
Text Design Delgado Design, Inc.
Cover Design Nancy Turner

Library of Congress Cataloging-in-Publication Data

Runkle, Gerald.
    Good thinking: an introduction to logic/Gerald Runkle;
illustration by Kermit L. Ruyle.—3rd ed.
      p. cm.
    Includes index.
    ISBN 0-03-030707-4
    1. Logic. I. Title.
    BC108.R79   1991
    160—dc20   90–41903
                                        CIP

ISBN 0-03-030707-4

Requests for permission to make copies of any part of the work should be mailed to: Permissions Department, Holt, Rinehart and Winston, Inc., 6277 Sea Harbor Drive, Orlando, Florida 32887.

Address for editorial correspondence: Holt, Rinehart and Winston, Inc., 301 Commerce Street, Suite 3700, Fort Worth, Texas 76102

Address for orders: Holt, Rinehart and Winston, Inc., 6277 Sea Harbor Drive, Orlando, Florida 32887. 1-800-782-4479, or 1-800-433-0001 (in Florida)

Printed in the United States of America

1 2 3 4 090 9 8 7 6 5 4 3 2 1

Holt, Rinehart and Winston, Inc.
The Dryden Press
Saunders College Publishing

To Randy, Liz, and Sarah

Preface to the Third Edition

Changes once again have been made throughout the book in order to clarify the material and provide pertinent examples.

The most significant changes are: (1) The creation of a new chapter called "Introduction to Symbolic Logic." This brings together earlier material on relations and the propositional calculus. What is new is a section on quantificational logic and a section on formal proofs involving relational statements. (2) The addition at the end of the text of answers to the odd-numbered problems in the exercises. Many students and teachers have suggested that the presence of answers would be helpful to students who wished to check their own work. (3) The addition of a "preview" section to most of the chapters. Each of these sections contains introductory remarks, a list of proficiencies to be attained, and a series of "warm-up" questions. (4) The addition of cartoons by Kermit L. Ruyle. It is hoped that his pictures will complement my words in the attempt to explain and illustrate the principles of logic.

The *Instructor's Manual* also contains revisions. Additional exercises (and their answers) may be useful for quizzes and examinations, as well as for classroom problems and discussions.

I am grateful to my colleagues at Southern Illinois University (Edwardsville) and elsewhere who have made suggestions. I am especially indebted to Professor John Barker, who was kind enough to read and comment on several manuscript pages of new material. I am also grateful to my chairperson, Thomas Paxson, and to my dean, David Butler, who have provided the material and facilities needed for completing the revisions.

I would also like to thank the following professors for reviewing the third edition manuscript and providing their comments: Steven Doty (Auburn University), Connie Kagan (University of Oklahoma–Norman), Nathan Oaklander (University of Michigan–Flint), Dr. Robert C. O'Brien (Fordham University), Dr. Clifton Perry (Auburn University), Dr. S. Petty (Indiana University–Purdue University at Indianapolis), Dr. Richard Van Iten (Iowa State University), and Dr. Dann Walker (McLennan Community College).

G. R.

Preface to the Second Edition

Changes have been made throughout the second edition to clarify certain sections and provide more instructive examples. The exercises have been both altered and extended. The material on form and function of sentences, tautology, probability (inductive and mathematical), and Mill's Methods has been re-worked. And, more extensive discussion of some emotional appeals has been provided.

The most signficant additions are: (1) a third subsection ("Mixed Forms") to the section in Chapter 3 called "Molecular Statements"; (2) a fifth subsection ("The Propositional Calculus") to the section in Chapter 6 called "Molecular Forms"; (3) a long chapter called "The Uses of Logic," containing sections entitled "What Does He Know?", "What Can I Claim?", "What Is the Answer?", and "What Should I Do?"

I am grateful to the following professors who made constructive criticisms of the first edition of *Good Thinking:* Charles E. Hornbeck (Keene State College), Wallace Roark (Howard Payne University), Benjamin F. Armstrong, Jr. (University of California at Santa Barbara), Irving Krakow (Camden County College), and Kevin W. Saunders (Northern Michigan University). The latter three also made valuable comments on the revisions. I am also grateful to my colleagues at Southern Illinois University (Edwardsville) who made useful suggestions: Professors John Barker, Edward Hudlin, George William Linden, Margaret Simons, and Robert Wolf. I should also like to thank my chairperson, Thomas Paxson, and dean, Carol Keene, who have mastered the administrative knack of encouraging and assisting their faculty in worthwhile endeavors.

Finally, I should like to acknowledge the consistent support and good advice of David P. Boynton, Philosophy editor at Holt, Rinehart and Winston.

G. R.

Preface to the First Edition

All of us, teachers and students, want to think as well as we can. The theoretical and practical advantages that good thinking has over bad are obvious. Who would not wish to increase his or her ability to reason soundly?

Most colleges and universities offer courses that are designed to do this. These courses carry such names as "Logic," "Critical Thinking," and "Formal Thought." They are usually offered on the lower level—perhaps on the assumption that the sooner students get their reasoning straightened out, the sooner they will begin to excel in their other courses.

This book is offered as a text for such a course. It is designed for undergraduate college students, whatever their major fields of study. It is suitable for the freshmen and sophomore levels at both community colleges and four-year institutions. It presupposes no previous training in logic, philosophy, mathematics, or rhetoric. The text will serve a course that is "terminal" for its students, but it will also lay the groundwork for such advanced courses as deductive logic, symbolic logic, inductive logic, and philosophy of science.

Good Thinking makes no heavy intellectual demands on students, but it does require them to learn to think formally or abstractly. The text provides many concrete examples for which general propositions are stated. If students can understand the principles involved in particular instances or problems, they can apply them to instances and problems they will encounter beyond the covers of this book.

Good Thinking is thus both an "informal" and a "formal" approach to logic. It is informal in the sense that a great deal of attention is paid to such topics as meaning, ambiguity, equivocation, definition, emotional appeals, and induction. The book also takes a formal approach to logic. It provides a formal analysis of statements and the relations between statements, and it presents a formal account of deductive arguments. This formal approach does not, however, carry us very far into the science of symbolic or mathematical logic.

The formal and the informal work together. In the areas of language, induction, and emotional appeals, the formal element is brought out and identified. That is, patterns of thought are recognized; rules and principles are stated. In the areas of statements, relations, and deduction, formal structures are illustrated by a host of examples. Patterns, rules, and principles are presented in the context of genuine statements and actual arguments.

This text provides one hundred exercises. Students may test their understanding of the principles of good thinking by applying them to the several hundred cases presented. Since the exercises require short answers, the instructor can grade them easily and return them promptly to the students. Students should try out their skills before examination time!

The organization of the book is apparent in the detailed Contents section. It proceeds naturally from words to statements, then to the relations between statements. This brings us to the kind of relations that statements have to one another in arguments. Two chapters on deduction and three on induction thus follow. Finally, there is a chapter on substitutes for argument: emotional appeals. The concluding chapter, containing some extended arguments, will be useful to instructors who feel that their students' experience with the shorter arguments presented earlier in the text should be supplemented. The appendix on Venn diagrams will be useful to instructors who like to depict statements, relations between statements, and syllogisms graphically.

Among the unusual featues of this book are: (1) The "informal fallacies" are not all presented in the same chapter. Fallacies of ambiguity are discussed in the chapter on words, in light of the discussion of meaning. Fallacies of induction are discussed at appropriate places in the chapters on induction. Fallacies of relevance are discussed in the chapter on emotional appeals. Each fallacy is taken up precisely at the point where it becomes most relevant. (2) Categorical and molecular statements are not separated from one another in major sections of the book. The basic categorical and molecular forms are presented in the same chapter—"these are the forms that statements exhibit." Tautology, self-contradiction, compatibility, equivalence, contradiction, and "immediate inference" are then shown to be concepts applicable to both kinds of statements. (3) An elementary account of the logic of relations is provided, including their properties and their function in deductive arguments. (4) Mathematical probability is shown to differ from inductive probability. The calculation of mathematical probability is thus presented as a kind of deductive inference. (5) The argument from analogy is presented in the chapter on generalization, for it is from generalizations that arguments from analogy derive whatever force they possess. (6) The chapter on causal relations deals not only with finding the cause, but also with finding the effect. (7) Since any emotion may be the basis for a fallacious argument, the chapter on emotional appeals contains a somewhat longer list of such appeals than is customary. (8) The conclusion presents brief discussions of some of the philosophical issues suggested by the logic of deductive and inductive inference. It also cites some other philosophical questions raised by logic in general. In addition it provides a bibliography for further study in logic. (9) The chapter on Venn diagrams deals with statements as well as syllogisms. It utilizes the "universe of discourse" concept in order to widen the applicability of the Venn approach. It is in this chapter that the question of "existential import" is dealt with and the traditional square of opposition "corrected." (10) Each chapter is divided into parts. Each part (except those in the Introduction) is devided into sections. At the close of each section (or part) there is a "Concluding Summary." In the Conclusion there is an outline-summary of the errors and fallacies discussed in the book.

* * * * * * * *

It is my pleasure to express my thanks to many of the people who helped me bring this book to completion.

I am grateful to several of my colleagues in the Department of Philosophical Studies at Southern Illinois University at Edwardsville. Professor John Barker and Ronald Glossop gave valuable advice. Professor Galen Pletcher read several sections of the manuscript and was especially generous with his time and counsel.

I am also indebted to the following professors who read and commented on the manuscript: John H. Dreher (University of Southern California), Dorothy Grover (University of Illinois, Chicago Circle), Henry W. Johnston, Jr. (Pennsylvania State University), Philip Kitcher (University of Vermont), Virginia Klenk (West Virginia University), David M. Rosenthal (City University of New York), John D. Schettler (Palomar College), Beatrice Stegeman (State Community College, East St. Louis).

The deficiencies that remain in *Good Thinking* must be attributed to the author however, rather than to these astute commentators.

I wish to express my appreciation for the consistent support provided me by my department chairperson, Professor G. William Linden, and by my deans, Professors Dale Bailey and Carol Keene. I am grateful to Southern Illinois University at Edwardsville for the grant of a sabbatical leave during the winter and spring quarters of 1976; it was then that I wrote the first draft.

Gratitude must also be expressed to Doris Franzi and her team of competent and cooperative workers in the stenographic pool of the School of Humanities.

Andrew Askin and Jeanette Ninas Johnson of Holt, Rinehart and Winston have, in their different ways, been encouraging, helpful, and patient.

Finally, I want to thank Mike Royko and the following publishers for permission to quote from works covered by their copyrights: Cambridge University Press, Ernest Benn, Ltd., Houghton Mifflin Company, The Macmillan Publishing Company, McGraw-Hill Book Company, Prentice-Hall, Inc., and the Reader's Digest Association. To all authors whom I have quoted (and to their publishers), I express my thanks.

G. R.

Contents

3. STATEMENTS

4. RELATIONS BETWEEN STATEMENTS

5. DEDUCTION: SYLLOGISM

6. MORE DEDUCTIVE INFERENCES

7. INTRODUCTION TO SYMBOLIC LOGIC

8. INDUCTION: GENERALIZATION

9. INDUCTION: CAUSAL RELATIONS

10. INDUCTION: HYPOTHESES

11. SEDUCTION: EMOTIONAL APPEALS

12. THE USES OF LOGIC

GOOD THINKING
An Introduction to Logic

Chapter 1

Introduction

GOOD THINKING

Good thinking has a signal advantage over bad thinking. It is more likely to lead us to truth, and truth is surely preferable to error. Good thinking permits us to discover what was the case in the past, what is the case in the present, and what will be the case in the future. It assures us that Caesar crossed the Rubicon, that no poodles are non-dogs, and that the sun will rise in the east tomorrow. Good thinking helps us to distinguish fact from fancy.

Bad thinking may on occasion lead us to truth also, but this would be accidental. Harry may buy a used car because the salesman has a firm handshake. The car may turn out to be a ''good buy,'' but Harry was very lucky in this instance. He will be more often disappointed if he continues to act on the assumption that firm handshakes mean honesty. Bad thinking is undependable.

Good thinking does not always lead us to truth. A careful coach may think very deeply about the best way to defend against a certain opponent, then see that team score five touchdowns against him. But good thinking is by definition that activity of the mind which is directed toward truth. It may sometimes miss its goal entirely. But it is the indispensable means for comprehending what is what. The best warrant for our beliefs is the quality of thought behind them. If truth is preferable to error, we must prefer thinking well to thinking badly.

Good thinking has its rivals. Some people profess to prefer intuition, instinct, faith, or authority to good thinking. These also, it is said, lead to truth. But their proponents must face up to certain questions: *How* does this other means lead to truth? *Under what circumstances* does it work, is it dependable? *Why* should we have confidence in it? Answers must appeal to our sense of what is reasonable. They must themselves be instances of good thinking. If intuition is indeed a source of truth, that fact must rationally be established. If it is, intuition (under specified circumstances) would itself be in the realm of good thinking. If a rational justification

1

can be provided for accepting certain beliefs on authority, then reliance on authority in certain situations would be a case of good thinking. Whatever value "alternative" approaches may have consists in their use under conditions specified by good thinking. Good thinking is indispensable whenever truth is our object.

Truth not only is valuable in itself, but it also has enormous practical value. It satisfies our curiosity to know that the chlorine content of the water is .016 percent, but if we are thinking of taking a swim in it, it is a useful fact as well. If we want to plan wisely, if we want to reach our objectives, if we want our actions to be successful, we must know certain truths about ourselves and that corner of the universe in which we perform. The *informed* investor, the *understanding* suitor, the *enlightened* reformer, and the *knowledgeable* basketball player will do better in their fields of endeavor than will their opposites (other things being equal). There is thus a practical advantage as well as a theoretical one in having true beliefs.

Aristotle called man "a rational animal." Most of the time, most of us think well (or at least adequately). But sometimes we do not. We may be tired or inattentive and hold inconsistent points of view. We may, while in the grip of a strong emotion, jump to conclusions. We may be confused by language and fall into verbal traps. We may be victimized by an unprincipled politician or advertiser who is more concerned to persuade us than to inform us. We may lose our bearings in unfamiliar or "difficult" material where customary beliefs are not present to help us out. It is in situations like these that we need explicit principles which distinguish good thought from bad. The purpose of this book is to bring to the fore those principles that we assume unconsciously when we are thinking well.

What exactly, is the nature of good thinking? We may answer with synonyms like 'reasonable,' 'critical,' and 'logical,' but these merely substitute one term for another. What does rationality really consist in?

It consists, in the first place, in being aware of the nature of *words*. What and how can they mean? What is the meaning of 'meaning'? How can the fact that words have two or more meanings help us and how can it hurt or deceive us? What are the purposes of definition and what kinds of definition are there? What are ambiguity and vagueness and how can they be dealt with?

The basic unit of speech and thought is the word. If we are not masters of the word, qua word, all that is composed of words will threaten us. Statements and arguments will hold us in thrall. We will be deflected from truth by confusions that are merely verbal. Before we can determine whether we *know,* we must first be clear on what we *mean.*

How old can bread be and still be *fresh?* If that dog is his and is a mother, does that mean that it is *his mother?* What does it mean to say that the announcer will return with *more important news?* Why is William so sure that all women are *bad drivers?* Is a fast turtle, since it is an animal, also a *fast animal?* Why do not three good acts necessarily add up to one good play?

The search after truth is peculiar to man.

—*Cicero,* De Officiis

The object, then, of the next chapter is to state the principles that help us to keep words in their place. We must know how they behave so that we can make them perform for us instead of against us. Knowledge of how words may be used assists us in the quest for truth. Knowledge of how they may be misused saves us from error.

The focus is shifted in the third chapter from words to sentences into which they have been combined. Sentences are found to serve various functions. Some express feelings, some ask questions, and some direct action. In what sense can we speak of the truth or falsity of sentences? And what kinds of disagreement may be present when two people utter different sentences?

We express our beliefs or judgments about reality in statements. Some statements are simple ("atomic"); some are compound ("molecular"). There are a few forms of each. It is very useful to understand each of the forms that statements may take, for when we do, we will understand the structure of the infinite number of statements that have (or may be translated into) one of these forms. Before we can determine whether we *know,* we must first be clear on what it is that has been *stated.*

Good thinking requires that one know exactly what he (or someone else) has committed himself to when he (or someone else) made that statement. Some statements are necessarily true (tautologies) and some are necessarily false (self-contradictions)—merely by virtue of their forms. But the truth or falsity of most statements is contingent upon the actual state of affairs in the universe. The statement either corresponds to this state of affairs or it does not. The third chapter, in dealing with the ways of making statements (or judgments or assertions) about the universe, is dealing with the ways of being right (true) or wrong (false).

Statements bear certain relations to one another. Any pair of statements is compatible or incompatible, contradictory or non-contradictory, equivalent or non-equivalent. On the basis of what these words mean to you, ask yourself whether each of the following pairs is compatible or incompatible, contradictory or non-contradictory, and equivalent or non-equivalent:

All reptiles are snakes.
All snakes are reptiles.

Some roses are red.
Some roses are not red.

No cats are dogs.
No dogs are cats.

All wars are crimes.
All non-crimes are non-wars.

All fish can swim.
Some fish cannot swim.

No generals are poets.
All poets are generals.

No tools are toys.
Some toys are tools.

No tools are toys and all implements are tools.
Either some tools are toys or some implements are not tools.

If she loves him, then she marries him.
If she marries him, then she loves him.

Stella is rich and good-looking.
Stella is not good-looking.

There should be no doubt in our minds about whether any two given statements (or judgments or beliefs or viewpoints) can be true at the same time, whether they contradict one another, and whether they assert the same thing. The fourth chapter shows how these distinctions may accurately be made. It is the mark of good thinking to recognize precisely what relations exist between any two statements.

Some relations between two statements are such that the one can be derived from the other. Whatever statement (or judgment or viewpoint or belief) one holds, it will point to certain other statements as its necessary implications. Which of these seem to be necessary implications?

All carnations are fragrant; therefore some fragrant things are carnations.

No crows are white; therefore all crows are non-white.

It is not the case that he is intelligent and industrious; therefore he is not intelligent and not industrious.

If wishes were horses, then beggars would ride; therefore if beggars do not ride, then wishes are not horses.

Good thinking requires us to be aware of the implications of what we (or anyone else) asserts.

INFERENCES AND ARGUMENTS

To say that a statement has implications is to say that inferences can be made from it. The fourth chapter thus introduces the important concept of *inference* and gives simple examples of it.

Inference in general consists of going from one or more stated reasons or premises to a stated conclusion of some kind. When this passage from premises to conclusion is warranted or justified, the inference is called *sound* or *valid;* when the passage is not warranted, the inference is called *unsound, invalid,* or *fallacious.*

> *Reason governs the wise man and cudgels the fool.*
> —*H. G. Bohn,* Handbook of Proverbs

Most of what we believe, we have inferred. These beliefs have something to rest on; they have reasons behind them. Are these reasons sufficient? Do they support the conclusion? If our derived beliefs are without adequate reason, they are unreasonable. Most of the rest of this book consists of distinguishing between good inferences and bad inferences, between validity and invalidity. Good thinking recognizes good inferences and employs them. It also recognizes bad inferences but rejects them.

A discourse containing premises and a conclusion and asserting that the latter has been inferred from the former is called an *argument*. The following are arguments:

(1) Since no scientists are actors and all actors are conceited, it follows that no scientists are conceited.

(2) All communists are opposed to private property. All socialists are opposed to private property. Therefore, all socialists are communists.

(3) All birds are mammals and all sparrows are birds. So all sparrows are mammals.

(4) Either Mondale will be a senator after the inauguration or he will be vice-president. It is the case that he will not be a senator. Hence he will be vice-president.

The following is not an argument:

(5) Scientists work long hours in the laboratory. They contribute greatly to our standard of living. Some are employed by universities, while some work for private corporations.

In the first four examples, there is a conclusion, and reasons for it are given. The conclusion is inferred from the reasons. It purports to follow from them. But the fifth example consists of assertions, none of which purports to follow from the others.

Some arguments are better than others. The strength of an argument is based on two things:

1. The truth of the premises (or reasons).
2. The soundness (or validity) of the inference by which the conclusion is derived from them.

Truth and *validity* must always be distinguished. Truth is a relation between the statement and reality. Does the statement correspond to what is the case? Validity is a relation between the premises and the conclusion. Do the premises support the conclusion? The first argument, above, is a very weak argument, for a premise is false and the inference is invalid. The second argument is also weak, for, while the premises are true, the inference is invalid. The third argument is also weak, for, while the inference is valid, one of the premises is false. The fourth argument is

---

No pleasure is comparable to the standing upon the vantage-ground of truth.
—Francis Bacon, Of Truth

strong, for the premises are true (1976) and the inference is valid. The strength of an argument is a matter of degree. The greater claim the premises have to being true and the inference to being sound or valid, the stronger is the argument.[1]

How can we tell whether inferences are sound or unsound (or valid or invalid)? We must first determine whether a given inference is deductive or inductive. In a *deductive* inference, the conclusion purports to follow *necessarily* from the premises; in an *inductive* inference, the premises purport merely to provide *evidence* for the conclusion.

These arguments contain deductive inferences (and are called deductive arguments):

(1) If the experiment were done correctly, a red precipitate would appear. But since a red precipitate did not appear, the experiment was not done correctly.

(2) If the experiment were done correctly, a red precipitate would appear. A red precipitate did appear. Therefore the experiment was done correctly.

These arguments contain inductive inferences (and are called inductive arguments):

(3) This white blue-eyed tomcat is deaf. I have known fourteen other white blue-eyed tomcats, and they were all deaf. A friend of mine tested a Himalayan white blue-eyed tomcat—he was also deaf. A scientist examined thirty white blue-eyed tomcats in Europe. Every one of them was deaf. I conclude that all white blue-eyed tomcats are deaf.

(4) I had a date with an actress last night. Boy, was she conceited. Two years ago I talked with an actress in California, and she was conceited also. I conclude that all actresses are conceited.

In a *good* deductive argument, the conclusion not only purports to follow from the premises, it actually *does*. It is impossible for the premises to be true and the conclusion false; the truth of the premises *guarantees* the truth of the conclusion. When this is the case, we call the deduction *valid;* when it is not the case, we call the deduction *invalid*. (1) above is valid, for the conclusion is actually necessitated by the premises.[2] It could be false only if one or more of the premises is false. (2) above is invalid, for the conclusion is not necessitated by the premises. It is quite possible for it to be false while the premises are true.

The fifth, sixth, and seventh chapters are devoted to deduction. They set forth the principles that distinguish valid from invalid deductive inference. Good thinking recognizes valid deduction and employs it. It also recognizes invalid deduction but rejects it.

In a good inductive argument, there is not only evidence for the conclusion, but it is the kind of evidence that would make the truth of the conclusion *probable*.

---

[1] Some writers employ the word 'sound' to refer to arguments containing true premises and valid inferences. But 'sound' in this book refers to inferences. Arguments that contain true premises and sound inferences are called *strong;* those that do not are called *weak*.

[2] It is to be understood that the expressions '(1),' '(2),' and so forth are not to be construed as parts of the displayed passages; they are rather the names or designators of the passages.

> *If any man can convince me and bring home to me that I do not think or act aright, gladly will I change; for I search after truth, by which man never yet was harmed.*
>
> —*Marcus Aurelius,* Meditations

Unlike the situation in deduction, the premises could be true while the conclusion is false, but a good inductive argument provides reasons for believing that the conclusion is true. The soundness of an inductive inference is thus a matter of degree, ranging from supporting evidence that is almost compelling to evidence that provides a slender basis for conjecture. It is better to call inductive inferences "more or less sound" than to call them "valid" or "invalid." (3) above is an argument that contains a rather sound (this vagueness is unavoidable) inductive inference, while (4) is a very weak argument, since it contains a very unsound inductive inference. We should have more confidence in the first conclusion than in the second, although both could be false.

The eighth, ninth, and tenth chapters are devoted to induction. They set forth the principles that distinguish sound from unsound inductive inference. Good thinking reposes greater confidence in conclusions based on sound induction than in those resulting from unsound induction.

We may call an argument valid or invalid (or sound or unsound) if the inference it contains is valid or invalid (or sound or unsound). Whether we are concerned with deduction or induction, we should try to focus our attention on the *form* of the argument. Just as we seek to master an infinite number of particular statements and their relations (in the third and fourth chapters) by concentrating on a few forms, so too can we master an infinite number of particular arguments by concentrating on a few argument forms. The rules and principles that apply to a given form will apply to all arguments having that form. Any deductive argument, for example, that has this form contains an invalid inference and would be called an *invalid argument:*

All P are M
All S are M
∴ All S are P

Any deductive argument that has this form contains a valid inference and would be called a *valid argument:*

p or q
Not-q
∴ p

Inductive arguments (and the inferences contained in them) will also be judged sound or unsound depending upon the forms they exemplify. Certain formal principles govern the drawing of such inductive conclusions as generalizations, causal statements, and hypotheses.

The eleventh chapter deals not with argument at all, but with substitutes for argument. These substitutes are often effective. They seduce us into accepting "conclusions" for which no reason whatever has been provided. They seek to persuade through emotional appeals rather than to convince with facts. They offer nothing relevant, nothing germane to the truth of the point of view being advanced. A rational person must resist substitutes for argument as resolutely as he resists bad arguments.

Finally, in the twelfth chapter, we will examine the "uses of logic" in acquiring knowledge, making claims, solving problems, and arriving at decisions.

THOUGHT ABOUT THOUGHT, WORDS ABOUT WORDS

'Logic' is from the Greek word, *logos,* which means 'reasoned discourse.' Derivatives from this Greek word are present in such English words as 'sociology,' 'anthropology,' 'psychology,' 'biology.' These disciplines are, respectively, reasoned discourses on society, the individual, the soul, and life. But 'logic' stands alone. Logic is not a reasoned discourse on anything! Quite literally, it is not about any *thing.* It is a case of thought turned back upon itself rather than being objectified in something external. What logic requires is that "thought think about thought," that it observe its own patterns and processes, that it distinguish forms.

It is this abstractness that distinguishes logic from the other disciplines, but which also makes it essential to them. Logic is the science of the sciences ("scientia scientiorum") because its principles, by their very generality, are indispensable to all sciences, and indeed to every enterprise where truth is the object. The most applicable is the most general, the most formal, the most abstract. The challenge for the student of logic lies in the injunction to think about ways of thinking!

'Logos' is sometimes translated as 'the word.' This suggests a somewhat more mundane challenge: that of speaking about speaking, or writing about writing.

Anyone who uses words to refer to other words is obliged to observe certain proprieties. Since throughout this book we will be talking about linguistic expressions (words, letters, symbols, phrases, etc.), this is a good time to set down some of these proprieties that govern us all.

When we refer to a linguistic expression, *as* a linguistic expression, we must use quotation marks (quotes). This indicates that we are *mentioning* the expression rather than using it. If we actually *use* the expression, we do not need quotes. Consider the following:

(1) Alexander is American.
'Alexander' is Greek.
(2) 'Short' is a shorter word than 'shorter.'
(3) Love is a many-splendored thing.
'Love' is a four-letter word.

Few persons care to study logic, because everybody conceives himself to be proficient enough in the art of reasoning already.
—*Charles Sanders Peirce,* The Fixation of Belief

(4) The Gateway Arch consists of stainless steel.
'The Gateway Arch' consists of three words.

In (1), the masculine name is first *used* to refer to the person. In the second statement, the masculine name is *mentioned* as a word. In the first, the name is the name of a person; in the second, the name, including the quotes, is the name of the name of a person. In (2), the middle word is used, while the first and last words are mentioned. Quotes are provided accordingly. In (3), the first word, since it is being used in its capacity to refer to certain feelings of the heart, does not need quotes. But in the second sentence, where attention is drawn to the word rather than its meaning, quotes are necessary. In (4), the first three words are used to refer to the structure beside the river and do not need quotes. But the second sentence is about the expression itself, and quotes are needed.

Whenever we mention an expression (and therefore employ quotes), the result is another expression, but one now with quotes on each end. This *resulting expression* is used, but it is used, not to refer to things in the "real" world, but to another expression.

The process of using a linguistic expression to refer to another linguistic expression may be carried on indefinitely. If we wanted to mention an expression for an expression (or a name for a name), we would need two sets of quotes; if we had to refer to a name for the name of a name, we would use three sets of quotes; and so on. For example:

The expression, 'The meaning of 'meretricious' is not widely known,' is a sentence.

'Alexander' is a name for a person, but ''Alexander'' is a name for the name of a person.

'''Chicago''' refers to ''Chicago,'' which refers to 'Chicago,' which refers to a city in Illinois.

Use of quotes is only one way to indicate that an expression is being mentioned rather than used. Two other ways are: (1) Place the expression on a line by itself. If this had not been done above, the examples would have required another set of quotes. (2) Italicize the term. Italics, however, are sometimes employed to serve another purpose: provide emphasis. In typescript, italicization is achieved by underlining.

Many works in logic use double quotation marks instead of the single ones used here. In this work we will reserve the use of double quotes for such occasions as these:

(1) ''Throw me a life preserver,'' said Christopher.
(2) We danced as the band played ''Begin the Beguine.''
(3) His ''argument'' was not very convincing.
Some ''amateurs'' make a pretty good living.
The pianist had to play a ''gig'' in another town.

The first use is to enclose a verbatim expression uttered or written by someone. It is used, literally, for *quotations*. The second use is to enclose the *title* of a song,

> *Chaos of thought and passion, all confused;*
> *Still by himself abused or disabused;*
> *Created half to rise, and half to fall;*
> *Great lord of all things, yet a prey to all;*
> *Sole judge of truth, in endless error hurled;*
> *The glory, jest, and riddle of the world.*
>   —*Alexander Pope,* Essay on Man

speech, movie, article, etc. Book titles, however, are usually italicized (or underlined). The third use is to convey the notion of *so-called.* It may indicate that the expression is being used in a very loose or figurative sense. It may indicate sarcasm. Or this third use may indicate a slang expression.

Those expressions for which double quotes would ordinarily be used (as described above) will be given single quotes when they appear *within* a quotation. For example:

"I don't understand," said the pilot, "what he could have meant when he said, 'Your landing-gear is not down.'"

She approached the bandleader and purred, "You played 'Fool on the Hill' beautifully!"

"I shall always be opposed," answered the Senator, "to 'right-to-work' laws."

There is one thing that both the single quotes and the double quotes have in common. By setting off a linguistic expression, they direct the reader's attention to words rather than the things the words refer to.

CONCLUSION

The author does not claim that all the prerequisites for good thinking are set forth in this volume. But some of them surely are, and these should sharpen the critical faculties of the reader who has mastered them. The quest for good thinking is a continuous one that began the day each of us was born and that will end on the day we die. A college course in "good thinking" will be one port of call along the way that helped a little in the quest.

EXERCISES[3]

Exercise 1

For each of the following, indicate whether true or false:

1. Good thinking consists of remembering lots of facts.
2. Critical thinking consists of raising objections.

[3] Answers to odd-numbered problems are provided at the end of the text.

3. Truth always results from good thinking.
4. Bad thinking always leads to erroneous results.
5. If an idea works, then it is true.
6. Emotions sometimes get in the way of good thinking.
7. Anyone who wants to think well should seek to eliminate his emotions.
8. Confusion over words sometimes gets in the way of good thinking.
9. Anyone who wants to think well should try to think without words.
10. To understand the relations between statements, it is necessary to know something about the structure of those statements.
11. Deductive inferences are valid or invalid.
12. Inductive inferences are either true or false.
13. Strong arguments contain true premises and sound inferences.
14. Deduction is better than induction.
15. Induction is better than deduction.

Exercise 2

Rewrite the following, supplying the needed quotation marks.

1. Penelope is Greek but Penelope is English.
2. Failure is not in my vocabulary.
3. Sam is the name of my uncle, but Sam is the name for that name.
4. Would you please sing Far, Far Away?
5. Pronounce Roosevelt correctly, she said.
6. The ambassador wrote, I have been instructed to say, we will give the suggestion due consideration.
7. He is a competent performer, but something of a hot dog.
8. Monosyllabic is polysyllabic.
9. Always capitalize Budweiser.
10. 1, 2, 3, and 4 denote cardinal numbers.
11. If you add an s to cares, which is plural, you get caress, which is singular.
12. Abby had a good answer for Downhearted in Downers Grove.
13. Able was I ere I saw Elba is a palindrome.
14. As an amateur, he earned $50,000.
15. Ave Maria is a Latin expression.
16. Ave Maria is a religious song.
17. Small is smaller than smaller.
18. Cross the t and dot the i.
19. His term paper consisted of a page of hastily scrawled notes.
20. The capital of Missouri is M.

Chapter 2

Words

PREVIEW

In this chapter we will study the building-blocks of language: words. Words have meaning, and it is this meaning that enables us to think and communicate. In order to think and communicate clearly, we must observe certain principles that govern the proper use of words. Among the things you should master in this chapter are the following:

1. The meaning of *meaning*.
2. The distinction between *extension* and *intension*.
3. The use of *connotative* meaning in setting the emotional tone.
4. The relation of meaning to *context*.
5. The nature and types of *ambiguity*.
6. Identification of the "fallacies of ambiguity": *equivocation, amphiboly, composition*, and *division*.
7. The nature of *vagueness* and how to avoid it.
8. The two basic *types of definition*.
9. The various *techniques* for formulating definitions.
10. Tests for determining the *adequacy* of definitions.
11. How *persuasive* and *question-begging* definitions can be used in a fallacious way.

Many of the concepts to be discussed in this chapter you already understand. Give yourself this little "diagnostic test" and see how you fare.[1]

1. Would you rather be called *skinny* or *slender?*
2. Do all nouns denote actual things?

[1] Answers are provided at the end of the text.

3. Can you rewrite this statement to eliminate ambiguity? *He had written out his address and left it on the desk.*
4. What two meanings can this statement have? *The newscaster will be back tomorrow with more important news.*
5. Are vagueness and ambiguity the same thing?
6. Does a writer or speaker always have to use a term the way society in general uses it?
7. Is there one and only one correct way to formulate definitions?
8. Show how a definition could be used to eliminate the vagueness of 'fresh' in this statement: *Bring home a loaf of fresh bread.*
9. True or false: The meaning of a word must never be permitted to shift during the course of an argument.
10. True or false: Proper definitions inform us of the nature of reality.

MEANING

Meaning as Use

Most of our thought and communication takes place by means of words. It is because certain meanings are regularly attached to certain words that we are able to use words to express and exchange views about the world. What is the meaning of *meaning?*

Like most words, 'meaning' has several meanings. It may mean 'significance' as in the sentence, 'What is the real meaning of Christianity?' It may mean 'the main point of a discourse' as in the sentence, 'I listened to his speech attentively but could not grasp his meaning.' It may mean 'purpose' or 'objective' as in 'The meaning of life is to grow in wisdom.' It may mean 'thought-provoking material' as in 'There is a lot of meaning in the New Testament parables.' It may mean 'intention' as in the sentence, 'William is an awkward but well-meaning person.' It may mean 'indicator' or 'sign of' as in the sentence, 'The meaning of a falling barometer is rain.'

We shall not be concerned with any of these meanings. What we are seeking is a sense of 'meaning' that applies to words and that seems to be involved in these uses of 'meaning':

What is the meaning of 'vorpal'?
If two terms have the same meaning, they are synonyms.
Definitions are attempts to specify meaning.
Not knowing the word's meaning, he employed it incorrectly.
Ambiguous terms have two or more possible meanings.
'Tbskt' is meaningless.
The etymology of a word is often helpful in determining its meaning.

Various theories have been formulated to expound the sense (or senses) of 'meaning' intended in these passages. What follows is one point of view on a very controversial subject.[2]

The meaning of a word is the *use* to which it can be put in the language of which it is a part. We know what a word means when we know how to *use* it correctly. A definition provides us with a word's meaning when it gives us another expression which may be used in the same context as the word being defined. To say that a group of people who speak the same language assume similar meanings for the words they communicate with is to say that they *use* words the same way. Damon uses 'triangle' to refer to rectilinear three-sided figures. So does Pythias. To use it in any other way (without explicit warning) would be to violate a convention of language governing its *use*. According to these conventions, some uses of a word are appropriate and some are not. If we want to be understood by others, we must use words conventionally. Those people who use words the same way are sharing common meanings. They are able to communicate.

Some uses abound in some circles, while others are preferred in other circles. The words 'cool' and 'rap' are used by one section of our society in a way not used by writers of scholarly articles. Many of the usages common to one group may be unknown to another group, although both groups profess to be speaking English.

The meanings of words change as their uses change. 'Stout' at one time meant 'valiant.' Today it is used to characterize people who are portly. 'Courtesan' once meant 'lady at court' and 'wench' meant any young girl. 'Get off,' according to Harper Barnes, "started as a drug term, became a sexual term and ended up meaning, more or less, to have a good time."[3] 'Sophomore' no longer means 'person with the wisdom of a moron,' and 'professor' no longer means 'person who has taken religious vows.' Some words have no contemporary meaning at all, and if they are listed in the dictionary are labeled "archaic" or "obsolete." We usually find the word 'prithee,' but most dictionaries no longer include such splendid terms from the past as 'snollygoster,' 'poopnoddy,' 'snodderclout,' 'bedswerver,' and 'mubblefubbles.'[4] Dictionaries not only have to record the various ways words are used but also must add and drop meanings and words from their lists. Their task is the difficult one of keeping abreast of gradually changing conventions, which, unlike legal statutes, are neither debated nor promulgated.

As new meanings emerge and old ones become obsolete, it occasionally becomes a bone of contention as to which is correct. Some usages may be called "standard," and some may be called "colloquial" or "informal." When enough more or less educated people are willing to use a word in a particular way, that usage has become standard, and a new meaning for the word has become established. Dictionaries do not prescribe correct usage but seek to indicate what is accepted in educated circles as standard usage and what is regarded as substandard. Sometimes they are thought

---

[2] This section utilizes some of the ideas of Ludwig Wittgenstein, Cambridge philosopher.

[3] See *St. Louis Post-Dispatch,* January 7, 1977, p. 3D.

[4] For the meaning of these and other dead words, see Susan Kelz Sperling, *Poplollies and Bellibones* (New York: Penguin Books, 1979).

to lag behind; sometimes they are deemed to be too permissive. Whatever its shortcomings, an up-to-date dictionary is an essential source for anyone who wants to know how words are used and their status.

Changing usage has given us many rich and interesting meanings. Sometimes, however, these changes seem to mark a deterioration of the language. A few people may begin to use a word inappropriately—in violation, that is, of the conventions of the language. Others may pick it up, and soon the new usage is fighting for recognition; it is establishing conventions of its own. The new meaning finds its way into the dictionary and eventually is listed without disparagement alongside the older meaning. Something of the sharpness of the language seems to be lost when a word can have meanings that are too similar.

The word 'hopefully' has for a long time been an adverb that means 'in a hopeful manner.' "He peered into the kitchen hopefully." Then it was "incorrectly" used to mean 'let us hope.' "The new administration will do something about the budget deficit—hopefully." This second meaning has now found its way into the dictionary and eventually may be as acceptable as the first. One of the meanings of 'irony' is 'an incongruity between what might be expected and what actually occurred.' It is now being used in a way synonymous with 'coincidence.' "Ironically, Jefferson died on the anniversary of the signing of the Declaration of Independence." *Real* irony is seen in the demise of the physical fitness advocate, James Fixx, who died from a heart attack that he experienced while jogging. But usage is a mighty talisman that can transform a gaffe into an acceptable social behavior. 'Litany' does not mean 'emotional outpouring,' nor does 'notorious' mean 'famous'—but some day they may.

> *What's in a name? That which we call a rose*
> *By any other name would smell as sweet.*
> —*William Shakespeare,* Romeo and Juliet

Concluding Summary: The meaning of a word consists of the way it is conventionally used. As usage varies from group to group and from period to period, meanings vary accordingly. Nevertheless, there is enough common usage within a society for its different segments to communicate and enough common usage in the history of a people for those of us living today to understand much of what our ancestors had to say.

Extension

It is sometimes said that "the most basic level of meaning" a word can have is its extension (or denotation). The extension (or denotation) of a word is that whole class of thing to which the word refers: the actual persons, events, animals, colors, or whatever. The extension (or denotation) of a word exists in that realm of actualities that language presupposes. If we are talking about *something,* our words have extension or "denotative meaning."

Most examples of extension are given in terms of nouns and noun phrases. 'Snow' surely has extension, but does 'rapidly melting'? 'Books that are green' has extension, but what about the word 'green'? Do adjectives and verbs denote or have extension? If one holds that extension consists of the things actually named by the word, he or she would have to answer in the negative, for only nouns and noun phrases can name things. But if one holds that the extension of a word is the class of things to which the word truly applies, he or she would answer in the affirmative. Most logicians take the second alternative. For them, the extension of 'rich' is the class of things to which the predicate 'is rich' truly applies. The extension of 'exploding' is the class of things to which the predicate 'is exploding' truly applies.

It is obvious that such terms as 'chair,' 'Margaret Thatcher,' 'water,' and 'tree' have extension and equally obvious what this extension consists of. In most universes of discourse these words all refer to things that exist. But what about words like 'Goldilocks,' 'unicorn,' 'perfect husband,' and 'Zeus'? We are surely not talking nonsense when we use these words. In some sense we are talking about something. If so, these words have extension—in some sense. If they do not exist in the world of time and space, may we not think of them as existing in some other world? Goldilocks in the context of fairy tales is real enough to experience hunger. Unicorns exist in the realm of legendary creatures, and it would be erroneous to picture them with two horns. Perfect husbands abound in the realm of female imagination. 'Zeus' denotes a real god in the context of classical mythology. Just about any noun or noun phrase has extension in some universe of discourse or other.[5]

It is when people assume that they are thinking or speaking in the same universe of discourse that difficulties may arise. Jane says that 'Santa Claus' has extension (or denotes), and June says that 'Santa Claus' does not have extension. Jane is correct if her universe of discourse is the realm of enacted, imaginary characters; June is correct if her universe of discourse is the realm of flesh-and-blood people.

In any case, to confront a term's extension is to have moved from the realm of language into a realm of existence. A term's extension does not ordinarily consist of other words. The extension of 'frog' is frogs. The extension of 'actress' is actresses. The extension of 'Metropolitan Museum of Art' is the Metropolitan Museum of Art. It is not very helpful to indicate the extension of a word in this way. It would be more helpful to draw a picture of a frog, to give examples of actresses, to point to the Metropolitan Museum of Art.

Sometimes words refer to other words. The extension of such words as 'preposition' exists in a language, but it is perhaps a different language than that containing the word 'preposition.' The extension of 'preposition' includes 'beyond,' 'under,' and the like. These and others are the words that 'preposition' refers to.

Since prepositions exist in some sense, as well as frogs, actresses, and the Metropol-

---

[5] *Universe of discourse* may be defined as the class that contains all the entities (and their negatives) referred to in a statement or argument.

> *It was common saying . . . that men ought not to investigate things from words, but words from things; for that things are not made for the sake of words, but words for things.*
> —*Diogenes Laertius*, Lives and Opinions of Eminent Philosophers

itan Museum of Art, 'preposition,' 'frog,' 'actress,' and 'Metropolitan Museum of Art' are said to denote. Such terms as 'chair,' 'left-handed dentist,' and 'rainbow' also refer to things that exist. These things comprise their extension or denotation. The words denote the things.

Strictly speaking, the extension of a word or an expression is not its meaning, since meaning consists not of a word's *reference* but of its *use*. It is possible for two terms to have the same extension but different meanings. 'Vice-president of the United States' and 'presiding officer of the senate' refer to the same person, yet have different meanings. The case of 'equiangular triangle' and 'equilateral triangle' is another common example of identical extension but different meaning.

While 'meaning' and 'extension' are not synonymous, it helps us to know what a word means (that is, its use) by knowing some of the things that the word refers to.

Concluding Summary: The extension or denotation of a term consists of all the things—past, present, and future—that it refers to. Although the meaning of a word does not consist of its extension or denotation, knowledge of what a term refers to is helpful in discovering what it means.

Intension

Another kind of "meaning" that words are said to have is intensional. While extension comprises the *things* a word refers to, *intension* comprises the *characteristics* that must be present for the word to be properly applied. The intension of a word is sometimes called its set of defining criteria.

It was said above that two terms may have different meanings even though they have the same extension. This is to say (in many cases) that their intensions are different although they refer to the same thing(s). The terms, 'smartest girl in North Snowshoe' and 'prettiest girl in North Snowshoe,' happen to refer to (or denote) the same person: Bertha Kilroy. But the intensions of these terms are obviously very different. The one involves brains; the other involves beauty. A common example of this phenomenon involves the terms 'man' and 'featherless biped.' They have the same extension but different intensions. So it would seem to be the case that intension comes closer to what we mean by 'meaning' than does extension.

Moreover, we find that many of the words that do not have extension and which would therefore be meaningless if extension were the same as meaning, do have intension. Adjectives, verbs, and other non-nouns have intension. The intension of 'graceful' is the characteristic of elegance of beauty or form. The intension of 'fly' is to move through the air on wings. Even some nouns have intension without extension. In most universes of discourse, 'unicorn' does not have extension, although its intension may be perfectly clear. We can state the characteristics of 'rhubarb ice cream,' although not even in the freezers of Baskin-Robbins does it have extension.

Despite these advantages of intension over extension, there are two good reasons for not holding that intension is the same as meaning:

(1) Some words have extension but no intension. Proper names and serial numbers are examples. Such an expression denotes a particular thing (person, city, building, piece of equipment, or whatever), but there is no intension for the expression. There is no set of essential qualities that must be present for the term to be applied. We may name our pet zebra 'Spot' if we like. The city, Cuyahoga Falls, does not have to contain a waterfall. Billie does not have to be a male person. The New York Giants do not have to be large or play their games in New York. And Philadelphia does not necessarily abound in brotherly love. So, if meaning is intension, these terms would have to be meaningless—which they are not.

(2) There are many words that have neither extension nor intension, but which do have meaning. Examples are: 'if,' 'and,' 'therefore.' These words have very important uses in our language.

We come back again, therefore, to our definition of 'meaning' in terms of use. All the words cited as examples in this section have conventional uses, so they have meaning. To state the uses they may serve in the language is to state their meaning. Words that have intension but no extension have meaning, words that have extension but no intension have meaning, and words that have neither extension nor intension have meaning. The meaning in all cases consists of the use to which they can be put in communication.

Just as knowing a word's extension is helpful in determining how a word is used, so too is knowing a word's intension. Indeed, in the case of words that have intension at all, the best way to state their use is to state those characteristics that comprise their intension. If I know that the intension of 'feather-weight boxer' is 'boxer who weighs between 118 and 126 pounds,' I know precisely how it is used; I know its meaning. In providing essential characteristics, the intension of a word provides the criteria for using the word.

Concluding Summary: The intension of an expression consists of those qualities or characteristics that must be present in a situation for the expression properly to be applied in that situation. To know an expression's intension is to know how to use it. But, since some meaningful expressions do not *have* intension, intension is not quite the same thing as meaning.

Connotation

Suppose we compare the terms 'firm' and 'obstinate' when used to describe a person. The intensions of the two words are very similar, yet their meanings seem to be very different. Anyone would rather be called firm than obstinate. Advertisers, when discussing coffee, pipe tobacco, and cosmetics, use the words 'aroma' and 'fragrance' instead of 'smell' or 'odor.' Real estate agents refer to their offerings as 'homes' rather than 'houses.' 'Highest quality filet mignon' on a menu seems more appetizing than 'first-class piece of dead cow.' This third kind of ''meaning,'' this ''meaning along with,'' is called *connotation*.[6]

Connotation is closely tied to feelings. When we hear a word that has a strong connotation, we react emotionally. It conveys something to us that is not simply factual but value laden as well. The speaker who uses words with strong connotations is evincing certain feelings and intends that the listener also experience these feelings.

Connotation obviously is not identical with what we have been calling 'meaning.' To state merely the connotation of a word would fall far short of stating its meaning. Since the connotative element of a word is neither informative nor descriptive, some people would make a distinction between extension and intension on one hand and connotation on the other, calling the former ''cognitive'' and the latter ''non-cognitive'' kinds of meaning. Others would not call connotation meaning at all.

But if we recall our sense of *meaning as use,* connotation must be at least *part* of the meaning of some terms. We choose to use the term 'gabby' when we want to evince or arouse feelings of disapproval in contexts where the more neutral word 'talkative' will not work. No account of the meaning of 'nigger' would be complete without including its reprehensible connotation. An adequate account of the way a word is used (and hence its meaning) would, if the word has palpable connotation, have to include its purpose of evincing or arousing certain feelings.

There is general agreement among the users of a language on what the extensions and intensions of words are, and there is agreement, too, on their connotations. While the latter are more personal, more subtle and elusive, most people would rather be ''appointed to a position'' than ''hired,'' be guilty of a ''miscalculation'' instead of ''goofing up,'' and be regarded as ''thrifty'' or ''economical'' instead of ''cheap.'' Connotation does vary from individual to individual, but there is enough agreement among people to support effective use of affective language.

It is possible to arrange terms, the extensions of which are the same and the intensions of which are nearly the same, from one connotative extreme to the other. Note how increasingly favorable the connotation becomes in the following sequence: 'stew-bum,' 'sot,' 'drunk,' 'alcoholic,' 'heavy drinker.' Another example: 'went nuts,' 'flipped,' 'became insane,' 'experienced a mental breakdown,' 'encountered severe

---

[6] The word 'connotation' is employed by many logicians to mean what we have been calling intension. We, however, intend to use 'connotation' in a way that is more in conformity to ordinary or popular usage.

psychological problems.' Another example: 'whore,' 'prostitute,' 'hooker,' 'call girl,' 'party girl.' The language one chooses to employ in discussing drunkenness, insanity, and prostitution sets a certain emotional tone.

There are honorific and derogatory words for almost everything. In Hollywood an association of extras recently demanded that they henceforth officially be known as 'atmosphere personnel.' Ponder these polarities: 'lady'—'broad,' 'statesman'—'politician,' 'budget account'—'charge account,' 'Ayran'—'Kraut,' 'native American'—'redskin,' 'custodian'—'janitor,' 'medical scientist'—'sawbones,' 'sanitary engineer'—'garbage man,' 'knight of the road'—'bum.'

Connotations not only arouse favorable or unfavorable feelings. They arouse more specific ones also. The Salvation Army uses this *hopeful* expression for death: 'promoted to glory.' The storyteller uses this *fearful* expression for animals that move at night: 'nocturnal creatures.' We evince *kindness* when we say 'visually handicapped' instead of 'blind as a bat.' The publisher gets closer to the *sexual* emotion when he calls his magazine 'Playboy' instead of 'Male Recreation.' And the feeling of *love* for our fellow man is easier to arouse when we speak of our 'brothers' rather than our 'male siblings.'

There are times when it is decent and wise to be concerned with connotations. As users of words, we want to choose words that will not arouse feelings that are inappropriate to the situation. One will not, for example, address the policeman who is writing a ticket as 'copper' or something worse. And he will not speak to a recently bereaved person of her loved one who has 'kicked the bucket.' Expressions not only convey information but they evince and arouse feelings as well. One should in his speech try to control the emotional dimension as well as the factual one. Concern for connotations helps him do this.

A poet who is trying to create a mood, the lover who is seeking to cast a spell, the salesperson who is anxious to sell, the candidate who wants to be elected, the preacher who is trying to save souls—these and others—must cultivate a sensitivity to connotation. For this ''meaning along with'' can make all the difference. It is no accident that bowling establishments now speak of 'lanes' instead of 'alleys' and 'channels' instead of 'gutters.'

It is possible, however, to go too far in this. If an individual arouses emotions to make a conclusion seem to follow when it does not, he commits a cardinal logical sin. He perpetrates a fallacy. Some of these fallacies are discussed later in this book. It is indeed a reprehensible thing to try to get people to believe certain things blindly—that is, on emotional grounds. Yet such attempts abound in advertising, politics, religion, journalism, and courtroom speeches. Many of them do succeed in getting people to suspend that which most makes them human: their rationality itself.

People may respond to the connotation of a term even when they are doubtful

---

Men are usually more stung and galled by reproachful words than hostile actions.

—Plutarch, Lives

or ignorant of its intension! According to *The Book of Lists 2*, George Smathers, in the 1950 Florida Democratic primary election for Senator, made several "accusations" against his opponent Claude Pepper. He charged that Pepper was "a known extrovert," his sister a "thespian," his brother a "practicing homo sapiens." Pepper, moreover, had "matriculated" at college and "practiced celibacy" before marriage. Smathers won the election.[7]

A term may be selected over another, not simply to arouse a more desirable emotion, but to mislead. When the President's press agent says that previous announcements are "inoperative," he conceals the fact that they are false. When the social worker talks about the "juvenile delinquent," he conceals the fact that his charge is a young criminal. When the young lady admits that she was somewhat "tipsy," she conceals the fact that she was drunk. When the car dealer advertises his "pre-owned" cars, he conceals the fact that they have been used. These terms are *euphemisms,* and while euphemisms have legitimate uses, they are employed here to obscure the truth.

Emotion is a fine and wondrous thing, but it should not be allowed to obscure the truth or distort the reasoning process.

Concluding Summary: The connotation of an expression consists of the emotional states that most people tend to experience when they use or hear the expression. For words that are used for their emotive force, connotation is part of their meaning. We should be sensitive to the nuances of connotation while disdaining to exploit it to win arguments.

EXERCISES

Exercise 3

Indicate by yes *or* no *whether the boldfaced words are used (more or less) properly. You may consult a dictionary.*

1. He is an original thinker, as his very **enervative** proposal for dealing with the trade imbalance shows.
2. If you win the lottery, you'll collect $50,000 a year for 20 years. Figure it out: You'll be an instant **millionaire.**
3. The air around the garbage dump had a definite **fetid** quality.
4. Are you **inferring** that I haven't read the assignment?
5. The child was sent to the **principal's** office.
6. She was a **fortnightly** visitor—every ten days without fail.
7. Bertha brought suit for adultery, naming Fifi as **correspondent.**
8. The horse, never having won a race, was called a **maiden.**

---

[7] See Irving Wallace *et al., The Book of Lists 2* (New York: William Morrow and Company, 1980), pp. 36–37.

9. Several **stalagmites** had grown from the roof of the cave.
10. Some plants consume insects and thus are called **carnivorous.**

Exercise 4

For each of the following, indicate the sense of "meaning" probably intended: extension, intension, *or* neither.

1. If you want to know what 'chartreuse' means, look at those drapes.
2. A birdie in golf means a score on a hole one stroke below par.
3. I'm playing golf tomorrow, and I mean to get some birdies!
4. The drought in the midwest means high food prices next year.
5. 'University' means Yale, Harvard, UCLA, etc.
6. 'Argument' means 'discourse containing premises and a conclusion drawn from them.'
7. 'Magnanimous' means 'noble of mind and heart.'
8. George is clumsy, but he means well.
9. 'Meretricious' means 'attractive in a gaudy or showy way.'
10. I mean to do my very best in the next exam.

Exercise 5

Indicate whether same, different, *or* unknowable:

1. 'athlete'—'football player'
   Extension: Intention:
2. 'tallest person in town'—'richest person in town'
   Extension: Intention:
3. 'triangle'—'plane, rectilinear, three-sided figure'
   Extension: Intention:
4. 'tallest person in town'—'Jason F. Heathcliffe'
   Extension: Intention:
5. 'snake'—'reptile'
   Extension: Intention:
6. 'spinster'—'middle-aged woman who has never been married'
   Extension: Intention:
7. 'brave'—'courageous'
   Extension: Intention:
8. 'oldest student in class'—'brightest student in class'
   Extension: Intention:
9. 'bluriosity'—'clorginess'
   Extension: Intention:
10. 'the author of *Hamlet*'—'William Shakespeare'
    Extension: Intention:

Exercise 6

Choose the expression with the most effective connotation:

1. Of course I enjoyed the song, but on the last note I thought you were (a trifle off pitch) (flat).
2. Come to me, my (sad) (melancholy) baby!
3. L&M cigarettes: "The (proud) (arrogant) smoke: product of a (proud) (arrogant) land."
4. If you (are greedy) (want to earn lots of money) and are willing to work, answer this ad today!
5. I don't want to frighten you, but as your doctor I must tell you that your lungs (show signs of injury) (are about shot).

Replace the boldfaced terms with terms having more suitable connotation:

6. Gargle every morning with Blisterine if you want to **avoid halitosis.**
7. Dear Sir: Thank you for letting us see your manuscript. We must return it, however, for it is **very badly written.**
8. Perhaps our marriage would be somewhat better, Mabel, if you were **not frigid.**
9. Before processing this loan, Mr. Jones, may I ask you how long you have been **flat broke?**
10. I have developed a delicious new candy bar. I think I will call it **"Mr. Fatstick."**

Exercise 7

Arrange each set in order of decreasingly favorable connotation:

1. assumes the inequality of the sexes
   male chauvinist
   prejudiced against women
   sexist pig
2. inflation
   rising prices
   skyrocketing prices
   upward-adjusting market
3. obscene
   pornographic
   realistic
   sexually explicit
4. expert
   know-it-all
   savant
   well-informed person

5. attractive
   beautiful
   pretty
   sensational
6. aging Lothario
   dirty old man
   sexy senior citizen
   victim of a Lolita-complex

AMBIGUITY

Context and Ambiguity

Most words have more than one meaning. Any good dictionary will list several definitions for the same word. If each word had one and only one meaning, we might be spared some confusion, but we would have to master a much larger vocabulary.

Most of the time the context will make clear which of two or more meanings is intended. The other words of the sentence or the other sentences in the paragraph usually indicate which meaning the word is to have. The context will rule out all but one meaning for the term.

Context is so important that dictionary makers and others who seek accurate knowledge about how words are actually used collect the contexts in which they are employed. Indeed, it is possible to derive the meaning of an unfamiliar word simply from looking at the contexts in which it appears: Consider the word 'zingle':[8]

In her new dress she fairly zingled!

Cherry trees zingle in the springtime.

The debate was interesting, although no one zingled.

This room is too dark; it will never zingle.

Use Peptic Toothpaste if you want teeth that really zingle!

No one zingles after working all night.

After perusing these contexts, we can feel pretty confident that we know what the hitherto unfamiliar word 'zingle' means.

The word 'address' has several meanings. Ordinarily this presents no problems.

(1) "Senator, that was the most moving address I've ever heard you deliver."
(2) Joe succeeded in obtaining Stella's address.
(3) He had written out the address and placed it in his brief case.

---

[8] For a similar approach to 'wanky,' see S. I. Hayakawa, *Language in Thought and Action* (New York: Harcourt, Brace and Company, 1941), p. 65.

In (1), it is obvious that 'address' means 'a public speech or oration.' The context assures us that this is the intended meaning. In (2), 'address' means something else. The context now excludes 'a public speech or oration.' This is not what Joe obtained from Stella. What he obtained from here was a street number, street, and city. He found out where she lived.

In (3), however, the context has not done its job. It is uncertain which of two possible meanings the word 'address' has. Was it a copy of the speech that was placed in the briefcase, or was it the notation of a street and city? Since there is this uncertainty in this context, we say that the word 'address' is *ambiguous in this context*.

Ambiguity is always relative to a context. No term is ambiguous in itself. The word 'address' in (1) was not ambiguous in that context, nor was it in the context of (2).

When a word is ambiguous in a particular context, something must be done. Uncertainty, which gets in the way of clear thought and expression, must be eliminated. In the case of ambiguity, any one of three actions may be taken:

(a) Alter the context. If the old context did not rule out all meanings but one, an altered one may. In the example above, instead of saying, ''He had written out the address and placed it in his briefcase,'' we can say, ''He had typed out all twenty pages of the address and placed them in his briefcase.'' If 'to the right of' is ambiguous in the context ''Harry stood to the right of Anne,'' we can say, ''Harry stood to the right of Anne in his political views.'' Or, if the other meaning is intended, we can say, ''Harry stood to the right of Anne in the club picture.''

(b) Replace the troublesome terms. One word may be ambiguous in a context while another one in the same context will be unambiguous. Sometimes, then, we need only change the term while leaving the context alone. In the examples above we could have said:

He had written out the *speech* and placed it in his briefcase.

Harry was *politically more conservative* than Anne.

(c) Indicate or provide a definition. We can state that 'address' means 'a speech' and that 'to the right of' means 'possessing more conservative views.' The nature and function of definition are discussed later in this chapter.

Sometimes ambiguity is harmless and deliberately used to be funny or arouse interest. An optometrist has a sign in his office saying, ''Where there is no vision, the people perish.'' His competitor also has a sign: ''We correct everything in sight.'' The jeweler across the street displays this one: ''We're the ring leaders!''

There are masked words abroad, I say, which nobody understands, but which everybody uses, and most people will also fight for, live for, or even die for, fancying they mean this, or that, or the other, of things dear to them.
—John Ruskin, Of King's Treasuries

Concluding Summary: When the context does not rule out all meanings for a term but one, that term is said to be ambiguous in that context. Ambiguity may be eliminated by altering the context, by replacing the term, or by providing a definition.

Equivocation

When an expression has an unambiguous meaning and retains that meaning throughout the passage in which it occurs, we will call it *univocal*. When an expression does not retain that one certain meaning, we will call it *equivocal*. These definitions do not quite conform to ordinary usage, but they serve the purpose of distinguishing between *one* occurrence of a word with two or more possible meanings (ambiguity) and *two or more* occurrences of a word with two or more possible meanings (equivocation).

An example of univocal is: "He *flung* himself from the room, *flung* himself upon his horse and rode madly off in all directions."[9] An example of equivocal meaning is:

The Pilgrims landed, worthy men,
   And saved from wreck on raging seas,
They *fell upon* their knees, and then
   Fell upon the Aborigines.[10]

In the first passage, 'flung' is used univocally; in the second, 'fell upon' is used equivocally. Equivocation is present in the second and absent in the first.

No harm is done by this case of equivocation. We all know what 'fell upon' means in each of its occurrences, and the juxtaposition of the two meanings deftly makes a point.

But equivocation *may* create uncertainty and confusion. When reading an equivocal passage, one may not know whether the meaning is supposed to change or not. He may not know which meaning to assign the first occurrence and which to assign the second. The words are the same, so he is inclined to assume the same meanings for them; but he can't be certain.

Consider this imaginary news report: "A mysterious *case* of whiskey was found early this morning on the front lawn of the Methodist Church. It was turned over to the police department, and Chief Johnson is now working on the case." Equivocation is present. 'Case' means one thing in the first sentence and something else in the second. It is not used consistently. This particular case of equivocation produces perplexity. We may believe (if only for a moment) that the case the chief is working on is the case that was found on the lawn.

Equivocation is most harmful when it is used to perpetrate a fallacy. A fallacious argument or process of thought is one in which the conclusion seems to follow

---

[9] Stephen Leacock, *Gertrude the Governess.*
[10] Arthur Guiterman, "The Pilgrims' Thanksgiving Feast."

from the premises or reasons when in fact it does not. A fallacious argument has some persuasive power while possessing no logical power. Equivocation may be employed in such a way as to make the conclusion only seem to follow. When this occurs, the argument is said to commit the *fallacy of equivocation*.

An expression may mean different things in the two premises of an argument:

> All *committed* individuals will get out and vote.

> Harvey has just been *committed* to a state institution.

The conclusion is then drawn that Harvey will get out and vote. Because of equivocation on the word 'committed,' this conclusion seems to follow when, logically, it does not.

Although the words are the same, the meanings are different. If we symbolize the different meanings with different letters, the complete lack of force of the argument becomes apparent:

> All A's will get out and vote.
> Harvey is a B.
> ∴ Harvey will get out and vote.

The conclusion is nothing but a *non sequitur*.[11]

If the meanings of the key term are made to remain the same, there is, of course, no equivocation and no fallacy of equivocation. But then one or the other of the premises becomes ridiculous and unacceptable.

The argument about Harvey is so crude that it would probably not fool anyone. But even when one knows that an argument is fallacious, he may find it useful for his own peace of mind or for purposes of making a rebuttal to state exactly why it is fallacious.

The following example of the fallacy of equivocation is somewhat more subtle:

> The instructor told us that he wants us to think for ourselves. Well, that's exactly what I did in the examination. When I didn't know the answer, I thought for myself and wrote down the results. He counted most of my answers wrong and flunked me in the exam. The instructor is a liar!

It is quite possible that the expressions about thinking for oneself have two different meanings. The instructor might have meant something like 'reason independently about the facts,' while the student meant 'employ my own judgment as to what the facts are.' Surely no instructor would encourage a student to dispute the fact that the atmosphere contains oxygen! The student has used an expression in two senses in an argument, so he has committed the fallacy of equivocation. If, however, what the instructor encouraged and what the student performed are exactly the same things, there is no equivocation, and the instructor, while perhaps not a liar, is culpable.

---

[11] 'Non sequitur' means 'it does not follow.' When the fallacy committed in drawing the conclusion has no name (often because it is so gross an infraction), the conclusion is generally called a non sequitur.

A person may be victimized by the fallacy of equivocation not only when it is employed by another, but also when, in his own thought processes, he permits one symbol to have different meanings. One may, for example, be accustomed to regarding man as the most intelligent of creatures. If he lets the meaning of 'man' shift in his thinking from 'human' to 'male person,' he will find himself believing that women are not among the most intelligent of creatures. Equivocation on the word 'man' has produced fallacious reasoning in that person's own mind.

Another kind of equivocation is present in these fallacious arguments:

> Clarence is a fast turtle
> Clarence is an animal
> ∴ Clarence is a fast animal

> Alice is a competent planner
> ∴ Alice is a competent governor

These arguments equivocate on the meanings of *relative terms*. In the premise of the first argument, 'fast' is relative to other *turtles*. 'Fast' relative to other *animals* is quite a different attribute, and being fast in *this* sense is not established by the premises. With respect to the second argument, it is not the case that competence in one activity guarantees competence in some other.

Concluding Summary: Although a word may have different meanings, it serves the cause of clarity if it is made to have a consistent meaning throughout the same passage. If it does not, it is equivocal. To employ equivocation to make a conclusion seem to follow when it does not is to commit the fallacy of equivocation.

Syntactical Ambiguity

The type of ambiguity that has been discussed and illustrated above may be called *semantical* ambiguity. In this kind of ambiguity there is uncertainty about which of two or more denotations or designations the term is intended to have. Semantical ambiguity involves things (objects or characteristics) outside the language itself. Does the word refer to *this* or *that*?

Another kind of uncertainty is involved in *syntactical ambiguity*. We may know what each word means, but we do not know what the statement means. The problem in syntactical ambiguity is not what the words mean but the relation of the words to one another.

Consider the statement:

All lizards are not poisonous.

Does this mean that not any lizards are poisonous or that some are not? Does 'not' deny 'poisonous' or does it qualify the universality of 'all'? We do not know. So the statement is syntactically ambiguous.

> *There is a weird power in a spoken word. . . . And a word carries far—very far—deals destruction through time as bullets go flying through space.*
> *—Joseph Conrad,* Lord Jim

The story is told about the blacksmith's ambitious assistant. He wanted to become a master blacksmith and asked his boss what he should do to satisfy this high hope. The master told him to obey immediately and unquestioningly all orders given him. One day the two of them were working over the anvil. The master had a piece of metal before him. ''When I nod my head,'' he ordered, ''hit it with the sledgehammer.'' A moment later he gave the signal, and his assistant hit his head with the sledgehammer. The master had been syntactically ambiguous in his directions. It was not clear whether the antecedent of the pronoun 'it' was 'piece of metal' or 'head.' So the apprentice is now the master blacksmith.

Sometimes it is unclear as to which of two or more words a word modifies. For example:

The instructor is demanding more original work.

She is a pretty little girl.

The doctor recommended a gentle woman's laxative.

In the first sentence, 'more' may modify 'original' or it may modify 'work.' In the second, 'pretty' may modify 'little' or it may modify 'girl.' In the third, 'gentle' may modify 'woman' or it may modify 'laxative.' The two meanings possible in each case are quite different.

Sometimes it is unclear as to what the subject or the object of a sentence is. In Shakespeare's play, *King Henry VI (Part II)*, the conjurer Bolingbroke asks:

First of the king: What shall of him become?

The spirit answers:

The duke yet lives that Henry shall depose;

If 'the duke' is the object of the verb 'depose,' things looks bright for Henry. But if 'the duke' is the subject and 'Henry' the object, the fates seem to be smiling on the duke. The spirit, having spoken ambiguously, would be right regardless of the outcome—so long, of course, as one of them deposed the other. The next line in the play, the one that completes the sentence, does not resolve the ambiguity:

But him outlive, and die a violent death.[12]

Syntactical ambiguity occurs when there is uncertainty about the ways that words are related to one another in a passage. Instead of saying that a *word* (or expression)

---

[12] See Act I, Scene IV.

is ambiguous (as we do in the case of semantical ambiguity), we say that the *sentence* or passage or paragraph is ambiguous.

It is possible for an expression to be both semantically and syntactically ambiguous at the same time. A government bureau recently asked its department heads to "provide a list of their employees broken down by sex." One administrator answered, "We don't have much of that around here, but a lot of our people drink too much." If 'broken down' modifies 'list,' it means one thing; if 'broken down' modifies 'employees,' it means something else. The meaning of 'sex' also changes, depending upon the syntax intended. The first meaning would be 'gender'; the second would be 'erotic activity.' Another example is this: "Toscanini's son did not know how to conduct himself."[13] In both examples, clearing up one kind of ambiguity will dispel the other kind also.

We eliminate syntactical ambiguity by rewriting the passage in such a way that the words may reasonably be understood to be related in only one way. We remove all doubt about such things as antecedents of pronouns, what modifies what, and whether a word functions as subject or object of the verb.

Below are more examples of syntactically ambiguous passages. Each has been rewritten in ways such that only one meaning can reasonably be derived.

> The skies are not cloudy all day.
> The skies are sunny all day.
> The skies are sunny at least part of every day.

> The gorilla is more like a human being than a chimpanzee.
> The gorilla is more like a human being than a chimpanzee is.
> The gorilla is more like a human being than it is like a chimpanzee.

> The sun also rises.
> The sun rises as well as sets.
> The sun, like the moon, rises.

> Reid's Criticism of Hume and His Reconstruction in Philosophy (title of Ph.D. dissertation)
> Reid's Reconstruction in Philosophy and His Criticism of Hume
> Reid's Criticism of Hume's Sceptical and Reconstructive Philosophy

> The company wishes to hire women, whatever their marital status, who have been denied their equal rights.
> The company wishes to hire those women whose equal rights have been denied; marital status is irrelevant.
> The company wishes to hire women, whatever their marital status.
> Women in general have been denied their equal rights.

Concluding Summary: A passage is syntactically ambiguous when, as a result of the ways the words within it can plausibly be related to one another, two or

---

[13] Borrowed from Samuel D. Guttenplan and Martin Tamny, *Logic: A Comprehensive Introduction* (New York: Basic Books, Inc., 1971), p. 294.

more different meanings are possible. Such ambiguity can (and should) be eliminated by rewriting the passage.

Amphiboly

Just as semantical ambiguity may be the basis for the fallacy of equivocation, syntactical ambiguity may be the basis for a fallacy. This fallacy is called *amphiboly*. The fallacy of amphiboly is committed when syntactical ambiguity is utilized in an argument to make a conclusion seem to follow when in fact it does not. As in the fallacy of equivocation, an expression is present that has two or more different meanings. The meaning is permitted to shift during the course of the argument from one sense to another.

Someone may read a notice announcing that a lecture will be given on deviant sexual behavior in the college auditorium. He may discuss this event, then conclude that he didn't know there was much sexual activity of *any* kind going on in the auditorium, and that it was a rather narrow topic, in any case, for a lecture.

A speaker may win acceptance of the premise that a man should love his family more than his mistress. Then point out that in fact he *does,* for his mistress can't *stand* his family.

In each of these rather racy examples we have a statement that is syntactically ambiguous. In the first, 'there will be a lecture on deviant sexual behavior in the college auditorium'; in the second, 'a man should love his family more than his mistress.' The first probably means that the lecture *will be held* in the auditorium; the second probably means that a man should love his family *more than he loves his mistress*. These interpretations will get ready acceptance, and the perpetrator of the fallacy of amphiboly realizes this. Having gotten this interpretation, he utters the statements again (with perhaps a different inflection to his voice) and derives a *different* interpretation—one, perhaps, that his opponent is not willing to make. In the first example, the perpetrator of the fallacy reinforces the interpretation that the subject of the lecture is deviant sex in the college auditorium; in the second, that a man should love his family more than his mistress loves his family. His opponent, having accepted the expression with *one* meaning, is now held responsible for the *other* meaning. The speaker wants to have it both ways; he wants to employ both meanings when he is entitled to only one.

It should be noted that the fallacy of amphiboly does not require that the ambiguous expression be repeated explicitly. A person may capitalize on the syntactical ambiguity of an expression by interpreting it in a manner clearly unintended by its sponsor. He ignores the meaning intended by his opponent in order to set forth his own. The following is such a truncated fallacy of amphiboly: "The sergeant said to pull the pin from the grenade and to throw it as far as possible. This is poor advice, for it would be very dangerous to throw the pin while continuing to hold the grenade itself."

One deals with this fallacy in the same way that one deals with the fallacy of equivocation. The critic points out the shift in meaning, insists that the meaning be kept consistent, and shows that, when this is done, either the argument becomes a simple *non sequitur* or a premise is patently false.

Concluding Summary: A passage must be made to carry the same interpretation throughout the course of the argument. To capitalize on syntactical ambiguity for the purpose of making a conclusion seem to follow when it does not is to commit the fallacy of amphiboly.

Composition and Division

There is still another type of fallacy of ambiguity. It is committed when we move illegitimately from the part to the whole (*composition*) or from the whole to the part (*division*).

Suppose we note that every part used in the construction of the airship Hindenburg was light in weight, then conclude that the airship as a whole was light. We would be committing the fallacy of composition. A coach may observe that every starter on his basketball team is very good and conclude from this that his starting team is very good. Again, the fallacy of composition. The whole does not necessarily possess the characteristics of its parts. What may be attributed *distributively* to every member of a class or every part of a whole does not necessarily belong *collectively* to that class or that whole.

This straw will not break the camel's back, nor will that or that or that. Yet *together* they may. One person may be too cowardly to break down the jail door, and this may be true for every individual gathered there. But the whole, the mob, may well possess a type of resolution absent from each of its members.

One commits the fallacy of composition when he overlooks the fact that the qualities of a whole are not simply a reflection of the qualities of its parts. This does not mean that we cannot generalize about a class on the basis of what has been found to be true about the members of that class. If each and every member of the class of college presidents is sagacious, we can indeed conclude that college presidents are sagacious, for we have consistently employed the *distributive sense of attribution*. But we could not say: "This college president earns less than one hundred thousand dollars, and so does that one, and many others. Therefore, the earnings of the whole class of college presidents are (total) less than one hundred thousand dollars." And the reason we cannot is that we began in the distributive sense and concluded in the *collective sense*. Our conclusion is not about an attribute possessed by *each and every* president but an attribute possessed by the class conceived *as a whole*.

The fallacy of division is the direct opposite of that of composition. The fallacy consists of inferring that what is true of the whole is also true of the parts. The United States of America may be a great nation, but it does not follow from this that each and every institution in the nation is great. A building may be well lighted but still have some shadowy places. To speak as if the parts must possess the qualities we recognize as adhering to the whole is to commit the fallacy of division.

> *Words are wise men's counters,—they do but reckon by them; but they are the money of fools.*
>
> —*Thomas Hobbes,* Leviathan

We may say that peaches are grown in many parts of the country. It does not follow from this that this particular peach, here in my hand, is grown in many parts of the country. We may say that honest politicians are scarce. It does not follow from this that Congressman Richards, being an honest politician, is scarce. In these examples we are going from what is collectively true to a distributive assertion. To do so is to commit the fallacy of division.

We can, however, go from what is distributively true of a class to a distributive assertion about its members. For example, if it is true that peaches contain pits, it follows that this particular peach in my hand contains a pit. 'Peaches contain pits' holds *distributively* for each member of the class of peaches, while 'Peaches are grown in many parts of the country' holds *collectively* for the class of peaches considered as a whole. We can infer from the whole to the parts when what we know is something about *every part* (distributive attribution), but we cannot infer from the whole to the parts when what we know is something about the whole *as a whole* (collective attribution).

Collectively, white sheep eat more than black sheep because there are more of them. Distributively, the average white sheep probably eats the same amount as the average black sheep. Collectively, conventional bombs did more damage in World War II than atomic bombs. Distributively, atomic bombs did more damage.

One last example: "Model T Fords have almost disappeared. This is a Model T Ford. Therefore this has almost disappeared." This argument commits the fallacy of division. What is true of the class of Model T Fords collectively need not be true of each of its members (distributively). On the other hand: "Model T Fords are black. This is a Model T Ford. Therefore this is black." This argument is valid. What is true distributively of the class of Model T Fords will also be true of each of its members.

Concluding Summary: The fallacies of composition and division occur when the difference between collective and distributive attribution is overlooked. The fallacy of composition assumes that what is true of the parts will also be true of the whole; the fallacy of division assumes that what is true of the whole will also be true of the parts.

EXERCISES

Exercise 8

Each of the following is ambiguous or contains an ambiguity. Identify the source of the ambiguity and indicate whether it is semantical *or* syntactical.

1. I'd invite you home for dinner, but my wife is mad.
2. He rents the house for $150 per month.
3. After the child watched the elephant perform, he was led back to the cage and locked up for the night.
4. The only person in sight was the sheriff; he stood there wiping his sweating neck on the courthouse steps.
5. Every household contains poisons that small children may drink.
6. "FOR SALE: Antique desk suitable for lady with curved legs and large drawers, also mahogany chest. Please write . . ." (Reprinted in the *Journal of the American Medical Association,* September 19, 1953.)
7. "This film is about a real person, Frank Serpico, who deals with equally real corruption in the New York City Police Department, and was shot this summer in New York, with full cooperation from the city and the police department." (Quoted in *The New Yorker,* December 3, 1973.)
8. That was a terrible fall. I hope I never experience another like it.
9. World War II slogan: HOMEMAKERS: SAVE SOAP AND WASTE PAPER.
10. "It won't be a real New England clam chowder unless you put your heart into it." (Reprinted in *The New Yorker,* June 12, 1954.)

Exercise 9

Rewrite the following in such a way as to eliminate the ambiguity:

1. "Wife Charged with Poisoning Her Fifth Husband." (newspaper headline)
2. "EPA Refuses to Get the Lead Out." (headline of an editorial criticizing the delay in banning leaded gasoline)
3. "The Democratic Party opposes quotas which are inconsistent with the principles of our country." (on "affirmative action" in 1984 party platform)
4. He posed for the picture with his prize racehorse, wearing jodhpurs and a gray Stetson.
5. "Buy these dresses for a ridiculous figure." (clothing store advertisement)
6. "Reagan to Youth: Lay Off Drugs, Drink." (newspaper headline)
7. Employees only may eat in the cafeteria.
8. The glasses had been left on the table.
9. If I had a mind to, I could write like Shakespeare.
10. All exams are not difficult.

Exercise 10

Each of the following arguments is fallacious. Indicate whether equivocation, amphiboly, composition, *or* division *is present.*

1. All adequate addresses contain a zip code. The President's address to the nation did not contain a zip code. It was, therefore, inadequate.
2. Every ingredient that went into the cake was good. So the cake is good.

3. Honest politicians are scarce. Paul Simon is an honest politician. So Paul Simon is scarce.

4. The paper said that after the child watched the elephant perform, he was led to a cage and locked up for the night. What a terrible way to treat a little kid!

5. America has a rich and varied racial heritage. Roger, therefore, has a rich and varied racial heritage, since he is an American.

6. The highest product of biological evolution is man. No woman is a man. Women, therefore, are not the highest products of biological evolution.

7. Dirty plates should be washed with a detergent. The umpire was therefore remiss when he simply dusted the plate off with a brush.

8. The American buffalo has all but vanished. Therefore that particular buffalo has all but vanished.

9. Every paragraph in the treatise is well constructed. The treatise itself must, therefore, be well constructed.

10. The 1954 Cleveland Indians was one of the few great teams in baseball history. Vic Wertz was on that team. Therefore, Vic Wertz was one of the few great ballplayers in baseball history.

Exercise 11

Each of the following arguments is fallacious. Indicate whether equivocation, amphiboly, composition, *or* division *is present.*

1. If we use the very best ingredients, we can be sure that the stew will be delicious.

2. Arguments are disagreeable and should be avoided. Therefore, you should refrain from marshaling premises and drawing conclusions, for to do so is to create arguments.

3. I checked this book out of the library. The library is famous all over the world. So this book is famous also.

4. He will vote for a strike against the company. I know this because he is a bowler, and bowlers like strikes.

5. 3 plus 2 times 5 is an odd number.

6. I live in one place. You live in one place. He lives in one place. She lives in one place. Everyone, apparently, lives in one place. It must be crowded!

7. A good man, as the song says, is hard to find. So if you meet one, write down his address and don't lose it!

8. Divorces are increasing. John and Mary are getting a divorce. So their divorce is increasing.

9. Every part of the wonderful one-hoss shay was built to last for a hundred years. So the shay will last for a hundred years.

10. I was having trouble with my breathing. My doctor said he would give me something to stop *that*. I think I should change doctors.

Exercise 12

Critically examine the following arguments:

1. He is an old baseball player. Therefore he is an old man.
2. He is a bearded baseball player. Therefore he is a bearded man.
3. Madge is a successful violinist. She must, therefore, be a successful person.
4. The ''Varmint'' is an inexpensive automobile, so it would be an inexpensive graduation present.
5. You say that that dog is a mother. And you admit that it is your dog. It follows, therefore, that that dog is your mother.

VAGUENESS

The Nature of Vagueness

Another kind of uncertainty is common in our language: *vagueness*. In ambiguity, there are two or more distinct possibilities; in vagueness, it is a question of degree. We know, for any vague word, conditions under which the word definitely would apply and conditions under which the word definitely would not apply. But between these areas of certainty there is a middle ground. Does or does not the word apply? There does not seem to be a line marking applicability from non-applicability.

Consider the word 'fresh.' Could we apply it to bread that has just this second come out of the oven? Yes, without doubt. Could we apply it to petrified bread that has been excavated at the site of an ancient city? No, unquestionably. Bread that is one second, one minute, five minutes, or even one hour old, is definitely *fresh*. Bread that is five thousand years, one thousand years, or six years old, is definitely *non-fresh*. Moving from each end, we seem to be approaching some line which will sharply demarcate fresh bread from non-fresh bread. But this is an illusion. There is no line. If there were a line, the word 'fresh' would not be vague. We would know where it properly applies and where it does not.

Instead of a line between applicability and non-applicability, there is an area of uncertainty. Would I call bread that is two days old 'fresh'? I do not know. It would depend upon how I happened to feel. You might or might not agree with me. Since we are somewhere in the area of uncertainty, neither of us should be very insistent.

There is a ''law of thought'' which says that everything either has a quality or does not.[14] Another ''law'' holds that something cannot both have a quality and not have it.[15] If something is *X*, it is not non-*X*; and if something is non-*X*, then it is not *X*. One or the other it must be, but not both. Vague words seem to defy these laws of thought. We cannot, with any confidence, call bread in the middle area

[14] The law of Excluded Middle.
[15] The law of Non-contradiction.

> *No one means all he says, and yet very few say all they mean, for words are slippery and thought is viscous.*
> —*Henry Brooks Adams*, The Education of Henry Adams

'fresh,' yet we are reluctant to call it 'non-fresh.' But it must be one or the other, and it cannot be both. Vague words seem to defy the basic principles of logic.

The wider the area of uncertainty between the areas of certain application and certain non-application, the more vague is the word. How much uncertainty has to be present before a word can be called 'vague'? The question has no answer. 'Vague' itself is a vague word.

Some ancient Greeks are supposed to have seated a bushy-haired man in the marketplace and plucked hairs, one at a time, from his head. They watched very closely to see precisely at what point he became *bald*. The experiment failed because their language had no rule to tell them how many hairs were necessary for a person not to be bald. The Greeks knew that everyone is bald or non-bald, but they could not know or discover the point at which the one begins and the other ends. A man with no hairs is bald. A man with fifty-thousand hairs is not. But in between is the area of uncertainty.

Where does the area of uncertainty begin? What are its boundaries? It would be as futile to seek these lines as to seek the line in the middle. There *are* no lines!

How pretty does a flower have to be before we can call it *beautiful?* How many pounds does a rock have to weigh before we can call it *heavy?* How high does the thermometer have to rise before we can call the weather *hot?* How much money does a person have to have before we can call her *rich?* It is fruitless to argue, for there are no answers. The words 'beautiful,' 'heavy,' 'hot,' and 'rich' are vague.

Vagueness and ambiguity are often confused. They are, however, two distinct kinds of verbal pitfalls. Vague words have areas of certain application; ambiguous words do not. Vagueness cannot be resolved by tampering with the context; ambiguity can. Vagueness is unavoidable when one uses natural language; ambiguity results from careless use of language. Vagueness confuses because of a *degree* of a quality; ambiguity confuses because of two or more *separate* qualities. A word may be vague without being ambiguous. And a word may be ambiguous without being vague.

Sometimes, however, we encounter a word that is both vague *and* ambiguous in a given context. The word 'democracy' is ambiguous in many contexts. It may mean 'government by the people' or it may mean 'government on behalf of the people.' Within each of these two distinct meanings, there is the element of vagueness. On the first meaning, what *degree* of popular participation is required before 'democracy' can be applied? Direct elections? Indirect? Everyone votes or only some? Everyone holds office or only some? On the second meaning, what degree of service to the public is required? Is everyone benefited or only the workers? How many workers? Party members only? How many party members? Thus, within each of the two distinct meanings of 'democracy,' there is a question of degree. So vagueness, while it does not have to, can occur along with ambiguity.

Concluding Summary: Vagueness, like ambiguity, is an obstacle to clear thought and expression. Words are vague when they designate qualities that may be present to a greater or lesser degree, and there is no generally known criterion to determine how much of the quality must be present before the word can properly be applied.

Precision

The opposite of vagueness is *precision*. If a word is not vague, it is precise. In the case of precision, our language does provide or imply a rule for applicability. In the sport of boxing, the term 'welterweight' is precise. A fighter is called a welterweight if and only if he weighs between 135 and 147 pounds. Thus, someone weighing a fraction of an ounce more than 147 pounds would *not* be a welterweight, while someone weighing a fraction of an ounce more than 135 pounds would indeed be a welterweight.

'Freezing weather' is a precise term, for there is a line setting 'freezing weather' off from 'non-freezing weather.' We know exactly how cold it has to be before the term can be applied. 'Lawful speed' is a precise term, for laws and signs tell us how much velocity our cars may reach before we enter the illegal zone.

It is, however, much easier to provide examples of vague words than precise words. Most words in our language that designate qualities are vague. We really do not know how much of a particular quality must be present before the term is applicable. Since clear expression and thought require precision, we often artificially provide what natural language does not give us: a rule. If there is no line, we draw one of our own.

The rule or the line may be stipulated in a definition. The teacher may *define* 'passing grade' as 'an average of 60 or above.' The association of retail grocers may define 'fresh bread' as 'twenty-four hours old or less.' The psychologist may define 'genius' as 'person scoring 160 or above on XYZ test.' A sociologist may define 'wealthy' as 'possessing goods of value in excess of $100,000.' The Internal Revenue Service may define 'dependent' as 'person deriving half or more of his support from someone else.'

Some of these definitions may seem somewhat arbitrary, but great clarity has been achieved in the spheres where they operate. When we hear or read these terms, we know the specific ranges where they apply. Vagueness has been eliminated.

Concluding Summary: If the language provides a line distinguishing the applicability of a word from its non-applicability, that word is *precise*. Precision is more often created by definition than found in natural language.

Exploiting Vagueness

The use of vague terms is a device to avoid being pinned down. Advertisers of cigarettes can say with perfect confidence that their product is *mild*—so long as it does not dissolve the lining of the throat. Sellers of golf balls can call them *lively*—so long as they bounce at all. Bakers can call their bread *fresh*—so long as it is free of mold. If these qualities are not clearly in the area of the word's non-application, who is to say they are not in the area of application? If there *is* no line, no one can prove that the quality (so long as it is not an extreme case) falls outside the area of the word's legitimate application. When one is speaking vaguely, he does not commit himself to much.

Consider this passage with its italicized vague words:

> Yesterday the weather was *warm,* so I went to *one of the finest* golf courses in the state, and played a *good* game. Afterwards, *thirsty* from the exercise, I drank *some* beer. I arrived home *tired* but *happy.*

What, actually, has the narrator committed himself to? The weather was above freezing, there is a golf course in the state that is inferior to the one he played on, his score was less than 150, he wanted a drink of something afterwards, he consumed at least one swallow of beer, and he arrived home in a state less energetic and morose than when he departed. The passage tells us how he spent his time but characterizes his actions and feelings hardly at all.

Although the user of vague words says very little, the listener often does not realize it. When the golfer says he had a good game, the listener may think of a score obviously in the 'good' range: low seventies. But all the golfer has said is that it was *outside* the not-good (or bad) area: it was not over 150. He is guaranteeing that the score was not at the extreme end of non-applicability, while the listener erroneously thinks he's committing himself at the other extreme (applicability). When the advertiser speaks of light biscuits, we think of fluffy things weighing a fraction of an ounce, but so long as the biscuits are not obviously outside the 'light' range (say, weighing a pound apiece), he cannot be shown to have misrepresented his product.

We have to be very wary. We must refrain from imputing more information to vague discourse than it actually contains. Vagueness is a way to seem to be saying a lot while not saying very much at all.

One last example—with a slightly different moral. If a man's wife or sweetheart asks him if she is beautiful, he has a vague word on his hands. Clearly Marilyn Monroe, Cybil Shepherd, and Raquel Welch are beautiful. On the other hand, Golda Meir, Nancy Walker, and Phyllis Diller are clearly in the opposite category of non-beautiful. Between these extremes are the vast majority of women, with no line to indicate where 'beautiful' stops and 'non-beautiful' begins. So if a man's wife or sweetheart asks him what *he* thinks, he should answer unhesitatingly that she is beautiful. Hearing this she will tend to place herself among the Monroes and Shepherds, but all the man is guaranteeing is that she is not at the opposite end of the scale with Walker and Diller. Strictly speaking, he has not lied. He had simply resorted to vagueness.[15]

Vague words may be the basis of a fallacious argument. A speaker may overlook (or try to get his listener to overlook) the fact that there is an area of uncertain application between two extremes. He thus presents two extreme alternatives as the *only* alternatives. He may argue that someone is beautiful or ugly (''not beautiful''), that Americans are free or oppressed (''not free''), that drinking is harmless or debilitating (''not harmless''), and insist that his listener espouse one or the other. If the listener declines to accept one of the extreme positions, he is forced to accept the other. This is the *black-or-white fallacy*.

The fallacy occurs when the question of *degree* (which may be very important) is ignored. No shades of gray are admitted to exist between that which is jet black and that which is snowy white. ''It's just a matter of degree,'' someone may say. ''If the party was not exciting, it must have been a bomb!'' Although there may not be a hard-and-fast line between exciting and nonexciting parties, there are differences in degree in the interest that a party may generate. Failure to qualify for one extreme does not mean that the *other* extreme is the case.

Concluding Summary: Vagueness makes possible two questionable strategies: (1) The speaker employs vague words to avoid being pinned down, but he hopes that his listener will understand his words to refer to an area of certain application. (2) The speaker, ignoring the area of uncertainty, seeks to pin his listener down to one or the other of the areas of certain application.

EXERCISES

Exercise 13

The following quotations are from advertising copy. Replace vague words with precise expressions:

1. ''A dollar back and long lasting energy, too.'' (power cell, Union Carbide)
2. La-Z-Boy Classics: ''Introducing a premium quality recliner with high fashion looks at an affordable price.''
3. ''Clark gets it done. You can count on it. Because the equipment is good to begin with.''
4. ''Had it with hot taste? Then put down what you're smoking and pick up the extra cool taste of Kool.''
5. ''Two great restaurants invite you to Thanksgiving turkey dinner.'' (Eisele's Black Forest, Bavarian Inn)

[15] This example is not intended to be sexist. It is a fact, however, that some women wish to be regarded as beautiful—just as some men wish to be regarded as handsome. In any case, we are speaking in this paragraph about a particular kind of physical beauty. That there are other kinds of physical beauty, as well as moral and intellectual beauty, is not denied.

6. True: "The low tar, low nicotine cigarette. Think about it."
7. "Seville Sale! Ten in stock to choose from at big savings!"
8. "Visit Penny's Remnant Room. . . . Find luxury Broadloom room-size rugs at low, low prices."
9. "Tom Jones": "A rollicking new play with music."
10. "A $200 million world-class golf course community in St. Charles County." (Whitmoor Country Club)

Exercise 14

A large office complex issued a dress code for its female employees. Indicate the rules that you think are too vague.

1. Fingernails shall be trimmed to a moderate length.
2. No earring may be longer than one inch.
3. Skirts shall be knee-length or lower.
4. Hair shall not be dyed a flashy or spectacular color.
5. Jeans may not be worn.
6. Heels must be three inches or shorter.
7. No underwear must be visible.
8. Good habits of personal hygiene and cleanliness must be observed.
9. Rouge and lipstick, if used at all, must be lightly applied.
10. Necklines shall be modest.

DEFINITION

The Nature and Types of Definition

A definition states the meaning of a particular expression (word, term, phrase, symbol). It sets forth the conditions for the appropriate use of that expression.

It is important to note that definitions are concerned with linguistic expressions. They often take these forms:

$$\text{'}X\text{'} =_{df} \text{'}X\text{'} \qquad \text{'}X\text{' means '}Y\text{'}$$

Definitions deal with the expressions with quotes around them. The one on the left in each case is the term-to-be-defined (definiendum); the one on the right is the defining term (definiens). Definitions are very different from descriptions. If we say that ice cream is a delicious dessert that is cold and comes in many flavors, we are not defining 'ice cream.' Instead we are describing the thing denoted by 'ice cream.' To define 'ice cream,' we must specify the conditions for using the term.

Those definitions which seek to state the meaning that the term ordinarily has among the people who use it are called *lexical* (or reportive or real) definitions. The defining term of a lexical definition tells us how the term-to-be-defined is actually used in society. Most of the definitions in dictionaries are lexical. We consult a dictionary to find out how terms are conventionally used.

There is another type of definition. It is also concerned with meaning and therefore with use. But it deals with individual use rather than social use. An individual proposes a *stipulative* (or nominal) definition when he says, in effect: "I don't care how other people use this word or even whether it is used at all. This is the word and this is how *I* intend to use it."

Lexical definitions seek to express an existing "rule of language." They are successful when they correctly reflect actual usage. Stipulative definitions prescribe a *new* "rule of language." They are successful when they serve the special purposes of their proposers. If we know how the defining term is used, we will know how the term-to-be-defined is to be used.

Consider these definitions:

'Glory' = $_{df}$ 'exalted honor, praise, or distinction accorded by common consent.'

'Glory' = $_{df}$ 'a good knockdown argument.'

The first is a lexical definition, taken from *The American Heritage Dictionary of the English Language*. It indicates how most of us use the word 'glory.' The second is a stipulative definition, taken from *Alice through the Looking Glass*. It indicates how Humpty Dumpty intends to use the word.

It sometimes happens that after a person has stipulated a new definition for an old word (or has coined one for the occasion), it becomes accepted in wider and wider circles. Time and usage thus change a stipulative definition into a lexical one:

'tiglon' = $_{df}$ 'offspring of a male tiger and female lion.'

'liger' = $_{df}$ 'offspring of a male lion and female tiger.'

'angel' = $_{df}$ 'a radar echo caused by something not visually discernible.'

'glitch' = $_{df}$ 'an unwanted brief surge of electrical power.'

'streak' = $_{df}$ 'run nakedly in public.'

Concluding Summary: A definition may state the conditions governing the use of an expression in society, or it may state the special conditions governing its use by the person doing the defining. The first type is lexical: how society uses the term. The second type is stipulative: how *I* use the term.

The Adequacy of Definitions

Definitions are better or worse, depending on how accurately, completely, and clearly they specify the conditions governing the use of the term-to-be-defined. Observation of the following principles would tend to promote the adequacy of a definition:

(a) The scope of an adequate definition is clearly understood. Because most words have several possible uses, it is often helpful to specify the scope of the term-to-be-defined. In what contexts is the defining term to apply?

In the scope (or within the context) of *sailing*, for example, 'brig' means 'two-masted vessel square rigged on both masts.' But in the scope of *naval discipline*, 'brig' means 'the compartment of a ship where prisoners are confined.' If the defining term is to be substituted for the term-to-be-defined, the substitution could take place only in the specified context. Sometimes the scopes overlap: 'Sam was thrown into the brig's brig.'

Where the scope is obvious, there is no need to specify it. If we are talking about baseball and someone defines 'strike' as 'act of swinging at pitched ball,' there is little danger than someone else will apply the defining term to fishing, bowling, or labor relations.

In the case of stipulative definitions, the speaker should state the contexts in which his new definition applies: "during this conversation," "throughout my speech," "in this book when I'm talking about space exploration."

(b) Adequate definitions are broad enough but not too broad. If we are defining a word by stating its intension, and it is the case that the word has extension, the defining term should be found to apply to all things denoted by the term-to-be-defined, but no more.

If we define 'triangle' as 'plane rectilinear figure with three sides of equal length,' we find that the defining term excludes things (right-angle triangles) denoted by 'triangle'; the definition is thus too narrow. If we define 'triangle' as 'plane figure with three sides,' we find that the defining term includes things (figures with *curved lines*) not denoted by 'triangle'; the definition is thus too broad.

We often have a clearer notion of a term's extension that of its intension, and we can use this knowledge to check the adequacy of a definition. A Supreme Court Justice said, "I can't define 'obscenity,' but I know it when I see it." In the case of a lexical definition, we ask, "Does it include all the things that people ordinarily use the term to denote, but no more?" In the case of a stipulative definition, we ask, "Does it include all the things that I want the term to denote, but no more?" This is called "the denotation test."

(c) Adequate definitions are not circular. The simplest kind of circularity consists of using the term-to-be-defined (or a derivative of it) in the defining term. It does not get us very far to define 'history' as 'that which is taught in history courses,' or to define 'poetry' as 'that which is composed by poets.' A definition is not circular when one of several words in a term-to-be-defined is repeated, provided that that word was not seriously in question. For example: 'Isosceles triangle' $=_{df}$ 'triangle having two sides of equal length.' But when all the terms are repeated, we are in trouble: 'Counter-culture' $=_{df}$ 'a culture, especially of the young, with values and mores that run counter to those of established society.'

If a term's meaning is already known, there is no point in defining it. If it is not known, it is futile to employ it in the defining term. Circularity seems so elementary a mistake that no one would be inattentive or desperate enough to commit it. But circularity does, in fact, occur frequently in students' examination papers (as well as in professors' textbooks).

> *Your noble son is mad;*
> *Mad call I it; for, to define true madness,*
> *What is't but to be nothing else but mad?*
>
> —*William Shakespeare*, Hamlet

A more subtle kind of circularity sometimes occurs when one is defining a *series* of terms.

There is no circularity in this pair of definitions:

'Philosophy' = $_{df}$ 'love of wisdom.'

'Philosopher' = $_{df}$ 'a person who espouses philosophy.'

But there is circularity in this pair:

'Philosophy' = $_{df}$ 'that which is espoused by a philosopher.'

'Philosopher' = $_{df}$ 'a person who espouses philosophy.'

In a careful report or essay, we should not employ definitions that ultimately come back to the term-to-be-defined with which we started. If we define 'acting justly' as 'giving everyone his due,' and define 'giving everyone his due' as 'recognizing natural rights,' and define 'recognizing natural rights' as 'acting justly,' we have traveled in a circle. Our set of definitions is seriously flawed.

The dictionary cannot avoid circularity, for it seeks to define all words. But since we do not, we can avoid circularity—simply by leaving some words undefined.

It is easy to fall into circularity when we use negatives. If we define 'brave' as 'not timid,' we might later define 'timid' as 'not brave.' However, there is nothing wrong in using negatives in definitions so long as circularity is avoided.

Use of synonyms also leads to circularity. It is tempting, after defining 'androgynous' as 'hermaphroditic,' to define 'hermaphroditic' as 'androgynous.'

Use of correlatives also tends to result in circularity. We may define 'cause' as 'that which produces an effect' while defining 'effect' as 'that which is produced by a cause.'

(d) Adequate definitions do not employ ambiguous or figurative language. They are direct and prosaic, and they must be unambiguous. We can call architecture 'frozen music' if we like, but we have not defined 'architecture.' It may be helpful to call time 'the moving image of eternity,' but it is not a definition. You can call a singles bar a place where aggressive people go who want to start something, but you have not provided a definition. The statement, 'The President is the shepherd of the University; the Dean is his crook,' is not an adequate definition of either 'president' or 'dean.'

(e) Adequate definitions do not employ obscure or needlessly technical language. With respect to this injunction, Dr. Samuel Johnson is the prime offender of all time:

'Eating' = ₍df₎ 'the successive performances of the functions of mastication, humectation, and deglutination.'

'Network' = ₍df₎ 'anything reticulated or decussated at equal intervals, with interstices between the intersections.'

Since the words in the defining term tend to be unfamiliar, the definition can hardly be expected to convey much information about what the term-to-be-defined means.

'Obscurity' is, of course, a relative term. What is obscure to Peter need not be obscure to Paul. The presence of 'karabiner' would be acceptable in the defining term of a definition addressed to mountain climbers, but not to the rest of us.

(f) Adequate definitions do not seek to bring about emotional reactions. The essential quality of definition is to provide a term's meaning and to show the conditions of its use, not to influence attitudes. Some ''definitions,'' while amusing, are not definitions:

'Explorer' = ₍df₎ 'bum with an excuse.'

'Fanatic' = ₍df₎ 'one who redoubles his efforts after he has forgotten his aim.'

'Marriage' = ₍df₎ 'social group consisting of one master, one mistress, and two slaves, making in all, two.'

'History' = ₍df₎ 'an account, mostly false, of unimportant events which are brought about by rulers, mostly knaves, and soldiers, mostly fools.'

These passages (most of them from Ambrose Bierce's *Devil's Dictionary*) are more concerned to evince and evoke feelings of contempt and cynicism than to state cognitive meaning.

(g) Adequate definitions state the word's connotation whenever it is a significant part of its use. The dictionary lists 'lean,' 'spare,' 'skinny,' 'scrawny,' 'lank,' 'lanky,' 'rawboned,' and 'gaunt' as synonyms. Most of these words have definite connotations, and good dictionaries cite them.

The importance of the injunction to specify connotation will depend in part on the occasion for which the definition is framed. It is indispensable when our concern is with the expressive function of language, but less important if we are concerned chiefly with the informative or descriptive function of language.

Concluding Summary: Adequate definitions provide or imply scope, pass the denotation test, avoid circularity, employ clear and literal language, avoid obscurity, and supply connotation (where it is helpful to do so). Here is a definition that seems to satisfy these principles fairly well:

'Male chauvinist' (in the context of the women's liberation movement) = ₍df₎ 'a person who believes that human males are intellectually and morally superior to human females' (connotation: scorn).

Denotative Definitions

One technique for formulating definitions is to cite all or some of the things denoted by the term-to-be-defined. This, as argued above, can be useful in stating the use to which the term can be put. Denotative definitions indicate the term's extension.

When the number of things denoted by the term is small, a denotative definition can *enumerate them.* 'Super Bowl contestants in 1977' can be denotatively defined as 'Minnesota Vikings and Oakland Raiders.' The defining term could be substituted in all contexts in which the term-to-be-defined occurs. It would be impossible, of course, to define 'Super Bowl contestant' in this way, for no one knows who will be playing in 1998. We can define 'element' by enumerating hydrogen, oxygen, and the rest of them, but, since new elements may be discovered, it would have to be understood that the definition is relative to the time in which it is formulated.

A more common way of employing the denotative technique is to *give examples.* No claim of completeness is made. To say that 'university' means places like Yale, Southern Illinois University, and Oxford is to indicate how the word is actually used.

Another form of the denotative definition is the *ostensive* definition. Here one simply points to one or more of the things denoted by the term-to-be-defined. To define 'Washington Monument,' we point to the Washington Monument. To define 'redness,' we can point to several occurrences of red surfaces. To define 'duckbilled platypus,' we point to some creatures in an Australian zoo.

There are drawbacks to denotative definitions. Many such definitions are not complete—e.g., those of 'university,' 'redness,' and 'duckbilled platypus.' Some may be made obsolete by future discoveries—e.g., that of 'element.' One obvious difficulty, then, is that the defining term cannot be substituted in the contexts in which the term-to-be-defined occurs without a disclaimer of some kind.

A more serious disadvantage is that we can never be sure that we have conveyed the actual meaning of the term in question. If we enumerate the Super Bowl contestants of 1977, one might think that an essential characteristic of such teams is to have a predatory name. If we give examples of universities, someone might think that institutions had to be English-speaking in order to qualify. And, if we point to the Washington Monument, someone might think that the denotation of 'Washington Monument' was a special kind of concrete block.

The examples given above happen to be lexical definitions. But much of what was said about them can also be said about stipulative definitions. We can stipulate that 'southern state' refers to Florida, Georgia, Mississippi, Texas, New Mexico, Arizona, and California (enumeration). We can stipulate that 'philosopher' refers to people like Will Rogers, Norman Vincent Peale, and Joan Rivers (examples). We can point to the snow as a case of redness (ostensive). And we run the same risk of being misunderstood when we stipulate denotatively as we do when we try to convey conventional use denotatively.

Concluding Summary: Denotative definitions may enumerate, give examples, or point to things denoted by the term-to-be-defined. They are helpful in conveying the way in which society uses an expression or the way the speaker intends to use it. There are, however, drawbacks.

Intensional Definitions

The most satisfactory way to define words that have intension is to state the intension. If we can discover (or stipulate) all the essential qualities that must be present before the word can be applied, we not only have an expression which can be substituted in certain contexts for the term-to-be-defined, but we have a complete statement of the necessary and sufficient conditions for their use. The formula ' 'X' = $_{df}$ 'Y' ' indicates that perfect synonymity has been achieved for the term-to-be-defined and the defining term.

The only difficulty with this view is that it is difficult if not impossible to provide a perfectly adequate lexical definition for a great many words. Though such words possess intension, no essential set of qualities can be stated for *all* the similar uses they have. Ronald Munson, after an instructive ''attempt'' to define 'ball,' writes: ''There is no one specific feature that all objects we refer to by the word 'ball' have in common—no thread that runs through them all, no necessary condition for using the word. Instead, there are a number of sets of properties which are sufficient for using the word.''[17] Ludwig Wittgenstein used 'game' as an example of a term which possessed *no one set* of defining criteria. Qualities W,X,Y,Z may be sufficient for the proper use of 'game' on one occasion; qualities V,X,Y,Z on another; qualities T,W,Y,Z on another; and qualities S,T,W,X on another. Games, he said, were a ''family,'' and the various uses of the term 'game' exhibited a ''family resemblance.''[18]

It is important to emphasize that what is involved here is not simply the fact that there are different meanings for the same term. This fact can be handled easily. When 'ball' means a great party, we define it one way; when 'ball' means an object used in sport, we define it another way. The problem is to define the term in *one* of its senses! The conventional uses differ, but not enough to produce a categorically different meaning. Wittgenstein's expression ''family of meanings'' puts us somewhere between *same* meaning and *different* meanings!

If Wittgenstein and his followers are right, we are doomed to failure if we try to give a complete intensional definition for some words. There simply is not the time and space to discover and specify all the components and their combinations in the family of meanings that clusters around such words as 'ball,' 'game,' and 'book.'

So where does that leave us? We must admit that just as the extensional or

---

[17] Ronald Munson, *The Way of Words* (Boston: Houghton Mifflin Company, 1976), p. 46.

[18] See Ludwig Wittgenstein, *Philosophical Investigations* (New York: The Macmillan Company, 1953), pp. 31ff.

denotational approach has limitations, so too does the approach to definition through intension. While we can formulate entirely adequate definitions for such terms as 'triangle,' 'three-base hit,' and 'welterweight boxer'—definitions that present term-to-be-defined and defining term as synonymous and interchangeable—we cannot do this with any confidence for a great many other terms. What can be said about the attempt to reflect or capture the entire conventional meaning of a term in an intensional definition is that it will be more or less successful.

Concluding Summary: Because the intension of an expression is that set of all qualities necessary for its use, a completely adequate definition is possible for some terms. The defining term will express the intension of the term-to-be-defined and can be substituted for it. But, for many expressions, this happy result cannot be achieved by means of a lexical definition. The reason is that the conventional use of these expressions is not entirely consistent. So, while one can aim at adequacy, one may sometimes have to settle for less.

> *Dictionaries are like watches; the worst is better than none, and the best cannot be expected to go quite true.*
> —*Samuel Johnson, quoted in Boswell's* Life of Dr. Johnson

Techniques for Formulating Intensional Definitions

(a) A very good way to formulate a definition (whether lexical or stipulative) is in terms of *genus and differentia.* One first cites the general category to which the term-to-be-defined belongs (genus), then distinguishes it from other things in that category (differentia). Aristotle defined 'man' as 'rational animal.' 'Animal' is the genus, while rationality is what differentiates man from other animals in that genus. 'Pentagon' may be defined as 'polygon with five sides.' 'Polygon' is the genus; 'with five sides' is the differentia. We first get into the ballpark, then we find our seats.

Sometimes it is convenient to employ a sub-genus before the final differentiation is made. The dictionary defines 'automobile' as 'a self-propelled land vehicle.' 'Vehicle' is the genus. 'Land' is a sub-genus, ruling out airplanes and ships. 'Self-propelled' is the differentia which rules out trailers and carts. Perhaps we need still another differentia to distinguish automobiles from trains and motorcycles.

In selecting genus and differentia, we try to select "essential" qualities. Aristotle's defining term for 'man' is better than 'featherless biped,' because the qualities of lacking feathers and having two feet are not thought of as essential to man by most people who use the term. The definition of 'man' as 'featherless biped' would meet the denotation test, but would fail to express the intension of the term-to-be-defined. We might agree that 'depiction of sexual behavior' is a suitable genus for a definition of 'pornography.' But is 'in a way that violates standards of propriety' or 'in a way designed to induce sexual excitement in the reader or observer' the better differentia?

It is thought in some quarters that genus and differentia have metaphysical significance and that a *true* definition will locate the thing denoted by the term-to-be-defined in its proper place in the chain of being. This issue will be dodged. We are concerned simply with more or less *adequate* definitions. How well does the definition reflect conventional use or stipulate a special use?

We will not even insist that the genus be more general than the differentia, although quite naturally it is. In the definition, ' 'stewardess' means 'female flight-attendant,' ' however, the differentia ('female') is more general than the genus ('flight-attendant').

It is often immaterial whether we view one quality or the other as the genus. For the definition, ' 'howdah' means 'canopied seat placed on the back of an elephant,' ' two acceptable views are possible: (1) 'Canopied seat' is the genus, while its location is what differentiates howdahs from other seats. (2) 'Placed on the back of an elephant' is the genus, while its being a canopied seat is what differentiates howdahs from other things placed on elephants' backs.

(b) Another good way to formulate a definition (whether lexical or stipulative) is to place the term-to-be-defined in a *context*. We may find it convenient to define such terms as 'grandparent,' 'ambiguous,' and 'vague' contextually:

> 'X is the grandparent of Y' $=_{df}$ 'there is a Z such that Z is the parent of Y and X is the parent of Z.'

> 'A term is ambiguous in a certain context' $=_{df}$ 'the context has not ruled out all meanings of the term but one.'

> 'A term is vague' $=_{df}$ 'there is no rule in the language to specify the degree to which a quality must be present in order for the term to be used.'

Although some of the words in the first expression are repeated in the defining expression, contextual definitions are not circular. The key term, 'grandparent,' 'ambiguous,' or 'vague,' is not repeated in the defining term.

It is permissible to be quite informal in stating contextual definitions. We can use 'if and only if' instead of '$=_{df}$' and we can omit quotation marks. A contextual definition may be written in this way:

> A line is perpendicular to another line if and only if it strikes that line at a ninety-degree angle.

It should be remembered, however, that while quotes are not used, we are still defining a *word* ('perpendicular') by trying to express its intension.

Contextual definitions are especially useful in defining words other than nouns. Most of the examples above were definitions of adjectives. Following are contextual definitions of a phrase and a verb:

> A ball is *on the green* (golf) if and only if some part of it touches the putting area.

A person *scrambles* in golf if and only if he makes especially good or lucky shots to compensate for poor shots.

Another advantage of a contextual definition is that it conveys something of the syntax of the term-to-be-defined by placing it with other words with which it naturally occurs. The term is placed in a sentence, and the defining term tells us what that sentence means.

The adequacy of any definition is enhanced when it indicates the context for which the definition is appropriate. Contextual definitions do this quite easily. Consider these definitions for two senses of the word 'strike':

A bowler is credited with a strike if and only if he or she knocks down all the pins with the first ball of the frame.

Workers engage in a strike if and only if they leave their jobs in order to win group benefits.

The first clearly indicates what 'strike' means in the context of bowling, while the second tells us what 'strike' means in the context of labor relations.

(c) Another kind of intensional definition is that which employs *one-word synonyms*. Such a definition may indicate quite neatly the meaning a word has. If we are told that 'obese' means 'fat,' we know how to use it; the intension of the two words is the same, so one could be substituted for the other. But this technique for defining words has serious limitations. First, many words do not have exact synonyms. Whether exact synonymity was achieved in the above example is debatable. Second, where an exact synonym is available, it may be too obscure to be helpful. If we don't know what 'doleful' means, we probably won't know what 'lugubrious' means either.

(d) Finally, we will look at a fourth technique for formulating intensional definitions: state that "the term is to apply to a particular case if the performance of specified operations in that case yields a certain characteristic result." This is Carl Hempel's definition of *operational definition*.[19] The technique is useful when we want to provide public and empirical criteria for the application of a term which might otherwise be abstract. It often takes the form of a contextual definition, but its distinctive feature is to specify a physical operation and to state the results of the operation what would justify the use of the term.

Such definitions can be lexical:

'X is harder than Y' $=_{df}$ 'when X and Y are rubbed together, X scratches Y.'

More often they are stipulative:

'X experiences brain activity' $=_{df}$ 'an electroencephalograph attached to the head of X shows oscillations.'

---

[19] See "A Logical Appraisal of Operationism," in Carl G. Hempel, *Aspects of Scientific Explanation* (New York: The Free Press, 1965), p. 123.

Where a term's meaning is not based on the results of physical operations, this kind of definition obviously is inappropriate.

Concluding Summary: There are at least four ways of expressing the intensional meaning of a term: by means of genus and differentia and by means of contextual, synonymous, and operational definitions. Each of these may be lexical or stipulative, and each has its applications and limitations.

Purposes of Definitions

The purposes of definition can be realized by means of lexical or stipulative definition or by a combination of the two basic types. Four such purposes are:

(a) *To increase vocabulary.* We may ask for a definition or look up a word in a dictionary because we are puzzled. We have heard a word (perhaps several times) and are curious about its meaning. Or we may not be able to understand a sentence in which it has just appeared. We want an accurate statement of its meaning. An explicit lexical definition thus serves the purpose of increasing our vocabulary. As someone once remarked, "If Julius Caesar had asked what 'Ides of March' means, he might be alive today!"

We may also increase our own vocabulary and perhaps that of others through stipulative definitions. We may coin a word and stipulate a meaning for it. A zoo keeper may coin the word 'liger' and define it as 'offspring of a male lion and female tiger.' Or he may coin the word 'tiglon' and define it as 'offspring of a male tiger and female lion.' He has increased his vocabulary—artificially but effectively. He is now able to use short words instead of long expressions. Stipulated meanings may pass over into common usage; they then are expressed in lexical definitions.

(b) *To eliminate ambiguity.* If a term is or might be semantically ambiguous in a certain context, we may not want to replace the term or alter the context. Instead we simply provide or indicate a definition. For example:

> I certainly support the democratic way of life—and by 'democracy' I mean the recognition of individual rights and freedoms.

This purpose is usually achieved by means of a lexical definition. There are two or more conventional meanings possible, and we indicate one of these by means of a definition.

We may want to use a word in a rather unusual way. To prevent ambiguity, we should explicitly stipulate the meaning the word is to have for us. The older or more common meanings are thereby ruled out. Much confusion can be avoided by the straightforward assertion that *this* meaning, whatever other meanings the word may have, is the one intended here.

(c) *To eliminate vagueness.* If the natural language does not provide a rule to distinguish applicability from non-applicability, the individual must do it himself. Reliance on lexical definition will not dispel vagueness; stipulation is necessary.

Consider the following definitions:

'Mountain' = $_{df}$ 'any elevation of the earth's surface to a point two thousand feet or more above the surrounding terrain.'

'Expensive dinner' = $_{df}$ 'a meal costing more than fifteen dollars, exclusive of drinks and gratuity.'

These definitions are partly lexical and partly stipulative. They are lexical in that their basic meanings correspond to actual usage. They are stipulative in that the exact amount of the quality required (elevation or price) is stipulated. The definitions accept a common meaning but draw a line where no line exists in ordinary usage.

(d) *To identify a theoretical idea.* A scientist or philosopher may wish to use a word to represent a fundamental idea in his theory. The defining term might well be complicated and lengthy. Comprehension of the term might be equivalent to the comprehension of an important aspect of the theory.

Such a definition could be partly lexical. The definer could take a common term and state a meaning that is similar to its ordinary usage. But, since the defined word refers to an idea that most people cannot be fully acquainted with, the theoretical definition will be partly stipulative. Einstein's definition of 'simultaneity' and Plato's definition of 'justice' are examples of theoretical definitions that are partly lexical and partly stipulative.

Einstein, to get away from an absolutist sense of the word, would put the matter this way: "Two events are simultaneous with respect to some local framework, for example, the world-line of some observer passing through P, if they are neither in the past nor the future of P."[20] Plato's definition is contained in this passage: "Justice in the state meant that each of the three orders in it was doing its own proper work. So we may henceforth bear in mind that each of us likewise will be a just person, fulfilling his proper function, only if the several parts of our nature fulfil theirs."[21]

Occasionally a scientist or philosopher will formulate a theoretical definition that is almost entirely nominal. Leibniz's definition of 'monads' as indivisible and impenetrable units of substance differing only in levels of awareness goes far beyond the simple meaning the Greek term originally had. Essential principles of his metaphysical theory are embodied in the meaning of the term itself. It is sometimes useful to formulate a definition in which the term-to-be-defined is a new word. Norbert Wiener thought so when he coined the word 'cybernetics' and defined it as 'the science of communication and control systems.'

It very important in ethical and legal matters to know exactly how a term is used. In these and other areas we must pin down the meaning. Is 'fetus' to be defined as a 'prenatal form of human life' or 'a potential form of human life'? Are 'pornographic' and 'obscene' really synonymous as Chief Justice Burger assumed in

---

[20] See Marx W. Wartofsky, *Conceptual Foundations of Scientific Thought* (New York: The Macmillan Company, 1968), p. 335.

[21] Plato, *The Republic,* translated by F. M. Cornford (New York: Oxford University Press, 1974), pp. 139–40.

Miller v. *California* (1973)? What is the actual difference between 'treason' and 'espionage'? The adherents of the Clean Air Act must provide a definition of 'clean air' in terms of permissible amounts of carbon monoxide, hydrocarbons, and other pollutants. Insurance companies and personnel people must know exactly what 'medically disabled' means. In many cases all four purposes of definition are achieved in achieving the *basic* purpose—that of indicating the actual or intended *use* of a term.

Definitions formulated to match a definite theoretical idea with an explicitly chosen term have this in common with other definitions: They are about *words,* and they do not, in themselves, tell us anything about the reality beyond the verbal sphere. Einstein's definition of 'simultaneity' may make the word very useful in talking about events in space and time. But whether events ever occur "simultaneously" is a factual question to be determined by investigation. Plato's definition of 'justice' assigns to that word a meaning characteristically Platonic. He has not established the nature of justice by defining the *term*. What justice really is, is something beyond the verbal realm where definition operates. If Plato convinces us that he's right, he does so by appealing to facts and ideals, not by making useful definitions. Definitions may serve, quite indirectly, the cause of truth. But truth is correspondence with reality, while definitions merely tell us the meanings of the words with which we talk and think about reality.

It is not a resolution to use certain words in certain ways that constitutes knowledge. The use to which words may be put is arbitrary; they are prescribed or stipulated by an individual or by society. Good definitions facilitate the search for truth. But truth lies not in the *words* but in the propositions that words permit us to assert.[22] Abraham Lincoln, it is said, asked someone this question: "If you call a tail a leg, how many legs has a dog?" The person answered, "Five." "No," said Lincoln. "Calling a tail a leg doesn't *make* it a leg."

Concluding Summary: Definitions—lexical and stipulative—may be employed to increase vocabulary, eliminate ambiguity and vagueness, and identify theoretical ideas.

Pitfalls in Choosing Definitions

Persons exercise a lot of choice in the meanings they may assume or the definitions they may formulate for the words they use. They may select one from among the several conventional meanings a term has, or they may choose to abandon conventional meanings entirely. These choices, when exercised properly, facilitate communication. When exercised improperly, through carelessness or design, they produce confusion and fallacy.

(a) *Quibbling.* When a party to a discussion gives a different meaning (lexically or stipulatively) to a word that has already been used and whose meaning is clear, he is quibbling. He may by his ill-advised action produce a disagreement that is

---

[22] For a discussion of propositions, statements, and sentences, see Chapter 3.

> *But the Idols of the Market-place are the most troublesome of all: idols which have crept into the understanding through the alliances of words and names. For men believe that their reason governs words; but it is also true that words react on the understanding; and this it is that has rendered philosophy and the sciences sophistical and inactive.*
>
> —*Francis Bacon,* Novum Organum

merely verbal. The parties to the dispute, if they are not alert, may as a result believe that they are in genuine disagreement (when they are not). Or they may become so confused they fail to recognize the nature of whatever genuine disagreement may be present.

Suppose a student says that History 306 is very difficult and points out that she has to study fifteen hours a week for that course. A second student then says that the course is not difficult at all, arguing that he understands all the concepts referred to in the lectures and the readings. The second student is quibbling on the word 'difficult.' The first student obviously meant 'requires lots of study time.' She is entitled to that meaning, and that meaning should prevail in the discussion. But the second student gratuitously shifts the meaning of 'difficult' to 'demanding great powers of comprehension.' What they are really arguing about is what 'difficult' shall mean—which is pointless. An argument in which disagreement is produced by differences in assumed meanings is a verbal argument, and the person who produces it is guilty of quibbling.

If the second student had avoided quibbling, his response would have consisted of remarking that he understood what was going on. It is not a very interesting or relevant observation, but quibbling has been avoided and no verbal disagreement has been produced. If he wanted to indicate real disagreement with the first student, he would have to deny that the course was difficult *in her sense of the word* 'difficult.' Another acceptable response on his part would have been to say, "That is not what I mean by 'difficult.' By 'difficult' I mean . . ." This expresses a willingness to argue about meaning, and if it is quibbling at all, it is not as reprehensible as the kind that operates covertly. That the disagreement is verbal is at least brought out into the open.

It is not the case that a dispute containing verbal disagreement is always *merely* verbal. Genuine disagreement may be present also. Consider the following discussion:

A. A falling tree in the north woods would produce no sound, for there are no beings there to experience the auditory sensations.

B. I'm sorry, but you are mistaken. There would indeed be sound, for the vibrations of the air would go out from the crash whether anyone picked them up or not.

A. You're quibbling on the word, 'sound.' I agree that in your sense of the word there would be sound. But in my sense of the word there would not be. Let's not waste our time arguing about how we intend to use the word, 'sound.'

B. OK. But even in your sense of the word, there is sound. There must be *some* creatures up there with ears. If trees can grow, some form of animal life must also exist.

A. Not necessarily!

The disputants have managed to resolve the verbal disagreement only to find that they have a genuine disagreement—which may (or may not) be worth arguing about.

(b) *Question-begging definition fallacy.* Begging the question occurs when one assumes in the premise of an argument the very thing he or she is trying to prove. The person who argues that the Bible is to be trusted because it declares itself to be the word of God commits the fallacy of begging the question. Another way of begging the question is by stipulating certain definitions for key words.

The car dealer who promises that "no reasonable offer will be refused" has not bound his hands, for any offer he did not choose to accept would fall outside his tacit definition of 'reasonable.' The wine merchant who guarantees that his product "will delight anyone with discerning taste" can blame the palate of anyone who does not find his wine delightful. Beware of individuals who begin their arguments with "all educated people believe . . ." and "any fair-minded person would . . ."

The person who exercises his stipulative privileges to the limit never seems to lose an argument. His confidence that all crows are black, that philosophers are always optimistic, that no women are good drivers remains unshaken, whatever evidence is brought to him. We should be suspicious of such a person, for matters of fact are seldom so certain.

If we brought our friend a yellow crow, he would deny that it is a crow. Why? Because he has defined 'crow' as having, among other things, the quality of blackness.

"What do you think Al means by 'reasonable offer'?"

And if we cite the case of the pessimistic philosopher, Schopenhauer, he would claim that he is not a genuine philosopher—since he lacks the crucial characteristic of discerning the ultimate purpose in the universe. And Ella Murphy, who hasn't so much as scraped a fender in fifty years behind the wheel of a truck? Well, she drives like a man. She's a good driver, all right, but it's because of the masculine side of her nature. Woman, qua woman, lacks the attribute of being a good driver.

So all these propositions are true—in some non-factual sense. They are tautologies: true by definition. They are like such statements as 'all bachelors are unmarried' and 'purple cows are purple.' They are true, not because the world is a certain way, but simply because certain meanings have been stipulated for words. They tell us nothing whatsoever about the universe that we did not know before.

The fallacy consists of winning, or trying to win, a factual argument by means of a definition. A factual conclusion *seems* to follow, when in reality it is only a tautology made possible by a tacit stipulative definition. When one gives a term a new meaning (which is one's privilege), he or she owes it to a listener to come right out with it, to make it explicit. If our friend had done so with his strange definitions of 'crow,' 'philosopher,' and 'woman,' the tautologous nature of his ''convictions'' would be apparent. And no one would argue with him.

Whether a statement is factual or non-factual depends on what its words mean. Ordinarily, 'all philosophers are optimistic' is factual, since its truth or falsity depends upon facts. But define 'philosopher' as 'optimistic lover of wisdom' and the statement becomes non-factual. That is, its truth or falsity is independent of any factual condition. Assuming the right definitions, any statement can stand as necessarily true. But no one should make the mistake of believing that it says anything specific about the world.

(c) *Persuasive-definition fallacy.* It was pointed out earlier that it is improper to formulate definitions for the purpose of arousing emotions. Good defining consists of stating a term's meaning, not evincing or arousing feelings about what it refers to.

Let us now shift our attention from the defining term to the term-to-be-defined. It is indeed a fact that certain words in most contexts have strong emotive force. A term (for example, 'murderer') may evoke the passions through its intension. In the section on connotation, examples were given of words that tend to evoke the passions over and above their simple intensions. It is this phenomenon of emotive force that makes the persuasive-definition fallacy possible.

This is the way it works: (1) Take a word that has strong emotive force. (2) Stipulate a *new* meaning for it. (3) Provide a context which will encourage its old emotive force. This is a fallacy because we are no longer entitled to the *old* emotive force after we have given the word a *new* meaning.

If we take the term 'god' and give it a new meaning—say, 'a set of moral ideals that inspire our best efforts'—we should not try to carry over the old emotive force of 'god,' which consists of faith and peace and confidence that virtue will ultimately triumph. If we define 'murderer' as 'a person who prevents a human life from coming into existence,' we may then assert that people who use contraceptives

> *Tell me what's wrong*
> *With words or with you*
> *That you don't mind the thing*
> *Yet the name is taboo.*
>
> —*D. H. Lawrence,* Conundrums

are murderers, but we are not entitled to all the negative connotations that 'murderer' formerly had. This fallacy is an attempt to eat one's cake (new meaning) and have it too (old emotive force).

Here is another example of the persuasive-definition fallacy: "I believe in free enterprise, for it is what made this country what it is today. Now what 'free enterprise' means is for everyone to look after Number One in as shrewd and ruthless a way as possible. Cheating on exams is engaging in free enterprise—provided you don't get caught. So don't criticize me! I'm just displaying the initiative and resourcefulness that characterize the American way of life!''

Emotional appeals, it will be argued later, do not belong in the realm of good thinking. It is bad enough to capitalize on aroused emotion, but to exploit the emotive force of a term that should no longer have this force is inexcusable.

Concluding Summary: We can choose definitions in ways that interfere with good thinking. Quibbling produces verbal disagreement. The question-begging definition fallacy makes an empty tautology look like a statement of fact. The persuasive-definition fallacy illegitimately preserves the old emotive force of a word that has been redefined.

EXERCISES

Exercise 15

Indicate whether the following "definitions" are extensional *or* intensional. *Where the former, indicate whether* enumerative, by example, *or* ostensive. *Where the latter, indicate whether* by genus/differentia, contextual, by synonym, *or* operational.

1. 'Extracurricular activities' are things like sports, dramatics, and music.
2. 'Liberty' = $_{df}$ 'freedom.'
3. "Home is the place where, when you have to go there, they have to take you in." (Robert Frost)
4. 'James Greenleaf Whittier' means James Greenleaf Whittier.
5. You want to know what I mean by 'chartreuse'? Just look at those drapes I'm pointing at.
6. An argument is valid if and only if its conclusion follows necessarily from the premises.
7. 'Sophomore' = $_{df}$ 'student who is in his or her second year of high school or college.'

8. The solution is alkaline if and only if the litmus paper turns blue.
9. 'College degree' refers to associate, bachelor's, master's, specialist's, and doctor's degrees.
10. 'Ratiocination' is 'thinking.'

Exercise 16

Examine the following inadequate definitions. Indicate the main flaw in each from this list of possibilities: does not state the essential qualities, seeks to produce an emotional reaction, is too broad, is too narrow, is circular, describes instead of defines, employs ambiguous or figurative language, employs obscure or needless technical language, is misleading.

1. The *conscience* is "the inner voice that warns us that someone may be watching." (H. L. Mencken)
2. 'Square' means 'polygon with four equal sides.'
3. 'Oats' = $_{cf}$ 'A grain which in England is generally given to horses, but in Scotland supports the people.' (Samuel Johnson)
4. "Political power, properly so called, is merely the organized power of one class for oppressing another." (Karl Marx)
5. "A *manuscript* is something that is submitted in haste and returned at leisure." (Oliver Herford)
6. 'Eft' means 'newt.'
7. 'Cactolith' means 'A quasi-horizontal chonolith, composed of anastomising ductoliths, whose distal ends curl like a harpolith, thin like a sphenolith, or bulge discordantly like an akmolith or ethmolith.' (See Willard R. Espy, *Words at Play,* p. 304.)
8. 'Musical instrument' means such things as trumpets, trombones, and tubas.
9. An outfielder in baseball is someone who plays in the outfield.
10. 'Fork' means 'eating utensil.'
11. 'Triangle' means 'rectilinear figure with three sides of equal length.'
12. *Vagueness* is what occurs when vague words are used.

Exercise 17

Choose a genus and a differentia from each list to define the words listed below.

Genus	Differentia
A. poetic composition	(a) consisting of an octave and a sestet.
B. prose composition	(b) narrating a people's heroic tradition.
	(c) presenting the personal views of the author on a single subject.
	(d) setting forth a long fictional narrative.
	(e) setting forth a short fictional narrative.
	(f) consisting of musical and narrative stanzas.

Genus	*Differentia*

(g) addressed to some praised object, person, or quality.

(h) which mourns for the dead.

(i) which aims at unity of characterization, theme, and effect in a brief fictional narrative.

(j) presenting an account of a person's life.

1. 'Ballad'
2. 'Biography'
3. 'Elegy'
4. 'Epic'
5. 'Essay'
6. 'Novel'
7. 'Novella'
8. 'Ode'
9. 'Short story'
10. 'Sonnet'

Exercise 18

Define all the terms below in terms of the following undefined terms and/or any of the terms previously defined:

'X is a female'

'X is the parent of Y'

1. 'X is a male' $=_{df}$ 'X is not a female'
2. 'X is the father of Y' $=_{df}$ 'X is the parent of Y and X is male'
3. 'X is the mother of Y' $=_{df}$
4. 'X is the child of Y' $=_{df}$
5. 'X is the daughter of Y' $=_{df}$
6. 'X is the grandparent of Y' $=_{df}$
7. 'X is the grandfather of Y' $=_{df}$
8. 'X is the sibling of Y' $=_{df}$
9. 'X is the sister of Y' $=_{df}$
10. 'X is the uncle of Y' $=_{df}$
11. 'X is the great-aunt of Y' $=_{df}$
12. 'X is the first cousin of Y' $=_{df}$

Exercise 19

Which function is probably intended by each of the following definitions? The term-to-be-defined is in boldfaced type.

Note: Dictionaries may be used.

Indicate your choice by the appropriate letter:

A—*to increase vocabulary*   C—*to eliminate vagueness*
B—*to eliminate ambiguity*   D—*to identify a theoretical idea*

1. ''By **substance,** I understand that which is in itself and is conceived through itself; in other words, that, the conception of which does not need the conception of another thing from which it must be formed.'' (Spinoza.)
2. Ted Williams was, without question, **a great hitter.** And to be a great hitter, you have to bat .400 or better in a full season.
3. When I say that good steaks are **rare,** I mean that they aren't put on the market very often.
4. ''An experienced datum is conceived as **epistemologically subjective** if it is not assumed to possess, and therefore to be capable of exhibiting, any 'intrinsic' quality or relation which the intended object of knowledge has within its own spatio-temporal limits.'' (Arthur O. Lovejoy, *The Revolt against Dualism.*)
5. For your information, **'disingenuous'** designates 'the quality of being crafty in a sneaky kind of way.' So the next time I call you that, you'll know what I mean.
6. Yes, I would call Vickie **tall.** She's over five feet ten inches in height.
7. **'Determinism'** may mean several things, but I prefer the definition of Lucius Garvin: ''the view that every natural event is due to previous natural events and would not have happened in just the way it did save for those previous events.'' (*A Modern Introduction to Ethics.*)
8. We need a word to designate 'the study of philosophical treatises.' Why not call it **'philosophology'?**
9. It doesn't matter how big the area of uncertainty is. If there's a doubtful area at all, I call the term **vague.**
10. When the navy speaks of ''officers and **men,''** they mean officers and noncommissioned personnel.
11. **'Cryptoscopophilia'** means 'the desire to look through windows of homes that one passes by.' (See Willard Espy, *Words at Play,* p. 304)
12. **'Melcryptovestimentaphilia'** means 'a fondness for women's black undergarments.' (See Espy, p. 304)

Exercise 20

The first speaker says: '' 'Affirmative action' means giving minorities an advantage when it comes to jobs and admission to educational programs. It is a case of compensatory justice. We've dealt unjustly with minorities in the past. In fairness, the pendulum must now swing the other way.'' Characterize each of these responses, using the appropriate letter:

A—*quibbling*
B—*not quibbling and not disagreeing in fact*
C—*not quibbling but disagreeing in fact*

1. Well, if it did, it would be a case of discrimination in reverse. That's not fair, either.
2. *Real* affirmative action consists of evaluating individuals on their own merits.
3. I'm in favor of affirmative action, but I don't think "quotas" is the way to do it.
4. If affirmative action means that the less qualified should be selected over the more qualified, I'm against it.
5. The legacy of past discrimination is the inability of present minorities to win out in open competition. That's why they need (and deserve) special treatment.
6. Affirmative action requires setting up rigid quotas. This is unfair to the white male.
7. Affirmative action calls for *goals*, not quotas. Still, it's not fair to target some for these goals while neglecting others.
8. I'm opposed to discrimination. We should respect the equal rights of all. So I'd be in favor of any kind of affirmative action that worked for this kind of attitude.
9. Affirmative action is an imperfect but temporary expedient for bringing all groups to the point where they can compete. Eventually, there will be no need for affirmative action.
10. Affirmative action is fatally flawed: It advocates one kind of preferential treatment in order to eliminate another kind of preferential treatment. It's like giving a drunkard scotch to drink in order to keep him away from bourbon.

Exercise 21

For each of the arguments below, indicate which fallacy is present:
A—question-begging definition fallacy
B—persuasive-definition fallacy

1. So-called "realism" in books and movies is really nothing more than an excuse to portray sexual behavior in a shocking and provocative way. Let's call it what it is—pornography—and ban those books and movies that depict sexual situations.
2. Euthanasia is a praiseworthy act. The term itself means "a good death." Anything that would bring about a death that is untimely, or premature, or mean-spirited would be wrong, because, by definition it would *not* be productive of a good death. It would not be a case of euthanasia.
3. The act of deliberately taking the life of an innocent human being is wrong. The fetus is a human being, an innocent person. Abortion, therefore, since it seeks to kill this person, is wrong.
4. Charitable acts are rightly praised. Indeed, one can even get an income-tax deduction for making charitable donations. Well, I'm putting money away for my retirement which is a charitable act on behalf of myself. If gift-

giving is such a good thing, you should not call me selfish for donating funds for my own future security. Charity begins at home!

5. As any person of discerning taste can tell you, Joyce Kilmer's poem, "Trees," is a literary masterpiece. You say that Louis Untermeyer sees no value in it? Well, that just shows that he is not a person of discerning taste.

Chapter 3

Statements

PREVIEW

The result of placing words together in a functional way is sentences. When sentences are used in order to inform, they are called statements. In this chapter we will look at the various forms that statements may take. If we can master the forms, we can master the countless statements that take these forms. Fortunately, these forms are few in number! Among the things you should learn in this chapter are:

1. How to determine whether a sentence is performing the *expressive, directive,* or *informative* functions.
2. How to determine whether a dispute represents a disagreement in *belief* or disagreement in *attitude*.
3. How to determine whether a disagreement is *real* or merely *verbal*.
4. How to express categorical statements in one or other of the *four standard forms*.
5. What *conjunctive* statements are.
6. What *disjunctive* statements are.
7. What *conditional* statements are.
8. What *tautologous* statements are.
9. What *self-contradictory* statements are.
10. What *synthetic* statements are.

Although much of this may sound rather technical, you already know many of these things. Give yourself a little test and see if you pass it:

1. Do all declarative sentences perform the informative function?
2. Do all interrogative sentences perform the directive function?
3. What does this sentence suggest: *George is even taller than William.*
4. Do these statements say the same thing?

Only fools buy lottery tickets.
All fools buy lottery tickets.

5. Do these statements say the same thing?

The only movies I like are westerns.
All movies that I like are westerns.

6. True or false? Paris is in France or the moon is made of green cheese.
7. True or false? Paris is in France and Rome is in Spain.
8. Can this statement possibly be false? *All wives are spouses.*
9. Can this statement possibly be true? *Some husbands are not spouses.*
10. True or false: Some statements are neither necessarily true nor necessarily false.

SENTENCES AND STATEMENTS

Form and Function

When one or more words are placed together in a functional grouping, they form *sentences*. Sentences in a discourse are separated from other sentences by terminating punctuation signs.

The class of sentences is often divided on the basis of grammatical form:

1. Declarative sentences. Something is asserted that is either true or false. Concluded with a period.
2. Interrogative sentences. A question is asked. Concluded with a question mark.
3. Imperative sentences. A command or request is given. Concluded with a period or exclamation point.
4. Exclamatory sentences. An emotion is expressed or evinced. Often concluded with an exclamation point.

This is a useful classification and suggests the basic *functions* of language: (1) to inform, (2) to direct, and (3) to express. Declarative sentences, because they make assertions, tend to serve the *informative* function. Interrogative and imperative sentences, because they request answers or other actions, tend to serve the *directive* function. And exclamatory sentences, because they express emotions, tend to serve the *expressive* function.

It is not the case, however, that this convenient correspondence always exists between form and function. We cannot always determine a sentence's function by ascertaining its grammatical form. Not all declarative sentences perform the *informative* function, and declarative sentences are not the only kind that do. Not all exclamatory sentences perform the *expressive* function, and exclamatory sentences are not the only kind that do. And not all interrogative and imperative sentences serve the *directive* function, and they are not the only kinds that do.

"Do you know where your parents are?"

(1) The informative function of language is served by such declarative sentences as these:

The book is on the table.

All dogs are poodles.

If the bough breaks, the cradle will fall.

But it is also served by such interrogative sentences as these:

Wasn't Napoleon a great general?

Aren't we responsible for the appearance of our own neighborhood?

Grammatically, these are questions. But they are more concerned to assert something than to elicit answers. The first is not asking about Napoleon's greatness; it is asserting it. The second is not asking about neighborhood responsibility; it is affirming it. Exclamatory sentences may also serve the informative function:

Franco Harris just scored a touchdown!

Thar's gold in them thar hills!

These sentences convey information, however excited the speakers may be.

(2) The directive function of language is served by the imperative sentence:

Raise your right arm.

And by the interrogative sentence:

Where were you last employed?

The first is a request for an action; the second is a request for specific information. Sometimes an interrogative sentence is a request for an answer to a question not literally asked by the sentence itself:

Do you know what time it is?

It is quite possible that such a sentence is asking not for a yes-or-no answer, but the specific time of day.

The directive function can also be served by declarative and exclamatory sentences:

The goldfish have not been fed in three days.

I'm dying for a drink!

What the speaker is directing be done is obvious in each case.

(3) The expressive function of language is served by such exclamatory sentences as:

I love you, Muriel!

Ouch!

But it may also be served by such interrogative sentences as:

Where will it all end?

How lucky can you get?

The speaker of such sentences is not requesting answers to specific questions. A listener who tried to provide them would have missed the intent of the utterances, which is to express emotions. Sometimes it is completely out of place to answer "questions." Finally, we may observe that some declarative sentences are more intended to express emotion than to convey information. Examples are:

"Loveliest of trees, the cherry now is hung with bloom. . . ."

"I have . . . miles to go before I sleep."

"Earth has not anything to show more fair. . . ."

There is no easy and mechanical way to determine the function of a sentence or passage. Some passages may serve two or more functions at the same time. Even a single sentence, although one purpose will usually be dominant, may serve two functions at the same time. The radio announcer who reported the Hindenburg disaster expressed his own sorrow while describing the flames that engulfed that airship. The intention of the speaker, difficult as this may sometimes be to ascertain, is the best guide for his language's function. And the more we know about the nature and situation of the speaker, along with the meaning and context of his utterance, the more we will know about his intention.[1]

Concluding Summary: Language may be used for the functions of informing, directing, and expressing. The grammatical forms that sentences have are less dependable indicators of which function is being served than the intention of the speaker.

Function and Truth

Declarative and exclamatory sentences that are informative in function are *statements*. The information they convey is either correct or incorrect. They state something about the universe, and what they state is actually the case or it is not. The relationships they assert either correspond to reality or they do not. Statements are either true or false.[2]

Most declarative sentences perform the informative function and are thus statements. Those declarative sentences the main function of which is to direct are not statements. The purpose of the sentence, 'I wish you would close the window' is not to inform us of what the speaker's wishes happen to be, but to direct us to close the window. One can treat the sentence *as if* it were a statement, but fundamentally it is not.[3]

Some exclamatory sentences perform the informative function as well as the expressive function. The sentence 'Coleman just stole second base!' has as an important function that of informing the listener what has just happened on the field. The statement involved is there—with an exclamation point tacked on. Whatever the emotion of the announcer reporting Coleman's theft of second base, it is or is not the case that he stole it. Many exclamatory sentences, of course, are not informative in any important way. The sentence 'Oh, what a beautiful morning!' clearly has the primary purpose of evincing feelings. One might suppose that such an utterance would not be made if the morning were wet and cold, but this is merely an inference. More difficult to classify would be the sentence 'I'm just thrilled to death!' One

---

[1] Some students of language would add a fourth function: *performative*. A sentence performs the performative function when its very utterance establishes or changes a certain situation or relationship. Examples: 'I christen thee Algernon.' 'I promise to repay the loan next week.' 'I'll take that bet.' 'I suggest that you watch your language.'

[2] The purpose of defining 'statement' is to avoid ambiguity and to identify a theoretical idea. The definition, since it departs from ordinary usage, is stipulative.

[3] Sentences that *perform* also have the declarative form, but are not statements. For example: 'I apologize for my rudeness.'

might argue that this, like the Coleman sentence, is informative as well as expressive. But since the former is neither the primary nor an important function of the sentence, the sentence should not be called a statement.

Some interrogative sentences have the primary or sole function of informing. They cannot themselves be called statements, but they do strongly *suggest* statements. 'Wasn't Napoleon a great general?' suggests that he was; and 'Aren't we responsible for the appearance of our own neighborhood?' suggests that we are. The statements 'Napoleon was a great general' and 'We are responsible for the appearance of our own neighborhood' are, like all statements, true or false. They assert something that may or may not be the case.

So, with all sentences performing the informative function, there is present or suggested a statement. This statement asserts something about the world that may or may not be true.

Some logicians speak of *propositions* and place them in various relationships with sentences and statements. The proposition is what the sentence or statement is supposed to assert. It is what corresponds or does not correspond to reality. The truth or falsity of the sentence or statement springs from the truth or falsity of the proposition. The concept of the proposition will virtually be ignored in this book. We will consistently speak of the truth or falsity of sentences (some) and statements (all, by definition). 'Proposition' is mentioned here only to point out an obvious truth: Two different statements may assert the same thing:

> The book is on the table.
> The table is under the book.
>
> J'ai faim.
> I'm hungry.

One may say that each pair asserts the same proposition (as some logicians say), or one may say that each pair asserts the same state of the world (as is said in this book).

What statements do is to assert some relationship or other about things in the universe. The things talked about either have this relationship or not. If they do, the statement that asserts it is true; if they do not, the statement that asserts it is false.

The question of truth and falsity is not crucial to directive discourse. Commands and requests may be proper or improper, justified or unjustified, but they are not true or false. They may be made in the light of beliefs that are true or false, but are not themselves true or false. Suppose that two people issue orders for two courses of action that cannot both be carried out. One person tells the quarterback to pass on the next play; the other tells him to hand off to a running back. The quarterback

---

To understand a proposition means to know what is the case, if it is true.
—*Ludwig Wittgenstein,* Tractatus Logico-Philosophicus

cannot obey both, but there is nothing contradictory in a universe that contains two people with different wishes. When the coach himself, in the heat of battle, issues contradictory commands, he may be said to be confused, but it would be improper to say that one of his commands is true and the other one false. Only when a command has been *converted* to a statement that it may suggest do we have something that is true or false. The *statement,* 'The correct play is a forward pass,' is either true or false and is contradictory to the *statement,* 'The correct play is not a forward pass.'

Questions, as instances of directive discourse, are not, strictly speaking, true or false. But they are, every one of them, uttered in the light of certain factual assumptions. The listener in answering them or considering what his answer will be accepts these assumptions. ''Where is the nearest gas station?'' assumes that a gas station exists somewhere in the general vicinity. ''Who won the basketball game last night?'' assumes that a basketball game was played. ''Why did he call and break the date?'' assumes that the action did occur and that there is a rational explanation for it. In these questions and most others, while the factual or informative element is present in the background, it is not the issue. It is to be taken for granted. The purpose of the question is to elicit an answer (directive), not to convey facts (informative).

There is, however, a rhetorical device in which the attempt is made to foist a particular point of view on someone by getting him to accept factual material behind a question that is *not* something that can be taken for granted. This is called the *fallacy of complex question.* The victim has not been alert enough to challenge the assumption behind the question. In answering it (or even considering an answer), he has conceded a point to his opponent. For example:

(1) Do you still think the Cubs will win the pennant?
(2) Why have the Republicans been fiscally more responsible than the Democrats?
(3) When will the United States land a woman on the moon?
(4) Who has been giving the President all that bad advice on Nicaragua?

The first assumes that the listener has indeed predicted a pennant for the Cubs. The listener, forced to answer yes or no, concedes by making an answer something that may not be true. The second assumes that the Republicans *have* been more responsible—which may not be the case. The assumptions in the third and fourth questions are obvious. The listener, even if he answered, ''I don't know,'' would seem to be conceding an important point to his opponent.

It is an easy matter to avoid being duped by the fallacy of complex question—provided, of course, that it is recognized for what it is. You simply refuse to answer a question that has built-in ''information'' that is debatable. You do not have to *refute* the assumption or prove that it is mistaken. You simply point out that the question contains material that the *speaker* has not established to be true. (1) What makes you think I ever made such a prediction? (2) You seem to believe that the Republicans are more responsible. What is your evidence? (3) Do you have any good reason for believing that this will occur? (4) How do you know that someone has been advising the President and why do you think the advice was bad? There is no logical reason why *you* should be on the defensive. The individual who seeks to perpetrate the fallacy should be placed on the defensive.

The question of truth and falsity is irrelevant also to expressive discourse. Emotions may be deep or superficial, genuine or feigned, expressed or merely evinced, but they are not true or false. They may be experienced in the context of a true comprehension of what is going on or a false one, but sentences that express these emotions can be neither true nor false. You may feel one way about strawberry-flavored yogurt; I may feel another way. But, again, there is nothing contradictory in a universe that contains two people with different feelings.

It is only when two people, using language in an informative way, assert incompatible things about the universe that something is wrong. Only when we are concerned with beliefs can there be a conflict in belief. In such a conflict, at least one of the beliefs must give way. Two opposing commands may both be justified; two exclusive emotions may both be genuine; but two incompatible beliefs can *not* both be true.

Concluding Summary: Sentences that primarily serve the informative function either are statements or strongly suggest statements. Statements make assertions about reality and are true or false. Sentences primarily serving the directive and expressive functions are not statements, nor do they strongly suggest statements. Since they make no assertions about reality, they are neither true nor false.

Kinds of Disagreement

If two people espouse statements such that both cannot be true, they are in disagreement. If two people espouse sentences that express (or evince) two very different emotions about the same thing, they are also in disagreement. The first kind is called *disagreement in belief;* the second kind is called *disagreement in attitude.*

If it is in our interest to resolve disagreement, we have to know what kind of disagreement is present. We may first check to make sure that it is not merely verbal. Do key words employed by the parties in the dispute have equivalent meanings? If they do, the disagreement is a real one. If the key words do not mean the same for both parties, they must be made to do so. If the disagreement dissolves away, it was merely verbal. What disagreement remains must be real.

The next step is to ascertain whether this real disagreement is based on belief or attitude or both.[4]

Suppose that A argues that John Locke, English philosopher and author of *Two Treatises of Government,* is a democrat, since he favors protection of individual rights. B argues that Locke is not a democrat, for he did not insist that the legislature be elected by the people. This looks like a verbal argument: Locke is a democrat on A's meaning of the term, but is not a democrat on B's meaning of the term. If

---

[4] The following discussion is based on the work done by Charles L. Stevenson in his book, *Ethics and Language* (New Haven: Yale University Press, 1944).

'democrat' were used consistently, there would be no disagreement. If A's meaning is chosen, B could simply agree, then point out Locke's lack of concern for popular sovereignty. If B's meaning is chosen, A could agree, then point out that despite Locke's lack of concern for popular sovereignty, he did believe in upholding individual rights.

But if B argues that John Locke had no real commitment to individual rights, there is disagreement in belief. The two views on Locke's commitment to individual rights are incompatible. At least one of the two views is, as a matter of fact, false. By the same token, if A argues that Locke favored a popularly elected legislature, there would be disagreement in belief. The two views on Locke's position on the legislature are incompatible. One of the two views is, as a matter of fact, false.

It is sometimes difficult to determine whether a point of view is primarily expressive (based on feeling) or informative (based on judgment) or a mixture of the two. Is the sentence, 'The conduct of intercollegiate sports is disgraceful,' an expression of feeling or an attempt to state something about reality? Its presence in a dispute, together with a conflicting point of view, will make it difficult to determine whether the disagreement is one of attitude or belief (or both). Some serious analysis may be necessary before the real issues can be identified.

How are disagreements in belief and attitude resolved, once they have been identified? Consider this example:

A: The waiter has served us spinach.

B: It is not spinach; it is dandelion greens.

This is a case of disagreement in belief. The parties to the dispute hold incompatible views on what the facts are.

The disagreement can be resolved by determining factually and logically what the green vegetable really is. The two may taste it, consult the menu, or question the waiter. When both parties are in possession of the same data relevant to what has been set before them and agree on the soundness of any inferences made from them, their disagreement should dissolve. They will be ready to agree that the vegetable is either spinach or dandelion greens (or something else).

Suppose that the exchange had been this:

A: The waiter has served us spinach.

B: The waiter has also served us iced tea.

Although the beliefs of A and B are different, they are not incompatible. They could both be correct. Since the beliefs could both be true at the same time, there is no conflict, and thus no disagreement. There is no disagreement in belief to resolve.

Consider this example:

Mother: Eat your spinach, Walter, it's delicious and very good for you.

Child: I know it's spinach and is loaded with vitamins, but I can't stand the taste of it.

How is this case of disagreement in attitude resolved? The obvious way to deal with an emotional disagreement is to make an appeal that will change the feelings of one of the parties to the dispute. The mother may eat some spinach with obvious gusto and enjoyment. She may call in the authority of Walter's father, who declares that if Walter will only taste it he will find it not so bad. Besides, he wants to have some dessert, doesn't he? The parents may paint a picture of a famous spinach eater who goes around ''beating up'' nefarious characters much larger than himself. Such appeals may (or may not) change Walter's feelings about spinach.

It should be noted that having *different* feelings about something does not in itself constitute a disagreement in attitude—just as having different views of the fact does not in itself constitute a disagreement in belief. For example:

Mother: Eat your spinach, Walter, it's delicious and very good for you.

Child: Thanks, mom, but I'm just not hungry tonight.

The mother has evinced a feeling of approval for spinach. Walter has evinced a feeling of not being hungry. These two emotions are different, but they could both be experienced at the same time by the same person. The one does not tend to *displace* the other. There is thus no disagreement in attitude, and therefore no disagreement to resolve.

It is often the case that one kind of disagreement sustains the other kind. A disagreement in belief may be the basis for a disagreement in attitude, and a disagreement in attitude may generate a disagreement in belief.

An example of the first occurred during the Watergate affair. One person was furious at Nixon for what he believed was Nixon's coverup of the break-in; he felt that Nixon was a crook. Another person felt that Nixon was an honorable man for trying to bring the perpetrators of the break-in to justice. It is quite possible that had both persons possessed the same beliefs about the facts of Watergate their feelings about Nixon would not have been in disagreement.

If two people have different attitudes toward a dish served at a dinner, it is quite possible that the conflict arises from a disagreement in belief on what in fact the dish is. One person may believe that it is rhubarb pie, the other that it is cherry pie. If they both believed that it in fact was cherry, they both might smack their lips.

It is wise, therefore, when the disagreement is in attitude, to ascertain whether there is an underlying disagreement in belief.

Let us now look at the other possibility: A disagreement in belief may be the result of a disagreement in attitude. James may argue that a particular scheme of socialized medicine can be soundly financed in the United States. Helen disagrees. In the dispute, many facts and arguments are exchanged, but the disagreement in belief persists. It is quite possible that feelings are so strong on both sides that the facts and arguments do not register. Both parties have closed minds. James refuses to examine Helen's data and inferences because of his great feeling of outrage that some citizens do not receive proper health care (a feeling that Helen does not share).

Helen is impatient with James' presentation because of her strong negative feelings about anything socialistic (a feeling that James does not share). Unless the emotional heat can be reduced somehow, it is unlikely that James and Helen will ever resolve their disagreement in belief—or even *understand* the opposing point of view.

It is wise, therefore, when the disagreement is in belief, to ascertain whether there is an underlying disagreement in attitude.

Concluding Summary: People may disagree in belief or attitude. The first is normally resolved by seeking more facts and argument; the second by resorting to emotional appeals. It is possible, however, that disagreement in belief is caused or sustained by disagreement in attitude, and that disagreement in attitude rests on some disagreement in belief. In such cases, it is profitable to try to resolve the basic disagreement first.

Suggestion

There is a fourth kind of thing that sentences can do. In addition to informing, directing, and expressing, they may *suggest*. It was observed above that some interrogative sentences, while not themselves statements, suggest statements, and thus may be said to serve the informative function. In the very asking of these questions, the speaker is conveying his own viewpoint.

This is the first way that suggestion can operate: by asking questions the answers to which are obvious. Other examples are:

Would I be here now if I were not serious?

Who would hire a man like that?

What is so rare as a day in June?

Aren't you perhaps feeling insecure?

The suggestions these questions make are expressed in these statements:

I would not be here now if I were not serious.

No one would hire a man like that.

Nothing is so rare as a day in June.

You are feeling insecure.

Statements may also be suggested by other statements:

Only ticket holders are admitted.

We don't litter the highway.

Harry Fletcher received a passing mark in my course.

Yvonne's current husband is Horace Carlyle.

I am not very good at small talk.

He never actually *said* he loved me.

The first states that all people admitted are ticket holders, but suggests that anyone with a ticket will be admitted. But this last is only a suggestion; the original statement does not guarantee admission to ticket holders. The second suggests that others litter the highway, but makes no accusation. The third suggests that Harry just squeaked by; in fact, he may have received an ''A.'' The fourth suggests that Yvonne has had many husbands. Actually, Horace is her first, and they will soon be celebrating their golden anniversary. The fifth suggests that the speaker is very good at conversation about major issues—which may or may not be true. The sixth suggests that he did everything *short* of telling her to her face that he loved her, when in fact he may not even have been acquainted with her.

When one takes a statement that someone else has made and chooses to emphasize certain words in order to give the statement a different meaning, he or she commits the *fallacy of accent*. Margaret may innocently remark that she and Ted had a good time last night. Irma then says, ''Oh, you had a good time *last night?* Your other dates with him were not so enjoyable, then?'' Irma has committed the fallacy.

As we can see from these examples, an assertion may be correct (or true) in what it states, but incorrect (or false) in what it suggests. A person certainly is

You have to do more than read lips

responsible for what he states. Is he responsible for what he suggests as well? Or is the listener at fault for imputing things to the speaker that he never said? Do we blame the user of suggestive speech or the suggestible listener? We should blame them both: the one for his deception, the other for being taken in by it.

Suggestion can be achieved by discourses of two or more statements as well as by single statements. Two statements may be made in such a way that the listener believes there is a connection between them. Consider:

> She had a lesson from the pro on Friday.
> On Saturday she shot the best game of her life.

> Jim was seen quarreling with Madge.
> Jim has been very irritable this week.

The first pair suggests that the good game was a result of the golf lesson. The week before, however, the day after the lesson, she shot the worst game of her life! The second pair suggests that the quarrel was caused by Jim's irritability. In fact, Jim could have been very patient and Madge the querulous one. It also suggests that the irritability was the result of the quarrel. So this one is ambiguous in its suggestibility!

Finally, we will look at *slanting*. It is possible to create an entirely erroneous impression through the use of a discourse containing statements that are all true. The discourse may be true in what it states, but false in what it suggests.

Slanting employs two major devices: (1) Selection. Cite only the facts that are favorable to your point of view. Never even hint at the unfavorable ones. Speak as if what you are saying is not only accurate but complete. The discourse will suggest that the partial truth is the whole truth. If you are describing a vacation spot, discuss the sunshine, the beautiful people, the exotic food. Do not mention the high prices, the insects, and the poor service. (2) Arrangement and emphasis. How you arrange and emphasize your material will have suggestive results. If you place certain facts in places of prominence and/or repeat them, they may be taken as more important than they really are. And something that is very important will not appear to be so if it is buried on another page at the end of your article. If you are writing up a case of murder, you can make the police look very good by emphasizing what they have done and have found out, keeping their mistakes out of the headlines. Compare the following accounts, both slanted:

HOSTAGES RELEASED

Fifteen children were released this morning unharmed by their captors. The kidnapers are still barricaded behind the doors of the Huntington Museum, where they have been for four days. They have repeated their demands: food and cigarettes now and independence for Greenland within one year. If these demands are not met, they have threatened to destroy every rare book in the museum. The children were glad to get out, but reported that they had been well treated.

TOTAL DESTRUCTION THREATENED

The terrorists in control of the Huntington Museum have vowed to annihilate the priceless treasures of the museum if their personal and political demands are not met. Now in their fifth day, they are known to possess ample dynamite and incendiary bombs. The men, believed to be American members of the fanatical H.A.T.E. organization, have demanded complete freedom for Greenland. Their leader, whose mother pleaded with him to surrender, refused to talk to her, but shouted his defiance of all imperialists. Fifteen children were released this morning, hungry and frightened. They were taken to a local hospital for examination.

Slanting presents facts that are incomplete and are emphasized in such a way as to suggest a distorted view of the actual situation. But a skillfully slanted account will contain no statements that are false!

Concluding Summary: There are several ways that language may be used to suggest: A question may suggest a positive statement, a statement may suggest another statement, a set of statements may suggest that there is a connection between them, and slanting may foist an erroneous viewpoint on the listener. Suggestion is a way to avoid responsibility for creating false or unproven conceptions.

Everything that can be thought at all can be thought clearly.
Everything that can be said can be said clearly.
   —*Ludwig Wittgenstein,* Tractatus Logico-Philosophicus

EXERCISES

Exercise 22

Indicate whether the function of language primarily served by each of the following is informative, directive, *or* expressive.

1. Gentlemen, start your engines.
2. "Damn posterity! What's posterity ever done for us?"
3. "The noblest prospect which a Scotchman ever sees is the high-road that leads him to England." (Samuel Johnson)
4. Except for milk, the potato is the food most consumed in the United States.
5. "There's a broken heart for every light on Broadway."
6. "Go west, young man." (John Soule)
7. "If anything can go wrong, it will." (Murphy's Law)
8. Murphy was an optimist.
9. Gabriel, Michael, and Lucifer are the only angels named in the Bible.
10. "Let sleeping dogs lie." (Charles Dickens)
11. "Please, sir, I want some more." (Charles Dickens)
12. "Be it ever so humble, there's no place like home." (John Howard Payne)

13. Don't cross the bridge till you come to it.
14. How many times have I told you to put your toys away?
15. Comfort the afflicted and afflict the comfortable.
16. Will you love me in December as you do in May?
17. Patrick Henry owned 65 slaves at the time of his death.
18. "Tell that to the marines—the sailors won't believe it." (Sir Walter Scott)
19. "What would the world do without tea?" (Sydney Smith)
20. "Can anybody remember when the times were not hard and money not scarce?" (R.W. Emerson)

Exercise 23

For each of the following, indicate what kind or kinds of disagreement (verbal, belief, *or* attitude) *is present.*

1. A. Elmer was not a violent man. I never knew him to strike a person or an animal, and he never fired a gun.
   B. His violence operated psychologically. He had an inner rage that caused him to needle his friends, torment his children, and humiliate his wife. Elmer was one of the most violent people I've ever known.
2. A. We rode our bikes all afternoon, racing through the most delightful countryside in all Europe. We covered at least forty miles.
   B. For forty miles or more we had to pedal those damned bikes along hot and dusty country roads.
3. A. Whittier was a great poet, but he did not write, "When the Frost Is on the Pumpkin."
   B. Another fine poem composed by James Greenleaf Whittier is, "When the Frost Is on the Pumpkin."
4. A. The evening star for next October 22 is Mercury.
   B. On October 22 Venus will be the evening star.
5. A. The decision on whether to abort a fetus or to give birth to it belongs solely to the woman who is pregnant. The fetus is, after all, only a condition of her own body.
   B. From the moment of conception, another life has begun to exist. And it has all the rights that other lives have. The fetus is not simply a condition of a pregnant body.
6. A. Abortion prevents the existence of unwanted children. It is humane for all concerned.
   B. Abortion is murder.
7. A. She served banana-cream pie for dessert, and it was delicious.
   B. After clearing the table, she wheeled out the rhubarb pie. I was *sick*.
8. A. The crash of the Hindenburg was caused by sabotage: someone wanted to strike a blow at Hitler Germany.
   B. I wouldn't call an impulsive act by some deranged crackpot an act of sabotage.

Exercise 24

State what each of these passages suggests:

1. He really didn't do any *harm* while he was working here. . . .
2. You must have been a beautiful baby.
3. The state mental hospital is on Route 140. Just beside it is the public golf course.
4. You should not speak ill of your *family!*
5. Will you please call out distinctly whether the ball is within the court or not? (origin of gamesmanship)
6. When he played ''I've Been Working on the Railroad'' on the piano, many of us were able to recognize it.
7. Who cares?
8. She wore her new dress downtown late this afternoon. A major traffic jam was reported on the 6:00 P.M. news.
9. She was as intelligent as she was good-looking.
10. The company hired Edwina. It has an ''affirmative action'' program.

Exercises 25

Indicate whether the fallacy of complex question *or* accent *has been committed.*

1. You say that he is the most competent violinist *in the orchestra.* In other words, you don't think he would compare very favorably with violinists in other orchestras?
2. Please try to answer this simple question: Why are you trying to conceal your knowledge of the whereabouts of the accused?
3. I think that if you could give me a yes or a no answer to this question, I would know how to invest my money: Will the prime interest rate remain at 8 percent for the rest of the year?
4. Well, I see you have arrived at work on time today. I think it should be duly noted that *today* you were right on the button!
5. You say that we should always be willing to help our *friends.* Apparently, then, you disagree with Jesus, who taught that we should help those who are *not* our friends?
6. ''Wanderers eastward, wanderers west,
   Know you why you cannot rest?'' (A. E. Housman)

ATOMIC STATEMENTS

Categorical Statements: Four Standard Forms

It is convenient to distinguish *atomic* or simple statements from *molecular* or compound statements. Atomic statements do not contain other statements as components; molecular statements contain at least two components, each of which could stand alone as a statement. The following are atomic or simple statements:

Some rock stars are weird.

Helen plays the harpsichord.

The following are molecular or compound statements:

Either some rock stars are weird or press reports are erroneous.

Helen plays the harpsichord and her parents are very proud.

These molecular statements assert something about their atomic components. The first, that at least one of them is true; the second, that both are true.

A great many atomic statements may be regarded as asserting a relation of inclusion or exclusion between two classes of things. Such atomic statements are called *categorical statements*.

If a categorical statement asserts that the subject class is included, wholly or partly, in the predicate class, is it said to be *affirmative*.

Consider this statement:

All geniuses are males.

It asserts that every single member of the class of things denoted by 'geniuses' is included in the class of things denoted by 'males.' If, somehow, we made a list of all the geniuses in the world and another list of all the males, we would find that every name on the first list is also on the second. The statement is *universal*, because *all* the subject class is included in the predicate class.

Suppose that we include only a part:

Some geniuses are males.

This means that *at least one* member of the subject class is included in the predicate class. If we compare our lists of geniuses and males, we would find, according to this statement, at least one name on both lists. This statement is *particular*, because only *part* of the subject class is asserted to be included in the predicate class.

If a categorical statement asserts that the subject class is excluded, wholly or partly, from the predicate class, it is said to be *negative*.

Consider this statement:

No geniuses are males.

To say that none is included is to say that all are excluded. The statement thus asserts that every single member of the class of things denoted by 'geniuses' is outside the class of things denoted by 'males.' If we looked at our lists, we would find, according to the statement, no name on both lists. This statement is universal, because *all* the subject class is excluded from the predicate class.

Suppose we exclude only part:

Some geniuses are not males.

> *If you want to know whether you are thinking rightly, put your thoughts into words. In the very attempt to do this you will find yourselves, consciously or unconsciously, using logical forms.*
> —*John Stuart Mill*, Inaugural Address at Saint Andrews

This means that at least one member of the subject class is excluded from the predicate class. If we go back to our lists, the statement asserts that there will be at least one name on the genius list which is not on the males list.

There are four ways of making assertions about classes of thing: all or part of one class is included in or excluded from another class. Corresponding to the four ways of making assertions are four kinds of categorical statement. If we know all the logical ramifications of these four basic statement forms, we will know how to handle the infinite number of particular statements that have these forms.

Concluding Summary: Any categorical statement will exhibit one of these four standard forms:

Universal affirmative (*A*): All *S* are *P*.

Particular affirmative (*I*): Some *S* are *P*.

Universal negative (*E*): No *S* are *P*.

Particular negative (*O*): Some *S* are not *P*.

The letters in parentheses represent the traditional ways of referring to them. The *A* and *I* are said to be positive in *quality;* the *E* and the *O* are negative in quality. The *A* and *E* are said to be universal in *quantity;* the *I* and *O* are particular in quantity.

Expressing Statements in Standard Form

We express a categorical statement in standard form when we make it conform to one of the four forms indicated above. Consider the statement:

Every president is overworked.

This statement can obviously be recast as an *A* statement. 'Every' may be translated as 'all,' and 'overworked' must be made into a noun class. We can thus write it as:

All /presidents/ are /overworked people/

The original statement is now in standard form. It can be abbreviated as:

All *P* are *O*.

The statement, 'Any diamond is valuable,' is also an *A* statement. Supplying a noun for the adjective, we get:

All /diamonds/ are /valuable things/

All *D* are *V*.

We not only convert adjectives to noun classes, but verbs as well. The statement, 'No Eskimos play the violin,' becomes:

No /Eskimos/ are /violin players/

No *E* are *V*.

The word, 'are,' in the standard forms means 'are included in the class of.' It is intended to be tenseless, since time is irrelevant to logical relations. Any temporal factor must be embodied in the classes. 'No St. Louis teams will win championships' is expressed in standard form in this way:

No /St. Louis teams/ are /teams that will win championships/

Since the 'will' in the predicate term makes the meaning of the statement relative to the time when it is uttered, we could express it somewhat differently:

No /St. Louis teams/ are /teams that win championships after November 1, 1990/

One problem in expressing statements in standard form is that of choosing the nouns with which to express the classes. Consider the statement:

Playing hockey is fun.

Is this statement about people, places, things, times, actions, or something else? A plausible answer to the question would provide us with a *universe of discourse:* that larger class which comprises both the subject and predicate classes (and their negatives). If we believe that the statement above is concerned with activities, then *activities* is its universe of discourse, and it becomes a simple matter to translate the statement into standard form:

All /activities that are hockey/ are /activities that are fun/

If we believe that the statement is about occasions, then *occasions* is its universe of discourse:

All /occasions when people play hockey/ are /occasions when people have fun/

Knowledge of the context in which the statement appears is helpful in choosing a plausible universe of discourse.

The following are examples of supplying universes of discourse in order to express statements in standard form:

To know him is to love him.
All /*people* who know him/ are /*people* who love him/

Whenever I think of Ireland, I get sad.
All /*times* that I think of Ireland/ are /*times* that I get sad/

Where there is no vision the people perish.
All /*places* where there is no vision/ are /*places* where the people perish/

If it's metallic, it's malleable.
All /*things* that are metallic/ are /*things* that are malleable/

What is done in haste can sometimes be forgiven.
Some /*actions* that are done in haste/ are /*actions* that can be forgiven/

The universe of discourse is indicated by the supplied noun (italicized in the above examples).

It is not necessary that *both* terms express the universe of discourse. For example:

All bears are fierce.
All /bears/ are /fierce *animals*/

Nor is it necessary that the universe of discourse be expressed at all:

Bears are mammals.
All /bears/ are /mammals/

The universe of discourse could be stated outside the statement as 'animals,' 'beings,' or something else. It could not be 'bears' or 'mammals,' for these terms are too narrow.

If the meaning of the original statement is to be preserved, the terms must appear in proper order. Consider the different ways to express 'He loveth well who prayeth well':

All /people who love well/ are /people who pray well/
All /people who pray well/ are /people who love well/

The first is incorrect; it changes the meaning of the original statement. The second is correct. 'Who prayeth well' modifies 'he' which is the subject of the statement. Similarly, the statement 'He jests at scars who never felt a wound' means:

All /people who have never felt wounds/ are /people who jest at scars/

and *not* the reverse.

Concluding Summary: To express categorical statements in standard form, it is necessary to make noun classes of both subject and predicate, eliminate tense from the 'are' that links them, provide a universe of discourse (in some cases), and place the terms in proper order.

Dealing with Universals

There are a great many words that indicate universality. Some have already appeared in the examples above: 'all,' 'every,' 'any,' 'he who,' 'whenever,' and 'no.' To these we can add such indicators of affirmative universality as 'wherever,' 'a,' 'anyone,' and 'everyone,' and such indicators of negative universality as 'none,' 'never,' and 'nothing.' Complete lists cannot be made.

Expressing in standard form is not an automatic matter. We have to grasp the meaning of the original statement and reflect this meaning in our translation. ''Tip-off words'' are helpful, but they do not tell the whole story. We can, however, illustrate some locutions that frequently occur and indicate how to deal with them.

The word 'only' is a difficult four-letter Anglo-Saxon word. It indicates universality, but usually in a reverse order. 'Only the brave deserve the fair' means:

All /people who deserve the fair/ are /brave people/

It does *not* mean the converse of this. 'Only dogs are poodles' means 'all poodles are dogs,' and not the converse. 'Only ticket holders are admitted' tells us nothing whatever about ticket holders, but a great deal about people who are admitted.

We have to be careful, however. The presence of the word, 'the,' may change everything. Consider the statement:

The only people here are adults.

We do not in this case reverse the terms. 'The only' here simply means 'all':

All /people who are here/ are /adults/

This is correct. To make 'adults' the subject would be incorrect.

'A' often means universality: 'A thing of beauty is a joy forever' means (less lyrically):

All /beautiful things/ are /joys that last forever/

And 'A person is not a machine' means:

No /persons/ are /machines/

But 'A' does not mean universality in this sentence: 'A squirrel is in the birdfeeder.' 'Nothing' and 'never' usually mean universality:

Nothing that walks on two legs frightens him.
No /beings that walk on two legs/ are /things that frighten him/

She never goes out without her compass.
No /times that she goes out/ are /times that she does not have her compass/

Some statements assert that a specified individual is included in or excluded from the predicate class. These are called *singular statements*. Such statements, when positive, may be treated as *A* statements:

Orion is a constellation.
All /things that are identical with Orion/ are /constellations/
All /Orion/ are /constellations/

The man on your immediate left is a spy.
All /beings identical with the man on your immediate left/ are /spies/
All /the man on your immediate left/ are /spies/

Such statements, when negative, may be treated as *E* statements:

> The Eiffel Tower is not insured.
> No /things that are identical with the Eiffel Tower/ are /insured things/
> No /Eiffel Tower/ are /insured things/

> The deepest river in the world is not blue.
> No /things that are identical with the deepest river in the world/ are /blue things/
> No /the deepest river in the world/ are /blue things/

Whether we use the awkward 'things that are identical with . . .' locution or the ungrammatical one that follows it, we are expressing the subject as a class that contains just one member.

Sometimes a word like 'but' appears after a universal indicator. This always tells us to negate something. For example:

> None but fish can swim.
> No /non-fish/ are /swimmers/

> All except freshmen are happy.
> All /non-freshmen/ are /happy people/

> All intruders except CIA agents will be arrested.
> All /intruders who are not CIA agents/ are /people who will be arrested/

> No one, unless he has applied before May, will be admitted.
> No /people who did not apply before May/ are /people who will be admitted/

> All but Indians are immigrants.
> All /non-Indians/ are /immigrants/

For every correct translation given in this chapter there are others that would be equally correct. We could have chosen different universes of discourse, we could have varied the words somewhat or, in some cases, we could have reversed the order of the terms. Any translation is correct that accurately conveys the meaning of the original statement. We could have said 'violinist' instead of 'violin player,' 'people who are not Indians' instead of 'non-Indians,' 'all occasions that' instead of 'all times that,' and so forth.

In addition to these minor differences, we could have reversed terms, negated classes, chosen *E*'s instead of *A*'s, or chosen *A*'s instead of *E*'s. For any statement, a great many *exactly equivalent* formulations can be given. For the statement, 'Only the brave deserve the fair,' we could write:

> All /people who deserve the fair/ are /brave people/
> No /people who deserve the fair/ are /people who are not brave/
> All /people who are not brave/ are /people who do not deserve the fair/
> No /people who are not brave/ are /people who deserve the fair/

These are all equivalent; they say the same thing. So any of them is correct.

But in the following list all are incorrect:

All /brave people/ are /people who deserve the fair/
No /brave people/ are /people who do not deserve the fair/
All /people who do not deserve the fair/ are /people who are not brave/
No /people who do not deserve the fair/ are /brave people/

These are equivalent to one another but not to the four above. They make the same inaccurate translation of the original statement.

Concluding Summary: There are several words that indicate that a statement is universal. Any universal may be expressed positively or negatively. Although there are always several correct translations possible, each must accurately reflect the meaning of the original statement.

Dealing with Particulars

The *I* and *O* statements mean, respectively, 'at least one . . . is . . .' and 'at least one . . . is not . . .' This is rather arbitrary, reflecting a nominal definition of 'some.' We do not want vagueness in standard forms.

Some examples of particular affirmative statements are:

(1) Some things are both plentiful and valuable.
   Some /plentiful things/ are /valuable things/
(2) There are amusing books that are also edifying.
   Some /amusing books/ are /edifying books/
(3) Many doctors are rich.
   Some /doctors/ are /rich people/
(4) A few lawyers are rich.
   Some /lawyers/ are /rich people/
(5) Most politicians are dishonest.
   Some /politicians/ are /dishonest people/

Some examples of particular negative statements are:

(6) Some things are plentiful but not valuable.
   Some /plentiful things/ are not /valuable things/
(7) There are amusing books that are not edifying.
   Some /amusing books/ are not /edifying books/
(8) Many doctors are not rich.
   Some /doctors/ are not /rich people/
(9) Few lawyers are rich.
   Some /lawyers/ are not /rich people/
(10) Not all candidates are candid.
   Some /candidates/ are not /candid people/

(11) All sports are not subsidized.
Some /sports/ are not /subsidized activities/

In looking over this list of statements, it may appear that for any *I* statement the corresponding *O* is also asserted, and that for any *O* statement the corresponding *I* is also asserted. In (4), for instance, if we say that *a few* lawyers are rich, aren't we also saying that many are not? And if we say in (10) that some candidates are not candid, aren't we also saying that some are? If we assert that *some are* because we cannot assert that *all are,* aren't we really saying that some are *and* some are not? And if we assert that *some are not* because we cannot say that *none is,* aren't we really saying that some are not *and* some are? The answer to all of these questions is *no.*

These other possibilities are *suggested,* but they are not asserted. If someone says that some poodles are dogs, he is not asserting that some poodles are not dogs. The fact that at least one poodle *is* a dog makes his statement (that some are) a true one. He is guaranteeing the doghood of just one poodle. What the rest of the poodles are is left open by the statement. It is often the case that one does not *know* whether the universal is true, so he only asserts a particular. But he will want to keep open the possibility that *all* are, as well as the opposite possibility that *some are not.* The fact, then, that someone refrains from asserting the universal does *not* mean that the universal is known to be false. I may say that some actresses are conceited (the only one I've been acquainted with), but I do not wish to be understood as asserting in addition that some actresses are *not* conceited. This *could* be true, but if 'all actresses are conceited' is true (and I don't know whether they are or not), then it (the negative assertion) is false.

Only when we are sure that a statement is asserting inclusion *and* exclusion, can we translate it into *two* statements, an *I* and an *O.* The statement 'Some cars are expensive and some are not' obviously translates into two atomic statements, an *I* and an *O.* The statement 'Apples are often red but not always' also translates into an *I* and an *O* statement. But the kinds of statements represented by the eleven examples above are not quite so unmistakable. In the absence of additional information from the speakers or writers of these statements, we must take them strictly on the level of assertion, ignoring what they may suggest.

Concluding Summary: There are several words that indicate that a statement is particular. It is often very difficult to distinguish between what a particular statement asserts and what it only suggests.

Two-Way Statements

Some statements make two assertions about the classes they are concerned with. They include the entire subject class in the predicate, and they include the entire predicate class in the subject. These two-way statements are called *identity statements.*

Consider the statement:

The president of the university is its chief officer.

It is a singular statement so should be treated as an *A:*

All /the president of the university/ are /the university's chief officer/

But the predicate is *also* singular, so the converse is also asserted:

All /the university's chief officer/ are /the president of the university/

The original statement thus asserts *two* statements, both *A*'s, the one the converse of the other.

Identity statements are not always singular. Consider:

The college graduates are the leaders of the nation.

To be happy is to be a fool.

The ones who complain the loudest are the very ones who refuse to do anything about it.

To express them in standard form:

All /college graduates/ are /leaders of the nation/ AND
All /leaders of the nation/ are /college graduates/

All /people who are happy/ are /fools/ AND
All /fools/ are /people who are happy/

All /people who complain the loudest/ are /people who refuse to do anything about it/ AND
All /people who refuse to do anything about it/ are /people who complain the loudest/

The two classes, in each of the examples, coincide. To be the one is to be the other.

All of our examples have been *A* statements. What about *E* statements? They obviously cannot be identity statements. Can they be "two-way statements"? 'Martha is not the chairperson' can obviously be reversed: 'The chairperson is not Martha.' This reversibility is the case for *all E* statements. 'No birds are fish' also means 'no fish are birds.' So a universal negative does not assert two *different* statements; it asserts two *equivalent* statements—and always does so. This situation is unlike that involving universal affirmatives. A universal affirmative *may* assert two different statements, the one the converse of the other, but it usually does not.

The *I* statement is like the *E* in that it always asserts two equivalent statements. 'Some politicians are statesmen' means 'some statesmen are politicians.' But these are equivalent statements; the second adds no information to that provided by the first. Unlike the two-way *A*, only one statement is necessary in the respective cases of the *E* and the *I*.

It should be noted that not all atomic statements are categorical. There are at least two kinds of atomic statements that are not categorical in the sense just discussed: (1) Statements that assert relations, not between a subject and predicate class, but between individuals. Relational statements will be discussed in the third part of Chapter 7. (2) Statements that are quantitative or statistical in nature. Statements expressing probability will be discussed in the second part of Chapter 6. The rest will be left to the science of mathematics.

Concluding Summary: Some categorical statements assert two *A* statements where the one is the converse of the other. These two-way statements assert that the classes denoted by the two terms coincide. If the two atomic statements are joined by 'and,' we pass from the region of atomic statements into that of molecular statements.

EXERCISES

Exercise 26

Express each of the following in standard form:

1. Some animals are dangerous.
2. Every story has a moral.
3. Cheaters never win.
4. A shortstop is an infielder.
5. A shortstop in the Brooklyn organization is left-handed.
6. When she is hungry, she eats.
7. Not every woman is dependent.
8. Socrates is mortal.
9. A few students are industrious.
10. Few students are industrious.

Exercise 27

Express each of the following in standard form:

1. "Whatever makes men good Christians, makes them good citizens." (Daniel Webster)
2. "Whom the gods love, die young." (Lord Byron)
3. "He prayeth best who loveth best all things both great and small." (Samuel Taylor Coleridge)
4. "Whenever a man's friends begin to compliment him about looking young, he may be sure that they think he is growing old." (Washington Irving)
5. "Happy is the house that shelters a friend." (R. W. Emerson)
6. Some foods are both tasty and nourishing.
7. "Nothing great was ever achieved without enthusiasm." (R. W. Emerson)
8. Whatever Lola wants, Lola gets.
9. Some fruits ripen after picking.
10. Some fruits do not ripen after picking.

Exercise 28

Express each of the following in standard form:

1. "When the going gets tough, the tough get going."
2. "I have nothing to offer you but blood, toil, tears, and sweat." (Winston Churchill)
3. Everything comes to him who waits.
4. None but the outgoing can succeed as tour leaders.
5. "To be great is to be misunderstood." (R. W. Emerson)
6. Not every job worth doing is worth doing right.
7. Students who hate to do homework are the very ones who should do homework.
8. Only people with good memories should set out to lie.
9. "Young men think old men are fools; but old men know young men are fools." (George Chapman)
10. "Every man desires to live long, but no man would be old." (Jonathan Swift)
11. All but the cobbler's child is well shod.
12. He jests at scars who never felt a wound.
13. There are a few TV programs that are educational.
14. The only books he owns are novels.
15. Many people who bet on the game will be disappointed.

MOLECULAR STATEMENTS

Conjunctions and Disjunctions

Two or more atomic statements may be combined into larger statements called molecular statements. Molecular statements can also be combined into still larger molecular statements. When the major components of a molecular statement are connected by 'and,' the molecular statement is called a *conjunction.*

A conjunction asserts that both (or all) parts are true. Its truth or falsity is thus determined by the truth and falsity of its parts (or conjuncts). No statement is partly true and partly false. It must be either true or false, but not both. The following conjunctions are false:

No dogs are poodles and some dogs are not mammals.
No dogs are poodles and all dogs are mammals.
Some dogs are poodles and some dogs are not mammals.

Each is false because at least one component is false. Conjunctions are true if and only if both conjunctions are true. This would be a true conjunction: 'Some dogs are poodles and all dogs are mammals.'

We will use '&' as an abbreviation for 'and.' We will also use it for words that have the same logical import as 'and.' The following, whatever their differences in suggestiveness, all state the same conjunction:

> Ruth went out with Don, but she had a good time.
> Ruth went out with Don; she had a good time nevertheless.
> Notwithstanding the fact that Ruth went out with Don, she had a good time.
> Ruth went out with Don; however, she had a good time.

We can connect the conjuncts in each case with '&':

> Ruth went out with Don & she had a good time.

It is not the case that all statements which contain the term 'and' are conjunctions. Consider the following:

> Elda and Morris are premed students.
> Elda and Morris are classmates.

The first can be expressed as a conjunction: 'Elda is a premed student and Morris is a premed student.' But the second does not assert that each person is a classmate. It asserts that they are classmates *of each other*. The statement asserts that Elda and Morris are related to one another in a certain way, not that each is a member of the class of classmates.

A *disjunction* is a combination of two or more statements connected by 'or.' The truth or falsity of disjunctions is also derived from the truth and falsity of its parts (or disjuncts).

But we have a special difficulty with 'or.' It is ambiguous in many contexts. Sometimes it means, 'at least one is the case, and maybe both.' That is what it means in these contexts:

> Karl is a citizen or he is married to one.
> (said about someone carrying a passport)

> Rebecca is very bright or she spent a lot of time studying.
> (said about someone who got an ''A'' on an exam)

> Homer possessed a bachelor's degree or a master's degree.

> Ann has traveled a lot or she is very well read.

For a disjunction of this kind to be true, at least one part must be true. But it is not falsified if both disjuncts are true. The disjunction is false only when both components are false. We will call this kind of disjunction a 'disjunction,' and we will replace the word, 'or,' with the symbol, 'v.'

Sometimes an expression with 'or' in it does *not* mean 'at least one is true.' It may mean, 'exactly one is true and exactly one is false.' This is what 'or' means in these contexts:

> Merle is in Memphis or he's in Nashville.

> We'll go to the movies this afternoon or we'll go swimming.
> (said to a child in a stern tone of voice)

All men are mortal or some men are not mortal.

It is snowing or it is not snowing.

These statements would be false if both components were false, and they would be false also if (somehow) both components are true. The speaker intends to assert a situation where the two possibilities exclude one another and where the disjuncts are opposite as far as their truth or falsity is concerned. We will call this kind of a disjunction a *strong* disjunction and will replace the word, 'or,' with the symbol '$\veebar$.'

For contexts in which it is not known for sure that a strong disjunction is intended, we should interpret the statement as an ordinary disjunction. Unless we are certain that 'or' means 'exactly one,' we should regard it as meaning, 'at least one.'

The symbols, '&,' 'v,' and '$\veebar$,' are called *statement connectives,* for they connect statements in such a way as to form larger statements. Since the truth or falsity of the resulting molecular statements is determined by (or is a function of) the truth or falsity of the component statements that the symbols connect, the symbols are said to be *truth-functional* statement connectives.

It is convenient to use the term *truth-value* when speaking of the truth or falsity of statements. The truth-value of true statements is *true;* the truth-value of false statements is *false.* We can now say that the truth-value of molecular statements such as conjunctions and disjunctions is determined by the truth-values of their component parts. Conjunctions and disjunctions are truth-functional statements.

A good way to show that these statements are truth-functional is to construct a table containing all possible combinations of their component parts. In the following tables, 'p' and 'q' are variables and stand for any two statements whatsoever.[5]

COMPONENT PARTS		CONJUNCTION $p \& q$	DISJUNCTION $p \vee q$	STRONG DISJUNCTION $p \veebar q$
p	q			
T	T			
F	T			
T	F			
F	F			

By alternating **T**'s and **F**'s in the first column and pairing them in the second, we have covered all possibilities: when both components are true (first line), when both are false (fourth line), and when they are opposite (second and third lines). We

---

[5] Lower-case letters will also be used as symbols referring to *particular* statements. Generally, letters from 'p' in the alphabet on will be used as variables, while other letters will stand for particular statements. In any case, the context will make clear whether the letters stand for variables or not.

draw a double vertical line after the component parts to indicate that all other truth-values are derived from the truth-values assigned to them.

Can we perform such derivations? Yes. Since conjunctions are true only when both components are true, we place **T** on the first line only, using **F**'s for the other spaces under '*p & q*.' Since disjunctions are false only when both components are false, we place **F** on the fourth line only, using **T**'s for the other spaces under '*p* v *q*.' Since strong disjunctions are true only when their components have opposite truth-values, we place **T**'s on the second and third lines only, using **F**'s for the other spaces under '*p* ⩔ *q*.' The completed table is called a *truth table*.

Concluding Summary: The truth table shows that the truth-values of conjunctive and disjunctive molecular statements are determined by the truth-values of their component parts. Such statements, as well as the connectives which make them possible, are thus said to be truth-functional.

p	*q*	*CONJUNCTION* *p & q*	*DISJUNCTION* *p v q*	*STRONG DISJUNCTION* *p ⩔ q*
T	*T*	*T*	*T*	*F*
F	*T*	*F*	*T*	*T*
T	*F*	*F*	*T*	*T*
F	*F*	*F*	*F*	*F*

Conditionals

When statements are connected by 'if . . . then . . .' the result is called a *conditional* statement. In the conditional statement, 'if she exercises, then she is hungry,' 'she exercises' is called the *antecedent,* and 'she is hungry' is called the *consequent.* A conditional statement presents an antecedent and a consequent; the former is a sufficient condition for the latter. The conditional statement guarantees that the consequent will occur whenever the condition specified by the antecedent is met.

Is 'if . . . then . . .' a truth-functional connective? Consider the statement:

If you meet the graduation requirements, you will receive a diploma.

Suppose you did meet the requirements, but the university declined to award you a diploma. In this case, the conditional is clearly false, for satisfying the prescribed condition did not bring about the promised result. Suppose that you met the requirements and were awarded the diploma. This, in light of the conditional, is what we would expect, so the conditional is not false. Nor would the conditional be false if you did not meet the graduation requirements and did not receive a diploma. What if you did not meet the requirements but the university, in its infinite generosity, awarded you a diploma anyway? This does not falsify the conditional because it did not assert that meeting graduation requirements was the *only* way to get a diploma. And any statement that is not false must be true.

It would appear, then, that the only way a conditional statement can be false is where the antecedent is true and the consequent false. If we use the symbol '→' for the conditional connective, we can construct a truth table for '$p \rightarrow q$' which reflects that it is always true except when the antecedent is true and the consequent false:

p	q	CONDITIONAL $p \rightarrow q$
T	T	T
F	T	T
T	F	F
F	F	T

If this truth table is an accurate representation of the meaning of 'if . . . then . . .' and the conditional statement that it generates, then it follows that conditionals are molecular statements and that 'if . . . then . . .' is a truth-functional connective.

It is the case, however, that this interpretation of 'if . . . then . . .' does not quite conform to the intended meaning of most conditional statements. Consider the following:

> If the United States had used atomic arms in Vietnam, then the war would have been over sooner.

> If the United States had used atomic arms in Vietnam, then the war would have lasted longer.

Since in fact the United States did not use atomic arms, the antecedents of both statements are false. Thus, according to the truth table, *both* conditional statements, despite their apparent conflict with one another, are true!

Consider these conditionals:

> If I take the antidote, then I survive the poison.
> If I do not take the antidote, then I survive the poison.

Suppose that I did survive the poison. The consequent is therefore true. Thus, according to the truth table, both conditional statements are true, regardless of the curative qualities of the antidote.

Equally disturbing is the fact that it is possible to assert true conditional "connections" between events that seem to be totally unrelated:

> If $2 \times 3 = 5$, then Atlanta is in Alabama.
> If $2 \times 3 = 5$, then Atlanta is in Georgia.

> If $2 \times 3 = 5$, then Carter is elected in 1976.
> If $2 \times 3 = 6$, then Carter is elected in 1976.

The first two statements of each pair are true, since the antecedents are false; and the second two are true, since the consequents are true. But what, in all four of these examples, is the *relevance* of antecedent to consequent or consequent to antecedent? Did the one really *condition* the other?

While the truth-table interpretation of 'if . . . then . . .' does not capture all the meaning of most conditional statements, it does reflect an important feature that all of them have in common: the impossibility of having a false consequent when the antecedent is true. All conditionals, whatever else they may say, assert that the consequent will occur whenever the condition specified by the antecedent is met.

We will say, then, that the arrow ('$\rightarrow$') is a truth-functional connective, but that it does not express *all* of what is expressed by 'if . . . then . . .' in most conditional statements. Whatever other kind of connection or implication there may be between antecedent and consequent, at least the kind of connection or implication indicated in the truth table is always present. This kind of connection or implication is called *material implication,* and it simply means that the consequent is never false when the antecedent is true. As we shall see in subsequent sections on equivalence and deduction, this *partial* translation of conditional statements has fruitful uses.

'If . . . then . . .' is not the only expression that can be represented by the arrow. For example,

> Whenever it rains, it pours.
> (it rains)$\rightarrow$(it pours)
> $r \rightarrow p$
>
> I'll attend, provided that I can be late.
> (I can be late)$\rightarrow$(I'll attend)
> $l \rightarrow a$
>
> Hard work always produces results.
> (if you work hard)$\rightarrow$(you get results)
> $w \rightarrow r$
>
> If we assume that the bough has broken, the cradle will fall.
> (the bough has broken)$\rightarrow$(the cradle will fall)
> $b \rightarrow f$

There is another expression that should be discussed here: 'only if.' While 'if' presents a sufficient condition, 'only if' presents a *necessary condition.* Consider the molecular statement:

> Only if she loves him does she marry him.

This asserts that love is necessary for marriage. That is, without her love there can be no marriage. Her love is not put forth as sufficient for marriage—she may love him, but marriage may be impossible (he may not love *her*).

Another way to express a necessary condition is to discard the 'only' and negate both parts: 'If she does not love him, then she will not marry him.' Still another way is to discard the 'only' and *reverse* the components: 'If she marries him, then she loves him.' Thus all three of these statements have the same meaning:

> Only if she loves him does she marry him.
> If she does not love him, then she does not marry him.
> If she marries him, then she loves him.

If we abbreviate the component statements and use the symbol '~' for 'it is not the case that,' they could be expressed as follows:

> Only if l, m
> $\sim l \rightarrow \sim m$
> $m \rightarrow l$

'Love is necessary for marriage' means that no love will result in no marriage, and that marriage guarantees that there was love.

Suppose, in addition to the above, that love on her part always leads to marriage. That is, love is not only a necessary condition for marriage, but a sufficient one as well. Now we can say:

> If and only if she loves him does she marry him.

The 'if' specifies love as sufficient for marriage; the 'only if' specifies love as necessary for marriage. Put them both together and we have a very powerful expression. Indeed, it is so powerful that we can seldom assert it with any confidence about matters of fact. It is useful, however, in stating definitions: the term-to-be-defined and the defining term point to each other and are substitutable for one another.

The "if and only if" statement is called a *biconditional*. It links two conditional statements: '$l \rightarrow m$' (by virtue of 'if') and '$m \rightarrow l$' (by virtue of 'only if'). Now it is certainly possible to write the second conditional this way: '$l \leftarrow m$.' Putting '$l \rightarrow m$' and '$l \leftarrow m$' together, we get a convenient expression for the biconditional: '$l \leftrightarrow m$.' Each leads to the other; each follows the other.

The truth table for the biconditional is:

p	q	BICONDITIONAL $p \leftrightarrow q$
T	T	T
F	T	F
T	F	F
F	F	T

It is false on the second line because p is necessary for q; it is false on the third line because p is sufficient for q.

Concluding Summary: When two statements are linked by 'if . . . then . . .' (or synonyms thereof), the resulting molecular statement is called a conditional. Conditional statements consist of an antecedent and a consequent; the former is a sufficient condition for the latter. The expression 'only if' gives us a necessary condition, although this relation may be expressed by conditional statements as well. When one statement can be presented as a sufficient *and* necessary condition for another, the resulting molecular statement is called a biconditional. We can express a very important part of all conditional relations by using the symbol for material implication ('→'), a truth-functional connective.

Mixed Forms

Some molecular statements contain other molecular statements. These in turn may contain molecular statements. There is no limit to the length and complexity of molecular forms.

Let us look at some examples of molecular statements that contain other molecular statements:

(1) The score is tied and if the Tigers are fouled they will win.

This is a conjunction, one conjunct of which is a conditional:

$t \ \& \ (f{\rightarrow}w)$

We use parentheses in order to avoid ambiguity. The statement is not a conditional the antecedent of which is a conjunction: '$(t \ \& \ f){\rightarrow}w$.'

(2) Either Marx has been misunderstood or Engels has made an important revision and Bernstein is not a Marxist.

This is ambiguous, but it is probably a disjunction, one disjunct of which is a conjunction. We could abbreviate it this way:

$x \ \text{v} \ (e \ \&{\sim}m)$

Once again, we employ parentheses and are careful to put them in the right place. Another example:

(3) If I get married and rent an apartment, then I will have to get a job or borrow some money.

The basic structure of this statement is conditional, but its antecedent is a conjunction and its consequent is a disjunction:

$(m \ \& \ r){\rightarrow}(j \ \text{v} \ b)$

One more example:

(4) If and only if he is not both energetic and dedicated, then he fails in his work and disappoints his parents.

The antecedent of this biconditional is a denied conjunction; the consequent is also a conjunction:

$\sim(e\ \&\ d)\leftrightarrow(f\ \&\ p)$

Suppose that in (1) we had added the expression, 'provided that Stanley is not the man fouled.' Now the statement is fundamentally a conditional and we must supply brackets to make this clear:

$\sim s\rightarrow[t\ \&\ (f\rightarrow w)]$

Suppose that in (2) we had added the expression, 'but in any case, if Bernstein is a revisionist, we have Engels to blame.' This would change the basic structure from a disjunction to a conjunction:

$[x\ v\ (e\ \&\ \sim m)]\ \&\ (r\rightarrow b)$

Suppose that in (3) we had added the expression, 'unless my wife does the right thing and either gets a job or robs a bank.' 'Unless' means 'if not . . . then . . .' and thus makes a conditional out of the original statement:

$\sim[w\ \&\ (g\ v\ o)]\rightarrow[(m\ \&\ r)\rightarrow(j\ v\ b)]$

'Unless' can also be translated as 'or,' in which case the statement as a whole is a disjunction (without the '$\sim$' before the first disjunct). Suppose that in (4) we had inserted the expression, 'or is placed on probation,' after 'fails in his work.' In this case, the statement remains a biconditional but the first conjunct of the consequent becomes a disjunction:

$\sim(e\ \&\ d)\leftrightarrow[\ (f\ v\ x)\ \&\ p]$

No matter how complex the expression becomes, the accurate use of parentheses and brackets indicates its basic form. Let us look at a very involved statement (abbreviations are indicated for each atomic part):

If I send in a pinch-hitter (p) and he is a right-hander (r), then the opposing manager will have him walked (w) or, if he has a right-handed reliever ready (h), replace his pitcher (e), provided that he wants to play the percentages (y); but if I let the pitcher bat (b), he is likely to strike out (f) and strand two base-runners (s).

Let us construct this statement in a step-by-step way: The first part is a conditional, the antecedent of which is: '$p\ \&\ r$.' The consequent is: '$w\ v\ (h\rightarrow e)$.' So we have:

$(p\ \&\ r)\rightarrow[w\ v\ (h\rightarrow e)]$

But this is predicated on the assumption that the opposing manager wants to play the percentages, so the expression above is itself a consequent:

$y\rightarrow\{(p\ \&\ r)\rightarrow[w\ v\ (h\rightarrow e)]\}$

The last part of the statement is introduced by 'but,' which tells us that the whole thing is a conjunction. The second conjunct is:

$b{\rightarrow}(f \mathbin{\&} s)$

So the complete translation is:

$[(y{\rightarrow}\{(p \mathbin{\&} r){\rightarrow}[w \lor (h{\rightarrow}e)]\}] \mathbin{\&} [b{\rightarrow}(f \mathbin{\&} s)]$

Although it is not immediately obvious what course of action we would take if we were manager, the structure of the original statement is clearly revealed to us. It is simply a conjunction with rather involved conjuncts. The first conjunct is a conditional, the consequent of which is another conditional. The antecedent of that conditional is a conjunction; the consequent is a disjunction, one disjunct of which is a conditional. The second conjunct is also a conditional, with a conjunction for a consequent.

Concluding Summary: Molecular forms of indefinite complexity can be expressed through proper use of parentheses and brackets. Any such form will basically be conjunctive, disjunctive, or conditional, and so will any part of it that is molecular.

EXERCISES

Exercise 29

For each of the following molecular statements, indicate whether it is a conjunction, disjunction, strong disjunction, *or* conditional:

1. "A nightingale dies for shame if another bird sings better." (Robert Burton)
2. Roses are red and violets are blue.
3. I make the putt or I lose the hole.
4. He either got mugged or was in an accident.
5. I'll send a valentine to Margaret or Glenda.
6. Whenever he's tired, he takes a nap.
7. Provided that the weather is good, we'll have the picnic.
8. Walter was at the party, but he did not play charades.
9. The game begins at 7:05 or 7:35 P.M.
10. Good study habits suffice for good grades.

Exercise 30

Express each of the following in an abbreviated form:

Example: God loves the sinner but hates the sin: 1 & h.

1. Signing up before Saturday is all you have to do to qualify for the drawing.
2. Being a resident of the city is a necessary condition for getting a library card.
3. Only if I get a raise can I afford to go to Europe.
4. If and only if I win the lottery will I ever be a millionaire.

5. He'll bid something with that hand or he will pass.
6. Unless I'm badly mistaken, that is a scarlet tanager on that tree.
7. The figure is either a pentagon or it is a hexagon.
8. You can be sure that his next book will be well-written or very exciting.
9. She was escorted by Reginald, who was wearing a tuxedo.
10. Whenever I go bowling, I get a pain in my back.

Exercise 31

Express each of the following in abbreviated form, indicating clearly what each letter means:

1. Early to bed and early to rise makes a man healthy, wealthy, and wise.
2. I haven't heard from him lately, but he is in Bangkok or Singapore.
3. If I can raise the money, I'll buy the house—unless, of course, they raise the price.
4. If the sun is shining and I can get off work, I'll play tennis or head for the golf course.
5. Only if the market takes a plunge or the interest rates go up would I consider selling out and investing in treasury notes.
6. If it's the case that if I drive to school I'll waste money and if I bike to school I'll arrive tired, then I'll either waste money or arrive tired, for I have to drive or bike to school.

TAUTOLOGY AND SELF-CONTRADICTION

Tautology

A *tautology* is a sentence which cannot possibly be false. The structure of the sentence itself guarantees its truth. Consider the sentences:

All purple cows are purple.
What will be, will be.
A rose is a rose.

We need not know anything about cows, history, or roses to know that these sentences are true. All we need understand is the syntax of the sentence. Our confidence is based not on a factual investigation of the world but on analysis of language.[6]

Are tautologies statements? It was said at the beginning of this chapter that statements make assertions about the world and that they are true or false depending upon whether what they assert is the case. But with respect to tautologies, we do not have to examine the world to discern conformity between assertion and reality. Tautologies are *necessarily* true.

---

[6] Many logicians decline to use the word 'tautology' for categorical statements, reserving its use for truth-functional statements. But ordinary usage supports the wider sense of the term employed here.

> *The truth of tautology is certain, of propositions possible, of contradiction impossible.*
> —*Ludwig Wittgenstein,* Tractatus Logico-Philosophicus

We will regard tautologies as statements. As statements they must be either true or false; it is when we recognize them *as* tautologies that we know which of the two they are. But if they are true, they must assert something that is the case. What they assert is that things in the world are what they are, that the universe obeys the law of non-contradiction. A tautology points out another instance of the general truth that what is, is. A tautology can be false only if it is not the case that what is, is.

Yet tautologous statements are regarded as trivial. They bear witness to the important law of non-contradiction, but it does not seem important since no one (except a few philosophers) doubts the law. They give us instances of a very broad (the broadest!) law which is never challenged in ordinary life. But they give us nothing that is specific and new. Tautologies, while true, convey no truth that we did not already know. There is nothing in them that anyone would care to dispute. There is, then, little point in asserting them.

People sometimes conceal the tautologous nature of their statements. They want to be taken as saying something specific, novel, constructive, controversial. They want to seem to be doing more than testifying to the consistency of the language and the orderliness of the universe. They want their contention to be seen as a proposition that *could* be false—had they not so astutely discovered otherwise.

The examples of tautologies given above are obvious. A word is repeated. If that word retains the same meaning, we know no more of the world than we did before. If the meaning shifts, what may look like a tautology (e.g., ''business is business'') may not really be one. But it is necessary to dig a little more deeply to expose some tautologies.

We may have to seek semantical meanings or ask for definitions. We can know that 'All bachelors are unmarried' is a tautology as soon as we read it, for we know what 'bachelor' means. But in the case of 'All crows are black,' we may have to discover the meaning the speaker places on 'crows' before we know whether it is a tautology. If someone maintains that sexual perversion is wrong, we need to know what he means by 'perversion.' If he wishes to define 'perversion' as 'deviation from a moral standard,' his assertion that sexual perversion is wrong is a tautology and there is no point in disputing the matter with him (although we might want to question the propriety of the definition). If, however, he means by 'perversion' something that deviates from social standards, his assertion that sexual perversion is wrong is not a tautology, since it does not necessarily follow that deviations from social standards are wrong. Suppose that the speaker, in addition to defining 'perversion' as 'deviation from social standards,' defines 'wrong' as 'any departure from social standards.' Then it would indeed be the case that 'sexual perversion is wrong' is a tautology. Its truth depends upon two definitions. What looks like a conclusion of an argument (all *P* are *D*, all *D* are *W*, therefore all *P* are *W*) is in reality merely a tautology: All cases of perversion (deviations from social standards) are wrong (deviations from social standards).

It is not always easy to discern how others are using words. In arguing with them we are not sure whether to question a factual assertion or an implied definition. The person who conceals or obscures the fact that her thesis is true simply because of meanings she has placed on key words is guilty of the *question-begging-definition fallacy*.[7] She succeeds in this because her listeners have neither been attentive enough to find these assumed meanings in the context of her discourse nor suspicious enough to elicit them from her.

In the case of molecular statements, tautology derives from the relation of the component parts. As a consequence of the meaning of truth-functional statement connectives, some molecular statements are necessarily true. The detection of tautologies can thus be a mechanical matter.

A favorite remark of sportswriters is "He may or may not break the record." And of political pundits: "He may or may not come up with enough votes." These do not tell us anything—except about the speaker's sense of uncertainty. Calvin Coolidge once remarked, "When a large amount of people are out of work, unemployment results." We can make truth tables for these kinds of assertion:

p	*~p*	*p* v *~p*
T	*F*	*T*
F	*T*	*T*

p	*p→p*
T	*T*
F	*T*

The disjunction, '*p* v *~p*,' is true on every line. The conditional, '*p→p*,' is true on every line. Because they cannot possibly be false, they are tautologous forms, and statements that have these forms deserve the "ho hum" treatment they usually get.

Any statement or statement form that can be placed on a truth table can be tested by a truth table. Consider the expressions:

(1) $\sim(p \ \& \ \sim p)$
(2) $\sim(p \ \& \ q) \ v \ p$
(3) $\sim q \ v \ (p \ v \ q)$

The truth table for (1) is:

[7] See pp. 55–56.

p	q	~p	p & ~p	~(p & ~p)
T	T	F	F	T
F	T	T	F	T
T	F	F	F	T
F	F	T	F	T

The truth table for (2) is:

p	q	p & q	~(p & q)	~(p & q) v p
T	T	T	F	T
F	T	F	T	T
T	F	F	T	T
F	F	F	T	T

The truth table for (3) is:

p	q	~q	p v q	~q v (p v q)
T	T	F	T	T
F	T	F	T	T
T	F	T	T	T
F	F	T	F.	T

To derive the truth-values in the final three columns, it was necessary to provide columns for all components of the expressions in question. We could thus move easily from the basic columns on the left, through the "intermediary" expressions, to the expressions being tested. Inspection of each of the three columns on the right shows nothing but **T**'s. Since there is no possibility of (1), (2), and (3) being false, they are all tautologous forms, and all statements that possess these forms are tautologies.

We may ascertain which of the following are tautologous by the same method:

(1) $(p \& q) \rightarrow p$
(2) $(p \rightarrow q) \leftrightarrow (\sim q \rightarrow \sim p)$
(3) $(p \& \sim q)) \vee (p \rightarrow q)$
(4) $(p \rightarrow q) \leftrightarrow (q \rightarrow p)$

The truth table for (1) is:

p	q	p & q	(p & q)→p
T	T	T	T
F	T	F	T
T	F	F	T
F	F	F	T

The truth table for (2) is:

p	q	~p	~q	p→q	~q→~p	(p→q)↔(~q→~p)
T	T	F	F	T	T	T
F	T	T	F	T	T	T
T	F	F	T	F	F	T
F	F	T	T	T	T	T

The truth table for (3) is:

p	q	~q	p & ~q	p→q	(p & ~q) v (p→q)
T	T	F	F	T	T
F	T	F	F	T	T
T	F	T	T	F	T
F	F	T	F	T	T

The truth table for (4) is:

p	q	p→q	q→p	(p→q)↔(q→p)
T	T	T	T	T
F	T	T	F	F
T	F	F	T	F
F	F	T	T	T

Because it is impossible for (1), (2), and (3) to be false, they are tautologous. Because it is not impossible for (4) to be false, it is not tautologous.

Concluding Summary: Tautologies may be regarded as statements serving the informative function. They are necessarily true as a consequence of the meanings of the terms they employ. They tell us nothing new or specific about the world, although the user of tautologies sometimes seeks to conceal this.

> *How can what an Englishman believes be heresy? It is a contradiction in terms.*
>
> —*George Bernard Shaw,* Saint Joan

Self-Contradiction

A self-contradiction is the direct opposite of a tautology; indeed it is the denial of a tautology. Such a statement cannot possibly be true. The structure of the sentence itself guarantees its falsity. Consider the sentences:

The green beer sold on St. Patrick's Day is not green.
The past can be changed.
Some roses are not roses.
He's so popular that no one likes him. (attributed to Yogi Berra)

We need to know nothing about beer, history, roses, or Yogi's acquaintance to know that these sentences are false.

Since they can be given the adjective *false,* they must be statements, for only statements are privileged to carry the attributes of 'true' and 'false.' But if they are statements, they must make an assertion about the world. What assertion do they make? In general, they assert that the universe is the kind of place that can have logically inconsistent phenomena. Specifically, they assert that this or that particular anomaly is to be found there. If we believe that words mean what they say and that the law of non-contradiction holds in the universe, we declare a self-contradiction to be false as soon as we recognize it to be self-contradictory.

The examples above are obvious, but it is not always easy to recognize a self-contradiction *as* a self-contradiction. We often have to determine meanings of certain

> *"Speak when you're spoken to!" the Queen sharply interrupted her.*
> *"But if everyone obeyed that rule," said Alice, who was always ready for a little argument, "and if you only spoke when you were spoken to, and the other person always waited for* you *to begin, you see, nobody would ever say anything, so that—"*
> *"Ridiculous!" cried the Queen.*
>
> —*Lewis Carroll,* Through the Looking Glass

words from the context itself or from asking the speaker, in order to conclude that a statement is self-contradictory. If someone says 'Some religions are atheistic,' he may or may not be expressing a self-contradiction. If he has explicitly or implicitly defined 'religion' in terms of gods, his statement is self-contradictory. When Voltaire said, "Common sense is not so common," he presumably meant two different things by 'common.'

It is not always easy to bring out the internal contradiction in a statement. It is not intuitively obvious that this statement asserts an impossible situation: 'There is a barber in Beaver Crossing, Nebraska, who shaves everyone in town who does not shave himself, and no others.' The impossible situation is that the barber will both have to shave himself and not shave himself.

Very close to a self-contradiction, is an *oxymoron*. An oxymoron places two qualities together that seem to work against one another. Examples are:

> It was an act of cruel kindness.
> He advised me to make haste slowly.
> The book was first-rate trash.
> The speaker was modestly arrogant.

Whether these statements are really self-contradictory is difficult to say. Is it possible for the cosmetic to be, as the ad declares, "honest makeup"? Incongruity alone does not constitute self-contradiction, and many oxymorons present little more than this.

We can determine whether truth-functional statements are self-contradictory by means of truth tables. Consider the expressions:

(1) p & $\sim p$
(2) $\sim q$ & $\sim(p \vee \sim q)$
(3) $(p \veebar q)$ & $(p$ & $q)$

The truth table for (1) is:

p	$\sim p$	p & $\sim p$
T	F	F
F	T	F

The truth table for (2) is:

p	q	$\sim q$	$p \vee \sim q$	$\sim(p \vee \sim q)$	$\sim q$ & $\sim(p \vee \sim q)$
T	T	F	T	F	F
F	T	F	F	T	F
T	F	T	T	F	F
F	F	T	T	F	F

The truth table for (3) is:

p	q	p ⩡ q	p & q	(p ⩡ q) & (p & q)
T	T	F	T	F
F	T	T	F	F
T	F	T	F	F
F	F	F	F	F

Since we get all "false" for each of these forms, they are all self-contradictory, and all statements of identical form are self-contradictions.

We may ascertain which of the following are self-contradictory by the same method:

(1) $(p \rightarrow q)$ & $(p$ & $\sim q)$
(2) $(p \rightarrow q)$ & $\sim(\sim p$ v $q)$
(3) $p \rightarrow \sim p$

The truth table for (1) is:

p	q	~q	p→q	p & ~q	(p→q) & (p & ~q)
T	T	F	T	F	F
F	T	F	T	F	F
T	F	T	F	T	F
F	F	T	T	F	F

The truth table for (2) is:

p	q	~p	~p v q	p→q	~(~p v q)	(p→q) & ~(~p v q)
T	T	F	T	T	F	F
F	T	T	T	T	F	F
T	F	F	F	F	T	F
F	F	T	T	T	F	F

The truth table for (3) is:

p	$\sim p$	$p \rightarrow\ \sim p$
T	F	F
F	T	T

Because it is impossible for (1) and (2) to be true, each of them is a self-contradictory form. Because it is not impossible for (3) to be true, it is not a self-contradictory form.

Conjunctions may be recognized as self-contradictory when the truth of one of their components is seen to be incompatible with that of another component. For example:

He'd rather fight than eat—and vice versa.
No one ever goes there—it's too crowded. (attributed to Yogi Berra)

In these cases we need not rely on truth tables but simply on our knowledge that conjunctions assert that all components are true.

Statements that are tautologous or self-contradictory have been called *analytic*. Tautologies are analytically true, self-contradictions are analytically false. Statements that are neither tautologous nor self-contradictory have been called *synthetic*. This distinction applies to atomic statements as well as molecular (or truth-functional) statements.

Concluding Summary: Self-contradictions are statements serving the informative function. They are necessarily false, because of the meaning of the terms they employ. They report specific cases of inconsistency in the world. Since no one (except a few philosophers) believes that this universe is self-contradictory, such statements are rejected as false, and no one wants to be found to have asserted one.

EXERCISES

Exercise 32

For each of the following, indicate whether tautologous, self-contradictory, *or* synthetic:

1. Disingenuous people are sneaky.
2. Disingenuous people are guileless.
3. Disingenuous people are intelligent.
4. The fetus is a person.
5. "Rookies don't have a lot of experience." (Yogi Berra)
6. A sloop has but one mast.
7. A rhombus has four sides.
8. Abstinence is a good thing if practiced in moderation.

9. "There are still standing-room only seats available." (Jay Randolph)
10. "I'll never say 'never,' never again."
11. "I can't trust my husband. He cheats so much I'm not even sure my last baby is *his.*" (Letter to Abigail van Buren)
12. "Every woman should marry—and no man." (Benjamin Disraeli)
13. "One dollar and eight-seven cents. That was all. And 60¢ of it was in pennies." (O. Henry, "The Gift of the Magi")
14. "The pictures that earn the most money at the box office . . . contain some of the ingredients that make for mass appeal." (Lloyd Shearer, *Parade*, February 28, 1988)
15. "We learn from experience that men never learn from experience." (G. B. Shaw)

Exercise 33

For each of the following, use the truth-table method to determine whether tautologous, *self-contradictory, or* synthetic:

1. Jan is married and Rose is engaged, but Jan is not married.
2. If it is the case that whenever it rains it pours, then it is the case that whenever it does not rain, it does not pour.
3. If Jan is married and Rose is engaged, then Jan is married.
4. If vitamins are necessary for health, then vitamins are sufficient for health.
5. If you're healthy, then you're happy, although you really can't be both at the same time.

Exercise 34

For each of the following, use the truth-table method to determine whether tautologous, *self-contradictory, or* synthetic:

1. $(p \rightarrow q)$ & $(\sim p \rightarrow q)$
2. $(p \rightarrow q) \leftrightarrow (q \rightarrow p)$
3. $[(p \lor q)$ & $\sim p] \rightarrow q$
4. $(p \lor q)$ & $(\sim p$ & $\sim q)$
5. $p \rightarrow (p \lor \sim q)$
6. $\sim(p \lor \sim p)$

Chapter 4

Relations between Statements

PREVIEW

Any pair of statements is compatible or incompatible. Any compatible pair is equivalent or non-equivalent. This chapter discusses these basic relations, as well as more specific ones. The relationships that statements have to one another can be determined simply on the basis of their forms. Among the concepts you should master in this chapter are the following:

1. Compatibility and incompatibility.
2. Equivalence and non-equivalence.
3. Contradiction and non-contradiction.
4. Conversion.
5. Obversion.
6. Contraposition.
7. Contrariety and subcontrariety.
8. Subalternation and superalternation.
9. Deduction and induction.
10. Truth tables.

Although you may be unfamiliar with many of these terms, you probably already know a lot about the ideas they express. Here is a little test:

1. If you reverse the terms of an A-statement, do you change its meaning?
2. If you reverse the terms of an E-statement, do you change its meaning?
3. Do these statements say the same thing?

   All stars are visible.
   No invisible things are stars.

4. Is it possible for both these statements to be true?

   No cats are dogs.
   Some dogs are cats.

5. Is it possible for both these statements to be true?

   The sun is shining and the grass is green.
   The sun is not shining and the grass is not green.

6. Is it possible for both the statements in (5) to be false?
7. Do these statements always have opposite truth-values?

   The sun is shining and the grass is green.
   The sun is not shining or the grass is not green.

8. If it is true that all students are industrious, does it follow that some are?
9. Pat maintains that if the temperature is at least 212°, the water boils; but Mike holds that if the water does not boil, the temperature is less than 212°. Are they in agreement?
10. 'All $\overline{S}$ are $\overline{P}$' is equivalent to 'All $\overline{P}$ are $\overline{S}$.' Is 'No S are P' equivalent to 'No $\overline{P}$ are $\overline{S}$'?

COMPATIBILITY AND INCOMPATIBILITY

The Basic Division

Two statements are *compatible* if and only if it is logically possible for them both to be true at the same time. We do not have to check on facts or concern ourselves with truth to determine whether statements are compatible. We merely have to examine their structures. It is not even necessary to know what all the words mean. Provided we know the statements' logical forms, we should be able to ascertain whether they are compatible.

'Compatible' and 'incompatible' mark a dichotomy. If two statements are not compatible, they are *incompatible*. And if they are not incompatible, they are compatible. We could have defined 'incompatible' first ('not logically possible for them both to be true at the same time'), then said that any two statements that are not incompatible are compatible.

A qualification must be noted here. Consider the statements:

   Melvin is a bachelor.
   Melvin is married.

These would seem to be incompatible, for they cannot both be true. But we know this only because we know that 'bachelor' means, among other things, 'unmarried.' If this knowledge is unavailable, however, we would have to call the statements compatible—just as we call the statements, 'Melvin is a bachelor' and 'Melvin is happy,' compatible. Factual knowledge could also have a bearing on whether we declare two statements to be compatible. Consider the statements:

A green light is in the lamp.
A blue light is in the lamp.

If we happen to know that the lamp in question has exactly one socket, we would regard the statements as incompatible. If we do not know this, we would call the statements compatible. This section, however, is concerned with that kind of compatibility that can be recognized from statements' forms, regardless of what other meanings or facts may be involved.

The most obvious examples of compatible statements are those that assert the very same thing. If the husband says to his wife, ''We will go to the movies tonight,'' and the wife responds, ''Tonight we'll go to the movies,'' they certainly have expressed compatible viewpoints. These statements are *equivalent,* and all equivalent pairs (with one qualification) are compatible.

The qualification is this: When each of two equivalent statements is self-contradictory, the pair would not be compatible in terms of our definition above. Since *neither* can be true, it is impossible for *both* to be true. They do not, however, conflict with *one another*.

Statements do not have to be equivalent in order to be compatible. Some statements are compatible without being equivalent. Suppose the wife in the previous example had responded, ''We will go out to dinner tonight.'' This does not assert the same thing that the husband asserted, but it is not in logical conflict with it. The joint truth of both statements is not impossible. The wife could have said, ''The stock market went down today.'' This too would have been compatible with the husband's statement.

Each of the following pairs is compatible:

(1) We will go to the movies tonight.
    Tonight we'll go to the movies.
(2) We will go to the movies tonight.
    We will go out for dinner tonight.
(3) We will go to the movies tonight.
    The stock market went down today.

The first pair is compatible because the statements are equivalent. The other two pairs are compatible because there is no logical conflict.

It is the case, then, that all compatible pairs are equivalent or nonequivalent. All equivalent pairs (except where each is self-contradictory) are compatible, but not all non-equivalent pairs are compatible. Some non-equivalent pairs, such as (2) and (3) above, are compatible, but some are not.

Those non-equivalent statements that are not compatible are, of course, incompatible. The wife could have responded, ''We will not go to the movies tonight.'' This is incompatible with the husband's statement. The two statements cannot both be true. At least one of them is false. In this case, *exactly* one of them is false and *exactly* one of them is true. The two statements are, therefore, *contradictories* of one another. When two statements are contradictory, they are incompatible, for two contradictory statements cannot both be true.

But statements do not have to be contradictory to be incompatible. Suppose the wife had answered, "We will *never* go to the movies." This position is certainly incompatible with that of her husband. Her statement is not, however, contradictory to the husband's statement. This is so because it is not the case that exactly one of them is true and one of them is false. Although the two statements cannot both be true, they *could* both be false. And they would indeed be false if the couple did not go to the movies that night but did go the next night.

We can thus say that some incompatible pairs are contradictory and some are not. All contradictory pairs are incompatible, but not all incompatible pairs are contradictory.

It should be obvious also that no equivalent pairs are contradictory and that no contradictory pairs are equivalent (or compatible). Non-equivalent pairs may be compatible or incompatible, and non-contradictory pairs may be compatible or incompatible.

Concluding Summary:

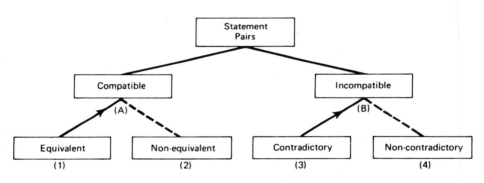

The arrows are intended to suggest that equivalence (with the qualification noted above) and contradiction lead, respectively, to compatibility and incompatibility. The dotted lines are intended to suggest this: While all compatible pairs are equivalent or non-equivalent, not all the latter are compatible; while all incompatible pairs are contradictory or non-contradictory, not all the latter are incompatible. The nature of any statement pair may be stated precisely by choosing one of the letter terms (middle rank) and one of the numbered terms (bottom rank).

> *Those that differ upon reason may come together by reason.*
> —*Benjamin Whichcote*, Moral Aphorisms

Contradiction: Categorical Statements

The contradiction of a categorical statement requires a change in the quality *and* a change in the quantity. *A*'s and *O*'s are thus contradictories of one another, and so are *E*'s and *I*'s.

Suppose that someone holds this position:

(1) All Christians are trustworthy.

To contradict it I have only to establish an *O*-statement:

(2) Some Christians are not trustworthy.

All I need do is find *one* Christian who is not trustworthy to establish the truth of that statement. And if my statement is *true,* my opponent's assertion is false, for the two statements are incompatible. I do not have to try to establish the truth of:

(3) No Christians are trustworthy.

To do so would also falsify my opponent's assertion, for these two statements are also incompatible. But an *E* statement is much more than I need.

(1) and (2) are *contradictory.* They must have opposite truth-values. Where one is true, the other is false; where one is false, the other is true. They cannot both be true *and* they cannot both be false. This is what is meant by contradiction.

(1) and (3) are *contrary.* They need not have opposite truth-values. They cannot both be true, but they can both be false.

Both pairs, (1) and (2) and (1) and (3), are incompatible, but the first pair is contradictory and the second is not.

What we have said about the *A* and *O* also holds for the *E* and *I*. To contradict the *E* statement,

(1) No fish are flyers.

I have only to establish the truth of the *I:*

(2) Some fish are flyers.

Finding one fish that flies would be enough to falsify my opponent's assertion. Just as we contradict *all are* by establishing *some are not,* we contradict *none is* by establishing *some are.* The universal affirmative,

(3) All fish are flyers.

is also incompatible with the original statement but goes much further than is necessary.

(1) and (2) are contradictory. They must have opposite truth-values. Where one is true, the other is false; where one is false, the other is true. They cannot both be true *and* they cannot both be false. This is what is meant by contradiction.

(1) and (3) are contrary. They need not have opposite truth-values. They cannot both be true, but they can both be false.

Both pairs, (1) and (2) and (1) and (3), are incompatible, but the first pair is contradictory and the second is not.

It is more difficult to establish the contradictories of particular statements. To deny that *some are,* we have to establish a universal: *none is.* And to deny that *some are not,* we must establish another universal: *all are.*

We can contradict the statement 'Some cars are safe' only by asserting the truth of 'No cars are safe.' And we contradict the statement 'Some wars are not justified' only by asserting the truth of 'All wars are justified.'

Just as we do not contradict a universal statement by asserting another universal statement, we do not contradict a particular statement by asserting another particular statement. I do not contradict 'Some cars are safe' by asserting 'Some cars are not safe.' These two statements are not even incompatible. They can both be true. They are compatible (but not equivalent). Similarly, we do not contradict the statement 'Some wars are not justified' by establishing the statement 'Some wars are justified.' The *I* and *O* statements are called subcontraries. They cannot both be false, but they can both be true.

It should be pointed out that those logicians who hold that particular statements *guarantee existence* and that universal statements do not would disagree with much of this section. They would argue that contraries would both be true if the subject does not exist and that subcontraries would both be false if their subject does not exist. For this existential approach, the reader is referred to the Appendix.[1]

Singular statements do not fit very neatly into either approach. Do we contradict 'Rudesheim is a town in Germany' by asserting that *some* Rudesheim *is not* a town in Germany? Do we contradict 'Fido is not a dog' by asserting that *some* Fidos *are* dogs? No. It is more natural to contradict the first by asserting that Rudesheim is not a town in Germany and to contradict the second by saying that Fido is a dog.

This would be to say that the contradiction of statements we treat as *A* and *E* statements are, respectively, statements we treat as *E* and *A* statements. But this relation is what we have been calling *contrary* rather than contradictory. It must be admitted that singular statements do not quite conform to the principles we have specified for the other categorical statements.

Consider these singular statements:

(1) The present governor of Virginia is a socialist.
(2) The present governor of Virginia is not a socialist.

So long as there *is* a governor of Virginia, these statements must have opposite truth-values. Thus they are contradictories. If, however, there were no governor of Virginia, the two statements could both be false. Thus they are contraries. In either case, whether Virginia has a governor or not, (1) and (2) are incompatible; they cannot both be true.[2]

---

[1] See especially pp. 404–406.
[2] For more discussion of singular statements see the Appendix, p. 407.

Concluding Summary:

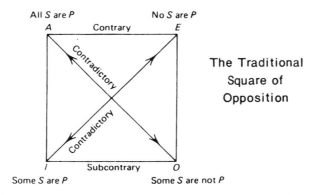

The Traditional
Square of
Opposition

Contradictories cannot both be true at the same time; they are thus incompatible. Nor can they both be false at the same time. They always have opposite truth-values. *A* and *O* are contradictories; *E* and *I* are contradictories. *Contraries* cannot both be true at the same time; they are incompatible. They can, however, both be false at the same time. *A* and *E* are contraries. Subcontraries can both be true at the same time; they are thus compatible. They cannot, however, both be false at the same time. *I* and *O* are subcontraries.

Look before you leap.

—Old saying

He who hesitates is lost.

—Another old saying

Contradiction: Molecular Statements

Contradiction means the same here as in the preceding section: Two statements are contradictory if and only if they always necessarily have opposite truth-values. Let us contradict the conjunction:

(1) The sun is shining and the grass is green.

An easy way to do it would be simply to assert: 'It is not the case both that the sun is shining and the grass is green.' But this does not get us very far.
Consider the statement:

(2) The sun is not shining and the grass is not green.

This is *incompatible* with (1); they cannot both be true. But it is not contradictory, because they could both be false. And they *would* both be false if one conjunct is true and the other is false. We have gone further here than we had to. We have denied too much.

To deny (1), we merely have to say that one or more of its parts is false. The contradiction of a conjunction is thus a disjunction:

(3) Either the sun is not shining or the grass is not green.

Statement (3) is contradictory to (1); they cannot both be true and they cannot both be false.

When we seek to contradict a disjunction, we find an interesting parallel:

(1) Either he is overworked or he is underpaid.

An easy way to contradict this disjunction would be simply to assert: 'It is not the case that he is either overworked or underpaid.' But this does not get us very far. Consider the statement:

(2) Either he is not overworked or he is not underpaid.

This is quite compatible with (1); they can both be true. And they *would* both be true if our worker were overworked and not underpaid. So (2) neither contradicts (1) nor is incompatible with (1). Although we have denied both disjuncts, we have not denied enough.

To contradict (1), we must change it to a conjunction and deny both parts. The contradiction of a disjunction is a conjunction:

(3) He is not overworked and he is not underpaid.

Statements (1) and (3) are contradictory; they cannot both be true and they cannot both be false.

We can prove our conclusions by means of a simple truth table:

p	*q*	~*p*	~*q*	*p* & *q*	~*p* v ~*q*	*p* v *q*	~*p* & ~*q*
T	T	F	F	T	F	T	F
F	T	T	F	F	T	T	F
T	F	F	T	F	T	T	F
F	F	T	T	F	T	F	T
				(5)	**(6)**	**(7)**	**(8)**

Note that columns (5) and (6) show opposite truth-values for all the possibilities set up in the first two columns and that (7) and (8) show opposite truth-values for all possibilities.

A truth table can also establish the contradictory of the strong disjunction. Since it is defined as asserting that exactly one of the disjuncts is true and exactly one of them is false, its contradictory would have to assert that either both are false or both are true.

p	*q*	~*p*	~*q*	*p* ∨ *q*	*p* & *q*	~*p* & ~*q*	(*p* & *q*) ∨ (~*p* & ~*q*)
T	T	F	F	F	T	F	T
F	T	T	F	T	F	F	F
T	F	F	T	T	F	F	F
F	F	T	T	F	F	T	T
(1)	(2)	(3)	(4)	(5)	(6)	(7)	(8)

The truth-values in column (8) derive from those in columns (6) and (7). All the truth-values, of course, derive ultimately from those stipulated in columns (1) and (2). Since columns (5) and (8) have opposite truth-values on every line, they are contradictories of one another.

A word of caution: In contradicting molecular statements, we also usually have to contradict atomic ones. And in doing the latter, we must adhere to the principles established in the preceding section. For example: The contradiction of the statement 'All knights are brave and some are chaste' is 'Either some knights are not brave or no knights are chaste.' It is *not:* 'Either all knights are not brave or some knights are not chaste.' And the contradiction of 'No dragons are civilized and some are not reluctant' is: 'Either some dragons are civilized or all dragons are reluctant.'

How do we contradict conditional statements? Recalling that a conditional is false when its antecedent is true and its consequent is false, we will want to assert the antecedent while denying the truth of the consequent. If someone asserts that if war is inevitable then civilization is doomed, we contradict him by arguing that while war is inevitable civilization is not doomed. Since this is the only way the conditional (when interpreted as a truth-functional statement) can be false, it is the only way it can be contradicted. The contradictory of '*w*→*d*' is '*w* & ~*d*.'

How do we contradict biconditional statements? Recalling that a biconditional is a conjunction of two conditionals, we will want to assert that at least one of these conjuncts is false. If someone asserts that you will receive a prize if and only if you return the coupon, you contradict him by arguing that either one or the other of these conditionals is false. The contradictory of '*p*↔*r*' is '~(*p*→*r*) ∨ ~(*r*→*p*).'

These results can be proved by truth tables:

w	*d*	~*d*	*w*→*d*	*w* & ~*d*
T	T	F	T	F
F	T	F	T	F
T	F	T	F	T
F	F	T	T	F

The last two columns show opposite truth-values on all four lines, so '$w{\rightarrow}d$' and 'w & $\sim d$' are contradictory.

p	r	$p{\leftrightarrow}r$	$p{\rightarrow}r$	$r{\rightarrow}p$	$\sim(p{\rightarrow}r)$	$\sim(r{\rightarrow}p)$	$\sim(p \rightarrow r)$ v $\sim(r \rightarrow p)$
T	T	T	T	T	F	F	F
F	T	F	T	F	F	T	T
T	F	F	F	T	T	F	T
F	F	T	T	T	F	F	F

The third and eighth columns show opposite truth-values on all four lines, so '$p{\leftrightarrow}r$' and '$\sim(p{\rightarrow}r)$ v $\sim(r{\rightarrow}p)$' are contradictory. Note that the expression '$p \lor\kern-0.5em\lor r$' would yield the same results as those in the last column, so it would also serve as the contradictory of '$p{\leftrightarrow}r$.'

Concluding Summary: A symbolic summary of contradictories follows. The first negation sign at the beginning of each line conveys the idea of 'the contradiction of . . .'

Conjunction:	$\sim(p$ & $q) = \sim p$ v $\sim q$
Disjunction:	$\sim(p$ v $q) = \sim p$ & $\sim q$
Strong disjunction:	$\sim(p \lor\kern-0.5em\lor q) = (p$ & $q)$ v $(\sim p$ & $\sim q)$
Conditional:	$\sim(p \rightarrow q) = p$ & $\sim q$
Biconditional:	$\sim(p \leftrightarrow q) = \sim(p \rightarrow q)$ v $\sim(q \rightarrow p)$

EXERCISES

Exercise 35

Contradict each of the following:

1. Some athletes are rich.
2. All spathling quiddities zingle marfully.
3. Some vegetables are not nutritious.
4. Vacation trips are always disappointing.
5. Not all ministers are virtuous.
6. Not a single student had done the homework.
7. Only metals expand when heated.
8. All rabbits are not fast.
9. Santa Claus has a white beard.
10. No threats of blackmail are justifiable.

Exercise 36

Contradict each of the following:

1. If he reports on time, there will be no penalty.
2. Some animals are not carnivorous and no reptiles are warm-blooded.
3. Gephardt is president or this newspaper is wrong.
4. The job is either dangerous or unnecessary.
5. The gate is up and a train is coming.
6. If and only if the weather is good will Wanda play golf.
7. If wishes were horses, then beggars would ride.
8. All roses are red and some violets are blue.
9. Only if the Soviet Union walks out will the summit be a failure.
10. He is a citizen or he is married to one.
11. Stella is good-looking, but she has an unpleasant personality.
12. If all weather forecasts were reliable, no farmers would go broke.
13. Some space shuttles are dangerous or I have been misinformed.
14. Unless he phones, he'll be on time.

EQUIVALENCE

Categorical Statements

We have already seen that there are different ways of saying the same thing. Statements that are worded differently may make the same assertion. When two statements make the same assertion, they are *equivalent*. It is important to be able to distinguish with perfect certainty between statements that are equivalent and those that are not equivalent.

Some equivalences are so common and so useful they have been given special names.

One kind of equivalence uses the word 'converse.' The *converse* of a categorical statement is simply a reversal of its terms. Sometimes the converse is equivalent; sometimes it is not. We call the former a *valid converse;* we call the latter an *illicit converse.*[3]

Let us examine an *A* statement:

(1) All poodles are dogs.

Its converse is:

(2) All dogs are poodles.

---

[3] We should not be misled by such traditional expressions as 'valid converse' and 'illicit converse.' Strictly speaking, such terms as 'valid' and 'illicit' refer to inferences, not to statements. It is thus not the converse itself which is valid or illicit but the *inference* of which it is the conclusion.

When we think about these statements, we realize that they are not equivalent. The first puts the entire poodle class somewhere inside the dog class, while the second puts the entire dog class somewhere inside the poodle class. Or, the first says that there are no poodles which are not dogs, while the second says that there are no dogs which are not poodles.

We can conceive of the first being true while the second is false. Thus the second cannot be derived from the first; it is the illicit converse of the first. And we can conceive of the second being true while the first is false. Thus the first cannot be derived from the second. (1) and (2) are illicit converses of one another.

While we know in fact that (1) and (2) are not both true, it is logically possible that they can both be true. They do not conflict in form or structure. They are thus not incompatible—which is to say that they are compatible. (1) and (2) are compatible but not equivalent.

That the *A* and its converse can both be true is indicated by the following:

All democrats believe in popular sovereignty.
All who believe in popular sovereignty are democrats.

These statements are in fact true. That the *A* and its converse can both be false is indicated by the following:

All Americans are democrats.
All democrats are Americans.

These statements are in fact both false. But, since one statement of a pair of converses *may* be true while the other is false, as in fact is the case in (1) and (2), *A* statements and their converses are not equivalent.

Let us next examine an *E* statement.

(3) No trains are planes.

Its converse is:

(4) No planes are trains.

These two statements assert the same thing. The two classes are entirely excluded from one another. It does not make any difference whether the subject is excluded from the predicate or whether the predicate is excluded from the subject. Complete exclusion is achieved in any case. We cannot conceive of the possibility of their having opposite truth-values. (3) and (4) are equivalent (and thus compatible).

Let us now examine an *I* statement:

(5) Some poets are prophets.

Its converse is:

(6) Some prophets are poets.

These two statements assert the same thing. They both say that the two classes overlap, that there is at least one person who is both poet and prophet (or who is both prophet and poet). (5) and (6) are equivalent (and thus compatible).

Finally, we look at an *O* statement:

(7) Some reptiles are not snakes.

Its converse is:

(8) Some snakes are not reptiles.

When we think about these statements, we recognize that they are not equivalent. The first excludes at least one reptile from the snake class, while the second excludes at least one snake from the reptile class. We are inclined to accept the first as true, since lizards are reptiles but not snakes; but we doubt the truth of the second, since we believe that *all* snakes are reptiles. If the two statements were equivalent, we could not entertain the possibility of different truth-values for them. (8) is the illicit converse of (7); it cannot validly be drawn.

While we know in fact that (7) and (8) are not both true, it is logically possible that they could be. 'Some engineers are not Indians' and 'Some Indians are not engineers' happen both to be true; so there is nothing in the statements' structure that conflicts. Thus we can say that the *O* and its converse are compatible but not equivalent.

In summary, then, the *E* and *I* have valid converses, while the *A* and *O* do not.

Another traditional equivalence is called the *obverse*. All statements have a valid obverse. Two things must be done to a statement to get its obverse: (1) change its quality, (2) negate its predicate. The first involves moving from *A* to *E* and vice versa, and from *I* to *O* and vice versa. The second requires us simply to attach a 'non-' to the predicate class.

The obverse of 'All men are mortal' is 'No men are non-mortal.' Including the entire class of men in the mortal class is equivalent to excluding the entire class of men from the non-mortal class. 'No metals are flammable' has as its obverse: 'All metals are non-flammable.' Excluding the entire class of metals from the flammable class is equivalent to including the entire class of metals in the non-flammable class.

The obverse of 'Some writers are boring' is 'Some writers are not non-boring.' The *I* is changed to an *O* and the predicate negated. To include part of one class in another is equivalent to excluding that part from the negative of that other class. The same principles operate when we obvert the *O* statement, 'Some men are not lawyers,' and get 'Some men are non-lawyers.'

Using a line over a class letter to indicate its negative or complement, we can summarize and generalize thus:

All S are P = No S are $\overline{P}$

No S are P = All S are $\overline{P}$

Some S are P = Some S are not $\overline{P}$

Some S are not P = Some S are $\overline{P}$

Note that the relation of obversion is, like that of conversion, a symmetrical one. That is, 'All S are P' is the obverse of 'No S are $\overline{P}$,' just as 'No S are $\overline{P}$' is the obverse of 'All S are P.' When any expression on the right is obverted, we get back to the expression on the left. Taking the right-hand expression on the third line:

Some S are not $\overline{P}$

We change its quality (that is, move from O to I) and get:

Some S are $\overline{P}$

Negating its predicate gives us:

Some S are $\overline{\overline{P}}$

Since to negate a negation is to remove that negation, the two 'nons' cancel out, and we are back to the left-hand expression:

Some S are P

Generalizing: If and only if x is the obverse of y, then y is the obverse of x.

The third kind of equivalence is the contrapositive. *Contrapositive* is defined as the obverse of the converse of the obverse. What this amounts to is reversing the terms and negating them both.

Drawing the contrapositive of an A in a step-by-step way we have:

(1) All priests are moral. [the original statement]
(2) No priests are non-moral. [obverse of (1)]
(3) No non-moral people are priests. [converse of (2)]
(4) All non-moral people are non-priests. [obverse of (3)]

(4) is the contrapositive of (1); (1) is the contrapositive of (4). They are equivalent.

Drawing the contrapositive of an O in a step-by-step way we have:

(1) Some students are not freshmen. [the original statement]
(2) Some students are non-freshmen. [obverse of (1)]
(3) Some non-freshmen are students. [converse of (2)]
(4) Some non-freshmen are not non-students. [obverse of (3)]

(4) is the contrapositive of (1); (1) is the contrapositive of (4). They are equivalent.

Since we now know that the A and O have valid contrapositives, we can draw them in a simpler way: reverse the terms and negate both.

But not all statements have valid contrapositives. This is because converses are involved, and some converses are illicit. If we sought to draw the contrapositive of an E statement, we would, by obversion, get an A statement. There we would have to stop, for A statements do not have valid converses. If we sought to draw the contrapositive of an I statement, we would, by obversion, get an O. There we would have to stop, for O statements do not have valid converses. If we wish to call 'No $\overline{P}$ and $\overline{S}$' the contrapositive of 'No S are P,' we would have to call it the *illicit* contrapositive. And 'Some $\overline{P}$ and $\overline{S}$' would be the *illicit* contrapositive of 'Some S are P.'

Every equivalent relation between atomic statements can be expressed in terms of converses and obverses. 'No people who are not brave are people who deserve the fair' is, for example, the converse of the obverse of 'All people who deserve the fair are brave.' And 'Some precious things are not non-jewels' is the obverse of the converse of 'Some jewels are precious.'

Concluding Summary:

ORIGINAL STATEMENT	ITS VALID CONVERSE	ITS VALID OBVERSE	ITS VALID CONTRAPOSITIVE
All S *are* P	*None*	*No* S *are* $\bar{P}$	*All* $\bar{P}$ *are* $\bar{S}$
No S *are* P	*No* P *are* S	*All* S *are* $\bar{P}$	*None*
Some S *are* P	*Some* P *are* S	*Some* S *are not* $\bar{P}$	*None*
Some S *are not* P	*None*	*Some* S *are* $\bar{P}$	*Some* $\bar{P}$ *are not* $\bar{S}$

Molecular Statements

Molecular statements may also be different in form and structure but identical in what they assert.

The conjunction 'The sun is shining and the grass is green' could just as well have been expressed 'The grass is green and the sun is shining.' Disjunctive statements can also be turned around without change of meaning. 'He is either very lucky or a good poker player' is equivalent to 'He is either a good poker player or he is very lucky.' Strong disjunctions are also reversible: 'It is either a seagull or a distant plane' is equivalent to 'It is either a distant plane or a seagull.'

Certain equivalences obtain between conjunctions and disjunctions. One has already been indicated. We have seen that the denial of a conjunction is a disjunction, both parts of which are denied. The contradiction, that is, of 'p & q' is '$\sim p$ v $\sim q$.' This is the same as saying that '$\sim(p$ & $q)$' and '$\sim p$ v $\sim q$' are equivalent. And, since the denial of a disjunction is a conjunction with both parts denied, '$\sim(p$ v $q)$' and '$\sim p$ & $\sim q$' are equivalent. They say the same thing and will always carry the same truth-values.

We tested supposed contradictories by means of truth tables. We can test supposed equivalences in the same way. If two molecular expressions *always* have the same truth-value, they are equivalent. Those equivalences expressed in the preceding paragraph will pass the test.

Every human proposition hath equal authority, if reason make not the difference.
                                    —Pierre Charon, De la Sagesse

Suppose that two expressions placed on a truth table do not always have opposite truth-values and do not always have identical truth-values. We would know that they are neither contradictory nor equivalent. What else would we know? If they are never both true on the same line, they are incompatible, since it is impossible for them both to be true. If they are both true on at least one line, they are compatible, for it is possible for them both to be true at the same time.

Let us examine two pairs on the same truth table. The first pair is:

(1) He did not write, but he did telephone.
(2) He did not telephone, but he did write.

The second pair is:

(3) He either telephoned or wrote.
(4) He either did not write or he did not telephone.

Abbreviating and symbolizing, we get:

(1) $\sim w$ & p
(2) $\sim p$ & w
(3) p v w
(4) $\sim w$ v $\sim p$

There are exactly four possible true-false combinations of the basic w's and p's from which everything else is derived, so our truth table will have four lines. Completed, it will look like this:

w	p	$\sim w$	$\sim p$	$\sim w$ & p	$\sim p$ & w	p v w	$\sim w$ v $\sim p$
T	T	F	F	F	F	T	F
F	T	T	F	T	F	T	T
T	F	F	T	F	T	T	T
F	F	T	T	F	F	F	T
				(1)	*(2)*	*(3)*	*(4)*

Comparing the columns above (1) and (2), we find that there is no line on which they are both true. This means that (1) and (2) are incompatible. We see that on lines 1 and 4 they do not have opposite truth-values. So they are not contradictory. (1) and (2) are incompatible but not contradictory.

Comparing the columns above (3) and (4), we find that they are both true on lines 2 and 3. This means that (3) and (4) are compatible. We see, however, that they have different truth-values on lines 1 and 4. So they are not equivalent. (3) and (4) are compatible but not equivalent.

The truth-table method is easy to use and certain in its results. If there were three basic components in an expression, we would need eight lines on the truth table. Four components would require sixteen lines to cover all the possibilities, and so on. So there are limits to the practicality of its manual use.

The conditional, when regarded as a truth-functional statement, may be expressed in terms of disjunction and conjunction:

(1) $p \rightarrow q$
(2) $\sim p \vee q$
(3) $\sim(p \And \sim q)$

This can be proved by means of a truth table:

p	q	$\sim p$	$\sim q$	$p \And \sim q$	$p \rightarrow q$	$\sim p \vee q$	$\sim(p \And \sim q)$
T	T	F	F	F	T	T	T
F	T	T	F	F	T	T	T
T	F	F	T	T	F	F	F
F	F	T	T	F	T	T	T
				(1)	(2)	(3)	

The expressions in columns (1), (2), and (3) have identical truth-values for all lines, so they are equivalent. Thus the following statements are truth-functionally equivalent:

If gold is precious, then Croesus is rich.
Either gold is not precious, or Croesus is rich.
Either Croesus is rich or gold is not precious.
It is not the case both that gold is precious and Croesus is not rich.

Consider these conditional statements:

(1) If you're prosperous, then you're happy.
(2) If you're happy, then you're prosperous.
(3) If you're not prosperous, then you're not happy.
(4) If you're not happy, then you're not prosperous.

Are they all equivalent? Let us abbreviate them and consult the truth table:

(1) $p \rightarrow h$
(2) $h \rightarrow p$
(3) $\sim p \rightarrow \sim h$
(4) $\sim h \rightarrow \sim p$

p	h	~p	~h	p →h	h →p	~p→ ~h	~h→ ~p
T	T	F	F	T	T	T	T
F	T	T	F	T	F	F	T
T	F	F	T	F	T	T	F
F	F	T	T	T	T	T	T

| | | | | *(1)* | *(2)* | *(3)* | *(4)* |

(1) and (2) can both be true, so they are compatible. But they do not always have the same truth values, so they are not equivalent. The same can be said about (3) and (4). When we compare the columns for (1) and (4), we see that they are identical. Therefore, '*p*→*h*' and '~*h*→~*p*' are equivalent. The same can be said about (2) and (3). These equivalent conditionals, where the component statements are negated and their order reversed, are called *contrapositives*.

Concluding Summary: The same questions may be asked about pairs of molecular statements that we asked about pairs of categorical statements. Are they compatible or incompatible? If the former, are they equivalent or non-equivalent? If the latter, are they contradictory or non-contradictory? These questions may be answered on the basis of an intuitive grasp of the statements' structure, by memorization of certain common equivalences and contradictories, or by means of constructing a truth table. The following principles hold for the truth-table method: (1) If the columns show one or more lines where both statements are true, the statements are compatible; otherwise they are incompatible. (2) If the columns show identical truth-values on all lines, the statements are equivalent. (3) If the columns show opposite truth-values on all lines, the statements are contradictory.

EXERCISES

Exercise 37

1. The converse of 'no grapes are juicy' is:
2. The obverse of 'all dictionaries are wordy' is:
3. The contrapositive of 'some bums are not taxpayers' is:
4. The obverse of 'some taxpayers are surly' is:
5. The contrapositive of 'all men are good drivers' is:
6. The obverse of 'no elms are healthy' is:
7. The converse of 'some birds are robins' is:
8. The obverse of 'some streets are paved' is:
9. The converse of the obverse of 'some winners are not good sports' is:
10. The obverse of the converse of 'no pens are pencils' is:

Exercise 38

For each of the following, state whether compatible *or* incompatible. *Where the former, state whether* equivalent *or* non-equivalent; *where the latter, state whether* contradictory *or* non-contradictory.

1. All birds are flyers.
   No birds are non-flyers.
2. All birds are flyers.
   All flyers are birds.
3. All citizens are taxpayers.
   No taxpayers are citizens.
4. Some reptiles are snakes.
   Some reptiles are not non-snakes.
5. No religions are superstitions.
   All superstitions are religions.
6. Some nests are feathered.
   Some nests are not feathered.
7. Some tests are unfair.
   No unfair things are tests.
8. Some tests are fair.
   Some non-fair things are non-tests.
9. All gasolines are flammable.
   No gasolines are inflammable.
10. All men are handsome.
    All women are beautiful.

Exercise 39

Some equivalent relationships are so useful in deductive logic that they have been expressed as transformation rules. *Some of these have already been confirmed as equivalences by the truth-table method:*

1. $\sim(p \lor q) = \sim p \,\&\, \sim q$ (De Morgan's law)
2. $\sim(p \,\&\, q) = \sim p \lor \sim q$ (De Morgan's law)
3. $p \to q = \sim p \lor q$ (law of Material Implication)
4. $p \to q = \sim q \to \sim p$ (Contraposition)

Construct truth tables for these other transformational rules:

5. $p = \sim(\sim p)$ (rule of Double Negation)
6. $p \,\&\, q = q \,\&\, p$ (law of Commutation)
7. $p \lor q = q \lor p$ (law of Commutation)
8. $p \,\&\, (q \lor r) = (p \,\&\, q) \lor (p \,\&\, r)$ (law of Distribution)
9. $p \lor (q \,\&\, r) = (p \lor q) \,\&\, (p \lor r)$ (law of Distribution)
10. $p \leftrightarrow q = (p \to q) \,\&\, (q \to p)$ (law of Biconditionals)

Exercise 40

For each of the following, state whether compatible *or* incompatible. *Where the former, state whether* equivalent *or* non-equivalent; *where the latter, state whether* contradictory *or* non-contradictory.

1. If he drinks, he shouldn't drive.
   If he doesn't drink, he should drive.
2. Charley is rich and good-looking.
   Charley is not rich and he is not good-looking.
3. I will read tonight or watch television.
   I will not watch television and I will not read.
4. If it is my ball, then it is a Maxfli.
   If it is not a Maxfli, then it is not my ball.
5. Logic is either a science or it is an art.
   Logic is either not a science or it is not an art.
6. All crows are black or some books are mistaken.
   All crows are black and some books are not mistaken.
7. Evelyn is witty and intelligent.
   Either Evelyn is not intelligent or she is not witty.
8. If she studies, then she passes.
   She studied and did not pass.
9. I dine out if and only if I can afford it.
   I can afford it if and only if I dine out.
10. Roses are red and violets are blue.
    Sugar is sweet and so are you.

Exercise 41

For each of the following state whether compatible *or* incompatible. *Where the former, state whether* equivalent *or* non-equivalent; *where the latter, state whether* contradictory *or* non-contradictory.

1. If abortion is murder, then so is contraception.
   Neither abortion nor contraception is murder.
2. Capital punishment is either cruel or unusual.
   Capital punishment is cruel, but it is not unusual.
3. Capital punishment is cruel and unusual.
   Capital punishment is not unusual and it is not cruel.
4. If you shop early, then you will avoid the rush.
   Either you shop early or you will not avoid the rush.
5. If you shop early, then you will avoid the rush.
   You will not avoid the rush, although you shop early.
6. Either fire burns or I've read the wrong books and am in deep trouble.
   Either fire burns or I've read the wrong books, and either fire burns or I'm in deep trouble.

7. If all poodles are dogs, then some reptiles are snakes.
   If some reptiles are not snakes, then no poodles are dogs.
8. Only if oxygen is present, then will combustion take place.
   If oxygen is present, then combustion will take place.
9. Only if the Equal Rights Amendment is passed, then will women receive their rights.
   Either the Equal Rights Amendment will be passed or women will not receive their rights.
10. $\sim(p \leftrightarrow q)$
    $p \leftrightarrow \sim q$

INFERENCES

"Immediate Inference"

The drawing of an equivalent statement from another statement has traditionally been called *immediate inference*. If the conclusion is indeed equivalent to the premise from which it is drawn, the process is not only an inference but a valid deductive one as well. The converses of the E and I statements have been called *valid* converses because they are equivalent, and the deducing of the one from the other is therefore valid. The same observation can be made of all obverses and the contrapositives of the A and O. The converses of the A and O statements, however, have been called *illicit* (or invalid) converses because they are *not* equivalent, and the deducing of the one from the other is not valid. The same observation can be made of the contrapositives of the E and I statements.

This should not suggest, however, that the *only* valid deductive inferences are from statements to their equivalents.

Another type of "immediate inference" is from a stronger form to a weaker form. Thus we can deduce an I from an A and an O from an E:

> All generals are bellicose
> ∴ Some generals are bellicose

> No Europeans are baseball fans
> ∴ Some Europeans are not baseball fans

If it is the case that all are, then it necessarily follows that *at least one* is; and if it is the case that none is, it necessarily follows that *at least one* is not. The particulars are called the subalterns of the universals.[4]

The universals are called *superalterns* of the particulars. To infer from the truth

---

[4] It is because of the validity of this inference that traditional logic can speak of "conversion by limitation" of an A-statement. We cannot go from 'all poodles are dogs' to 'all dogs are poodles.' But we can convert the *subaltern* of 'all poodles are dogs.' The result, 'some dogs are poodles,' is called the "converse by limitation" ("per accidens") of the original statement.

of the latter to the truth of the former would be going from the weaker to the stronger, which would be invalid. But we can reason from the *falsity* of the particulars to the falsity of their superalterns. If the statement of limited scope is not true, then, a fortiori, the one of greater scope cannot be true either.[5]

Let us complete the traditional Square of Opposition originally shown on p. 115.

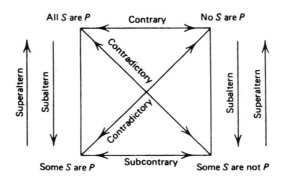

On the basis of what we now know about categorical statements, we should, once we know whether a statement is true, be able to infer something about the statements at the other three corners. Indeed, we should be able to infer something about *any* statement that contains the same terms (or their complements), whatever their order, even if it is simply that *nothing* can be known about the statement in question. For example:

Let us assume that

(1) All *S* are *P*

is true. If this is so, then

(2) No *S* are *P*

is false, for it is the contrary of the original statement, and two contraries, being incompatible, cannot both be true.

(3) Some *S* are *P*

---

[5] Those who hold that particulars guarantee existence and that universals do not will take issue with this and the preceding paragraph. They would insist that the qualification, "only if there is existence in the subject class," be added. 'All perfect husbands are understanding' would not necessarily yield 'some perfect husbands are understanding,' for the former does not guarantee existence, while the latter does. Conversion by limitation would also be impossible in those cases where existence cannot be assumed. We could not, therefore, deduce 'some living beings are Martians' from 'all Martians are living beings.' See Appendix, pp. 405, 409.

is true, being the subaltern of (1), a true statement; and being the contradictory of (2), a false statement.

(4) Some S are not P

is false, being the contradictory of (1), a true statement.

(5) All P are S

is unknown, being the illicit converse of (1).

(6) No $\overline{P}$ are S.

is true, being the equivalent (converse of the obverse) of (1), a true statement.

(7) Some $\overline{P}$ are not $\overline{S}$

is false, being the equivalent (contrapositive) of (4) which is false.

Let us assume that

(1) All S are P

is false. If this is so, then

(2) No S are P

is unknown, for, while contraries cannot both be true, they can both be false. (1) and (2) are incompatible, but not contradictory.

(3) Some S are P

is unknown, since it may be true or false, depending upon what (2) is—which is unknown.

(4) Some S are not P

is true, being the contradictory of (1), a false statement.

(5) All $\overline{P}$ are $\overline{S}$

is false, being equivalent (contrapositive) to (1), a false statement.

(6) All S are $\overline{P}$

is unknown, being equivalent (obverse) to (2), which is unknown.

(7) Some $\overline{P}$ are S

is true, being equivalent (converse of the obverse) to the contradictory of (1), which is false.

Let us assume that

(1) No S are P

is true. If this is so, then

(2) All *S* are *P*

is false, being the contrary of (1), a true statement.

(3) Some *S* are not *P*

is true, being the subaltern of (1), a true statement; and the contradictory of (2), a false statement.

(4) Some *S* are *P*

is false, being the contradictory of (1), a true statement.
Let us assume that

(1) No *S* are *P*

is false. If this is so, then

(2) All *S* are *P*

is unknown since it is neither equivalent nor contradictory to (1).

(3) Some *S* are *P*

is true, since it is the contradictory of (1), a false statement.

(4) Some *S* are not *P*

is unknown, being neither equivalent nor contradictory to (1); being neither equivalent nor incompatible with (3); and being the contradictory of (2), which is unknown.
Let us assume that

(1) Some *S* are *P*

is true. If so, then

(2) No *S* are *P*

is false, being the contradictory of (1), a true statement.

(3) All *S* are *P*

is unknown, being the superaltern of (1), which is true; being neither equivalent nor contradictory to (2); and being neither equivalent nor incompatible with (1).

(4) Some *S* are not *P*

is unknown, being the contradictory of (3), which is unknown; being neither equivalent nor incompatible with (1); and being neither equivalent nor contradictory to (2).

(5) Some *P* are *S*

is true, being the valid converse of (1), which is true.

Consistency thou art a jewel.

—*Common saying*

(6) All S are $\overline{P}$

is false, being equivalent (obverse) to (2), which is false,
Let us assume that

(1) Some S are P

is false. If this is so, then

(2) All S are P

is false, being the superaltern of (1), which is false.

(3) No S are P

is true, being the contradictory of (1), which is false.

(4) Some S are not P

is true, being the contradictory of (2), which is false; the subcontrary of (1), which is false; and the subaltern of (3), which is true.

(5) Some P are S

is false, being equivalent (converse) to (1), which is false.

(6) No $\overline{P}$ are S

is false, being equivalent (converse of the obverse) to (2), which is false.

(7) All P are S

is false, being the superaltern of (5).
Let us assume that

(1) Some S are not P

is true. If so, then

(2) All S are P

is false, being the contradictory of (1), which is true.

(3) No S are P

is unknown, being neither equivalent nor contradictory to (2); and being neither equivalent nor incompatible with (1).

(4) Some S are P

is unknown, being the contradictory of (3), which is unknown; being neither equivalent nor incompatible with (1); and being neither equivalent nor contradictory to (2).
Let us assume that

(1) Some S are not P

is false. If so, then

(2) All *S* are *P*

is true, being the contradictory of (1), which is false.

(3) Some *S* are *P*

is true, being the subcontrary of (1), which is false; and being the subaltern of (2), which is true.

(4) No *S* are *P*

is false, being the superaltern of (1), which is false; being the contrary of (2), which is true; and being the contradictory of (3), which is true.

These examples all use statements containing the same terms (and their complements). When we have two categorical statements which do *not* have the same terms (or their complements), knowledge of the truth-value of one will not help us in determining the truth-value of the other. Knowledge of the truth-value of 'All *S* are *P*' will not help us determine the truth-value of, say, 'All *X* are *Y*.' So, for the latter, we would have to say, "unknown."

Concluding Summary: We can make "immediate inferences" from categorical statements. These include inferences to equivalents and to weaker forms. We can also, given the truth or falsity of any categorical statement, infer to the truth, falsity, or unknowability of any other categorical statement.

Molecular Statements

The inference from a molecular statement to one that is equivalent to it is a valid deduction. From the premise, 'Jones is in Lincoln or he is in Omaha,' we can indeed deduce, 'Jones is in Omaha or he is in Lincoln.' And from 'If she is a paperchild, then she owns a bike,' the equivalent, 'If she does not own a bike, then she is not a paperchild,' can be deduced.

But, as was the case with respect to atomic statements, equivalences are not the only conclusions that can validly be deduced from single premises. The following simple arguments are valid:

All the food is eaten and the money is spent
∴ The money is spent

He is happy if and only if he prospers
∴ If he prospers he is happy

There is tea in China
∴ There is tea in China or I'm a monkey's uncle

He who says there is no such thing as an honest man, you may be sure is himself a knave.

—*George Berkeley,* Maxims Concerning Patriotism

It is not the case that she is rich or good-looking

∴ She is not good-looking

In these and other arguments, a conclusion is validly inferred from a premise that is wider in scope. We can infer from the premise to the conclusion, but we *cannot,* as we do with equivalent expressions, infer both ways.

We can also start with individual molecular statements presumed to be true or false and state whether other statements are true, false, or unknown. If the other statement is equivalent, we know it will have the same truth-value as the original. If the other statement is contradictory, it will have a truth-value opposite to that of the original. If the original statement is presumed true, then any statement incompatible with it is false. If the other statement seems to be "contained in" the original and the original is presumed true, then the other statement is true (that is, any statement validly deducible from a true statement is true). If the other statement seems to go beyond the original and the original is presumed false, then the other statement is false. If none of these conditions obtains, then the other statement must be declared *unknown.*

Suppose, for example, that 'a' stands for 'Arnold is extravagant, 'b' stands for 'Betty is forgetful,' and 'c' stands for 'their bank account is overdrawn':

(1) If 'a & b' is true, then '$\sim b$' would be false, for it is incompatible with the conjunction.
(2) If '$a \rightarrow b$' is false, then '$\sim b \rightarrow \sim a$' is false, for it is equivalent to the conditional.
(3) If 'a v b' is true, then 'b' is unknown.
(4) If 'a v $\sim b$' is false, then 'b & $\sim a$' is true, for it is contradictory to the first.
(5) If 'a' is true, then 'a & b' is unknown.
(6) If 'a' is false, then 'a v b' is unknown.
(7) If 'a' is true, then 'a v b' is true, since it can be deduced from 'a.'
(8) If '$(a$ v $b) \rightarrow c$' is true, then '$a \rightarrow c$' is true, for it is "contained in" the original.
(9) If '$(a$ v $b) \rightarrow c$' is false, then '$a \rightarrow c$' is unknown.
(10) If 'a & b' is false, then '$(a$ & $b)$ & c' is false, since it goes beyond what is already false.

The validity of these "immediate inferences" can easily be shown by means of truth tables:

a	b	$\sim a$	$\sim b$	a & b	$a \rightarrow b$	$\sim b \rightarrow \sim a$	a v b	a v $\sim b$	b & $\sim a$
T	T	F	F	T	T	T	T	T	F
F	T	T	F	F	T	T	T	F	T
T	F	F	T	F	F	F	T	T	F
F	F	T	T	F	T	T	F	T	F

(1) Wherever '*a* & *b*' is true (first line), '~*b*' is false.

(2) The statements '*a*→*b*' and '~*b*→~*a*' have the same truth-values on all lines.

(3) In two cases where '*a* v *b*' is true (first and second lines), '*b*' is true, but on the third line '*a* v *b*' is true while '*b*' is false.

(4) Wherever '*a* v ~*b*' is false (second line), '*b* & ~*a*' is true.

(5) In one case where '*a*' is true (first line), '*a* & *b*' is also true; but on the third line, '*a*' is true while '*a* & *b*' is false.

(6) In one case where '*a*' is false (fourth line), '*a* v *b*' is also false; but on the second line, '*a*' is false while '*a* v *b*' is true.

(7) While '*a*' and '*a* v *b*' do not always have the same truth-values, wherever '*a*' is true (first and third lines), '*a* v *b*' is also true.

To construct a truth table for an expression with three basic components, we need eight lines to provide all the possibilities:[6]

a	*b*	*c*	*a* v *b*	(*a* v *b*) →*c*	*a* →*c*	*b* →*c*	*a* & *b*	(*a* & *b*) & *c*
T	T	T	T	T	T	T	T	T
F	T	T	T	T	T	T	F	F
T	F	T	T	T	T	T	F	F
F	F	T	F	T	T	T	F	F
T	T	F	T	F	F	F	T	F
F	T	F	T	F	T	F	F	F
T	F	F	T	F	F	T	F	F
F	F	F	F	T	T	T	F	F

(8) While '(*a* v *b*)→*c*' and '*a*→*c*' do not always have the same truth-values, wherever '(*a* v *b*)→*c*' is true (first, second, third, fourth, and eighth lines), '*a*→*c*' is also true.

(9) In two cases where '(*a* v *b*)→*c*' is false (fifth and seventh lines), '*a*→*c*' is also false; but on the sixth line '(*a* v *b*)→*c*' is false while '*a*→*c*' is true.

(10) In all cases where '*a* & *b*' is false (all lines but first and fifth), '(*a* & *b*) & *c*' is also false.

Concluding Summary: We can make "immediate inferences" involving molecular statements. These include inferences to equivalents and to weaker forms. In the context of molecular statements, given the truth or falsity of any statement, we can also infer to the truth, falsity, or unknowability of any other statement.

---

[6] The formula for the number of lines needed is 2^x, where '*x*' stands for the number of components.

Deduction and Induction

In this chapter we have discussed the relations that one statement may bear to another: compatible, incompatible, contradictory, subaltern, superaltern, subcontrary, equivalent, converse, obverse, contrapositive. And in this section we have talked about another relation between statements: that of *being inferred from*.

It is very important to be able to say what can be inferred from a statement. Various examples of inferences from a single premise have been given in this section. In chapters to come we will look at arguments in which conclusions are inferred from two or more premises.

Before we embark on the study of various kinds of arguments and the inferences they contain, we should recall what was said in the introduction about the nature of inference and its two types.

Inference is a process of reasoning in which we go from what we "know" to what we do not know. It consists of moving from starting points called 'premises' to resting points called 'conclusions.' Having accepted certain statements, we move out from them to see what else is true. What do these statements entail or imply? What is their consequence? What conclusion can they support?

The act or process of inferring conclusions is more or less sound. The conclusion is firmly established by the premises, well supported, or hardly supported at all. It is a sound inference if we have proceeded properly from premises to conclusion; it is an unsound one if we have not. The science of logic seeks to distinguish 'good,' 'proper,' 'sound,' and 'cogent' reasoning from 'bad,' 'improper,' 'unsound,' and 'fallacious' reasoning; it seeks to uncover the rules and principles of logical inference and to state what it means to have good reasons for a conclusion.

Inference may be divided into two types: deductive and inductive. Arguments containing deductive inferences are called deductive arguments; those containing inductive inferences are called inductive arguments.

An inference is *deductive* when the conclusion is related, or purports to be related, to the premises in such a way that it is necessitated by those premises. The conclusion simply brings out, or seems to bring out, what was already tacitly contained in the premises. A deductive argument is one in which the truth of the premises guarantees, or seems to guarantee, the truth of the conclusion. In a deductive argument it is impossible, or seems to be impossible, for true premises to lead to a false conclusion.

Sound deductive arguments contain inferences in which the conclusion *actually is* necessitated or guaranteed by the premises. Such inferences and arguments are called *valid*. *Unsound* deductive arguments contain inferences in which the conclusion only *seems* to be (or is purported to be) necessitated or guaranteed by the premises.

The beliefs which we have most warrant for, have no safeguard to rest on, but a standing invitation to the whole world to prove them unfounded.
                                        —*John Stuart Mill*, On Liberty

Such inferences and arguments are called *invalid*. A deductive inference is valid if and only if it is impossible for its premises to be true while its conclusion is false.

The premises do not *in fact* have to be true in order for a deductive inference to be valid. It is possible for a conclusion to follow validly from false premises:

> All Canadians are hockey players
> All hockey players are healthy
> ∴ All Canadians are healthy

This is a valid argument, because, *if* the premises were true, then the conclusion would have to be true. The inference is valid because the conclusion is already "contained in" the premises, whether these premises are true or false. The conclusion necessarily follows from the premises—whatever their status. We do not have to know whether premises are true to determine the validity of inferences made from them.

It is useful to reiterate the difference between truth and falsity and between validity and invalidity. The former are properties of statements and denote a relation between what is asserted and what is the case (do they correspond?). The latter are properties of deductive inferences and arguments and denote a relation between premises and a conclusion (does the conclusion necessarily follow?). With this distinction in mind, we can state the requirements for *proof*.

A deductive argument constitutes a proof when two requirements are met:

(1) The inference is valid.
(2) The premises are true.

When these two requirements are met, the conclusion must be true; it has been proved. What if they are not both met? Then the conclusion may be either true or false, and we have no basis for saying which one it is.

It is possible to get a true conclusion from a valid argument with false premises:

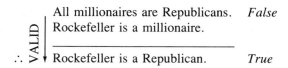

> All millionaires are Republicans.   *False*
> Rockefeller is a millionaire.
> ∴ Rockefeller is a Republican.   *True*

But we are just as likely to get a false conclusion:

> All millionaires have two heads.   *False*
> Rockefeller is a millionaire.
> ∴ Rockefeller has two heads.   *False*

We only know that the conclusion is true when *both* requirements are met.

It is possible to get a true conclusion from an invalid argument with true premises:

INVALID
All millionaires are wealthy.   *True*
Rockefeller is wealthy.   *True*

∴ Rockefeller is a millionaire.   *True*

But we are just as likely to get a false conclusion:

INVALID
All Greek shipowners are wealthy.   *True*
Rockefeller is wealthy.   *True*

∴ Rockefeller is a Greek shipowner.   *False*

We know the conclusion is true only when we know that *both* requirements are met.

It is even possible to get a true conclusion from an invalid argument which has false premises:

INVALID
All millionaires have two heads.   *False*
Rockefeller has two heads.   *False*

∴ Rockefeller is a millionaire.   *True*

But this is a matter of sheer luck. The aim of good thinking is to eliminate or reduce the element of chance. If the deductive argument is valid, the conclusion follows necessarily. And if, in addition, the premises are true, then it is impossible for the conclusion to be anything *but* true.

It is not, however, always possible to meet the two requirements of proof. We may have to settle for less than absolute certainty. We may have to resort to another type of inference.

The other type of inference is induction. In *induction* the conclusion goes beyond the premises (or evidence). There is no certainty: The premises could be true while the conclusion is false. In deduction we can say, "It therefore necessarily follows. . . ." But in induction we have to say something like, "I have good evidence that . . . is probably true."

In deduction 'valid' and 'invalid' mark a dichotomy, but in induction the difference between a good inference and a bad one is a matter of degree. We speak of more or less soundness, greater or lesser probability. There are indeed principles that distinguish good inductive reasoning from bad, but the difference is not so categorical as the difference between valid and invalid deduction.

If deduction seems to have an advantage over induction in the rigorous and undebatable nature of the reasoning process, induction would seem to have an advantage in the certainty of its starting points or premises. Such premises are usually facts of observation. One can challenge the truth of the premises in a deductive argument, but not, if it is valid, the inescapability of its conclusion. One can always raise questions about the soundness of even the best inductive inferences, while usually accepting the truth of the premises or evidence.

Consider the following arguments:

(1) All ruminants have horns.
     All giraffes are ruminants.
     ∴. All giraffes have horns.

(2) This giraffe has horns.
     That giraffe has horns.
     That giraffe over there has horns.
          . . .
          . . .
     ∴. All giraffes have horns.

(3) If Spike's fingerprints are on the gun, he committed the murder.
     His fingerprints are on the gun.
     ∴. Spike committed the murder.

(4) Spike was seen quarreling with the victim.
     Spike was observed purchasing a gun.
     Spike was apprehended on the Mexican border.
     ∴. Spike committed the murder.

(1) is a deductive argument. It is a valid one. The conclusion follows necessarily from the premises. Are we sure that the premises are true? Only to the degree that we are, can we be sure that the conclusion is true. (2) gets at the same conclusion inductively. There is no question about the truth of the premises. But is our sampling technique sound? With what degree of confidence can we generalize about the whole class of giraffes on the basis of the sample we have examined?

(3) is a valid deductive argument. Given the premises, we *have* to accept the conclusion. But we don't have to accept the *truth* of the conclusion unless we are prepared to accept the truth of the premises. (4) is an inductive argument. Unlike (3), it is possible for the premises to be true and the conclusion false. The hypothesis that Spike committed the murder accounts for the facts from which it derives, but it is not the *only* hypothesis that does.

Concluding Summary: Inference, which is a process of drawing conclusions from premises, is of two kinds. One, deduction, has the essential quality of necessity. If the deduction is carried out validly, the conclusion, provided the premises are true, cannot be false. The other, induction, can at best aspire to probability. Even if the inductive process is soundly carried out, the conclusion makes a leap beyond the premises or evidence. Each type of inference has its strengths and its weaknesses. Both are indispensable for science and ordinary life.

EXERCISES

Exercise 42

Make the indicated assumption, then state what, if anything, can be known about the other statements.

1. 'All philosophers are consistent' is true.
   (a) No philosophers are consistent.
   (b) All inconsistent people are non-philosophers.
   (c) All consistent people are philosophers.
   (d) Some philosophers are consistent.
   (e) No inconsistent people are philosophers.
   (f) Some inconsistent people are philosophers.
   (g) Some philosophers are not consistent.
2. 'Some soldiers are officers' is true.
   (a) Some officers are soldiers.
   (b) Some soldiers are not officers.
   (c) All soldiers are officers.
   (d) No officers are soldiers.
   (e) All soldiers are non-officers.
   (f) Some officers are not non-soldiers.
   (g) Some sailors are brave.
3. 'No urgs are blooks' is true.
   (a) All urgs are non-blooks.
   (b) No blooks are urgs.
   (c) No non-blooks are non-urgs.
   (d) Some urgs are blooks.
   (e) Some urgs are not blooks.
   (f) Some non-blooks are not non-urgs.
   (g) All blooks are urgs.
4. 'Some vacations are not expensive' is true.
   (a) Some vacations are inexpensive.
   (b) Some expensive things are not vacations.
   (c) All inexpensive things are non-vacations.
   (d) No vacations are expensive.
   (e) All expensive things are vacations.
   (f) Some inexpensive things are not non-vacations.
   (g) Some non-vacations are expensive.
5. 'No trees are evergreens' is false.
   (a) All trees are non-evergreens.
   (b) No evergreens are trees.
   (c) No non-evergreens are non-trees.
   (d) Some trees are evergreens.
   (e) Some trees are not evergreens.

    (f) Some non-evergreens are not non-trees.

    (g) All trees are evergreens.

6. 'Some courageous people are not lucky' is false.

    (a) Some courageous people are unlucky.

    (b) Some courageous people are lucky.

    (c) No courageous people are lucky.

    (d) All unlucky people are uncourageous.

    (e) No courageous people are unlucky.

    (f) Some unlucky people are not uncourageous.

    (g) Some soldiers are lucky.

Exercise 43

1. Assume that this statement is *true:* 'He is a scholar and he is a gentleman.' What, if anything, can be known about each of the following?

    (a) He is a gentleman.

    (b) It is not the case that he is either not a scholar or not a gentleman.

    (c) He is not a gentleman.

    (d) He reads a lot.

2. Assume that this statement is *true:* 'If the temperature goes up, then the pressure increases.' What, if anything, can be known about the following?

    (a) If the pressure increases, then the temperature goes up.

    (b) The temperature goes up, but the pressure does not increase.

    (c) If the pressure does not increase, then the temperature does not go up.

    (d) The temperature goes up and the pressure increases.

3. Assume that this statement is *false:* 'All graduates are successful or some advisers are incompetent.' What, if anything, can be known about each of the following?

    (a) Some graduates are not successful or no advisers are incompetent.

    (b) All advisers are competent and some graduates are unsuccessful.

    (c) No advisers are incompetent.

    (d) Some advisers are not competent or all unsuccessful people are non-graduates.

4. Assume that this statement is *true:* 'Arnold was a loyalist.' What, if anything, can be known about each of the following?

    (a) Arnold was a loyalist and Adams was a traitor.

    (b) Arnold was a loyalist or Adams was a traitor.

    (c) Adams was not a traitor, and Arnold was not a loyalist.

    (d) Patrick Henry was a rebel.

5. Assume that this statement is *false:* 'Admiral Byrd was a fine sailor and an experienced pilot.' What, if anything, can be known about each of the following?

    (a) Admiral Byrd was not a fine sailor.

    (b) It is not the case that Admiral Byrd was both a fine sailor and an experienced pilot.

(c) Either Admiral Byrd was not an experienced pilot or he was not a fine sailor.

(d) Admiral Byrd was a scholar and a gentleman.

Exercise 44

Use the truth-table method to determine the validity of the following "immediate inferences":

1. $p \leftrightarrow q, \therefore q \rightarrow p$
2. $p \rightarrow q, \therefore \sim p \vee q$
3. $p \rightarrow q, \therefore p \vee \sim q$
4. $\sim(p \rightarrow q), \therefore p$
5. $\sim(p \rightarrow q), \therefore q$
6. $(p \mathrel{\&} q) \rightarrow r, \therefore p \rightarrow r$

Exercise 45

Indicate for each of the following arguments whether deductive or inductive:

1. Arlene is secretary of the Swahili Club, treasurer of her chapter of the Future Farmers of America, and captain of the field hockey team. She must be a very responsible person.
2. I enjoyed *Hamlet, King Lear,* and *Macbeth.* I haven't read *Othello* yet, but when I do, I expect to enjoy it too.
3. All plays by Shakespeare are edifying. *Othello,* therefore, is edifying, since it is by Shakespeare.
4. All television debates are boring, and some expensive projects are boring. Therefore, all television debates are expensive projects.
5. If the weather is bad or Liz can't come, then we'll postpone the picnic and study all day. As it happens, Liz is not able to come. It follows, therefore, that we will study instead of having the picnic.
6. He used the correct ingredients and measured them accurately. But the cake was terrible. The recipe must not have been any good.
7. "No one without shoes will be admitted" is what the sign says. It therefore necessarily follows that everyone with shoes will be admitted.
8. This odd-numbered highway runs north and south. The one we saw yesterday also was north-south. Come to think of it, every highway route I've ever seen with an odd number ran north and south. Therefore, all highways with odd numbers proceed in a north-south direction.
9. He means what he says. Therefore, we can be sure he says what he means.
10. There's not much of a line at the box office. It must be a lousy show.

Exercise 46

The following passage is about deduction. Substitute the appropriate terms from this list:

> *true*   *valid*
> *false*   *invalid*

Statements are either _____ or _____. If what a statement asserts is the case, the statement is _____. If what it asserts is not the case, the statement is _____.

We never call arguments or inferences _____ or _____. A sound deductive argument or inference is called _____; a bad one is called _____.

If the premises are _____ and the inference is _____, then the conclusion must be _____. If the conclusion is _____, then we know that either one or more premises is (or are) _____ or the inference is _____. If the inference is _____ and the premises are true, then the conclusion is _____ or _____. If the premises are _____ and the inference is _____, then the conclusion is unknown.

If one premise is true and the inference is valid and the conclusion is false, then the other premise must be _____.

Chapter 5
Deduction: Syllogism

PREVIEW

It was more than 2,000 years ago when Aristotle systematized the logic of the syllogism. While no longer holding its position as the most valuable kind of deductive inference, syllogistic reasoning is still regarded as an important way of deriving conclusions from categorical premises. In order to be able to handle syllogisms, you should:

1. Memorize the definition of 'syllogism.'
2. Know the meaning of the technical term, 'distribution.'
3. Memorize the rules of syllogistic inference.
4. Know how to apply the rules.
5. Be able to express informal arguments in syllogistic form.
6. Know how to reduce arguments that are equivalent to syllogisms to arguments that meet the definition of 'syllogism.'
7. Be able to supply the missing statement when only two-thirds of a syllogism is present.
8. Be able to arrange premises in a manner that creates a syllogistic chain with suppressed conclusions.

Aristotle was not the first to think syllogistically. Indeed, many people think syllogistically without even knowing what a syllogism is or the rules that govern its validity. See how well *you* do in this preliminary quiz:

1. Valid or invalid:
   (a) No idiots are responsible
   <u>All voters are responsible</u>
   ∴ No voters are idiots

    (b) All contentious people are stubborn
        All conservatives are stubborn
    ∴ All conservatives are contentious

    (c) No tigers are dogs
        Some mammals are tigers
    ∴ Some mammals are not dogs

    (d) No cats are dogs
        No bears are cats
    ∴ No bears are dogs

    (e) Some teachers are unfair
        Some left-handers are teachers
    ∴ Some left-handers are unfair

2. Where *possible,* complete the argument in such a way as to make a valid syllogism:

    (a) All men are mortal
        Socrates is a man
    ∴ [

    (b) All poodles are dogs
        [
    ∴ Some mammals are dogs

    (c) [
        All Senators are politicians
    ∴ No politicians are statesmen

    (d) All the apples in this bag are delicious
        [
    ∴ No apples in this bag are wormy

    (e) No Christians are Muslims
        [
    ∴ Some Frenchmen are not Muslims

REGULAR SYLLOGISMS

Definitions

A *syllogism* is a deductive argument consisting of three categorical statements, two of which are premises and one a conclusion. It contains exactly three terms, each appearing twice but never twice in the same statement. 'Term' means something more specific here than 'word' or 'group of words'; it means 'that expression which denotes one of the classes talked about by the categorical statement.'

According to this definition of 'syllogism,' the following argument qualifies: All executives are careful planners, and some bank robbers are careful planners; therefore some bank robbers are executives. Setting it up in standard form:

> All /executives/ are /careful planners/
> Some /bank robbers/ are /careful planners/
> ∴ Some /bank robbers/ are /executives/

It is easily seen that there are three terms and that each occurs twice. Whether it is a *valid* syllogism is another question.

The following is not a syllogism: Pericles rules Greece and Aspasia rules Pericles; therefore Aspasia rules Greece. Expressing its premises and conclusion as *A* statements, we get:

> All /Pericles/ are /rulers of Greece/
> All /Aspasia/ are /rulers of Pericles/
> ∴ All /Aspasia/ are /rulers of Greece/

We find that there are four terms instead of three and that two of them occur but once. This may be a valid *argument,* but it is not a syllogism.

Consider the argument that sociologists delight in seeing their names in the paper, because they are interested in society and all society people delight in seeing their names in the paper. We can express the argument as:

> All /people interested in society/ are /people who delight in seeing their names in the paper/
> All /sociologists/ are /people interested in society/
> ∴ All /sociologists/ are /people who delight in seeing their names in the paper/

If the premises have any plausibility whatever, it is because 'society' in the first premise means 'the social life of wealthy, prominent, or fashionable persons,' while 'society' in the second is concerned with whole communities of human beings. The argument, depending as it does on the same expression having different meanings in its two occurrences, commits the fallacy of equivocation.

Is the argument a syllogism? It actually deals with *four* classes of objects instead of the three that *syllogisms* are supposed to deal with. But while there are four *classes* involved, there seems to be only three *terms.* However, if we invoke the rule that terms must have a consistent meaning throughout the course of an argument, we will have to alter the language in one of the premises. If we change the subject term of the first premise to 'people interested in the social life of wealthy, prominent, or fashionable persons,' we have an argument that now has *four* terms. It is not, then, by our definition a syllogism.

Abbreviating this argument, we can express the form it *appeared* to have in (1) and the form it *actually* has in (2):

(1)	All X are D	(2)	All Q are D
	All S are X		All S are X
$\therefore$	All S are D	$\therefore$	All S are D

Let us now look at an argument that is a syllogism and clarify some more expressions.

All pollutants are maleficences
No snowflakes are maleficences
$\therefore$ No snowflakes are pollutants

The *major term* is the term that appears as the predicate of the conclusion. 'Pollutants' is thus the major term. The *minor term* is the term that appears as the subject of the conclusion. 'Snowflakes' is thus the minor term. The *middle term* is the term that appears in each of the premises, but not in the conclusion. 'Maleficences' is thus the middle term. The *major premise* is that which contains the major term, while the *minor premise* is that which contains the minor term. It is immaterial whether the major premise or the minor premise is stated first. In the argument above, the first premise happens to be the major premise; the second premise happens to be the minor premise.

Concluding Summary: A syllogism consists of a major premise containing the major term and the middle term, a minor premise containing the minor term and the middle term, and a conclusion containing a minor term (subject) and a major term (predicate).

> *But God has not been so sparing to men to make them barely two-legged creatures, and left it to Aristotle to make them rational. . . . I say not this any way to lessen Aristotle, whom I look on as one of the greatest men amongst the ancients. . . . I readily own, that all right reasoning may be reduced to his forms of syllogism.*
> —*John Locke,* Essay Concerning Human Understanding

Rules of Syllogistic Inference

Since each of the three statements constituting a syllogism may take any one of the four standard forms, there are 64 (four to the third power) possible combinations of A's, E's, I's, and O's in syllogisms. So there are at least 64 possible syllogistic forms.

But for each of these there are four possible configurations, depending upon the position of the middle term. The following are different forms, although they all employ the *All* combination:

(1) All *M* are *P*
    Some *S* are *M*
∴ Some *S* are *P*

(2) All *P* are *M*
    Some *S* are *M*
∴ Some *S* are *P*

(3) All *M* are *P*
    Some *M* are *S*
∴ Some *S* are *P*

(4) All *P* are *M*
    Some *M* are *S*
∴ Some *S* are *P*

These four ways of positioning the middle term have been called the *figures of* a syllogism. When the middle term is the subject of the major premise and the predicate of the minor premise, the syllogism is said to be in the first figure. When the middle term is the predicate of both premises, the syllogism is said to be in the second figure. When the middle term is the subject of both premises, the syllogism is said to be in the third figure. And when the middle term is the predicate of the major premise and the subject of the minor, the syllogism is said to be in the fourth figure.

If there are 64 possible combinations of statement forms and 4 possible figures, there must be 256 possible syllogistic forms (64 × 4). Every particular syllogism will fall into one of these syllogistic forms.

Some of these forms are valid and some are not. How do we determine which is which? There are three infallible ways.

One way is to memorize the valid forms. They are much less numerous than the invalid forms. The medieval schoolmen had names for them and various mnemonic devices in Latin rhymes. The valid forms in the first figure were called Barbara, Celarent, Darii, and Ferio. The second figure gives us Cesare, Camestres, Festino, and Baroco. In the third figure, Darapti, Disamis, Datisi, Felapton, Bocardo, and Ferison are valid. And the valid forms in the fourth figure are Bramantip, Camenes, Dimaris, Fesapo, and Fresison. The vowels tell us the statement forms.

A second way is to draw pictures of the arguments, using circles for classes. The Euler and Venn methods have been popular.[1] And Lewis Carroll worked out a grid system for determining validity.

The third way is to memorize a few rules and ascertain whether the syllogism meets these rules. If it does, it is valid; if it does not, it is invalid. It is this third

---

[1] The method of Venn diagrams is presented in the Appendix. This method is also useful in determining whether or not statement pairs are compatible, contradictory, and equivalent. The first section of the Appendix (pp. 401–410) deals with single statements and statement pairs. The second section (pp. 411–418) deals with syllogisms.

way which will be explained and recommended in this chapter. It requires less memorizing than the first way and less time and space than the second.

To state two of these rules, it is necessary to use a technical term—'distributed.' A term is *distributed* in a statement if and only if the statement says something about all members of the class of things denoted by that term.

Consider the *A* statement: 'All mines are dark.' The subject term is distributed, because the statement asserts that *every* member of the class of mines has the characteristic of being dark. But the predicate term is not distributed, because nothing has been said that is true of every member of the class of dark things. The subject class is *entirely* contained in the predicate class, but the predicate class is not necessarily wholly contained in the subject class.

Consider the *E* statement: 'No saints are sinners.' The subject term is distributed, because the statement asserts that *every member* of the class of saints lacks the characteristic of being a sinner. The predicate term is also distributed, because the statement asserts that *every member* of the class of sinners lacks the characteristic of being a saint. The subject class is *entirely* excluded from the predicate class, and the predicate class is *entirely* excluded from the subject class.

Consider the *I* statement: 'Some slippers are glass.' The subject term is not distributed, since the statement fails to commit itself on every member of the class of slippers. The predicate term is not distributed either, since nothing has been said about the class of glass things in its entirety. Only part of the subject class is guaranteed to be in the predicate class, and only part of the predicate class is guaranteed to be in the subject class.

Consider the *O* statement: 'Some dogs are not poodles.' The subject is not distributed, since the statement does not commit itself on every member of the class of dogs. The predicate term, however, is distributed, for the statement excludes at least one dog from the *entire* class of poodles.

It is therefore the case that the subjects of universals and the predicates of negatives are distributed. All other terms are undistributed.

DISTRIBUTED TERMS

	SUBJECT		PREDICATE	
Universals {	Yes	A	No	
	Yes	E	Yes	} Negatives
	No	O	Yes	
	No	I	No	

The *E* statement distributes both its terms, being universal and negative. The *I* statement distributes neither of its terms, since it is neither universal nor negative.

We will now state the rules of syllogistic inference:

1. At least one premise must be affirmative.
2. If a premise is negative, the conclusion must be negative; and if the conclusion is negative, a premise must be negative.
3. The middle term must be distributed at least once.
4. Any term distributed in the conclusion must also be distributed in a premise.

There are other general principles or "rules" that hold true for all valid syllogisms. But so far as determining validity, they are superfluous. The four rules stated above will catch all invalid syllogisms, and any syllogism that meets these four rules will be valid.

These rules must be memorized. The student will find, however, that applying them a few times will itself virtually bring about memorization.

One more point must be mentioned in this section. It is the possibility of another rule. Those logicians who hold that particular statements guarantee existence and that universal statements do not would add this rule: If the conclusion is particular, at least one premise must be particular. Such a rule would prevent concluding about existence when no existence has been asserted in the premise. Consider these arguments:

(1) All perfect women are moral
All perfect women are intelligent
∴ Some intelligent beings are moral

(2) All frictionless fluids are precious
All precious things are expensive
∴ Some frictionless fluids are expensive

According to this rule, nothing would follow from the premises in (1). In (2) we would be able to conclude that all frictionless fluids are expensive but could say nothing about *some* frictionless fluids. If the reader agrees that particulars guarantee existence while universals do not, he or she should embrace "Rule 5."[2]

Concluding Summary: A method must be selected for determining which of the 256 syllogistic forms are valid and which are invalid. The method selected here is that of memorizing and applying four or five rules.

Applying the Rules

In this section we will apply the rules to particular syllogisms.

It is important, first of all, to make certain that the argument one is examining *is* a syllogism. These are rules of *syllogistic* inference and apply only to syllogisms. It is unreasonable to expect arguments that are not syllogisms to conform to these rules. The argument above about Pericles and Aspasia is neither a valid nor invalid

---

[2] The question of existence is discussed in the Appendix.

syllogism, for it is not a syllogism at all. The argument about people interested in "society" is not a syllogism, so the rules cannot be used to determine its validity. We saw, however, once the equivocation was eliminated, that it was simply a *non sequitur*. *Before* we apply the rules, we must make sure that we are dealing with a three-term argument.

Let us consider the argument:

> No cats are dogs
> No dogs are horses
> ∴ No cats are horses

After ascertaining that this is indeed a syllogism, we find that it runs afoul of Rule 1. It is thus not valid. It commits the "two negative premises" fallacy. The conclusion in this argument happens to be true—we know this on independent grounds. But we could just as easily have got a *false* conclusion with this way of reasoning. The form of the syllogism is:

> No S are M
> No M are P
> ∴ No S are P

Another argument having this form is:

> No poodles are giraffes
> No giraffes are dogs
> ∴ No poodles are dogs

The premises are true, but the conclusion is false. So the argument *must* be invalid. And all arguments of this *form* are invalid. All of which confirms what Rule 1 told us.

Let us examine this argument:

> All well-read people are happy
> Some Americans are not well-read
> ∴ Some Americans are happy

After ascertaining that this is indeed a syllogism, we find that it passes Rule 1 but runs afoul of Rule 2. The argument has a negative premise but not the required negative conclusion. So the syllogism is invalid.

Is there any conclusion that can validly be drawn from these premises? As Rule 2 tells us, it would have to be negative. It would thus have a distributed predicate. But, since neither 'happy' nor 'Americans' is distributed in the premises, neither term could appear as the predicate of the conclusion without violating Rule 4. So there is no syllogistic conclusion whatever that can validly be drawn from the two premises of this argument.

Let us look at this syllogism:

All dogs are mammals
All poodles are mammals
∴ All poodles are dogs

There can be no difficulties with the first two rules, for there are no negatives in the argument. But when we apply Rule 3, we find that 'mammals' (being the predicate of affirmative statements) is not distributed in either premise. So this argument commits the fallacy of "undistributed middle term." No conclusion can validly be drawn from premises neither of which distributes the middle term.

We can confirm that this particular form:

All *P* are *M*
All *S* are *M*
∴ All *S* are *P*

"I can prove I'm right by means of an EAE syllogism in the second figure."

is invalid by thinking of particular instances of it that have true premises and false conclusions—which would be impossible if it were valid. For example:

All dogs are mammals	All communists oppose private property
All cats are mammals	All socialists oppose private property
∴ All cats are dogs	∴ All socialists are communists

In all these instances, if the major premise were reversed—that is, if the converse had been stated instead—the argument would be valid. But who would want to assert that all mammals are dogs or that all people who oppose private property are communists?

Let us examine this argument:

Some convicts are rehabilitated
All convicts are felons
∴ Some felons are not rehabilitated

After ascertaining that this is indeed a syllogism, we find that it passes Rules 1 and 3, but founders on Rules 2 and 4. It has a negative conclusion but lacks a negative premise. Also (although one violation is enough to invalidate it), the major term 'rehabilitated' is distributed in the conclusion but not in the premise. So this instance of the form:

Some *M* are *P*
All *M* are *S*
∴ Some *S* are not *P*

is invalid, and all instances of the form are invalid. They commit the fallacy of "illicit process of the major term."

We might note that this pair of premises does yield a valid conclusion: 'Some *S* are *P*.' The argument:

Some convicts are rehabilitated
All convicts are felons
∴ Some felons are rehabilitated

does satisfy all the rules and is valid.

Consider this syllogism:

All card players are munchers
No dieters are card players
∴ No dieters are munchers

The requirements of the first two rules are met, since we have an affirmative premise and a negative conclusion to go with the negative premise. The middle term, 'card player,' is amply distributed. The conclusion, being universal negative, distributes both its terms. Rule 4 tells us to check back to the premises and make sure that the major and minor terms are distributed there also. The minor term 'dieters' is. But the major term 'munchers' is not. So Rule 4 is not quite met. Which means that it is *not* met and that the argument is invalid. It commits the fallacy of "illicit process of the major term."

Note that the conclusion 'some munchers are not dieters' does follow validly from the premises if we do not employ Rule 5: If the conclusion is particular, a premise must be particular.

Let us look at another way of violating Rule 4:

> All followers of Calvin are Presbyterians
> All followers of Calvin believe in predestination
> ∴ All Presbyterians believe in predestination

Here it is the minor term 'Presbyterians' that is distributed in the conclusion but not in the premise. The argument commits the fallacy of "illicit process of the minor term."

Note that the conclusion 'some Presbyterians believe in predestination' does follow validly from the premises if, once again, we decline to invoke Rule 5.

The only time we do not have to worry about Rule 4 is when the conclusion is an *I* statement. Since there are no distributed terms in an *I*, there is no possibility of violating the rule. When the conclusion is an *E*, however, we must check both terms. When it is an *A*, we check the minor only; and when the conclusion is an *O*, we check the major only.

One more argument:

> All cows are common
> All purple cows are cows
> ∴ All purple cows are common

Is this a syllogism? If it is, it meets all the rules and is a valid argument. But it is not a syllogism. The first premise does not really mean that each and every cow is common (distributive sense); it means that cows *collectively* possess the quality of being numerous. The conclusion also employs the collective sense of attribution, rather than the distributive sense. Syllogistic statements, however, must all be distributive, for this is what class inclusion/exclusion means. If we phrased the statements of this argument distributively while preserving their original meaning, we would have to make the first premise and the conclusion *singular:*

> All /the class of cows/ are /classes with many members/
> All /purple cows/ are /cows/
> ∴ All /the class of purple cows/ are /classes with many members/

The argument really has five terms, although it *appeared* to have only three. So it is not a syllogism. Is it valid? No, it is a *non sequitur*. Because of the ambiguity, the conclusion seems to follow. The argument commits the fallacy of division.[3]

---

[3] The term 'distribution' is not used the same way in this paragraph as it is used in Rules 3 and 4.

> *With the study of logical forms Aristotle made the decisive step that led to the science of logic.*
> —*Hans Reichenbach,* The Rise of Scientific Philosophy

Concluding Summary: Arguments that look as though they might be syllogisms should be set up in standard form. If and only if the argument fits the definition of 'syllogism,' it can then be subjected to the requirements of the four (or five) rules for syllogistic inference. If and only if the syllogism meets the requirements of all the rules, it may be pronounced valid.

Placing Arguments in Syllogistic Form

Once an argument is in syllogistic form, it is quite easy to apply the rules check for validity. The three terms are conspicuously present, each appearing twice in exactly the same words. The type of each statement is obvious, and distribution is easily recognized. The premises are clearly marked off from the conclusion. There is nothing extraneous. We may even abbreviate the terms with single letters. The pure form of the syllogism now shines forth.

Unfortunately, except in textbooks and intelligence tests, arguments do not present themselves in standard form. People who wish to evaluate them must express arguments in such a way that their form becomes apparent. And this often is a difficult task. But to determine the validity of *any* argument, syllogistic or otherwise, we have to expose its form. We must determine its pattern or structure.

We can do this either mentally or in black and white. Let us try the latter on the following informal argument:

> In these perilous and challenging times, it is obvious to all of us who have thought deeply about it that only an experienced public servant, one who has served the nation long and faithfully in a variety of public trusts, can give this country the kind of leadership it needs in the years ahead. Now it is indisputable that Senator Frump has over the years held a great many offices in this great land of ours. Not even his enemies can deny the length and depth of his experience. Yes, Senator Frump has proved himself, and it thus follows that he is the man of the future, the man who, at this crucial juncture of our history, can at last provide the needed leadership. Vote for Frump for president!

Behind this welter of words is a simple argument. Let's try to find it.

It is usually helpful first to try to get the drift of the argument. Where is it headed? What is it trying to prove? This argument seems to be saying something favorable to Frump, namely, that he will be an excellent leader. The expression, 'it thus follows,' is the tipoff. It tells us that a conclusion is about to be stated. In this argument, the conclusion comes at the end. The conclusion is:

> Senator Frump can provide the country with the leadership it needs.

'He is the man of the future' is redundant, being a rather emotional way of saying the same thing. 'At this critical juncture of our history' is expressive language reinforcing the appeal to fear initiated at the beginning of the argument with the expression, 'in these perilous and challenging times.' All this is extraneous because it is irrelevant. The last sentence is purely directive and thus irrelevant and extraneous to any attempt to derive a conclusion from premises.

What reasons does the argument present for the conclusion that Frump can provide the needed leadership? One appears at the beginning of the argument:

> Only an experienced public servant can provide the country with the leadership it needs.

This reason or premise is introduced by the expression 'it is obvious to all of us who have thought deeply about it.' The only function of this expression is to beg people to accept the truth of the statement to follow, so it may be ignored as extraneous to the argument. 'One who has served the country long and faithfully in a variety of public trusts' may also be ignored, since it only dramatizes what is meant by 'experienced public servant.' 'Public servant,' incidentally, is used instead of 'politician' because of its better connotation.

There is still another premise buried in the paragraph. It would be convenient if it employed two of the three terms we have already unearthed, the two that have only appeared once: 'Senator Frump' and 'experienced public servant.' This indeed is what we find to be the case. The passage beginning with 'now it is indisputable' and ending at the point where the conclusion is tipped off, swelled in length by rhetoric and repetition, simply says:

> Senator Frump is experienced.

The expressions 'it is indisputable' and 'not even his enemies can deny' serve to seek support for the truth of the premise that follows. The speaker wants his argument not only to be thought valid but to be thought to contain true premises as well.

Putting together the statements we have isolated, we get this argument:

> Only an experienced public servant can provide the country with the leadership it needs.
> Senator Frump is experienced.
> ∴ Senator Frump can provide the country with the leadership it needs.

Expressing the statements of this argument in standard form, we get:

> All /people who can provide the country with the leadership it needs/ are /experienced public servants/
> All /Senator Frump/ are /experienced public servants/
> ∴ All /Senator Frump/ are /people who can provide the country with the leadership it needs/

The argument conforms to the definition of 'syllogism,' and because its statements are in standard form and the premises distinguished from the conclusion, we will say that it is in standard syllogistic form.

We now apply the rules of syllogistic inference. Since the argument contains no negatives, there is no problem with Rules 1 and 2. But it does violate Rule 3. The middle term 'experienced public servants' is nowhere distributed. So the argument is invalid.

The premise that would have made the argument valid is the (illicit) converse of the major premise that actually appears. If it had been 'All experienced public servants can provide the country with the leadership it needs,' Rule 3 (and all others) would have been satisfied. But who would have accepted the *truth* of such a premise?

Consider the following argument from the *Summa Theologica* (Part I, Q. 98) of Thomas Aquinas:

> What is natural to man was neither acquired nor forfeited by sin. Now it is clear that generation by coition is natural to man by reason of his animal life, which he possessed even before sin, as was above explained, just as it is natural to other perfect animals. This is made clear by the corporeal member deputed to do this work. So we cannot allow that these members would not have had a natural use, as other members had, before sin.

It is easier here to start with the premises. The first sentence appears to be one:

(1) What is natural to man was neither acquired nor forfeited by sin.

Then, prefaced by the words 'Now it is clear that,' we encounter another premise:

(2) Generation by coition is natural to man.

The last statement gives us a conclusion:

(3) We cannot allow that these members would not have had a natural use before sin.

Expressing the numbered statements in standard form, we get:

(*1*) All /actions natural to man/ are /actions neither acquired nor forfeited by sin/
(2) All /cases of generation by coition/ are /actions natural to man/
_____
(*3*) All /cases of generation by coition/ are /actions neither acquired nor forfeited by sin/

The translation of (3) to (*3*) might be considered questionable, but St. Thomas, in denying that the sexual organs had no natural use before Adam and Eve sinned, is affirming that they *did* have this natural use. That is, the act of generation was not something inflicted on mankind as a result of man's fall—which is covered by the (*3*) formulation.

There is other material in this paragraph to buttress the truth of the second premise. St. Thomas is perhaps recalling an earlier syllogism:

All /actions done by perfect animals/ are /actions natural to man/
All /cases of generation by coition/ are /actions done by perfect animals/
_____
(2) All /cases of generation by coition/ are /actions natural to man/

Both of these syllogisms are valid. They are AAA in the first figure, "Barbara," the form most preferred by medieval writers.

Before leaving this interesting argument, we might note that, although St. Thomas taught that sexual intercourse would have taken place in the garden of Eden even had Adam and Eve *not* eaten the forbidden fruit, he held that it would have taken place without concupiscence or immoderate passion. The union of the sexes would be through "deliberate action" rather than "lustful desire."

But philosophers are not always infallible. Consider this argument from Book III of David Hume's *A Treatise of Human Nature:*

> Since morals, therefore, have an influence on the actions and affections, it follows, that they cannot be deriv'd from reason; and that because reason alone, as we have already prov'd, can never have any such influence.

'It follows, that' leads to the conclusion. 'Since' and 'and that because' lead to the premises. The argument is thus:

> Morals have an influence on the actions and affections
> Reason alone cannot influence actions and affections
> ∴ Morals cannot be derived from reason

If we are in a hurry we might think we see this form:

> All *M* are *I*
> No *R* are *I*
> ∴ No *M* are *R*

And call the argument valid. But this is not quite the form the argument has. Let us go back:

> All /moral sentiments/ are /influences on actions and affections/
> No /acts of reason/ are /influences on actions and affections/
> ∴ No /moral sentiments/ are /things derived from acts of reason/

The subject of the second premise and the predicate of the conclusion are not the same term. So the argument has four terms and is not a syllogism. Its form is this:

> All *M* are *I*
> No *R* are *I*
> ∴ No *M* are *X*

The premises give no basis whatever for the conclusion. What *can* be deduced is that moral sentiments are not acts of reason. There is nothing in the premises to rule out the possibility that moral sentiments may be *derived* from acts of reason.

Let us look at one more informal argument:

> As the history of track and field teaches us, all records, however amazing they may be, are eventually broken. Some broadjumping performances in Mexico City, therefore, will be bettered, for they were records.

A preliminary translation:

> All track and field records are eventually broken.
> Some broadjumping performances that took place in Mexico City were records.
>
> Some broadjumping performances that took place in Mexico City will be bettered.

Expressed in standard syllogistic form:

> All /track and field records/ are /records that will eventually be broken/
> Some /broadjump performances that took place in Mexico City/ are /track and field records/
>
> Some /broadjump performances that took place in Mexico City/ are /records that will eventually be broken/

This is a syllogism and it obeys all the rules. So it is valid.

Concluding Summary: In placing arguments into standard syllogistic form, we must identify the premises and conclusion, determine what the three classes are and where they occur, express all three statements in standard form, and ignore all extraneous material. Having determined that an informal argument is indeed a syllogism and having ascertained its particular form, we can decide its validity easily and mechanically by applying the rules.

EXERCISES

Exercise 47

For each of the following syllogisms, indicate whether valid or invalid. If the latter, indicate the number of the rule that is violated.

1. All *M* are *P*
   Some *S* are not *M*
   ∴ Some *S* are not *P*

2. No *S* are *M*
   No *M* are *P*
   ∴ No *S* are *P*

3. All *P* are *M*
   All *S* are *M*
   ∴ All *S* are *P*

4. All *P* are *M*
   Some *S* are not *M*
   ∴ Some *S* are not *P*

5. Some *M* are not *P*
   All *M* are *S*
   ∴ Some *S* are not *P*

6. Some *M* are not *P*
   All *M* are *S*
   ∴ Some *P* are not *S*

7. Some *P* are *M*
   All *S* are *M*
   ∴ All *S* are *P*

8. Some *M* are not *P*
   Some *S* are not *M*
   ∴ Some *S* are not *P*

9. No *P* are *M*
   All *S* are *M*
   ∴ No *S* are *P*

10. No *P* are *M*
    All *M* are *S*
    ∴ No *S* are *P*

Exercise 48

Using the information given earlier about Barbara, Celarent, and the rest, set forth the nineteen valid syllogistic forms:

1. *First Figure* (middle term is subject of major, predicate of minor premise): four forms.
2. *Second Figure* (middle term is predicate of both premises): four forms.
3. *Third Figure* (middle term is subject of both premises): six forms.
4. *Fourth Figure* (middle term is predicate of major, subject of minor premise): five forms.

Exercise 49

For those arguments that are syllogisms, indicate whether valid or invalid. If valid, indicate the rule number.

1. Some fattening foods are not rich desserts
   All chocolate eclairs are rich desserts
   ∴ All chocolate eclairs are fattening foods

2. Some snakes are not dangerous animals
   All snakes are reptiles
   ∴ Some reptiles are not dangerous animals

3. All supporters of popular government are democrats
   All Democrats are opponents of the Republican Party
   ∴ All supporters of popular government are opponents of the Republican Party

4. No parrots are pests
   Some pets are parrots
   ∴ Some pets are not pests

5. All munchkins are prurient
   Some onangers are prurient
   ∴ Some onangers are munchkins

6. All vaarks are emus
   Some gnus are vaarks
   ∴ Some gnus are emus

7. No dogs are felines
   All cats are felines
   ∴ No cats are dogs

8. All singers are performers
   All actors are performers
   ∴ All actors are singers

9. All wastrels are nonchalant
   Harold is not a wastrel
   ∴ Harold is not nonchalant

10. St. Louis is north of Little Rock
    Chicago is north of St. Louis
    ∴ Chicago is north of Little Rock

11. Some wars are not profitable
    All crusades are profitable
    ∴ Some wars are not crusades

12. All perfect men are understanding
    All understanding men are forgiving
    ∴ Some perfect men are forgiving

Exercise 50

Set up in standard syllogistic form and ascertain validity:

1. Whenever it's cold, she wears her blue coat. She's not wearing her blue coat today, so it must not be cold.
2. Louise weeps whenever Patrick speaks sharply to her. He must have spoken sharply to her, for she is weeping now.

3. Only the brave deserve the fair. Clifford, then, deserves the fair, for he is brave.

4. All men are mortal, so Socrates, being a man, is mortal.

5. Only a moron would laugh at that joke. So I guess that makes the present company morons, for they all laughed at the joke.

6. Since no one passes unless he studies and some athletes passed, some athletes must have studied.

7. The only good songs are old songs. Some hymns, then, are good songs, since some of them are old.

8. All brokers are honest, but none of them is a saint. Therefore, no saints are honest.

Exercise 51

Set up in standard syllogistic form and ascertain validity:

1. No successful man has failed to give great credit to his mother. Roger must be a successful man, since he is always giving credit to his mother.

2. No one who likes major-league baseball wants to see an end to the reserve clause, so not all those who like major-league baseball are fans, since many fans want to see an end to the reserve clause.

3. Reports of miracles run counter to natural law, to the best and most exceptionless generalizations we have of human experience. Such reports, therefore, should not be believed, for anything that conflicts with universal and extensive human experience should be doubted.

4. "The proud man loves the presence of parasites or flatterers, and hates that of the noble minded," for "pride is a joy arising from a man's having too high an opinion of himself," and all men who have too high an opinion of themselves love to be flattered. (Spinoza.)

5. There are good reasons for my belief that all college students should take a course in logic. In the first place, it is true that only people who wish to improve their powers of reasoning should take such a course. And it is indisputable that college students, whatever their major, do want to improve the quality of their thinking.

"IRREGULAR" SYLLOGISMS

Arguments Equivalent to Syllogisms

It is sometimes possible to reduce an argument that has four or more terms to one that has three. Some arguments, therefore, that do not appear to be syllogisms because of excessive terms may be transformed into genuine syllogisms. Another way to put it: Some arguments, while technically not syllogisms, are equivalent to syllogisms.

Consider the familiar argument:

Those who can, do. Those who can't, teach. Therefore, teachers are not doers.

Setting it up in standard form:

All /people who can/ are /people who do/
All /people who cannot/ are /teachers/

∴ No /teachers/ are /people who do/

Technically, this is not a syllogism, because it contains four terms. It would thus be wrong to apply the rules to the argument as it now stands.

The argument can be reduced to a three-term argument by contraposing the major premise and obverting the conclusion:

All /people who do not/ are /people who cannot/
All /people who cannot/ are /teachers/

∴ All /teachers/ are /people who do not/

The result, which is equivalent to the original argument, is a syllogism. We can now apply the rules. When we do, we find that 4 is violated. The syllogism commits the fallacy of illicit process of the minor term.

The particular transformation made is not the only way to achieve a reduction of terms. We might have contraposed the minor premise and obverted the converse of the conclusion:

All /people who can/ are /people who do/
All /non-teachers/ are /people who can/

∴ All /people who do/ are /non-teachers/

But no matter how we shift things around, so long as we are faithful to the meanings of the original statements, we end up with an invalid argument.

It is the case that *whenever* the excessive terms are complements, reduction can be made to three terms. Another example:

All mechanics are competent
All tax assessors are incompetent

∴ No tax assessors are mechanics

Here we need only obvert the minor premise:

All mechanics are competent
No tax assessors are competent

∴ No tax assessors are mechanics

'Non-incompetent' is taken to be synonymous with 'competent.' The syllogism meets all the rules, so is valid.

Here is an argument with five terms:

> All unscientific people are unsuccessful
> Some astrologers are not scientific
> ∴ Some astrologers are not successful

It is reduced to a syllogism simply by contraposing the first premise:

> All successful people are scientific
> Some astrologers are not scientific
> ∴ Some astrologers are not successful

Only now can we apply the rules of syllogistic inference. And when we do, the syllogism meets them, so it is valid.

Finally, we will look at an argument with six terms:

> All relevant arguments are reverent
> All irrelevant arguments are irreligious
> ∴ No religious arguments are irreverent

What needs to be done? Take the contrapositive of the second premise and the obverse of the conclusion:

> All relevant arguments are reverent
> All religious arguments are relevant
> ∴ All religious arguments are reverent

Or we could have taken the contrapositive of the first premise and the obverse of the second:

> All irreverent arguments are irrelevant
> No irrelevant arguments are religious
> ∴ No religious arguments are irreverent

Or we could have taken the contrapositive of the first premise and the obverse of the converse of the conclusion:

> All irreverent arguments are irrelevant
> All irrelevant arguments are irreligious
> ∴ All irreverent arguments are irreligious

Whichever way we go, we end up with equivalent syllogisms. And they are all valid.

Concluding Summary: All statements have equivalent formulations in which negatives are added or removed. Thus it is always possible to reduce an argument whose excessive terms are complements to a syllogism. The original argument and the resulting argument are equivalent to one another, but the rules of the syllogism can only be applied to the latter.

Incomplete Syllogisms

We sometimes encounter a syllogistic argument that is incomplete. Either the conclusion or one of the premises has been omitted. Such an argument, two-thirds of a syllogism, is called an *enthymeme*.

An example of a syllogism with a missing premise is:

Dogs are not ruminants, for they do not chew the cud.

Supplying the missing premise (in brackets), we get this valid syllogism:

No /dogs/ are /animals that chew the cud/
[All /ruminants/ are /animals that chew the cud/
∴ No /dogs/ are /ruminants/

An advertisement might say, "Joe Hubcap does a big volume of business! You know he'll give you a good trade-in on your old car." How do we know this? It does not follow from the stated premise. But if we provide an additional premise (bracketed), it does follow, for we have a valid argument:

All /Joe Hubcap/ are /dealers who do a big volume of business/
[All /dealers who do a big volume of business/ are /dealers who give good trade-ins/]
∴ All /Joe Hubcap/ are /dealers who give good trade-ins/

Why are premises sometimes omitted? There are at least two different reasons: (1) The identity and truth of the missing premise are so *obvious* that they do not need to be stated. (2) The truth of the missing premise is *suspect*. To state it would call attention to it. Moreover, the listener, if left to himself, might assume as the missing premise a more plausible statement than the one needed to make the argument a valid one. The speaker is thus spared the odium of sponsoring a false premise or an invalid argument.

The enthymeme about the dogs seems to be an instance of the first reason. That the missing premise is 'All ruminants chew the cud' is obvious and so is its truth.

But the enthymeme about the car dealer seems to be an instance of the second reason. The missing premise is patently false, so the conclusion cannot be known to be true. If the listener supplies a somewhat different premise, 'All dealers who give good trade-ins are dealers who do a big volume of business,' we have a more plausible premise. But the argument is now invalid, since the middle term is undistributed.

In supplying missing premises, we choose as our terms those that have only occurred once each. In putting them together, we keep the requirements of the rules before us. If the conclusion is negative and the given premise is not, the premise we supply must be negative. But if the given premise is negative or the conclusion is affirmative, the premise we supply must be affirmative. If the middle term is not yet distributed, we must distribute it now. And if the major or minor term (whichever one is in the supplied premise) is distributed in the conclusion, we distribute it in the supplied premise.

Is it possible for an enthymeme to be invalid? Yes, when there is no conceivable premise that could be added to make a valid syllogism. Perhaps we should call such an argument a *pseudo-enthymeme*. The following are examples of partial syllogisms:

(1) No trees are plants, inasmuch as all shrubs are plants.
(2) All lizards are reptiles, since some animals are reptiles.
(3) All dogs are blunks, for no dogs are cats.

Whatever premise is supplied for (1), the argument would be invalid, for 'plants' is distributed in the conclusion but not in the given premise.

The missing premise for (2) must include 'lizards' and 'animals.' 'Lizards' must be distributed because it is distributed in the conclusion; 'animals' must be distributed since it is the middle term, and it is not distributed in the given premise. The only kind of statement that will distribute both terms is the *E*. But this is a negative and, according to Rule 2, unacceptable for the affirmative conclusion.

All this suggests a third reason for stating a syllogistic argument enthymematically: There exists no valid way to complete it. If invalidity is to be perpetrated, let it be done by the listener!

(3) looks like an easy one. Doesn't the fact that there is an affirmative conclusion and a negative premise (in violation of Rule 2) necessarily invalidate any complete syllogism we might come up with? Not necessarily. We can change the conclusion to an *E* statement by obverting: 'No dogs are non-blunks.' Rule 2 is now satisfied. Now all we need do is to supply an affirmative premise that includes 'cats' and distributes 'non-blunks.' The missing premise is 'All non-blunks are cats.' So (3), contrary to our first impression, is a valid enthymeme. When distribution rules are not violated at the outset, an enthymeme can often be set up as a valid argument.

Another type of enthymeme is a syllogistic argument in which the conclusion is omitted. The three reasons for doing this are similar to those above: (1) The valid conclusion is obvious; one does not have to bother stating it. (2) The speaker hopes that the listener will draw the wrong conclusion. (3) There is no valid conclusion that can be drawn. Examples of each are:

(1) A moralist may say to a friend: "An honest man would have reported the overpayment. You, however, did not." It is clear to one and all that he is saying that his friend is not honest. There is no need actually to *draw* the conclusion. It is obvious.

(2) A department store may proclaim: "The only things on sale this weekend are tires! Only things on sale are covered by the guarantee!" It is hoped that the reader or listener will draw the conclusion that all tires are covered by the guarantee, whereas the valid conclusion is something else. The validly completed enthymeme is:

All things that are on sale are tires
All things covered by the guarantee are on sale
∴ [All things covered by the guarantee are tires]

The advertising claim does not cover *all* tires. It may be limited to a very special (and unpopular) kind. The only things that are covered by the guarantee are tires, but not necessarily all of them—not even those on sale.

(3) This argument is taken from Monroe Beardsley's *Practical Logic:* "I deny that some of my friends are disloyal to the government, and I also deny that all those who appeared on that platform are my friends. You may draw your own conclusion."[4] Well, there is no conclusion that can validly be drawn.

The denial of the first statement is:

> No friends of mine are disloyal to the government.

The denial of the second statement is:

> Some people who appeared on the platform are not friends of mine.

Both of these premises are negative. According to Rule 1, any syllogism containing two negatives would seem to be invalid, whatever its conclusion might be. But we should not be too hasty. The premises might be equivalent to statements that meet the requirements of Rule 1.

We note that the first premise could be changed to an affirmative statement without creating any extra terms. So we would have as our pair of premises:

> All friends of mine are loyal to the government.
> Some people who appeared on the platform are not friends of mine.

What now can be concluded? The conclusion (according to Rule 2) must be negative and involve 'people loyal to the government' and 'people who appeared on the platform.' One or the other of these terms will be the predicate and thus be distributed. But neither one of these is distributed in a premise, so any negative conclusion would violate Rule 4. No matter how we manipulate the premises, no valid conclusion is possible.

It is sometimes the case that two negative premises *do* validly yield a conclusion. Consider the following:

> No *A* are *B*
> Some *A* are not *C*

These premises can never be premises of a valid syllogism when the same terms, 'B' and 'C,' appear in the conclusion. Rule 1 holds for all complete and genuine syllogisms. We can, however, make one or more of the premises affirmative by means of obversion and draw a valid syllogistic conclusion:

All A are $\overline{B}$	No A are B	All A are $\overline{B}$
Some A are not C	Some A are $\overline{C}$	Some A are $\overline{C}$
∴ [Some $\overline{B}$ are not C]	∴ [Some $\overline{C}$ are not B]	∴ [Some $\overline{B}$ are $\overline{C}$]

---

[4] Monroe C. Beardsley, *Practical Logic* (Englewood Cliffs, N.J.: Prentice-Hall, Inc., 1950), p. 253.

Note that these conclusions contain, respectively, '$\overline{B}$' instead of 'B,' '$\overline{C}$' instead of 'C,' and '$\overline{B}$' and '$\overline{C}$' instead of 'B' and 'C.'

When we have two premises that do not rule out a valid conclusion, we take the two terms that have appeared but once in the premises and try to combine them in a way that will satisfy the rules. On the basis of Rule 2, we decide whether the conclusion is affirmative or negative. And, in the light of Rule 4, we distribute only those terms that are distributed in the premises.

Finally, we may cite a syllogistic argument that is even shorter than an enthymeme. Someone says:

> All men are dishonest.

Adding the obvious premise that the speaker is a man, we can conclude that *he* is dishonest. If a married person asserts that every spouse cheats on his or her mate, we can be sure that the speaker does also.

Concluding Summary: One should be skeptical of syllogistic arguments that lack one of the three statements. Some of these arguments can be validly completed and some of them cannot. Even those that can be validly completed may be found to have a false premise.

Syllogistic Chains

It is often the case in deductive argumentation that the conclusion of one argument is used as a premise for the next. Before one arrives at a final conclusion, he may have paused along the way for intermediate conclusions. The entire argument may be likened to a chain with many links. When the conclusion of a syllogism is used as a premise for another one, we have a *syllogistic chain* or, as it is traditionally called, a "sorites."

The following is an example:

(1) No one takes the *Times* unless he is well educated
(2) Those who cannot read are not well educated
   ∴ [Everyone who takes the *Times* can read]
(3) No hedgehogs can read
   ∴ No hedgehogs take the *Times*

This argument, like all other sorites in this chapter, was composed by Lewis Carroll. It is a chain with two links and one intermediate conclusion, which is enclosed in brackets. The intermediate conclusion is used as a premise in the second link. The three original premises (numbered) lead up to the final conclusion about hedgehogs and the *Times*.

To easily determine its validity, we express the argument in standard form:

> All /beings who take the *Times*/ are /beings who are well educated/
> All /beings who are well educated/ are /beings who can read/
> ∴ [All /beings who take the *Times*/ are /beings who can read/]
> No /hedgehogs/ are /beings who can read/
> ∴ No /hedgehogs/ are /beings who take the *Times*/

Both links are valid, so the chain (or sorites) is valid.

Let us work another sorites. Lewis Carroll gives us four basic premises:

(1) Things sold in the street are of no great value.
(2) Nothing but rubbish can be had for a song.
(3) Eggs of the Great Auk are very valuable.
(4) It is only what is sold in the street that is really rubbish.

Placing the statements in standard form, and starting out with (1) and (3), which have a term in common, we arrive at the following valid sorites:

(1) No /things that are sold in the street/ are /things of great value/
(3) All /eggs of the Great Auk/ are /things of great value/
∴ [No /eggs of the Great Auk/ are /things that are sold in the street/]
(4) All /things that are rubbish/ are /things that are sold in the street/
∴ [No /eggs of the Great Auk/ are /things that are rubbish/]
(2) All /things that can be had for a song/ are /things that are rubbish/
∴ No /eggs of the Great Auk/ are /things that can be had for a song/

If we started with (1) and (4), which also have a term in common, or with any of several other pairs, we would also have used up all the premises and come out with the same final conclusion. The intermediate conclusions, however, would have been different.

The longest sorites that Carroll has left us has these premises:

(1) The only animals in this house are cats.
(2) Every animal is suitable for a pet, that loves to gaze at the moon.
(3) When I detest an animal, I avoid it.
(4) No animals are carnivorous, unless they prowl at night.
(5) No cat fails to kill mice.
(6) No animals ever take to me, except what are in this house.
(7) Kangaroos are not suitable for pets.
(8) None but carnivora kill mice.
(9) I detest animals that do not take to me.
(10) Animals that prowl at night always love to gaze at the moon.

If the sorites is valid (and it is), we should expect it to consist of nine (ten minus one) valid links, with eight intermediate conclusions before the final conclusion. There are a great many places to start, but, again, we get the same conclusion regardless of where we start.

(1) All /animals in this house/ are /cats/
(5) All /cats/ are /mice killers/
   ∴ [All /animals in this house/ are /mice killers/]
(6) All /animals that take to me/ are /animals in this house/
   ∴ [All animals that take to me/ are /mice killers/]
(8) All /mice killers/ are /carnivora/
   ∴ [All /animals that take to me/ are /carnivora/]
(4) All /carnivora/ are /night prowlers/
   ∴ [All /animals that take to me/ are /night prowlers/]
(10) All /night prowlers/ are /animals that love to gaze at the moon/
   ∴ [All /animals that take to me/ are /animals that love to gaze at the moon/]
(2) All /animals that love to gaze at the moon/ are /animals suitable for pets/
   ∴ [All /animals that take to me/ are /animals suitable for pets/]
(9) All /animals that I do not detest/ are /animals that take to me/
   ∴ [All /animals that I do not detest/ are /animals suitable for pets/]
(3) All /animals that I do not avoid/ are /animals that I do not detest/
   ∴ [All /animals that I do not avoid/ are /animals suitable for pets/]
(7) No /kangaroos/ are /animals suitable for pets/
   ∴ No /kangaroos/ are /animals that I do not avoid/ =
   All /kangaroos/ are /animals that I avoid/ =
   I ALWAYS AVOID A KANGAROO

In getting premises that would have the right terms, it was often necessary above to take an obverse or contrapositive or some equivalent formulation of the most natural expression of the given premises. But no meanings were changed.

As it happened, all the sorites examined here were valid. Obviously, however, fallacies must be looked for in sorites as well as any other syllogistic argument. If a fallacy occurs at any link of a syllogistic chain, the argument breaks down. The sorites is invalid, and every conclusion drawn from the fallacious point to the end is under suspicion.

Concluding Summary: Syllogisms linked together in such a way that the conclusion of one becomes a premise for another constitute a sorites or syllogistic chain. The validity of the chain can best be determined by expressing its statements in standard form and applying the rules of syllogistic inference.

EXERCISES

Exercise 52

Set up as syllogisms and ascertain validity

1. No drinkers are men in perfect physical condition
    Some men in perfect physical condition are not non-athletes
    ∴ Some nondrinkers are athletes

2. All mortals are imperfect beings
   No humans are immortals
   ∴ All perfect beings are nonhumans
3. No worldly goods are immaterial
   No material things are unchangeable
   ∴ All changeable things are worldly goods
4. All things present are non-irritants
   All visible things are absent
   ∴ No irritants are invisible
5. Since all ambiguous arguments are unreasonable, and no reasonable arguments are invalid, it follows that all valid arguments are unambiguous.
6. All consistent discourses are unimpassioned and some philosophies are impassioned. Therefore, some philosophies are inconsistent.
7. Those who sing can also dance. Those who don't sing are actors. Therefore, actors are not dancers.
8. Some Irishmen are dishonest, for no politicians are honest and some Irishmen are politicians.
9. All writers are literate, and some writers are not intelligent. Therefore, some stupid people are not illiterate.
10. Only linguists are comfortable when abroad, and only people who are comfortable when abroad really enjoy themselves. Therefore, all people who are not linguists are people who do not enjoy themselves.

Exercise 53

Where possible, complete the argument in such a way as to make a valid syllogism:

1. [
   Susan has red hair
   ∴ Susan has a temper

2. [
   All students are overworked
   ∴ No students are happy

3. All noise is distracting
   Some music is not distracting
   ∴ [

4. All private detectives are softhearted
   [_____
   ∴ All softhearted people are tough

5. Some near-sighted people wear glasses
   Some professors are near-sighted
   ∴ [

6. No cats are dogs
   Some dogs are not poodles
   ∴ [

7. Some trees are cedars
   [
   ∴ Some trees are fragrant

8. No predicaments are endless
   [
   ∴ No traffic jams are endless

9. All urban areas are crowded
   All cities are urban areas
   ∴ [

10. Some phrenaxes are poodles
    [
    ∴ Some dogs are not poodles

Exercise 54

At least three of the following syllogistic chains are valid. Where valid, set up and draw the intermediate and final conclusions. Where invalid, indicate the point where the argument breaks down.

1. (1) My saucepans are the only things I have that are made of tin.
   (2) I find all your presents useful.
   (3) None of my saucepans are of the slightest use.
2. (1) No terriers wander among the signs of the zodiac.
   (2) Nothing that does not wander among the signs of the zodiac is a comet.
   (3) Nothing but a terrier has a curly tail.
3. (1) The only articles of food my doctor allows me are not very rich.
   (2) Anything suitable for supper agrees with me.
   (3) Wedding cake is always very rich.
   (4) My doctor allows me all articles of food that are suitable for supper.
4. (1) No birds, except ostriches, are nine feet high.
   (2) There are no birds in this aviary that belong to anyone but me.
   (3) No ostrich lives on mince pies.
   (4) I have no birds less than nine feet high.

Exercise 55

Both these sorites are valid. Draw the intermediate and final conclusions:

1. (1) No interesting poems are unpopular among people of real taste.
   (2) No modern poetry is free from affectation.
   (3) All your poems are on the subject of soap bubbles.
   (4) No affected poetry is popular among people of real taste.
   (5) No ancient poem is on the subject of soap bubbles.
2. (1) No shark ever doubts that it is well fitted out.
   (2) A fish that cannot dance a minuet is contemptible.
   (3) No fish is quite certain that it is well fitted out unless it has three rows of teeth.
   (4) All fishes, except sharks, are kind to children.
   (5) No heavy fish can dance the minuet.
   (6) A fish with three rows of teeth is not to be despised.

Chapter 6

More Deductive Inferences

PREVIEW

Since the time of Aristotle, logicians have developed several kinds of deductive inference. In this chapter, we will look at arguments that contain molecular statements. The validity of these arguments depends upon the meaning of such terms as 'and,' 'or,' and 'if . . . then.' Truth tables provide a mechanical method for testing validity—or confirming intuitive judgments. Calculating the probability of particular outcomes can also be a matter of deduction. The same kind of necessity operates in deducing the degree of probability for an event that operates in drawing a conclusion, say, in a disjunctive argument. The following aims must be achieved by the student of molecular deduction:

1. Determining the validity of disjunctive arguments.
2. Determining the validity of conditional arguments.
3. Understanding the nature of the dilemma and knowing how to ''answer'' one.
4. Evaluating deductive arguments that contain a mixture of molecular forms.
5. Mastering a truth method for determining validity.

The following skills must be attained by students of mathematical probability:

1. Know how to calculate the initial probability of a single event by relying on equal possibilities.
2. Know how to calculate the initial probability of a single event by relying on statistical possibilities.
3. Know how to calculate the probability of two or more disjunctive (or exclusive) events.
4. Know how to calculate the probability of conjunctive (or independent) events.
5. Know how to calculate the probability of combinations of events that are neither exclusive nor independent.

6. Know how to calculate the value of a bet when the probability of the event that is bet on is known.

Here is a little test on molecular deduction. Ask yourself what, if anything, follows from the premises:

1. She is very intelligent or she works hard
   She is not very intelligent
   ∴ [

2. She is very intelligent or she works hard
   She is very intelligent
   ∴ [

3. If all tests are positive, he is OK'd for the space shot
   He is OK'd for the space shot
   ∴ [

4. If all tests are positive, he is OK'd for the space shot
   He is not OK'd for the space shot
   ∴ [

5. If all tests are positive, he is OK'd for the space shot
   Some tests were not positive
   ∴ [

Following are five questions on mathematical probability:

6. Which is more probable—throwing a seven with two dice or guessing a number between one and ten?
7. Which is more probable—surviving a domestic flight on an airline or a 2,000-mile trip by car?
8. If "1" is certainty, what is the probability of guessing a coin toss twice in a row?
9. If a player has guessed wrong 40 times in a row at the roulette table, is he or she, in some sense, "due" at the next spin of the wheel?
10. If a person has a one in ten chance of guessing right, what odds should he or she expect in a bet?

MOLECULAR FORMS

Disjunctive Arguments

A very common type of deductive argument is one in which we conclude that one of two alternatives is true because the other one is not. For example, while riding my bike, I find that my pedaling suddenly ceases to drive the rear wheel. I say to myself:

> The chain has slipped off the sprocket or the gear cable is loose.

I look down and see that the chain has not slipped off the sprocket. So I conclude that the gear cable must be loose. This is a valid argument and has this form:

$$p \lor q$$
$$\underline{\sim p}$$
$$\therefore \quad q$$

If I had checked the gear cable first and discovered that it was not loose, I would have concluded that the chain had slipped off the sprocket. This would, of course, also have been valid:

$$p \lor q$$
$$\underline{\sim q}$$
$$\therefore \; p$$

When two alternatives appear in a premise, the denial of one of them necessitates the other.

Disjunctive premises may present any number of alternatives (or disjuncts). Before one of them can be concluded, all other alternatives must be denied:

$$p \lor q \lor r \lor s$$
$$\sim p$$
$$\sim q$$
$$\underline{\qquad \sim r \qquad}$$
$$\therefore \qquad\qquad s$$

What we *cannot* do in a disjunctive argument is to conclude that one alternative is not the case on the basis of having discovered that the other one is. In the bike example, I would have reasoned invalidly if, after looking down and finding that the chain had come off, I had concluded that the gear cable was not loose. Such an argument would have this form:

$$p \lor q$$
$$\underline{p} \qquad \textit{Invalid}$$
$$\therefore \; \sim q$$

Remembering that 'or' usually means 'at least one is the case and maybe both,' we realize that the chain may have come off *and* the cable may be loose. The occurrence of one does *not* rule out the occurrence of the other.

The physician who knows that two diseases cause the symptoms and rules out one disease simply because she has found out that the other one is present may be making a fatal mistake. The teacher who concludes that the student is *not* especially bright after discovering that he studies a lot may be doing the student an injustice.

The popular girl who, apparently, is very personable or very good-looking may indeed be both.

The only time we can draw a negative conclusion from an 'either . . . or' premise is when the premise is a *strong* disjunction, when we are sure that the connective means, 'exactly one is the case.' The following arguments contain such a strong disjunction as a premise and appear, therefore, to be valid:

(1) Rhoda is either pregnant or she is not pregnant
Rhoda is pregnant
∴ It is not the case that she is not pregnant

(2) Her husband is either in Chicago or New York
Her husband is in Chicago
∴ Her husband is not in New York

(3) The baby will be a boy or a girl
The baby will be a boy
∴ The baby will not be a girl

The premise in (1) is known to be a strong disjunction because the alternatives are contradictory: Exactly one is true and exactly one is false. The premise in (2) is known to be a strong disjunction because it is impossible for a person to be in two places at the same time. The premise in (3) is known to be a strong disjunction because the alternatives, boy and girl, are exclusive; a baby cannot be both a boy *and* a girl. Given these strong disjunctions, all three arguments are valid.

In addition, of course, the inferences valid from ordinary disjunctions are valid from strong disjunctions. This is because strong disjunctions say not only that the two alternatives cannot both be true but also that they cannot both be false. This is what it means to say 'exactly one is the case.' So all four of these forms are valid:

$$p \veebar q$$
$$\sim p$$
$$\therefore \quad q$$

$$p \veebar q$$
$$\sim q$$
$$\therefore \ p$$

$$p \veebar q$$
$$p$$
$$\therefore \quad \sim q$$

$$p \veebar q$$
$$q$$
$$\therefore \ \sim p$$

The form in the lower left is that exemplified in the three arguments earlier about Rhoda.

The strong disjunction, like the ordinary disjunction, may contain any number of disjuncts. Also like the disjunction, we would have to deny all but one before we could conclude that that one is the case. But unlike arguments with ordinary disjunctions, if we can assert in the second premise that one is the case, we can deny all the other alternatives:

Joe is in Chicago, Detroit, or New York
Joe is not in Detroit
Joe is not in New York

∴ Joe is in Chicago

Joe is in Chicago, Detroit, or New York
Joe is in Chicago

∴ Joe is not in Detroit and Joe is not in New York

Both these arguments are valid.

Concluding Summary: Disjunctive arguments contain a disjunctive statement as a premise. It is always valid to infer from the denial of all but one of the disjuncts to the affirmation of the remaining one. Only if the premise is a *strong* disjunction, however, can we reason from the affirmation of a disjunct to the denial of the other(s). All this is confirmed by the truth table test.

I have found you an argument. I am not obliged to find you an understanding.
                    —Samuel Johnson, quoted in Boswell's Life of Dr. Johnson

---

Conditional Arguments

We can put two conditionals together to get a valid argument:

If the bough breaks, then the cradle falls
If the cradle falls, then the baby cries

∴ If the bough breaks, then the baby cries

Another "conditional syllogism" is:

If Dorothy was nervous, she skated badly
If she won the gold medal, then she did not skate badly

∴ If she won the gold medal, then Dorothy was not nervous

The forms of these two valid deductive arguments are:

$p \rightarrow q$
$q \rightarrow r$
∴ $p \rightarrow r$

$p \rightarrow q$
$r \rightarrow \sim q$
∴ $r \rightarrow \sim p$

In some arguments containing conditional statements, the second premise is an atomic statement. It may affirm or deny one of the components of the conditional statement. Sometimes a conclusion follows validly and sometimes it does not.

Let us take as our first premise:

If you go out with Stella, then you have a good time

If the second premise is:

You went out with Stella

Then it does indeed follow that you had a good time, for going out with Stella is asserted as a sufficient condition for having a good time. Whenever a sufficient condition is met, that for which it suffices must be the case. This is called "affirming the antecedent."

Suppose the second premise had been:

You did not go out with Stella

From these two premises we cannot deduce anything. It would be fallacious to infer that you did not have a good time. You may very well have had a good time— watching television, working logic problems, or chatting with Yvonne. The first premise did not assert that going out with Stella was the *only* way to have a good time. If one infers the denial of the consequent from two such premises, he has committed the fallacy of "denying the antecedent."

Suppose the second premise had been:

You had a good time

Here again, since the first premise does not say that going out with Stella is the only way to have a good time, it would be fallacious to conclude anything about the other component of the conditional statement. To conclude that you must have gone out with Stella would be to commit the fallacy of "affirming the consequent."

Finally, let us suppose the second premise is:

You did not have a good time

This is a case of "denying the consequent." From such a denial we can validly deny the antecedent. If the result did not occur (good time), then that which would have sufficed for it (going out with Stella) could not have occurred either.

So, of these four arguments, two are valid and two are invalid. Their forms are:

$$
\begin{array}{cc}
\begin{array}{c} p \rightarrow q \\ \underline{p} \\ \therefore \quad q \end{array} \quad Valid
&
\begin{array}{c} p \rightarrow q \\ \underline{\sim q} \\ \therefore \quad \sim p \end{array}
\end{array}
$$

$$
\begin{array}{cc}
\begin{array}{c} p \rightarrow q \\ \underline{\sim p} \\ \therefore \quad \sim q \end{array} \quad Invalid
&
\begin{array}{c} p \rightarrow q \\ \underline{q} \\ \therefore \quad p \end{array}
\end{array}
$$

A form that is sometimes mistaken for an *if* statement is the *only if* statement. While *if* statements give us a sufficient condition for some consequent, *only if* statements give us a necessary condition. Consider these arguments:

(1) Only if he has a ticket will he be admitted
      He has a ticket
  ∴ He will be admitted

(2) Only if he has a ticket will he be admitted
      He does not have a ticket
  ∴ He will not be admitted

(3) Only if he has a ticket will he be admitted
      He is admitted
  ∴ He had a ticket

(4) Only if he has a ticket will he be admitted
      He is not admitted
  ∴ He does not have a ticket

(1) is an invalid argument. Having a ticket is not presented as a sufficient condition, so it is not necessarily the case that the ticket holder will be admitted. There may be additional requirements for admission such as adulthood or proper attire. (2) is a valid argument, since what is presented as necessary for admission is lacking. (3) is also valid. Since the person was admitted, all conditions necessary for admission must have been met, including the one stated in the first premise. (4) is invalid. That he was not admitted is not necessarily the result of his not having a ticket. He may indeed have had a ticket (a necessary condition) but may have appeared at the door drunk and disorderly.

We see then that precisely those forms that are valid for *if* arguments are invalid for *only if* arguments, and those that are invalid for *if* arguments are valid for *only if* arguments.

Only if p, q		Only if p, q
$\sim p$	*Valid*	q
∴ $\sim q$		∴ p
Only if p, q		Only if p, q
p	*Invalid*	$\sim q$
∴ q		∴ $\sim p$

There are many terms that mean the same as 'if' and 'only if.' Since the validity rules are just opposite for arguments involving the two connectives, it is very important that these other expressions be recognized for what they really are. 'Whenever' and 'provided that,' for example, present *sufficient* conditions, while 'is essential to' and 'is indispensable for' follow *necessary* conditions.

The *if* and *only if* statements, while very different, can be expressed in terms of one another. 'Only if *x*, then *y*' is equivalent to 'if ~*x*, then ~*y*' (~*x*→~*y*) and also to 'if *y*, then *x*' (*y*→*x*). But it is *not* equivalent to 'if *x*, then *y*' (*x*→*y*). One always has a choice of several equivalent forms for expressing sufficient and necessary conditions, but he must know the difference between them in order to avoid erroneous formulations.

The word 'unless' sometimes creates problems. What it means is 'if not.' 'Unless he loses count of trumps, he will make the contract' means '*If* he does *not* lose count of trumps, then he will make the contract.' The word precedes a negative sufficient condition.

Since conditional statements (when interpreted truth-functionally) can always be expressed as disjunctions, we can derive an even simpler meaning for 'unless':

$$\sim p \rightarrow q = p \vee q$$

'Unless it rains, the crops will die' may thus be translated as: 'It either rains or the crops will die.' Whatever can be deduced from the '~*p*→*q*' form can also, of course, be deduced from the '*p* v *q*' form, and conversely.

The biconditional statement presents both a sufficient condition and a necessary condition. 'If and only if he is sober is he dependable' tells us that being sober suffices for dependability (*s*→*d*), and that it is also necessary for dependability (~*s*→~*d*). The latter could have been written '*d*→*s*.' This in turn can be written '*s*←*d*.' If we put '*s*→*d*' (sufficient condition) and '*s*←*d*' (necessary condition) together, we get '*d*↔*s*.'

The biconditional provides such a powerful premise for an argument that all four deductive forms are valid:

(1) If and only if *p*, then *q*   *p*↔*q*

$$\underline{\hspace{3cm} p \hspace{3cm}} \qquad \underline{\hspace{1cm} p \hspace{1cm}}$$

∴   *q*   ∴   *q*

(2) If and only if *p*, then *q*   *p*↔*q*

$$\underline{\hspace{3cm} q \hspace{3cm}} \qquad \underline{\hspace{1cm} q \hspace{1cm}}$$

∴   *p*   ∴ *p*

(3) If and only if *p*, then *q*   *p*↔*q*

$$\underline{\hspace{3cm} \sim p \hspace{3cm}} \qquad \underline{\hspace{1cm} \sim p \hspace{1cm}}$$

∴   ~*q*   ∴   ~*q*

(4) If and only if *p*, then *q*   *p*↔*q*

$$\underline{\hspace{3cm} \sim q \hspace{3cm}} \qquad \underline{\hspace{1cm} \sim q \hspace{1cm}}$$

∴   ~*p*   ∴ ~*p*

(1) and (4) are valid by virtue of the sufficient condition ("if . . . then . . ."); (2) and (3) are valid by virtue of the necessary condition ("only if . . . then").

Concluding Summary: The conditional argument is valid when, in the second premise, we affirm the antecedent or deny the consequent. When, however, we conclude something on the basis of denying the antecedent or affirming the consequent, we are arguing fallaciously. The *only if* argument may be translated into a conditional argument or treated as an independent argument with its own set of (opposite) rules. It is almost impossible to err in biconditional arguments, since all four deductive forms are valid.

> *The value of deduction is grounded in its emptiness. For the very reason that the deduction does not add anything to the premises, it may always be applied without a risk of leading to a failure.*
> —*Hans Reichenbach,* The Rise of Scientific Philosophy

The Dilemma

The dilemma is one of the arguments we get when we mix molecular statements. A *dilemma* contains three premises: two conditionals and one disjunction. The disjuncts of the disjunction affirm the antecedents or deny the consequents of the conditionals. The conclusion consists of the consequents or the negative of the antecedents of the conditionals.

When the antecedents are affirmed by the disjunctive premise, we have a *constructive* dilemma:

$$
\begin{array}{ll}
(1)\ p \rightarrow q & (2)\ p \rightarrow q \\
\quad\ r \rightarrow q & \quad\ r \rightarrow s \\
\quad\ \underline{p \vee r} & \quad\ \underline{p \vee r} \\
\therefore\ q & \therefore\ q \vee s
\end{array}
$$

When the consequents are denied by the disjunctive premise, we have a *destructive* dilemma:

$$
\begin{array}{ll}
(3)\ p \rightarrow q & (4)\ p \rightarrow q \\
\quad\ p \rightarrow r & \quad\ r \rightarrow s \\
\quad\ \underline{\sim q \vee \sim r} & \quad\ \underline{\sim q \vee \sim s} \\
\therefore\ \sim p & \therefore\ \sim p \vee \sim r
\end{array}
$$

(1) and (3) are called *simple* dilemmas, for the conclusion is not a disjunction. (2) and (4) are called *complex* dilemmas, for the conclusion is a disjunction.

The dilemma is an old but still useful argument. It has been likened to a charging bull who aims two sharp horns at his antagonist. If the antagonist manages to elude one of the horns, he or she is necessarily impaled on the other. The dilemma is valid, and the conclusion does indeed follow necessarily from the premises.

Consider this situation: You are in command of a platoon of infantry. Just to the south is a swift and treacherous river. To the north is the enemy, superior in number and firepower. You may see the situation in the form of a complex, constructive dilemma:

> If we advance, we are killed by machine-gun fire
> If we retreat, we drown in the river
> We advance or we retreat
> ∴ Either we are killed by machine-gun fire or we drown in the river

Since a dilemma usually (but not always) has an undesirable conclusion, it is of some importance to know how to "meet" a dilemma. How can we avoid the conclusion forced upon us?

It usually does no good to challenge the validity of the argument. The four forms are all valid. A genuine dilemma is by definition a valid argument. Still, one should check to make sure that he is not dealing with a "pseudo-dilemma," an invalid argument that looks like a dilemma:

> $p \rightarrow q$
> $r \rightarrow s$ *Invalid*
> $q \vee s$
> ∴ $p \vee r$

But the military example above is not of this form. It is a genuine dilemma and is thus valid.

If the argument is valid, the conclusion follows necessarily from the premises. But we do not have to *accept* the conclusion unless we accept the premises. If we can show that one or more of the premises is false, then one of the elements of proof is missing. The conclusion, though it necessarily follows from the premises, is not necessarily *true*. The good ways of meeting a dilemma all consist of challenging the truth of a premise.

Suppose, in the example above, your second-in-command points out that attacking and retreating do not exhaust the possibilities. This challenges the truth of the third premise, which states that no action is possible beyond the two that are given—advance or retreat. But it is possible to do neither. We might dig in and hold our position until rescued. Or we might move eastward to the protective forest there. This method of meeting a dilemma is called "slipping between the horns"—adding a possibility to the two that are given. If the disjunctive premise is refuted or placed under suspicion, we are relieved of the necessity of accepting the conclusion as true.

Someone else in the platoon might challenge the truth of the first conditional premise, arguing that death by machine-gun fire is *not* the inevitable result of attacking. The enemy would be so surprised by our bold action that he would be disorganized and soon overrun. Another bright non-com might challenge the truth of the other conditional premise, arguing that drowning is *not* the inevitable result of retreating. Rubber boats are available and, under the cover of night, the men could be ferried across the river. This method of meeting the dilemma is called "grasping a horn." One of the alternatives is accepted but its harmful consequence is denied.

A third way of refuting a dilemma is by means of another dilemma. This has great rhetorical effect but is very difficult to accomplish. The conclusion of a refuting dilemma must be *incompatible with* that of the dilemma it is seeking to meet.

We do *not* refute the military dilemma by arguing:

> If we advance, we do not drown in the river
> If we retreat, we are not killed by machine-gun fire
> Either we advance or we retreat
> _____
> ∴ Either we do not drown in the river or we are not killed by machine-gun fire

This is cold comfort indeed. The expressions 'k v d' (conclusion of the original dilemma) and '$\sim d$ v $\sim k$' (conclusion of the "rebutting" dilemma) are quite compatible. They could both be true at the same time—and they *would* both be true if we died one way but did not die the other. What has to be proved is that we *neither* drown in the river *nor* are killed by machine-gun fire.

This method of refuting by counterdilemma tries to do too much. We do not have to prove a position of our own in order to refute an opponent. All we have to show is that he has not proved his position. And we can do this by questioning the validity of his argument or the truth of his premises. The method of refuting by means of a counterdilemma sets out to do more than is necessary and usually ends by doing less.

So it is best to forget about counterdilemmas. When faced with a dilemma whose conclusion you do not like, ascertain whether you are being arbitrarily restricted in the alternatives held out to you. Or determine whether the results attached to each of these alternatives really are their consequents.

Concluding Summary: A dilemma is a valid argument containing two conditional premises, one disjunctive premise, and a conclusion (usually unpleasant) consisting of the consequences of the disjuncts. One can avoid the necessity of accepting the truth of the conclusion by questioning the truth of the premises. If she or he successfully questions the truth of the disjunctive premise, she or he has slipped between the horns. If he or she successfully questions the truth of one of the conditional premises, he or she has grasped one of the horns.

> *If you say what is just, men will hate you;*
> *if you say what is unjust, the gods will.*
> —*Quoted in Aristotle,* Art of Rhetoric

Other Mixed Forms

The number of possible ways to combine conjunctive, disjunctive, conditional, and atomic statements into valid and invalid arguments is indefinite. The dilemma is one of the few that have received special treatment; it was given a name, a classification, and a set of rules. We will in this section illustrate some of the nameless valid deductive arguments involving molecular statements.

Suppose we had a conditional premise, the antecedent of which is a disjunction and the consequent of which is a conjunction:

> If Hart is inaccurate or Metcalf can't play, then the Cardinals lose and I am unhappy.

Let us abbreviate the parts of the statement and use the statement as a premise in several arguments:

(1) $(\sim a \lor \sim p) \to (l \& \sim h)$
    $\underline{\sim a \lor \sim p}$
    $\therefore l \& \sim h$

(2) $(\sim a \lor \sim p) \to (l \& \sim h)$
    $\underline{\sim (l \& \sim h)}$
    $\therefore a \& p$

(3) $(\sim a \lor \sim p) \to (l \& \sim h)$
    $\underline{\sim a}$
    $\therefore l \& \sim h$

(4) $(\sim a \lor \sim p) \to (l \& \sim h)$
    $\underline{l \& \sim h}$
    $\therefore \sim a \lor \sim p$

(5) $(\sim a \lor \sim p) \to (l \& \sim h)$
    $\underline{\sim l \lor h}$
    $\therefore a \& p$

(6) $(\sim a \lor \sim p) \to (l \& \sim h)$
    $\underline{\sim l}$
    $\therefore a \& p$

(7) $(\sim a \lor \sim p) \to (l \& \sim h)$
    $\underline{\sim (\sim a \lor \sim p)}$
    $\therefore \sim (l \& \sim h)$

(1) is valid. It is simply a case of affirming the antecedent in a conditional argument. (2) is valid. It is a case of denying the consequent in a conditional argument. The more obvious conclusion is '$\sim (\sim a \lor \sim p)$' but, remembering that the denial of a disjunction is a conjunction both parts of which are denied, we can express it as

'~ ~a & ~ ~p' or 'a & p.' (3) is also valid. Inaccuracy *itself* on the part of Hart suffices for the consequent. In affirming one part of a disjunction we affirm it all. So, having affirmed the antecedent, we can, as the conclusion does, affirm the consequent. (4) is invalid, being a case of affirming the consequent. (5) is valid, for the second premise is the denial of '*l* & ~h.' Having denied the consequent, we can, as the conclusion does, deny the antecedent. The denial of '~a v ~p' is 'a & p.' (6) is also valid. Since the consequent is a conjunction, it is incompatible with '~l.' Having asserted '~l' in the second premise, we have in effect denied '*l* & ~h.' So we can validly conclude the denial of the antecedent. If the Cardinals did not lose, then Hart was accurate and Metcalf played. (7) is invalid, being a case of denying the antecedent.

We have seen, above, that to affirm a disjunct is to affirm the whole disjunction, and to deny a conjunct is to deny a whole conjunction. But we cannot say that to affirm a conjunct is to affirm a whole conjunction, for the other conjunct may be false. And we cannot say that to deny a disjunct is to deny the whole disjunction, for the other disjunct could be true. Therefore, while the following arguments are valid:

$$(p \lor q) \rightarrow r \qquad p \rightarrow (q \ \& \ r)$$
$$\underline{p} \qquad\qquad\qquad \underline{\sim q}$$
$$\therefore \ r \qquad\qquad \therefore \ \sim p$$

These are invalid:

$$(p \ \& \ q) \rightarrow r \qquad\qquad p \rightarrow (q \lor r)$$
$$\underline{p} \qquad\qquad Invalid \qquad \underline{\sim q}$$
$$\therefore \quad r \qquad\qquad\qquad \therefore \ \sim p$$

Concluding Summary: By obeying the basic rules of disjunctive and conditional inference, denials, and equivalences, one can determine the validity of arguments of indefinite complexity.

Truth Tables

The validity of most of the molecular arguments discussed above can be recognized most of the time by most people intuitively—or by direct inspection. Knowing as we do what 'and,' 'or,' and 'if' mean, we usually can ascertain quite confidently whether the conclusion of an argument really *is* implied by its premises. Any doubts can be clarified by utilizing the truth table method first presented in the last section of Chapter 4.

The method consists of creating truth tables for all the premises in the argument, then asking this question: Is the conclusion always true when all the premises are? If and only if the answer is in the affirmative is the argument valid. For example:

(1) $p \vee \sim q$

$$\frac{q}{\therefore \quad p}$$

	Concl.	Prem.			Prem.	
	p	**q**		**~q**	**p v ~q**	
	T	T		F	T	✔
	F	T		F	F	
	T	F		T	T	
	F	F		T	T	

(2) $\sim p \rightarrow q$

$$\frac{p}{\therefore \quad \sim q}$$

	Prem.			Concl.	Prem.	
p	**q**		**~p**	**~q**	**~p → q**	
T	T		F	F	T	✔ !
F	T		T	F	T	
T	F		F	T	T	✔
F	F		T	T	F	

(3) $(p \vee q) \rightarrow r$

$$\frac{q}{\therefore \quad r}$$

	Prem.	Concl.			Prem.	
p	**q**	**r**		**p v q**	**(p v q) → r**	
T	T	T		T	T	✔
F	T	T		T	T	✔
T	F	T		T	T	
F	F	T		F	T	
T	T	F		T	F	
F	T	F		T	F	
T	F	F		T	F	
F	F	F		F	T	

(4) $(p \ \& \sim q) \rightarrow r$

$$\frac{\sim q}{\therefore \quad r}$$

		Concl.	Prem.			Prem.	
p	**q**	**r**		**~q**	**p & ~q**	**(p & ~q) → r**	
T	T	T		F	F	T	
F	T	T		F	F	T	
T	F	T		T	T	T	✔
F	F	T		T	F	T	✔
T	T	F		F	F	T	
F	T	F		F	F	T	
T	F	F		T	T	F	
F	F	F		T	F	T	✔ !

'(1)' is valid, for on the first line, the only line on which both premises are true, the conclusion is also true. '(2)' is invalid, for on the first line we can see that it is possible for the premises to be true and the conclusion false. '(3)' is valid, for on both lines on which the premises are true, the conclusion is also true. '(4)' is invalid, because there is a line, the eighth, where the premises are true and the conclusion false.

Concluding Summary: The truth table method exhibits the truth or falsity of the statements of a molecular argument for every possible T/F combination of its basic, atomic components. Validity is graphically demonstrated when the conclusion is seen to be true whenever the premises are. The method is a mechanical way to confirm (or disconfirm) our intuitive judgments.

The Shorter Truth Table Method

The truth table method works very nicely when we have but two components (say, 'p' and 'q'). But it becomes rather tedious if we have three components and have to make eight lines. A complex dilemma containing four components would require sixteen lines. And if we were faced with an argument involving 'p,' 'q,' 'r,' 's,' and 't,' we would surely look for an alternate to the ordinary truth table method.

Isn't there a shorter way to use the truth table principle to check validity? Yes. We will call it the *shorter truth table method*. While it is not so mechanical as the ordinary method, it does save time and space. But it requires a little thinking.

The logic of the method is expressed in this rule: An argument is valid if and only if it can be expressed as a tautology. A valid argument, when expressed in one statement, cannot possibly be false. We can express an argument in statement form by making it a conditional: The premises are the antecedent and the conclusion is the consequent. For example:

(1) $p \lor q$
$\underline{\quad p \quad}$ $=$ $[(p \lor q) \mathbin{\&} p] \rightarrow \sim q$
$\therefore \ \sim q$

(2) $p \lor q$
$\underline{\quad \sim p \quad}$ $=$ $[(p \lor q) \mathbin{\&} \sim p] \rightarrow q$
$\therefore \qquad q$

(3) $(p \lor q) \rightarrow r$
$\underline{\qquad\quad p \qquad}$ $=$ $\{[(p \lor q) \rightarrow r] \mathbin{\&} p\} \rightarrow r$
$\therefore \qquad\quad r$

(4) $(p \ \& \ q) \rightarrow r$

$$\frac{p}{\therefore \quad r} = \{[(p \ \& \ q) \rightarrow r] \ \& \ p\} \rightarrow r$$

Is it possible for '(1)' to be false? In order for it to be false, its antecedent would have to be true and its conclusion false. Let's see whether such a situation is possible:

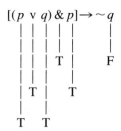

On the second line we had to assign 'T' to 'p v q' and to 'p' because they are conjuncts of an expression that we assumed to be true on the first line. The 'T' dropping down from the wedge refers to the whole disjunction—just as the 'T' dropping down from the ampersand refers to the whole conjunction. The third (bottom) line presents no problem: 'p' is true because it is true on the second line; 'q' is true because '~q' is false on the first line. The demand of 'p v q' that at least one disjunct be true is amply met.

We found no difficulty in carrying out our assumption that the statement is false. Every component receives a truth value, and no absurdity crops up. This proves that it *is* possible for the original statement to be false. It is not, therefore, a tautology, and the argument it represents is not a valid one.

Let us approach (2) in the same way:

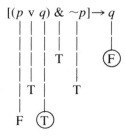

On the second line we are constrained to assign a 'T' to both 'p v q' and '~p.' On the third (bottom) line, we must assign an 'F' to 'p' since '~p' has already been assigned 'T.' The disjunction, 'p v q,' is true, so at least one of its disjuncts is true. This would have to be 'q,' but a 'T' for 'q' would conflict with the 'F' we assigned to it at the very beginning. We have been forced into absurdity (highlighted by the circles) by our assumption that the statement could be false—which means that it cannot *possibly* be false. This is to say that it is necessarily *true*—and that the argument it represents is valid.

We will now check (3):

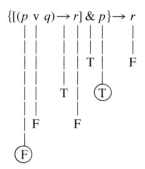

On the first line we indicate the same *assumption* with which we always begin: that the antecedent is true and the consequent false. This is the only way the entire statement can be false. Once again we assign truth values in accordance with this assumption. On the second line, both '(p v q)→r' and 'p' are true, for they are conjuncts of a true conjunction. On the third line we assign an 'F' to 'r'—this is dictated by the value of 'r' on the first line. The only way we could have a false consequent 'r' in a true conditional ('(p v q)→r') is for the antecedent ('p v q') to be false. In order for 'p v q' to be false, both disjuncts must be false. But this cannot be the case, for 'p' (according to the second line) is true. Having encountered absurdity (self-contradiction), we must conclude that our original assumption that (3) is not necessarily true is indeed false. That is, the statement *is* necessarily true. Since it is a tautology, the argument that it represents is *valid*.

Finally, we will apply the method to (4):

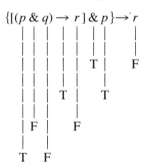

It is possible to carry through on our original assumption without encountering absurdity. This means that the original statement could possibly be false. The argument that it represents, therefore, is invalid.

Let us, finally, use this short method to test the validity of a complex, destructive dilemma. We might note that if we used the normal method we would need sixteen lines and twelve columns—a total of 192 'T's' and 'F's.'

$$p \rightarrow q$$
$$r \rightarrow s$$
$$\underline{\sim q \ v \ \sim s}$$
$$\therefore \ \sim p \ v \ \sim r$$

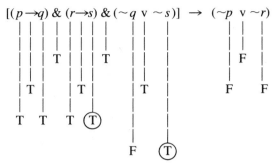

We cannot avoid absurdity: both 's' and '~s' must be true. The advantage of the short method is obvious: Only fourteen 'T's' and 'F's' were needed.

Concluding Summary: The steps in applying the shorter truth table method are: (1) express the argument as one conditional statement, (2) assume that the statement is false, (3) draw out all the implications of this assumption. If absurdity appears, the argument is valid; if it does not, the argument is invalid.

EXERCISES

Exercise 56

Use the truth table method to determine the validity of each of these deductive forms, indicating the crucial lines:

1. $\sim p \ v \ q$
    $$\underline{\hspace{1.2cm} \sim p}$$
    $\therefore \qquad q$

2. $p \rightarrow \sim q$
    $$\underline{\hspace{1cm} \sim q}$$
    $\therefore \qquad p$

3. $p \rightarrow q$
    $$\underline{\hspace{0.8cm} \sim p}$$
    $\therefore \ \sim q$

4. $p \leftrightarrow q$
    $$\underline{\hspace{1cm} q}$$
    $\therefore \qquad p$

5. $(p \rightarrow q) \lor r$

$\quad\quad r$

$\therefore \quad \sim q$

6. $p \lor q \lor r$

$\quad p \lor r$

$\therefore \quad \sim q$

7. $p \lor q \lor r$

$\quad\quad \sim p$

$\therefore \quad q \lor r$

8. $p \rightarrow (q \,\&\, r)$

$\quad\quad \sim r$

$\therefore \quad \sim p$

Exercise 57

Abbreviate and symbolize the following arguments and indicate whether valid or invalid:

1. He will either phone or write. He did not phone. Therefore, he will write.
2. Only if the weather is good will the course be open. The weather is good, so the course will be open.
3. If he has not heard the joke, he will laugh. He is laughing. Therefore, he has not heard the joke.
4. It is either raining or not raining. It is raining. Therefore, it is not the case that it is not raining.
5. Whenever he's ill, he stays home. He did not stay home, for he was not ill.
6. The solution is either acid or alkaline. I happen to know it is alkaline. It is not, therefore, acid.
7. The grass is green. Therefore, either the water is blue or the grass is green.
8. Regular exercise is both necessary and sufficient for good health. I do exercise. Therefore, I will be healthy.
9. He'll buy the car only if he has enough money. He doesn't have enough money, so he will not buy the car.
10. Either the East German athletes are very talented or East Germany has an excellent training program. The country does have an excellent training program, so the athletes are not very talented.

Exercise 58

Abbreviate and symbolize the following arguments and indicate whether valid or invalid:

1. If all poodles are dogs, then some violets are blue. No violets are blue. No poodles, therefore, are dogs.
2. Unless Congress acts soon, the Social Security system will go broke. Congress will not act soon. The Social Security system, therefore, will go broke.
3. If everyone keeps his mouth shut, no one will know. Someone must not have kept his mouth shut, for some people do know.
4. If the bough breaks, the cradle falls, and if the cradle falls, the baby cries. Thus, if the baby does not cry, the bough has not broken.
5. Only if the Cardinals win will all their fans be happy. The Cardinals do not win. So none of their fans is happy.
6. Some joggers are crazy or all psychologists are mistaken. Some joggers are not crazy. All psychologists, therefore, are mistaken.
7. If you have money, you're comfortable, and if you're comfortable, you're happy. Therefore, if you do not have money, you're unhappy.
8. Validity is necessary for proof. The argument is not a proof. Therefore, it is not valid.
9. He answers only when he's sure. He's not answering now, so he must not be sure.
10. All reptiles are snakes or some dogs are poodles. Some reptiles are not snakes, so some dogs are poodles.

Exercise 59

For each of the following valid dilemmas, abbreviate and symbolize its form. Show how you would meet the dilemma.

1. If the Soviet leadership gives in to the demands of its various nationalities, it will lose control of the overall economy. But if it doesn't make some concessions to their demands, it will be subject to continued outbreaks of defiance. Clearly, it must give in or make concessions. Therefore, the Soviet leadership will lose control of the overall economy or it will be subject to continued outbreaks of defiance.
2. If the Vice President runs on the record of the previous administration, he is blamed for all its mistakes. While if he dissociates himself from that record, he can claim no credit for its success. He must either run on the record or dissociate himself from the record. Therefore, he will be blamed for its mistakes or be denied credit for its successes.
3. If he is permitted to shoot, then he will score well from the field. And if he is guarded closely, then he will draw many fouls. Either he will not score well from the field or he will not draw many fouls. Therefore, he will not have been permitted to shoot or he will not have been guarded closely.
4. If I take eighteen hours, my GPA will go down. And if I take only twelve hours, I won't have enough hours to graduate this year. Since I must take

eighteen or twelve, either my GPA will go down or I won't graduate this year.

5. If you say what is just, men will hate you. And if you say what is unjust, the gods will hate you. Since you say what is just or unjust, someone is sure to hate you!

6. If I go to Quebec, I'll suffer from the cold; and if I go to Acapulco, I'll suffer from the heat. Since (according to the gift certificate) I must go to Quebec or Acapulco, I'll suffer either from the cold or from the heat.

7. If you sell the house, you'll have to take a loss. If you don't sell it, you'll have to pay the taxes. You will either have to take a loss or pay the taxes, for it's obvious that you must sell it or not sell it.

8. If I watch television tonight, I'll be bored. And if I attend the concert, I'll be bored. It looks like I'll be bored, because I'll either watch television or I'll go to the concert.

Exercise 60

Abbreviate and symbolize the following arguments and indicate whether valid or invalid:

1. If he has the time and has the money, he will attend the concert. He does not attend the concert. He therefore does not have the money or does not have the time.

2. If the plane lands, Gertrude will board it and fly to Milwaukee. She did not fly to Milwaukee. Therefore, the plane did not land.

3. If the sun is shining, we'll go biking or hiking. We did not go hiking. The sun must not, therefore, have shone.

4. If Smith is ill or Jones is away, then Williams will take charge. Williams does not take charge. It follows, then, that Jones is not away and Smith is not ill.

5. Either he really was in Borneo or he has a fertile imagination and tells a good story. He does not have a fertile imagination. So he must have been in Borneo.

6. If the book is correct, then rule 4 is applicable and the argument is invalid. The book must be incorrect, for the argument is valid.

7. He is in Chicago or he is in Detroit and having a good time. He is in Chicago. So he is not having a good time.

8. If the weather is bad or Stella can't come, then we'll postpone the picnic and study all day. The weather is not bad and Stella can come. Therefore, it is not the case that we'll postpone the picnic and study all day.

9. Whenever the stock market goes up, he is happy in spirit and generous in action. The stock market did go up. Therefore, he is generous in spirit.

10. If I practice I'll become perfect or if I exhibit virtue I'll be rewarded. I do exhibit virtue without being rewarded. But I'll not become perfect. Therefore, I don't practice.

Exercise 61

Use the shorter truth table method to determine the validity of the following deductive forms:

1. $p \rightarrow \sim q$
   $\underline{q\qquad\qquad}$
   $\therefore \sim$

2. $p \rightarrow q$
   $\underline{q \rightarrow r\qquad}$
   $\therefore \sim r \rightarrow \sim p$

3. $(p \mathbin{\&} q) \rightarrow r$
   $\underline{\quad q \qquad\qquad}$
   $\therefore \quad r$

4. $(p \mathbin{\&} q) \rightarrow r$
   $\underline{\quad r \qquad\qquad}$
   $\therefore p \mathbin{\&} q$

5. $p \lor q \lor r$
   $\underline{\sim p \mathbin{\&} \sim q}$
   $\therefore \qquad r$

6. $(p \lor q) \rightarrow (r \mathbin{\&} s)$
   $\underline{\qquad \sim r \qquad\qquad}$
   $\therefore \sim p \mathbin{\&} \sim q$

7. $(p \lor q) \rightarrow (r \mathbin{\&} s)$
   $\underline{\qquad q \qquad\qquad}$
   $\therefore \quad s$

8. $p \rightarrow q$
   $r \rightarrow s$
   $\underline{p \lor r}$
   $\therefore q \lor s$

9. $p \lor q \lor r$
   p
   $\underline{q \qquad\qquad}$
   $\therefore \sim r$

10. $(p \leftrightarrow q) \lor r$
    $\underline{\sim r \qquad\qquad}$
    $\therefore q \rightarrow p$

11. $p \lor (q \mathbin{\&} r)$
    $\underline{\sim r \qquad\qquad}$
    $\therefore p$

12. $p \rightarrow q$
    $\underline{q \rightarrow r\qquad}$
    $\therefore r \rightarrow p$

13. $(p \lor q) \veebar r$
    $\underline{p \qquad\qquad}$
    $\therefore \sim r$

14. $(p \mathbin{\&} q) \rightarrow r$
    $s \rightarrow \sim r$
    $\underline{\quad s \qquad\qquad}$
    $\therefore \sim q$

15. $p \rightarrow (q \lor r)$
    $s \rightarrow \sim r$
    $\underline{\quad s \qquad\qquad}$
    $\therefore \sim p$

MATHEMATICAL PROBABILITY

Kinds of Probability

It may seem strange to discuss probability in a chapter on deductive inference. Deduction deals with inferences in which conclusions *necessarily* follow. But the kind of probability we are concerned with here also involves necessity. Given specific knowledge of the past (or of the logical possibilities), an assumption about the future, and a few mathematical principles, we can *deduce* the degree of probability that some events and sets of events have of occurring. If the premises are true, the conclusion must be true. That is, the event does have this calculated degree of probability. While the truth of the premises may be a matter of dispute, the necessity of that which is deduced from them is not.

The conclusion that the probability of a black card being drawn from the deck is one-half (or .5) may indicate something about the state of our knowledge as well as about the state of the world (which is the case for all uses of 'probability'), but that our expectation should be precisely .5 and not something else is a necessary consequence of premises that are not implausible.

The sense of probability we are concerned with here is far different from the kind we will be dealing with in the three chapters on induction to come. *Mathematical probability* tells us the exact degree of expectation we rationally should have—in view of the known possibilities and statistics at hand—that a certain event will occur. *Inductive probability,* on the other hand, has to do with *how well* the inductive premises support a categorical conclusion, but we do not assign degrees of probability to that conclusion. Inductive probability is concerned with the strength of the evidence relative to the conclusion derived from it. Is the inductive conclusion more or less warranted than some other inductive conclusion? What additional evidence can be sought?

In order to determine mathematical probability, we must make a deductive calculation from statements setting forth possibilities and frequencies. The conclusion that an event has a specific probability of occurring follows necessarily from the premises, however accurate or inaccurate those premises may be. In an inductive argument where the conclusion is inductively probable, the premises may be true while the conclusion is false. But in a deductive argument where the conclusion expresses a calculated degree of probability, the conclusion cannot be false if the premises are true. The doubt that may attach to inductive probability is a function of the relation between the premises and conclusion. The doubt that may attach to mathematical probability is a function of the doubt about the accuracy of the mathematical premises.

There are two approaches to mathematical probability. The first, "mathematical" in the narrow sense, has been called the *classical theory* of probability, or the *a priori* approach. It is based on the assumption that we should, *if we have no reason to believe otherwise,* regard all possibilities as having an equal chance of occurring. We believe that, if the roulette wheel is evenly balanced and the casino employees are not controlling it in any way, each of the 38 numbers has an equal chance of coming up. And any one of the six sides of a die has as much chance of being thrown as any other. This is not to say that we believe that there is chance in the

---

Probabilities direct the conduct of the wise man.
                                   —*Cicero,* De Natura Deorum

universe, that probability characterizes the events themselves. Presumably, if we knew all the physical forces operating at the moment the ball is tossed on the spinning wheel or the die is hurled against the board, we could make our prediction on the basis of the laws of motion. But since we do not, we are restricted to possibilities that we have no reason to believe are unequal. So we say that the chance of the ball stopping on 26 is one out of 38, that the chances of a 3 coming up on a die are one out of six. Probability is calculated from these possibilities or chances. The probability, therefore, that the ball will stop at 26 is 1/38 or .026; the probability that a 3 will come up on a die is 1/6 or .167. The moment we have reason to believe the wheel is fixed, the die is loaded, or that anything else is at work that could interfere with "pure chance," we abandon the classical approach (unless we want to develop a whole new set of outcomes equally possible).

If the classical theory is based on the belief that we have nothing more to go on than the logical possibilities, the other approach to mathematical probability says we have much to go on. This approach, which is mathematical in the broader sense, has been called the empirical or *a posteriori* approach to probability, or the *relative frequency theory*.

If a bowler goes up to the line, we may wonder whether he will get a strike. It would be foolish to say that his chances were one in eleven, that he could knock down 0, 1, 2, 3, 4, 5, 6, 7, 8, 9, or 10 pins, and that the last possibility had a probability of 1/11 or .091. If we knew absolutely nothing about bowling, though, I suppose this is what we would have to say. But if we had statistics from the bowling league reporting that exactly 26 percent of the frames (or turns) bowled by its people were strikes, then, using the relative frequency method, we could say that the probability that this bowler would get a strike was .26. And if we had had statistics on this *particular* bowler, we would use them instead in assigning a probability.

The statistical statements expressing relative frequency are usually inductive generalizations—that is, they are based on examination of only a part of the class generalized about. The statement, 'Thirty-four percent of children reared in foster homes go to college,' is an example. We may use this information to calculate the probability of a past event or a future event. If we know that Enid (age thirty) was reared in a foster home, we can say that the probability of her having gone to college is .34. If we know that Timmy (age six) is now being reared in a foster home, we can say that the probability of his going to college is .34. The second case, unlike the first, would seem to require the assumption that the future will resemble the past, that what happened to foster children who reached college age in the past will also hold for such foster children in the future. Use of relative frequency in calculating the probability of future events would seem to require the assumption of "the uniformity of nature."

Just as the classical approach had to be abandoned or applied differently in the

---

A reasonable probability is the only certainty.

—*E. W. Howe,* Sinner Sermons

case of the die which was thought to be loaded, the relative frequency method breaks down when the event in question is significantly different from those on which we have statistics. If we know that the bowler is drunk or is bowling left-handed instead of right-handed, has just had lessons, or is trying out a new ball, the relative frequency in the past will not be very useful. We would now need statistics on drunken performances, left-handed deliveries, and so on. If we know that Timmy has an I.Q. of 168, we would seek other relative frequency statements than the one about foster children in general. The two methods of deducing probability operate on the assumption that no factors are at work to make the event in question different, respectively, from the logical possibilities posited in the classical approach or the actual events utilized in the empirical approach.

It would appear that there is a convenient division of labor here. We can use the classical approach in areas where ''chance'' operates—that is, where the causes are too elusive or complicated to work with. And we can use the relative-frequency method when we have some good statistical summaries of the past. We assign coin flipping, card drawing, dice casting, and roulette to the classical theory, but go to the relative-frequency theory when we want to determine probabilities for such things as longevity, divorce rates, scores in games of skill, and graduation prospects. Each approach would be useless and irrelevant outside its own obvious domain.

Unfortunately, this happy situation is not quite the case. In the first place, some cases of calculating probability seem to utilize both the a priori and empirical approaches. In the case of Enid (above), our information about foster children was derived empirically, but we resorted to ''chance'' when calculating the probability of her having gone to college. Enid's chances were deemed similar to those of a number on a roulette wheel, although the nature of our knowledge of the fate of foster home children was far different from that of the fate of the roulette numbers. In the second place, we may operate on the basis of *complete* knowledge of a class of events (instead of an inductive generalization) and make different uses of this knowledge. If we know, for example, that sixty-five percent of all American presidents have had blue eyes, we can calculate that the probability of Millard Fillmore having had blue eyes is .65 *and* that the probability of the *next* president having blue eyes is .65. But in the former case, we are using the classical approach, while in the latter case we are using the empirical approach and assuming that the future will resemble the past. In the third place, we may operate on an unlimited inductive generalization about a whole class of events (past, present, and future). If our empirical generalization is that sixty-one percent of all Americans have blood type ''O,'' we would seem to be borrowing from the classical approach when we assert that the probability that the next American we meet will have blood type ''O'' is .61.

Finally, we may note that the two approaches have partisans and that these partisans engage in theoretical disputes. The RF people might say that the probability of the coin coming up heads is .514 rather than .500, and they have evidence to back them up. The classicists retort that *in the long run* the figure moves toward .500 and that it would be foolish to depend upon the accidents of the recent past. The classicists challenge the RF adherents to prove or even show the likelihood that

> *I don't know whether he will lead a spade, but the probability that he will is .5, for there are only two possibilities: he leads it or he does not.*
> —*Donald L. Taylor (bridge player)*

nature is uniform, that the future tends to resemble the past—an assumption on which all their calculations are based. The RF people reply that they are in no worse shape than the classicists on this point, and that the classicists could not so confidently say that certain alternative events have equal likelihood had the past not confirmed them. We cannot readily resolve these and other issues.

Despite the difficulties of keeping the two approaches in their place, we can proceed with the task of calculating probabilities on the basis of whatever information we possess, a priori or empirical, expecting particular events to occur with the same frequency as they are believed to occur in the class as a whole.

Concluding Summary: Mathematical probability may be derived by means of a classical approach and an approach based upon relative frequency. The first looks to logical possibilities; the second looks to past experience. The first deals with equal possibilities, the second with statistical possibilities. Both methods rely on mathematics in calculating the probability of events, and agree that calculation proceeds deductively.

Calculating Probability

Fortunately, the mathematical calculations of probabilities by the classicists and the relative frequency people are about the same. The classicists divide the number of favorable possibilities by the total number of possibilities in order to get the probability of a single event. The others divide the number of favorable observations by the total number of observations. Thus we arrive at the probability of a single event (''initial probability''). This figure will be between *zero,* which is impossibility (the event cannot occur), and *one,* which is full certainty (the event must occur).

The manner in which these initial probabilities are dealt with to calculate the probability of a complex event is also similar for the two approaches, and its basic principles will concern us in this section.

In calculating the probability of disjunctive or *exclusive* events, we simply add their probabilities. Events *a* and *b* are exclusive events if the occurrence of one rules out the occurrence of the other. Whether a 3 or 4 will be thrown with a die is a case of exclusive events; whether a 3 or an odd number will be thrown is not. The formula is:

P of ($a \lor b$) = (P of a) + (P of b)

The probability of drawing a spade or a club from a 52-card deck is:

1/4 + 1/4 = 1/2

The probability of drawing a spade, club, heart, or diamond is:

$$1/4 + 1/4 + 1/4 + 1/4 = 1$$

There are 36 possible results in throwing a pair of dice. Since there are 6 ways to throw a 7 and 2 ways to throw an 11, the probability of throwing a 7 or 11 is:

$$6/36 + 2/36 = 8/36 = 2/9 = .222$$

It is important that these events be mutually exclusive. We cannot apply the formula to events both of which may be true. The probability of throwing a 3 or 4 with one die is $1/6 + 1/6$, but the probability of throwing a 3 or an odd number is not $1/6 + 1/2$. What is the probability of drawing a spade in one or more of two draws? The expression, 'one or more,' links the two events into a dependent relation. Similarly, it would be a mistake to argue that in four draws we are certain $(1/4 + 1/4 + 1/4 + 1/4)$ to come up with at least one spade. 'At least one' does not designate exclusivity. This is a different kind of problem entirely, which we shall come back to.

In calculating the probability of conjunctive or *independent* events, we simply multiply their probabilities. The formula is:

$$P \text{ of } (a \ \& \ b) = (P \text{ of } a) \times (P \text{ of } b)$$

If the probability that I will be divorced this year is .162 and the probability that I will be involved in a non-fatal automobile accident is .248, the probability of *both* happening is:

$$.162 \times .248 = .040$$

If I bet on a *natural* in a craps game and my wife bets on *red* in a roulette game, the probability of both of us winning is:

$$2/9 \times 18/38 = 2/19 = .105$$

If the probability of my expected baby (the first) being a girl is .484 (relative frequency), having blue eyes is .865, the baby surviving is .916, and my winning a million dollars in the Illinois lottery is .043, then the probability of my becoming the rich father of a blue-eyed daughter is:

$$.484 \times .865 \times .916 \times .043 = .016$$

The third kind of basic problem the probability calculus deals with is that involving combinations of events that are neither exclusive nor independent. The problem of drawing a spade in two draws is such a case. The two events are not exclusive, for we could get a spade in both draws. They are not independent, for what we need on the second draw depends on what happened on the first draw. We seem to be able neither to add nor to multiply.

One way of calculating such *dependent* events is to reduce them to *one* event, as it were, and to calculate an initial probability. That is, divide the favorable possibilities by the total possibilities. How many possible events are there in drawing two cards? Abbreviating the suits and linking the two separately drawn cards together as single events, we have: SS, SH, SD, SC, HH, HS, HD, HC, DD, DS, DH, DC, CC, CS, CH, and CD. There are 16 possibilities, of which 7 are favorable. So the probability of getting at least one spade in two draws from a full deck is 7/16 or .438.

The probability of tossing heads with a coin within three throws is calculated similarly. Seven of the eight possibilities are favorable (all, that is, but the possibility where all tosses are tails), so the probability is 7/8 or .875. The more tosses we make, the closer we come to 1 or certainty, but we never reach it. With each toss the numerator and the denominator get larger, but the numerator remains one less than the denominator.

This suggests another way of calculating the probability of dependent events. It may be easier to work with their non-occurrence than with their occurrence. If we know the probability that something will *not* occur, we merely have to subtract that figure from 1 in order to get the probability that it *will* occur. In the case of trying to get a heads in three tries, we turn the problem around and ask about the chances of *not* getting heads in three times. In other words, what are the chances of getting three straight tails? Now we can use the formula for conjunctive or independent events:

$$1/2 \text{ (first toss)} \times 1/2 \text{ (second toss)} \times 1/2 \text{ (third toss)} = 1/8 = .125$$

Subtracting .125 from 1, we confirm our answer above: .875.

In the spade problem, we can also figure the probability of not getting a spade. The probability in the first draw is 3/4, and in the second draw it is 3/4. Multiplying them, we find that the probability of *not* drawing a spade is 9/16. That of drawing a spade is thus 1 minus 9/16, or 7/16.

In some problems of dependent combination, we can only work from this direction. If the probability that I will live until my child reaches the age of 21 is .475 and that of my wife is .533, what is the probability that at least one of us will live until our child is 21? There are no events, favorable and total, to count. So we figure the chances that we will both be dead, taking them as independent events:

$$.525 \text{ (for myself)} \times .467 \text{ (for my wife)} = .245$$

If the probability that we will both be dead is .245, then the probability that at least one of us will be alive is .755 (1 minus .245).

Suppose, during a poker game, we need a 6 to fill an inside straight, and we only have one more card to do it with. If we see one 6, there are, among the 36 cards we do not see, three 6's remaining. The probability of getting a 6 is thus 3/36 or 1/12 or .083. If, however, we are trying to complete a straight that is open at both ends, either a 3 or an 8 would do. If we see two 3's and no 8's and there are 36 cards remaining, the probability of completing the straight is 6/36 or 1/6 or .167.

If we have *two* chances or two cards to make our straight (and the other data remain the same), we are dealing with dependent events. How can we not get a straight? For the inside straight we would have to take the probabilities for not getting a 6 in either card:

$$33/36 \times 33/35 = 1089/1260 = 121/140 = .864$$

Subtracting this from 1, we get .136 as the probability of filling the inside straight in two draws. To calculate the open straight, we again first calculate how *not* to get it:

$$30/36 \times 30/35 = 5/7 = .714$$

Subtracting this from 1, we find the probability of filling a straight open at both ends (in this situation) is .286.

Finally, we may look at combinations of exclusive and independent events. What are my chances of being dealt five hearts (flush) in five cards? First, I'll need a heart. The probability of getting one is 13/52. Then I'll need another heart, but there is one card gone from the deck now, so the chances are 12 out of 51. The probabilities for the other three hearts are 11/50, 10/49, and 9/48. The probability of combining these independent events is their product:

$$13/52 \times 12/51 \times 11/50 \times 10/49 \times 9/48 = 33/66640 = .000495$$

But if I would be satisfied with any flush at all, my chances are increased fourfold:

$$33/66640 + 33/66640 + 33/66640 + 33/66640 = 132/66640 = 33/16660 = .001981$$

This solution may be reached another way. For the first card, any suit will do, so the first initial probability is 1. The initial probability of the second card being the same suit is 12/51. The initial probability of the third card matching them is 10/50. For the fourth card it is 9/49, and for the fifth it is 8/48: Multiplying these independent events, we get:

$$1 \times 12/51 \times 11/50 \times 10/49 \times 9/48 = 11880/5997600 = 33/16660 = .001981$$

Concluding Summary: It should be emphasized that the probability calculus involves much more than has been presented here. It employs advanced mathematics and can be very complex. But these principles are fundamental in the system and are useful for the layman: (1) When you have exclusive events, add their probabilities. (2) When you have independent events, multiply their probabilities. (3) When you have dependent events, calculate the probability of their not occurring and subtract from 1.

Bets: Good and Bad

In buying insurance, making investments, or gambling in the casinos of Las Vegas, we are making bets. Other things being equal, if we bet at all, it is reasonable to bet on the most likely possibility, the most probable event. But another factor enters: How much do I stand to win and is it worth the risk? Pascal argued that the nonbeliever should cultivate a belief in God, not because God's existence could be shown to be more probable than his nonexistence, but because of the big payoff that would accrue to the believer if he should turn out to be correct. So it is not simply a matter of betting the greatest probability but betting where the odds are most favorable, where you get the most for your betting dollar.

If someone is willing to give you two to one odds on the toss of a coin provided you bet on heads, and only even money if you bet on tails, the first is by far the better investment (provided, of course, that no cheating takes place). If you bet heads, the "expected value" of your dollar is $1.50. If you bet tails, the expected value is $1.00. Expected value is calculated by multiplying the sum of the bet and the possible return by the probability that the event bet on will occur. To the degree, then, that expected value exceeds your bet (or the "price"), you have a good bet. To the degree that it drops below, you have a bad bet. In the coin-tossing example, the expected value of your bet on heads is half again as great as its price. So, if you bet, you should bet on heads.

Suppose we are tempted to bet that a craps shooter will make his 8 before he rolls a 7. The "house" will pay us even money if we are right. Is it a good bet? What is the expected value of every dollar we bet this way? The possibilities of rolling an 8 (favorable) are 5. The possibilities of rolling a 7 (unfavorable) are 6. Since all other numbers are irrelevant, we can ignore them and take 11 (5 + 6) as the total possibilities. So our betting dollar is worth:

$$5/11 \times (1 + 1) = 10/11 = 91¢$$

If a casino pays 6 to 1 for a 10 "the hard way" (two 5s), the expected value is:

$$1/9 \times (1 + 6) = 7/9 = 77.8¢$$

What it "should" pay is 8 to 1, for there are exactly 8 times as many ways of getting a 7 or an "easy way" 10 as there are of getting a "hard 10." The value of the bet would then be equal to its price:

$$1/9 \times (1 + 8) = $1.00$$

But then, of course, there would be no reason for a casino to be in business.

There is no game in Las Vegas in which the bettor receives full value for his betting dollar. Roulette looks tempting until we see the green zero and double-zero. The expected value of dollars bet, respectively, on black, even, 23, and a column of 12 is:.

$$18/38 \times (1 + 1) = 94.7¢$$
$$18/38 \times (1 + 1) = 94.7¢$$
$$1/38 \times (1 + 35) = 94.7¢$$
$$12/38 \times (1 + 2) = 94.7¢$$

But it is still a far better game than blackjack, poker, or keno.

All gambling run by organizations that wish to make money, from lotteries run by the state to insurance policies, employ probability inferences to make sure that the individual who bets with them is denied full value for the price he pays. Unless, therefore, he is constrained to bet, one is foolish to do so. If one must gamble, he is wiser to do so with his friends, for all the money stays in the game instead of a good percentage being skimmed off the top.

It does make sense to bet if you have reason to believe that the odds are in your favor: that the dice are loaded in some way, that the roulette wheel has a magnetized 23, that you'll die within three weeks of taking out the life insurance policy, that you'll need major surgery two weeks after taking out a hospitalization policy, that you are more proficient than most of the other players in a private poker game, that the company whose stock you are buying will be selected to build 5,000 airplanes for the government. But unless one has an edge, something extra going for him, he is foolish to bet and expect to win. Probability, in the long run, is what wins or loses for the bettor, not *luck*.

Often the horse bettor feels he has that edge, and sometimes he does. If the track is offering 12 to 1 odds on Stardust, Harry may think that the horse has a better chance than that, say 7 to 1. Now, there is no objective way to determine which is closer to the truth. The "true" odds on roulette or craps can be calculated (classical approach) and so can the odds on living, marrying, divorcing, and dying (relative frequency), but how can we figure probabilities in horse races? Harry, apparently, has done so, for he thinks that the probability of Stardust winning is 1/8. If Harry is right, what is the expected value for each dollar bet on Stardust at the track odds?

$$1/8 \times (1 + 12) = \$1.625$$

So, while he does not believe that Stardust will win, to bet on him makes sense.

If Harry thought that Lido had a better chance than any other horse, he would not bet on her if he felt that the probability of her winning was 1/3 and the posted odds were only 3 to 2:

$$1/3 \times (1 + 1.50) = \$.833$$

Concluding Summary: There is a simple formula for calculating "expected value":

Probability of winning event × *(amount bet + winning return)* = *expected value*

If one wants to bet and can get an expected value of more than the price he pays to make the bet, he has a good bet. If the expected value is less than the price, he has a bad bet. But in order to apply the formula, one needs to know the probability of the event that is bet on or how to calculate it.

EXERCISES

Exercise 62

Calculate the probability of each of the following simple events:

1. Drawing a one-eyed jack from a 52-card deck.
2. Winning a raffle for which 312 tickets were sold and you bought four of them.

3. An odd number coming up in roulette after nine consecutive even numbers.
4. Guessing the suit of a card.
5. Guessing a number between 1 and 10.
6. Hitting a straight golf shot after slicing or hooking twelve of the last fifteen.
7. That the next fire will be accidental, if 67.7 percent of the fires in the neighborhood in the last five years were cases of arson.
8. Drawing the only black jelly bean from a jar containing 655 other jelly beans.
9. Guessing the day of the week that Leif Erickson discovered America.
10. Picking up a vowel when there is one tile for each letter of the alphabet.

Exercise 63

Calculate the probability of each of the following complex events:

1. Drawing a deuce or a one-eyed jack from a 52-card deck.
2. Rolling four straight "naturals" (7 or 11) in craps.
3. Correctly picking the winners in three football games between closely matched teams (excluding ties).
4. Guessing at least one out of five answers correctly in a multiple-choice exam offering five answers for each question.
5. Of black or red coming up on a roulette wheel containing two greens.
6. That the next number to come up on the roulette wheel will be black and even.
7. Guessing the suit of a card at least once in three times.
8. Of hitting the jackpot on a slot machine with four wheels, each containing sixteen symbols, one of which is "jackpot" (assuming that the machine is not "set").
9. Of Reggie Smith (batting .312) getting a hit or striking out (13 times in 242 appearances at the plate so far this season) in his next official time at bat.
10. You are scheduled for four blind dates with four different persons at Cougar University. What are your chances that at least one of these persons is in the top tenth of his or her class?

Exercise 64

Exactly how good is each of these bets?

1. You are offered 4 to 1 odds if you can guess the suit of a card.
2. You bet someone $6 to $1 that he cannot call the flip of a coin correctly three straight times.
3. You place a wager that you can draw a red or yellow jelly-bean from a bottle containing ten of each, plus 20 black ones.
4. You bet someone else even money that you can draw a red or yellow jelly-bean in two tries from a bottle containing ten of each, plus 20 black ones.

5. Five out of six inhabitants of a particular city are Caucasian. You accept 5 to 1 odds that the first person randomly selected from its population is not Caucasian.

6. You bet at 1 to 2 odds that you can roll a 10 before a 7.

7. Joe Vosmik is batting .300. You bet even money that he will get at least one hit in four official times at bat in the game today.

8. Averill homers about once in every 26 games, and makes an error once in every 14 games. You bet one dollar against twenty that he will hit a homerun and not make an error in today's game.

9. You get 1000 to 1 odds and bet that neither heads nor tails will come up.

10. You bet even money that either Lopez or Bradley will win the tournament, figuring Lopez's chances at 1 in 3 and Bradley's chances at 1 in 4.

Chapter 7

Introduction to Symbolic Logic

PREVIEW

In this chapter we will examine some basic symbolic techniques for handling deductive arguments. We will use truth-functional connectives and lower-case letters to express molecular statements and forms—as we have done in earlier chapters. We will also symbolize "quantificational" statements and forms, but not in the way we have done previously when dealing with categorical statements. Finally, we will discuss relational statements and forms (hitherto ignored) and show how to symbolize them. All this is preliminary. The objective of the chapter is to show how these various statements or forms can be used in formal proofs, each step of which is justified by an appeal to a specific rule of inference or rule of equivalence. The proficiencies that you need to develop include the following:

1. Expressing molecular, quantificational, and relational statements in acceptable symbolic form.
2. Understanding and remembering the various rules of proof that are available.
3. Constructing formal proofs for stipulated conclusions having been given the premises.
4. Knowing when and how to utilize the methods of conditional and indirect proof.
5. Knowing the conditions for removing quantifiers.
6. Knowing the conditions for supplying quantifiers.
7. Knowing the properties that relations can have.

Although all this seems quite abstract and utterly removed from ordinary thought, there is much in it that is quite in accordance with "common sense." This preliminary test is based on some of the ideas important in the science of symbolic logic:

1. True or false? If every step of a series of deductive inferences is valid, then the series itself is valid.

2. True or false? If two expressions can each be deduced from the other, the two expressions can be said to be truth-functionally equivalent.
3. Suppose, within a proof, we assume 'p' and then go on to establish 'q & r.' What expression does this permit us to assert?
4. Complete: The denial of a universal statement is a _____ statement; the denial of a particular statement is a _____ statement; the denial of a singular statement is a _____ statement.
5. If Bill loves Joyce, does it follow that Joyce loves Bill? Does it follow that Joyce does not love Bill?
6. If Clarence is taller than Roger, does it follow that Roger is not taller than Clarence?
7. If someone likes everyone, does it follow that someone likes himself?
8. If Philip is richer than Robert, and Agnes is richer than Philip, what can we say about Agnes and Robert?
9. If Philip likes Robert, and Agnes likes Philip, what can we say about Agnes and Robert?
10. If it is true that all golfers are liars, can we deduce that if Rudolph is a golfer, then he too must be a liar?

THE PROPOSITIONAL CALCULUS

Formal Proofs and the Rules upon Which They Are Based

In addition to the methods discussed in Chapter 6, there is another way to establish the validity of deductive arguments containing truth-functional statements. This method employs the *propositional calculus,* a formalized system based on explicit rules. The calculus permits us to express premises of indefinite complexity and to show in a rigorous way what follows from them.[1] We need not depend on the vagaries of "common sense" or lengthy and tedious truth tables.

Instead, we construct a formal proof: a systematic technique of repeatedly applying valid rules, not only to initial premises, but subsequently to the new information obtained. We state the premises first and make deductions in a step-by-step way. Each step in the proof is justified by appeal to a specific rule. The proof terminates when the intended conclusion is reached. This conclusion follows, directly or indirectly, from the premises. It is the end of a chain of reasoning every step of which is supported by a sound rule. It has been shown to be the conclusion of a valid deductive argument.

What are these rules? They fall into two categories: *rules of inference* and *rules of transformation.* The first tells us what deductions we can make, and the second tells us what equivalent expressions we can employ. We can be sure that the rules are sound, for they can be validated by truth tables.

---

[1] What is presented here is simply an introduction to the system.

How many rules do we need? It is possible to get by with a very short list, and this is considered "economical" and "elegant." But with a somewhat longer list, we can save ourselves some steps in our deductive proofs. The longer the list, the more we will have to remember, but the shorter the proofs. The following lists are moderate in length and permit us to construct a great many deductive proofs:

Rules of Valid Inference

p, q, therefore p & q. Conjunctive argument (C.A.).
p & q, therefore p. Simplification (Simp.).
p, therefore p v q. Addition (Add.).
$p{\rightarrow}q$, p, therefore q. Modus ponens (M.P.).
$p{\rightarrow}q$, $\sim q$, therefore $\sim p$. Modus tolens (M.T.).
$p{\rightarrow}q$, $q{\rightarrow}r$, therefore $p{\rightarrow}r$. Conditional syllogism (C.S.).
p v q, $\sim p$, therefore q. Disjunctive argument (D.A.).

Rules of Transformation (equivalences)

$p = \sim\sim p$. Double negation (D.N.).
$(p$ v $q) = (q$ v $p)$. Commutation (Comm.).
$(p$ & $q) = (q$ & $p)$. Commutation (Comm.).
$p = (p$ v $p)$. Tautology (Taut.).
$p = (p$ & $p)$. Tautology (Taut.).
$(p{\rightarrow}q) = (\sim q{\rightarrow}\sim p)$. Contraposition (Contrap.).
$(p{\rightarrow}q) = (\sim p$ v $q)$. Material implication (M.I.).
$(p{\leftrightarrow}q) = [(p{\rightarrow}q)$ & $(q{\rightarrow}p)]$. Biconditional (Bic.).
$(p \veebar q) = [(p$ & $\sim q)$ v $(\sim p$ & $q)]$. Strong disjunction (S.D.).
$\sim(p$ v $q) = (\sim p$ & $\sim q)$. DeMorgan's law (D.M.).
$\sim(p$ & $q) = (\sim p$ v $\sim q)$. DeMorgan's law (D.M.).

Each of these rules has a name, and its abbreviation may be cited when it is appealed to.

It is to be understood that in using the Rules of Transformation that the expression on one side of the '=' may replace the expression on the other side *wherever* it occurs in a proof, whether the equivalence is an entire line of a proof or merely a part of a line. The Rules of Valid Inference, however, can be applied only to entire lines of a proof.

Examples

Consider this argument:

If Nicklaus sinks his putt, Watson will drop out of the lead. Watson either holds his lead or gets a tie. Nicklaus sinks his putt. Therefore, Watson gets a tie.

First we abbreviate, label, and number the premises, placing what we want to prove, 'Watson gets a tie,' opposite the last premise. Then we make deductions and transformations, indicating the expressions and rules utilized. Use of modus ponens in (4) and disjunctive arguments in (5) quickly gives us the conclusion:

1. s→~l	*premise*	
2. l v t	*premise*	
3. s	*premise*	/∴ t
4. ~l	*1, 3 (M.P.)*	
5. t	*2, 4 (D.A.)*	

Here is another one:

Harriet is in New York or Philadelphia. If she is not in Philadelphia, she got lost. Since she did not get lost, she is not in New York.

1. n ⩔ p	*premise*	
2. ~p→l	*premise*	
3. ~l	*premise*	/∴ ~n
4. (n & ~p) v (~n & p)	*1 (S.D.)*	
5. ~~(n & ~ p) v (~n &p)	*4 (D.N.)*	
6. ~(n & ~p)→(~n & p)	*5 (M.I.)*	
7. ~~p	*2, 3 (M.T.)*	
8. p	*7 (D.N.)*	
9. p v ~n	*8 (Add.)*	
10. ~n v p	*9 (Comm.)*	
11. ~~(~n v p)	*10 (D.N.)*	
12. ~(n & ~p)	*11 (D.M.)*	
13. ~n & p	*6, 12 (M.P.)*	
14. ~n	*13 (Simp.)*	

The key here is to replace the strong disjunction (1) with an equivalent disjunction (4), then to transform that disjunction into a conditional (5). When we see that the conclusion is contained in the consequent of that conditional, we build up '*p*' (7) in order to get the antecedent of that conditional. We do so in (11), and the rest is easy.

Let us now use the method of formal proof to validate a constructive dilemma:

1. p→q	*premise*	
2. r→s	*premise*	
3. p v r	*premise*	/∴ q v s
4. ~~p v r	*3 (D.N.)*	
5. ~p→r	*4 (M.I.)*	
6. ~p→s	*5, 2 (C.S.)*	
7. ~q→~p	*1 (Contrap.)*	

8. ~q→s   7, 6 *(C.S.)*
9. ~~q v s   8 *(M.I.)*
10. q v s   9 *(D.N.)*

We saw that some conditional syllogisms are possible if we transform (3) into a conditional, so we did so in (5). The first conditional syllogism yielded (6). Realizing that we must bring '*q*' and '*s*' into the same expression, we ponder the possibility of having '~*p*→*s*' (6) and '*p*→*q*' (1) serve as premises of another conditional syllogism. This can be done if we first contrapose '*p*→*q*,' so we did so in (7). In (9) we simply replace the conclusion of the second conditional syllogism (8) with a disjunction.

Let us now construct a formal proof of validity for the following argument:

> If the draft is resumed or Poland attacks, then Gloria is drafted and leaves school, provided that the U.N. does not solve the crisis. Although the draft was resumed, Gloria did not leave school. Therefore, the U.N. solved the crisis.

Our first task is to express the statements in molecular forms, abbreviating the components. The first premise contains a conditional, the antecedent of which is a disjunction, the consequent a conjunction:

$(r \lor a) \to (d \mathbin{\&} l)$

This conditional itself is consequent to the U.N. not solving the crisis, so the entire first premise is:

$\sim s \to [(r \lor a) \to (d \mathbin{\&} l)]$

The second premise is a conjunction:

$r \mathbin{\&} \sim l$

We are now ready to construct the proof:

1. ~s→[(r v a)→(d & l)]   *premise*
2. r & ~l   *premise*   /∴ s
3. ~l   2 *(Simp.)*
4. ~l v ~d   3 *(Add.)*
5. ~d v ~l   4 *(Comm.)*
6. ~(d & l)   5 *(D.M.)*
7. r   2 *(Simp.)*
8. r v a   7 *(Add.)*
9. (r v a) & ~(d & l)   8, 6 *(C.A.)*
10. ~~(r v a) & ~(d & l)   9 *(D.N.)*
11. ~[~(r v a) v (d & l)]   10 *(D.M.) (D.N.)*
12. ~[(r v a)→(d & l)]   11 *(M.I.)*
13. ~~s   12, 1 *(M.T.)*
14. s   13 *(D.N.)*

In this proof we had to work up to the denial of the consequent of the first premise by separating the components of the second premise and building on them.

In the following proof, the reasons are left for the reader to supply:

1. $[(a \lor b) \to \sim c] \,\&\, (\sim c \to f)$ *premise*
2. $x \to \sim(f \,\&\, g)$ *premise*
3. $g \,\&\, (b \,\&\, d)$ *premise* $/\therefore \sim x$
4. $(a \lor b) \to \sim c$
5. $b \,\&\, d$
6. b
7. $b \lor a$
8. $a \lor b$
9. $\sim c$
10. $\sim c \to f$
11. f
12. g
13. $f \,\&\, g$
14. $\sim\sim(f \,\&\, g)$
15. $\sim x$

Conditional and Indirect Proofs

There is another technique which is very useful: that of *conditional proof*. It consists of making an assumption and finding out where it leads. The assumption and the result can then be joined as the antecedent and consequent of a conditional statement. The *rule of conditional proof* (C.P.) could be added to our list of rules of inference. Some proofs are impossible without it. This is how it works:

1. $(b \,\&\, c) \to \sim a$ *premise*
2. b *premise* $/\therefore a \to \sim c$
3. a *assumption*
4. $(b \,\&\, c) \to \sim a$ *1 (Reit.)*
5. $\sim(b \,\&\, c)$ *4, 3 (M.T.)*
6. $\sim b \lor \sim c$ *5 (D.M.)*
7. b *2 (Reit.)*
8. $\sim c$ *6, 7 (D.A.)*
9. $a \to \sim c$ *3–8 (C.P.)*

Since the conditional we wanted to establish has '*a*' as an antecedent, we took that as our assumption in (3). It serves as a premise in a subordinate proof, so we indented the expression and drew a vertical line to set it off from the main proof. We can always bring an expression from the main proof into the subordinate [as we did in (4) and (7)], and this is justified by the *rule of reiteration* (Reit.). Our assumption '*a*' did lead to '~*c*,' so we could go back to the main proof (terminating the line) and assert '*a*→ ~*c*.' Its justification is the whole subordinate proof (3–8).

Here is another example of conditional proof:

> If China is in Asia, then if Peking is in Europe then Denver is in Africa. But either Denver is not in Africa or the atlas is wrong. Since the atlas is not wrong, if China is in Asia then Peking is not in Europe:

1.	c→(p→d)	*premise*	
2.	~d v w	*premise*	
3.	~w	*premise*	/∴ c→~p
4.	⌐ c	*assumption*	
5.	c→(p→d)	*1 (Reit.)*	
6.	p→d	*5, 4 (M.P.)*	
7.	~d v w	*2 (Reit.)*	
8.	~w	*3 (Reit.)*	
9.	~d	*7, 8 (D.A.)*	
10.	~p	*6, 9 (M.T.)*	
11.	c→~p	*4–10 (C.P.)*	

Whenever we seek to establish a conclusion which has the conditional form, the method of conditional proof can be tried. Sometimes the conclusion, a conditional, contains conditionals. We may then find it convenient to construct conditional proofs within conditional proofs. Let us, for example, deduce '*p*→[*q*→(*r*→*s*)]' from '[(*p*→*q*)→*r*]→*s*.'

1.	[(p→q)→r]→s	*premise*	/∴ p→[q→(r→s)]
2.	⌐ p	*assumption*	
3.	⌐ q	*assumption*	
4.	⌐ r	*assumption*	
5.	[(p→q)→r]→s	*1 (Reit.)*	
6.	r v ~(p→q)	*4 (Add.)*	
7.	~(p→q) v r	*6 (Comm.)*	
8.	(p→q)→r	*7 (M.I.)*	
9.	s	*5, 8 (M.P.)*	
10.	r→s	*4–9 (C.P.)*	
11.	q→(r→s)	*3–10 (C.P.)*	
12.	p→[q→(r→s)]	*2–11 (C.P.)*	

We can also use the method of conditional proof to establish material equivalence. We simply show that the two expressions lead to one another—that is, they form a biconditional. The rule of transformation called ''association'' (which we did not include on our original list) can be established in a proof where there are no premises but two assumptions each leading to the other.

1.	p v (q v r)	assumption
2.	~(p v q)	assumption
3.	~p & ~q	2 (D.M.)
4.	~p	3 (Simp.)
5.	~q	3 (Simp.)
6.	p v (q v r)	1 (Reit.)
7.	q v r	6, 4 (D.A.)
8.	r	7, 5 (D.A.)
9.	~(p v q)→r	2–8 (C.P.)
10.	(p v q) v r	9 (M.I.)
11.	[p v (q v r)→[(p v q) v r]	1–10 (C.P.)
12.	(p v q) v r	assumption
13.	~(q v r)	assumption
14.	~q & ~r	13 (D.M.)
15.	(p v q) v r	12 (Reit.)
16.	~r	14 (Simp.)
17.	p v q	15, 16 (D.A.)
18.	~q	14 (Simp.)
19.	p	17, 18 (D.A.)
20.	~(q v r)→p	13–19 (C.P.)
21.	(q v r) v p	20 (M.I.)
22.	p v (q v r)	21 (Comm.)
23.	[(p v q) v r]→[p v (q v r)]	12–22 (C.P.)
24.	{[p v (q v r)]→[(p v q) v r]} & {[(p v q) v r]→ [p v (q v r)]} 11, 23 (C.A.)	
25.	[p v (q v r)] ↔[(p v q) v r]	24 (Bic.)

Various other useful material equivalences can be proved, and they can serve as additional rules of transformation.

There is another very useful technique for proving the validity of arguments. It is called *indirect proof* and it utilizes the principle of *reductio ad absurdum:* any statement that leads to a self-contradiction is false. This is a sound principle because self-contradictions are necessarily false and any conditional statement that contains one in the consequent must, if it is to be true, contain a false antecedent. If, after assuming that the denial of our conclusion is true, we encounter a self-contradiction, we must conclude that the denial of our conclusion is *not* true. That is, our conclusion is necessarily true.

Here is a simple example:

1.	(p v q)→r	*premise*
2.	q	*premise* /∴ r
3.	└─ ~r	*assumption*
4.	(p v q)→r	*1 (Reit.)*
5.	~(p v q)	*4, 3 (M.T.)*
6.	~p & ~q	*5 (D.M.)*
7.	~q	*6 (Simp.)*
8.	q	*2 (Reit.)*
9.	q & ~q	*8, 7 (C.A.)*
10.	~r→(q & ~q)	*3–9 (C.P.)*
11.	~~r	*10 (R.A.)*
12.	r	*11 (D.N.)*

We were able to show that '~*r*' leads to a self-contradiction (3–9), so '~*r*' must be false—i.e., '*r*' is true. The principle appealed to in (11) is *reductio ad absurdum* (R.A.).

Here is another example of indirect proof:

1.	p→q	*premise*
2.	r→s	*premise*
3.	~q v ~s	*premise* /∴ ~p v ~r
4.	─ ~(~p v ~r)	*assumption*
5.	~~p & ~~r	*4 (D.M.)*
6.	~~p	*5 (Simp.)*
7.	p	*6 (D.N.)*
8.	p→q	*1 (Reit)*
9.	q	*8, 7 (M.P.)*
10.	~~r	*5 (Simp.)*
11.	r	*10 (D.N.)*
12.	r→s	*2 (Reit.)*
13.	s	*12, 11 (M.P.)*
14.	~q v ~s	*3 (Reit.)*
15.	~~s	*13 (D.N.)*
16.	~q	*14, 15 (D.A.)*
17.	q & ~q	*9, 16 (C.A.)*
18.	~(~p v ~r)→(q & ~q)	*4–17 (C.P.)*
19.	~~(~p v ~r)	*18 (R.A.)*
20.	~p v ~r	*19 (D.N.)*

This particular form is, of course, that of the destructive dilemma, and could be included in our list of permitted inferences: (*p*→*q*) & (*r*→*s*), ~*q* v ~*s*, therefore ~*p* v ~*r*.

If there should be inconsistency in the premises themselves, anything whatever can be deduced from them. This is so because inconsistency (or incompatibility) implies a contradiction. Contradictory expressions, through the use of the rule of addition, may be used to prove whatever we want to prove, no matter how ridiculous. It is thus very important that the premises be consistent with one another.

We can indeed deduce that the moon is made of green cheese ('x') from these premises:

If the weather is good, the picnic is held and everyone is happy.

The weather is good.

Some people are not happy.

1. $g \rightarrow (e \& a)$ *premise*
2. g *premise*
3. $\sim a$ *premise* $/\therefore x$
4. $e \& a$ 1, 2 (*M.P.*)
5. a 4 (*Simp.*)
6. $a \lor x$ 5 (*Add.*)
7. x 6, 3 (*D.A.*)

Concluding Summary: The propositional calculus provides the means for constructing formal deductive proofs. Each step in the proof relies on a specific valid rule of inference or transformation. Conditional proofs may be used to establish conditional statements. Such a statement may be the conclusion sought, an element of a truth-functional equivalence, or the basis of a *reductio ad absurdum*.

> When reason is against a man, a man will be against reason.
> —*Thomas Hobbes*

EXERCISES

Exercise 65

Employing the rules stated on p. 210, construct a formal proof of validity for each of the following arguments:

1. Premises: $p \rightarrow q$, $p \lor r$
   Conclusion: $\sim r \rightarrow q$
2. Premises: $(p \lor q) \rightarrow (r \& s)$, q
   Conclusion: s
3. Premises: $p \& q$, $p \rightarrow (r \lor s)$, $\sim s$
   Conclusion: $q \& r$
4. Premises: $\sim p \lor q$, $\sim r \lor q$, $r \lor p$
   Conclusion: q
5. Premises: $p \lor q$, p
   Conclusion: $r \lor \sim q$

6. Premises: If I buy a Cadillac or lease a Lincoln, then I have good transportation and a big debt. If I have a big debt, I must work harder. I cannot work harder.
   Conclusion: I do not buy a Cadillac.

7. Premises: Either the path leads to the river or the map is wrong and we are lost. If the path leads to the river, the ground is soft. The ground is not soft.
   Conclusion: We are lost.

8. Premises: If and only if you study do you pass. You do not study. You either study or watch TV.
   Conclusion: You watch TV and do not pass.

9. Premises: Either Rousseau is correct or Locke is uninformed. It is not the case that both Rousseau is correct and Hobbes is not superficial.
   Conclusion: If Locke is informed, then Hobbes is superficial.

10. Premises: He will either write or phone and she will be surprised or happy. If he is distracted, he will not write and she will be unhappy.
    Conclusion: He will phone and she will be surprised.

11. Premises: Stella is rich (r) and good-looking (g). Only if Stella wins the lottery (w) can she be rich. If Stella wins the lottery, she will make a donation to the United Fund (d).
    Conclusion: Stella is good-looking and made a donation to the United Fund.

12. Premises: Horace played golf (p) but went to the bank (b) as well, or he went to the bank but did not cash a check (c). If Horace played golf, then he stopped at the clubhouse (s). He did not stop at the clubhouse.
    Conclusion: Horace did not cash a check.

13. Premises: If I give all my books to the library (g), then I'll have nothing to read (n). If I have nothing to read, I'll get into trouble (t). I give all my books to the library or I keep some of them (k). If I keep some of them, I have to make some difficult choices (d).
    Conclusion: If I don't make some difficult choices, I'll get into trouble.

14. Premises: If he puts all his money on the stock market (a), he risks severe financial losses (r). If he does not play the stock market (p), his savings will be eroded by inflation (e). If he is not victimized by bad advice (v), he will not risk severe financial losses. His savings will not be eroded by inflation unless he is victimized by bad advice. He is not victimized by bad advice.
    Conclusion: He does not put all his money on the stock market but he does play the stock market.

15. Premises: If I attend school (s), I'll have to borrow money (b). If I borrow money, I'll not prosper (f). If I don't attend school, I'll earn some money (e). If I earn some money, I'll prosper.
    Conclusion: If and only if I don't attend school will I prosper.

Exercise 66

Employing the rules stated on p. 210 and using the method of conditional proof, construct a formal proof of validity for each of the following arguments:

1. Premise: $(a \text{ \& } b) \text{ v } c$
   Conclusion: $\sim b {\rightarrow} c$
2. Premises: $\sim p {\rightarrow} \sim q$, $\sim p \text{ v } (r {\leftrightarrow} s)$
   Conclusion: $q {\rightarrow} \sim (r \text{ \& } \sim s)$
3. Premises: $\sim p \text{ v } \sim s$, $(q \text{ v } t) {\rightarrow} r$
   Conclusion: $p {\rightarrow} [q {\rightarrow} (r \text{ \& } \sim s)]$
4. Premise: $(p \text{ v } q) {\rightarrow} [(r \text{ v } s) {\rightarrow} t]$
   Conclusion: $\sim [(r \text{ v } s) {\rightarrow} t] {\rightarrow} \sim p$
5. Premise: t
   Conclusion: $p {\rightarrow} \{q {\rightarrow} [r {\rightarrow} (s {\rightarrow} t)]\}$

Exercise 67

Employing the rules stated on p. 210 and using the method of conditional proof, construct a formal proof for each of these pairs of truth-functional equivalences:

1. $(p \text{ v } q) {\rightarrow} r$, $\sim r {\rightarrow} (\sim p \text{ \& } \sim q)$
2. $p {\rightarrow} (q \text{ v } r)$, $\sim (\sim q \text{ \& } \sim r) \text{ v } \sim p$
3. $\sim (p {\rightarrow} q)$, $p \text{ \& } \sim q$ (denial of conditional)
4. $\sim (p \text{ w } q)$, $p {\leftrightarrow} q$ (denial of strong disjunction)
5. $p \text{ \& } (q \text{ \& } r)$, $(p \text{ \& } q) \text{ \& } r$ (rule of association)

Exercise 68

Employing the rules stated on p. 210 and using the method of indirect proof (reductio ad absurdum), *construct a formal proof of validity for each of the following arguments:*

1. Premises: $p {\rightarrow} \sim q$, $p {\rightarrow} (p \text{ \& } q)$
   Conclusion: $\sim p$
2. Premises: $p {\rightarrow} (q {\rightarrow} r)$, $\sim p {\rightarrow} (q {\rightarrow} r)$
   Conclusion: $q {\rightarrow} r$
3. Premises: Stella is rich or good-looking. If Stella is rich or intelligent, then she is popular and well-dressed. Stella is not popular.
   Conclusion: Stella is good-looking.
4. Premises: If I study Greek, I'll be edified. If I study Latin, I'll be edified. I study either Greek or Latin.
   Conclusion: I'll be edified.
5. Premises: If we issue an ultimatum, there will be war; and if we don't issue an ultimatum, we'll be humiliated. We will not be humiliated.
   Conclusion: There will be war.

QUANTIFICATIONAL LOGIC

Symbolizing Statements

The propositional logic just discussed enabled us to deal with molecular statements and the various arguments in which they take part. We utilized rules of equivalence and validity in which each atomic particle preserved its own basic meaning while entering into many interesting relations with other atomic particles. The 'p's,' and 'q's,' and the 'a's,' and 'b's' stood for statements that were self-contained. While we examined the molecular structures of which they were components, we did not analyze the structure of these atomic particles themselves.

Symbolic logic finds it very fruitful to make this analysis. The result is a "predicate" or "quantificational" logic that makes possible a rigorous and systematic treatment of atomic statements in general. Aristotle and his followers approached the logic of categorical statements from the point of view assumed in Chapters 3–5. Modern logic employs the symbolic techniques presented here—in a very elementary and introductory way.

In symbolizing quantificational statements, we will use lowercase letters to indicate subjects and uppercase letters for predicates. We will take 'subject' in a very broad sense to indicate persons, places, times, or things—whatever is our universe of discourse. We will also take 'predicate' in a very broad sense to include qualities or properties—whatever is attributed to the subject. For example:

'Ja' could stand for 'Adam is a jogger.'

'Ib' could stand for 'Betty is intelligent.'

'Bt' could stand for 'The Taj Mahal is beautiful.'

Each of the small letters is a constant, denoting an individual in some universe of discourse or another. The capital letter represents the property that it possesses.

These are singular statements. How do we present particular and universal statements? Here we must introduce two new symbols.

The first is the *existential quantifier:* '∃x.' This means 'there exists at least one element in our universe of discourse such that . . .'

'(∃x)Bx' could stand for 'There is at least one thing that is beautiful.'

'(∃x)(Wx & Ux)' could stand for 'There is at least one thing that is a wedding present and is useful.'

'(∃x)Lx' could stand for 'There is at least one thing that is loyal.'

Whether these are true, of course, depends upon whether in fact an x exists which does have the property indicated. The term 'x' is a variable that can stand for anything in the whole range of elements constituting the selected universe of discourse.

Our second new symbol is the *universal quantifier:* '(x).' This means 'for any x in the universe of discourse . . .'

'(x)Bx' could stand for any of the following:

'For any x, x is B.'

'For anything in the universe, it is beautiful.'

'Everything in the universe is beautiful.'

'(x)(Bx → Px)' could stand for any of the following:

'For any x, if x is B, it is P'

'For anything in the universe, if it is beautiful, then it is precious'

'If anything is beautiful, it is precious'

'All beautiful things are precious'

'(x)[Px→(Ox→Gx)]' could stand for any of the following:

For any x, if x is a P, then if x is O, then x is G'

'For anything in the universe, if it is a person, then if it is an officer, then it is a gentleman'

'If anyone is an officer, then he or she is a gentleman'

'All officers are gentlemen'

The four standard forms taken by categorical statements can be expressed this way:

A	**(x)(Sx→Px)**
E	**(x)(Sx→~ P)**
I	**(∃x)(Sx & Px)**
O	**(∃x)(Sx & ~Px)**

The A and O are contradictories, and so are the E and I. They will thus always have different truth values. But none of the other "immediate inferences" cited in the Traditional Square of Opposition on p. 115 can be made from these statements as interpreted by quantificational logic.

Subalterns cannot be deduced from their superalterns, for to do so would be going from a statement which says nothing about existence to one in which existence is guaranteed. Can contraries both be true? Yes, provided that there is no x possessing the subject property. 'All perfect women are thoughtful' and 'No perfect women are thoughtful,' for example, are both true if it is the case that perfect women are nonexistent. A universal rules out its contrary only if we can assume that at least one element of the subject class exists. Similarly, subcontraries can both be false—provided that no members of their subject class exist.[2]

---

[2] See below, p. 226.

Let us symbolize the following:

(1) Everything is black or white.
(2) Every girl is friendly or hostile.
(3) If everything is extended, then something is colored.
(4) Anything colored is also extended.
(5) If something exists which is colored, then something exists which is extended.
(6) All members of the human race are both rational and passionate.
(7) Some builders are either incompetent or dishonest.
(8) If no humans are mortal, then some philosophies are in error.
(9) Everything is finite but important.

Taking *things* as our universe of discourse and using natural abbreviations for predicates, we get:

(1) (x)(Bx v Wx)
(2) (x)[Gx→(Fx v Hx)]
(3) (x)Ex→(∃y)Cy
(4) (x)(Cx→Ex)
(5) (∃x)Cx→(∃y)Ey
(6) (x)[Hx→(Rx & Px)]
(7) (∃x)[Bx & (~Cx v ~Hx)]
(8) (x)(Hx→~Mx)→(∃y)(Py & Ey)
(9) (x)(Fx & Ix)

Concluding Summary: Atomic statements are not irreducible. Categorical statements of any kind can be expressed as singular statements involving constants and predicates or as general statements involving variables bound by quantifiers.

Constructing Formal Proofs

In order to construct formal proofs involving quantificational statements, we must utilize the rules of equivalence and inference listed on p. 210, as well as the rule of conditional proof. But these alone are not enough. We must devise a way of removing the quantifier so that we can work with the variables that they bind. And we must also devise a way of adding the quantifiers to singular statements or to expressions that would not otherwise be statements.

These four rules demonstrate what we are justified in doing with quantifiers during the course of a formal proof:

(1) *Universal Instantiation* (UI). Since the quantifier is universal, we can remove it and infer any substitution instance of the expression it binds. The following inferences, for example, are valid:

1. (x)(Ax→Bx) *premise*
2. Ab→Bb *1* (UI)

1. (x)(Ax v Bx)   *premise*
2. Ax v Bx   *1* (UI)

(2) *Universal Generalization* (UG). When something is the case for any arbitrarily selected individual, it is the case for *all* individuals. But we must be careful. We cannot introduce the universal quantifier to a premise, nor can we bind a variable that has been derived from Rule 3 (EI). In the following argument, for example, step 6 is valid, because no restrictions had been placed on the x occurring in the preceding line:

1. (x)(Ax→Bx)   *premise*
2. (x)(Bx→Cx)   *premise*
3. Ax→Bx   *1* (UI)
4. Bx→Cx   *2* (UI)
5. Ax→Cx   *3, 4* (C.S.)
6. (x)(Ax→Cx)   *5* (UG)

But step 2 in the following is *not* valid. We cannot be sure that all things will have the qualities that the individual *a* has:

1. Ma & Pa   *premise*
2. (x)(Mx & Px)   *1* (UG)   **NO!**

Step 3 in the following is *not* valid. Just because some instance or another of x has attributes F and G does not permit us to say that *all* of them do:

1. (∃x)(Fx & Gx)   *premise*
2. Fx & Gx   *1* (EI)
3. (x)(Fx & Gx)   *2* (UG)   **NO!**

(3) *Existential Instantiation* (EI). Since the quantifier guarantees the existence of at least one instance, we can remove it and arbitrarily infer some instance or another that has *not* previously been mentioned in the proof. The constant is making its first appearance, and it cannot denote any specific individual. The next two arguments, for example, are valid. We simply assign a constant to represent the existence that is guaranteed in the first premise:

1. (∃x)(Ax→Bx)   *premise*
2. Ax→Bx   *1* (EI)

1. (∃x)(Ax v Bx)   *premise*
2. Aa v Ba   *1* (EI)

But step 3 in the next argument is *not* valid. The constant (*a*) occurring in the first premise denotes a specific individual. No existential instantiation can denote a specific individual; it merely indicates some individual or another. There is no basis for believing that the existence guaranteed in step 2 is the same specific individual indicated in step 1.

1. Ba   *premise*
2. (∃x)(Ax & Bx)   *premise*
3. Aa & Ba   *1* (UI)   **NO!**

Step 4 in the following argument is *not* valid, because we cannot be sure that the thing denoted in step 4 is the same thing instantiated in step 3. Whenever we intend to instantiate both universally and existentially, we must do the latter first.

1. (x)(Fx v Gx)   *premise*
2. (∃x) ~ Gx   *premise*
3. Fx v Gx   *1* (UI)
4. ~Gx   *2* (EI)   **NO!**

This *is* a valid argument:

1. (x)(Fx v Gx)   *premise*
2. (∃x)~Gx   *premise*
3. ~Gx   *2* (EI)
4. Fx v Gx   *1* (UI)

When we instantiate from a universal, *anything* is open to us.

(4) *Existential Generalization* (EG). If a particular constant has been shown to possess a quality, we can generalize and say that there exists at least one thing that has it. The following arguments are thus valid:

1. Pa   *premise*
2. (∃x)Px   *1* (EG)

1. (x)(Px v Qx)   *premise*
2. Px v Qx   *1* (UI)
3. (∃x)(Px v Qx)   *2* (EG)

This last argument might seem to be rather questionable, since we go from a universal statement where no existence is guaranteed to an existential statement. It does indeed require an additional assumption: That there is at least one thing in the world. This is not too great an assumption to make!

Following are some formal proofs that utilize these rules. The first two proofs are syllogisms:

(1) All men are mortal. Plato is a man. Therefore, Plato is mortal.

1. (x)(Mx→Ox)   *premise*
2. Mp   *premise   /∴* **Op**

3. Mp→Op	*1* (UI)
4. Op	*3, 2* (M.P.)

(2) No Olympians are modest. Some Americans are Olympians. Therefore, some Americans are not modest.

1. (x)(Ox→~Mx)	*premise*
2. (∃x)(Ax & Ox)	*premise* /∴ (∃x)(Ax & ~Mx)
3. Aa & Oa	*2* (EI)
4. Oa→~Ma	*1* (UI)
5. Oa	*3* (*Simp.*)
6. ~Ma	*4, 5* (*M.P.*)
7. Aa	*3* (*Simp.*)
8. Aa & ~Ma	*7, 6* (*C.A.*)
9. (∃x)(Ax & ~Mx)	*8* (EG)

(3) All athletes are strong and fast. Some athletes are drug addicts. Therefore, some drug addicts are strong.

1. (x)Ax→(Sx & Fx)	*premise*
2. (∃x)(Ax & Dx)	*premise* /∴ (∃x)(Dx & Sx)
3. Aa & Da	*2* (EI)
4. Aa→(Sa & Fa)	*1* (UI)
5. Aa	*3* (*Simp.*)
6. Sa & Fa	*4, 5* (*M.P.*)
7. Da	*3* (*Simp.*)
8. Sa	*6* (*Simp.*)
9. Da & Sa	*7, 8* (*C.A.*)
10. (∃x)(Dx & Sx)	*9* (EG)

(4) All office buildings are both impressive and dangerous. All skyscrapers are office buildings. Therefore, all unimpressive things are non-skyscrapers.

1. (x)[Ox→(Ix & Dx)]	*premise*
2. (x)(Sx→Ox)	*premise* /∴ (x)(~Ix→~Sx)
3. | ~Ia	*assump.*
4. | (x)[Ox→(Ix & Dx)]	*1* (*Reit.*)
5. | Oa→(Ia & Da)	*4* (UI)
6. | ~Ia v ~Da	*3* (*Add.*)
7. | ~(Ia & Da)	*6* (*D.M.*)
8. | ~Oa	*5, 7* (*M.T.*)
9. | (x)(Sx→Ox)	*2* (*Reit.*)
10. | Sa→Oa	*9* (UI)
11. | ~Sa	*10, 8* (*M.T.*)
12. ~Ia→~Sa	*3–11* (*C.P.*)
13. (x)(~Ix→~Sx)	*12* (UG)

It is convenient to add two rules to the list of equivalences. To do so shortens the proofs. These rules may be called *quantifier negation* (QN) and may be stated this way:

$$\sim(x)Fx = (\exists x)\sim Fx \qquad (QN)$$

$$\sim(\exists x)Fx = (x)\sim Fx \qquad (QN)$$

That these are equivalent should be intuitively obvious: If it is not the case that a universal holds, it is the case that there is at least one negative instance—and conversely. And if it is not the case that there is at least one positive instance, then it is the case that all instances are negative. These equivalences hold for *any* bound expression, no matter how complex. For example:

$$\sim(x)[(Ax \ \& \ Bx)\rightarrow(Cx \ v \ Dx)] = (\exists x)\sim[(Ax \ \& \ Bx)\rightarrow(Cx \ v \ Dx)]$$

We can rather automatically switch a negation sign from one place to the other, while changing the quantifier.

Proof 5 shows how we can infer that a contrary is false after making an existential assumption (second premise). Proof 6 shows how we can infer a true subcontrary from a false I-statement. These two arguments, as well as the next two, utilize the *QN* rule.

(5)		
	1. (x)(Ax→Bx)	premise
	2. (∃x)Ax	premise /∴ ~(x)(Ax→~Bx)
	3. Ax	2 (EI)
	4. Ax→Bx	1 (UI)
	5. Bx	4, 3 (M.P.)
	6. Ax & Bx	3, 5 (C.A.)
	7. ~~(Ax & Bx)	6 (D.N.)
	8. ~(~Ax v ~Bx)	7 (D.M.)
	9. ~(Ax→~Bx)	8 (M.I.)
	10. (∃x)~(Ax→~Bx)	9 (EG)
	11. ~(x)(Ax→~Bx)	10 (QN)

(6)		
	1. ~(∃x)(Ax & Bx)	premise
	2. (∃x)Ax	premise /∴ (∃x)(Ax & ~ Bx)
	3. Ax	2 (EI)
	4. (x)~(Ax & Bx)	1 (QN)
	5. ~(Ax & Bx)	4 (UI)
	6. ~Ax v ~Bx	5 (D.M.)
	7. Ax→~Bx	6 (M.I.)
	8. ~Bx	7, 3 (M.P.)
	9. Ax & ~Bx	3, 8 (C.A.)
	10. (∃x)(Ax & ~Bx)	9 (EG)

(7) It is not the case that all lemons are tart. All grapefruits are tart. It is not the case that some lemons are not citric. Some citric things, therefore, are not grapefruits.

1. ~(x)(Lx→Tx)   *premise*
2. (x)(Gx→Tx)   *premise*
3. ~(∃x)(Lx & ~Cx)   *premise* /∴ (∃x)(Cx & ~Gx)
4. (∃x)~(Lx→Tx)   *1 (QN)*
5. ~(La→Ta)   *4 (EI)*
6. ~(~La v Ta)   *5 (M.I.)*
7. La & ~Ta   *6 (D.M.)*
8. ~Ta   *7 (Simp.)*
9. Ga→Ta   *2 (UI)*
10. ~Ga   *9, 8 (M.T.)*
11. (x)~(Lx & ~Cx)   *3 (QN)*
12. ~(La & ~Ca)   *11 (UI)*
13. ~La v Ca   *12 (D.M.)*
14. La   *7 (Simp.)*
15. ~~La   *14 (D.N.)*
16. Ca   *13, 15 (D.A.)*
17. Ca & ~Ga   *16, 10 (C.A.)*
18. (∃x)(Cx & ~Gx)   *17 (EG)*

(8) All philosophies either attract a following or inspire opposition. There does not exist a cosmology that attracts a following. Therefore, anything that is both a philosophy and a cosmology must inspire opposition.

1. (x)[Px→(Ax v Ix)]   *premise*
2. ~(∃x)(Cx & Ax)   *premise* /∴ (x)[(Px & Cx)→Ix]
3. | Pa & Ca   *assump.*
4. | (x)[Px→(Ax v Ix)]   *1 (Reit.)*
5. | Pa→(Aa v Ia)   *4 (UI)*
6. | Pa   *3 (Simp.)*
7. | Aa v Ia   *5, 6 (M.P.)*
8. | ~(∃x)(Cx & Ax)   *2 (Reit.)*
9. | (x)~(Cx & Ax)   *8 (QN)*
10. | ~(Ca & Aa)   *9 (UI)*
11. | ~Ca v ~Aa   *10 (D.M.)*
12. | Ca   *3 (Simp.)*
13. | ~Aa   *11, 12 (D.A.)*
14. | Ia   *7, 13 (D.A.)*
15. (Pa & Ca)→Ia   *3–14 (C.P.)*
16. (x)[(Px & Cx)→Ix]   *15 (UG)*

It should be noted that in most of these proofs both universal instantiation and existential instantiation took place. In these cases, the *EI* step was taken first. From a universal we can instantiate anything we please, but from an existential expression we cannot instantiate any element that has already appeared in the proof. It should also be noted that in the fourth and eighth proofs, where the rule of indirect proof was used, we arbitrarily chose an individual as an assumption. Since it led to a consequence which would have followed from *any* individual having the property, we were justified in universally generalizing (*UG*) on the last line. Finally, note that we could *not* have instantiated from the negative premises in the seventh and eighth proofs. In order to instantiate, we had to remove the negation sign from the left of the quantifier. We executed this by the rules of quantifier negation (*QN*).

Concluding Summary: Formal proofs of indefinite complexity can be constructed using the notation of quantificational statements. The list of transformational rules given on p. 210 must be supplemented with the rules of *UI*, *UG*, *EI*, *EG*, and *QN*.

EXERCISES

Exercise 69

Symbolize the following statements:

1. Some weapons systems don't work.
2. No diet is both tasty and effective.
3. There is a man who is neither loved nor hated.
4. Either some books are trash or all reviewers are incompetent.
5. Nothing is both finite and important.
6. Everything that happens has a purpose.
7. If someone tells, everyone will know.
8. Some rabbits are white and some are not.
9. Everything that is reasonable and well-defended is useful and important.
10. There is no such thing as a bad boy.

Exercise 70

Construct a formal proof for each of these arguments. Take persons *as your universe of discourse wherever it is convenient to do so.*

1. All lieutenants are officers and all officers are gentlemen. Therefore, anyone who is not a gentleman is not a lieutenant.
2. If all ghosts are white, then all ghost stories are misleading. There are no ghosts. There are ghost stories. Therefore, some things are misleading.
3. If anyone is a winner, then someone is a loser. Sam, a person, is a winner. Therefore, it is not the case that no one is a loser.
4. If there are any anarchists, then all liberals are anarchists. If there are any democrats, then all anarchists are democrats. Therefore, if there are any democrats who are anarchists, then all liberals are democrats.
5. If Clarence were honest, he would have confessed to taking the apple. And if he had confessed to taking the apple, everyone would have known about it. But Jeanette didn't know about it. Clarence, therefore, is dishonest.

6. All roses (O) are red (E) or some violets are blue. No violets are blue—unless the botanists (T) are all wrong. At least one botanist is not wrong. At least one rose exists. Therefore, at least one red thing exists.

7. If some pitchers (P) are wild (W), then all batters (B) stay loose (L). If all batters stay loose, then they will not hit well (H). Therefore, if some pitchers are wild, then no batters will hit well.

8. It is not the case both that some abortions (A) are justified (J) and that some doctors (D) are not responsible (R). If all doctors are responsible, then no regulations (G) are needed (N). Therefore, if some abortions are justified, then no regulations are needed.

RELATIONAL LOGIC

Relational Statements

We have already seen that in categorical statements subject and predicate classes are *related* to one another (wholly or in part) by inclusion or exclusion. And we have seen how statements can be *related* to one another as equivalences, contradictories, and so on. Also we saw in the previous section how properties can be *related* to variables and constants by attribution. In this section we will discuss relations between or among *individuals*. These relations are specific and almost endless in number. Consider the following:

Tom is older than Harriet.

Pericles rules Greece.

Jean and Glenn are not married to one another.

Mexico is between the United States and Guatemala.

Don, Leo, Bill, and Art played bridge together.

Although it is possible to express some of these as categorical statements or as constant-predicate statements, doing so would be an injustice to the intended meaning. The intent of the speaker is not to include or exclude something in or from a class or a predicate, but to assert that:

The relationship of *older than* holds between Tom and Harriet.

The relationship of *ruling* holds between Pericles and Greece.

The relationship of *marriage* does not hold between Jean and Glenn.

The relationship of *lying between* holds for Mexico with respect to the United States and Guatemala.

The relationship of *playing bridge* holds for Don, Leo, Bill, and Art.

The number of entities that may be related to one another depends on the particular relation. The first three are binary (or dyadic) relations; the fourth is a ternary (or triadic) relation; and the fifth is a quaternary (or tetradic) relation.

We could abbreviate the relation and symbolize the statements in this way:

Oth

Rpg

~Mjg

Bmug

Pdlba

We can also express generalized relational statements. In the following, we will take *people* as our universe of discourse:

Someone likes Bertha: $(\exists x)Lxb$

Everyone likes Bertha: $(x)Lxb$

Bertha does not like anyone: $(x)\sim Lbx$

Everyone likes everyone: $(x)(y)Lxy$

Everyone likes someone or another: $(x)(\exists y)Lxy$

Someone likes everyone: $(\exists x)(y)Lxy$

Someone is liked by everyone: $(\exists x)(y)Lyx$

Anyone who likes Bertha likes Karen: $(x)(Lxb \rightarrow Lxk)$

If we had not taken *people* as the universe of discourse, the first expression would have meant 'something in the universe likes Bertha,' and the second would have meant 'Everything in the universe likes Bertha.' To prevent conveying these and similar meanings, we would have had to enlarge our expressions by supplying *person* as a predicate: '$(\exists x)(Px \ \& \ Lxb$,' '$(x)(Px \rightarrow Lxb)$,' and so on. *Things* is the widest universe of discourse and is assumed when nothing is said to the contrary. But convenience sometimes dictates a narrower one—such as *people*.

We can also express quantificational statements containing both relational and non-relational components:

Anyone who is a teacher is resented: $(x)[Tx \rightarrow (\exists y)Ryx]$

Good drivers are not always appreciated: $(\exists x)(\exists y)(Gx \ \& \sim Ayx)$

A Cadillac is more expensive than any foreign import: $(x)(y)[(Cx \ \& \ Fy) \rightarrow Mxy]$

Every dog has his day: $(x)[Gx \rightarrow (\exists y)(Dy \ \& \ Hxy)]$

Everything comes to those who wait: $(x)[(Px \ \& \ Wx) \rightarrow (y)Cyx]$

Some doctors do not heal themselves: $(\exists x)(Dx \ \& \sim Hxx)$

Some philosophers disagree with everyone: $(\exists x)[Px \ \& \ (y)Dxy]$

Concluding Summary: Some statements of everyday language can be more accurately expressed as assertions of relations rather than as assertions about subjects and predicates. They can be symbolized and used in the propositional and quantificational systems discussed above.

Properties of Binary Relations

A relation is said to be *symmetrical* when it necessarily goes both ways. If *a* bears this kind of relation to *b*, *b* must bear the same relation to *a*. Examples of symmetrical relations are:

   . . . is identical to . . .

   . . . is married to . . .

   . . . is parallel with . . .

   . . . is the obverse of . . .

A symmetrical relation is defined in the formula: $(x)(y)(Rxy \rightarrow Ryx)$.

If, however, the relation is such as to *forbid* the reversal, it is said to be *asymmetrical*. If *a* bears this kind of relation to *b*, *b* cannot bear that relation to *a*. Examples of asymmetrical relations are:

   . . . parent of . . .

   . . . hotter than . . .

   . . . lies to the left of . . .

   . . . subaltern of . . .

An asymmetrical relation is defined in the formula: $(x)(y)(Rxy \rightarrow \sim Ryx)$.

The first two properties are not contradictories, so another property is possible. A relation which is neither symmetrical nor asymmetrical is called *non-symmetrical*. If *a* bears this kind of relation to *b*, *b* may or may not bear it to *a*. Nothing is guaranteed. The truth of 'Rab' tells us nothing about 'Rba.' The following relations are non-symmetrical:

   . . . loves . . .

   . . . brother of . . .

   . . . votes for . . .

   . . . understands . . .

Any relation that does not meet either of the first two definitions is non-symmetrical.

Another set of properties concerns reflexivity. Can a thing bear a relationship to itself? Yes, this is a possibility: 'Raa.' A relation is *reflexive* when everything has that relation to itself. The following relations are reflexive:

. . . identical to . . .

. . . equal to . . .

. . . not less than . . .

A reflexive relation is defined in the formula: (x)Rxx.

If, however, things can never bear that relationship unto themselves, the relation is *irreflexive*. The possibility of 'Raa' is denied. The following are irreflexive relations:

. . . less than . . .

. . . an ancestor of . . .

. . . taller than . . .

An irreflexive relation is defined in the formula: (x)~Rxx.

Those relations that are neither reflexive nor irreflexive are *non-reflexive*. Such relations relate things which may or may not bear that relationship to themselves. 'Raa' may be the case, but 'Rbb' may not. The following relations are non-reflexive:

. . . loves . . .

. . . shoots . . .

. . . gives haircut to . . .

Any relation that does not meet the previous two definitions are non-reflexive.

The property of transitivity also has three different types. The following relations are *transitive:*

. . . descendant of . . .

. . . east of . . .

. . . older than . . .

. . . equivalent to . . .

A transitive relation is defined in this formula: (x)(y)(z)[(Rxy & Ryz)→Rxz]

A relation is *intransitive* if it meets the requirement of this formula: (x)(y)(z)[(Rxy & Ryz)→ ~Rxz]. The following are intransitive relations:

. . . mother of . . .

. . . best friend of . . .

. . . contradictory of . . .

Those relations that are neither transitive nor intransitive are *non-transitive*. Tom may be the friend of Dick and Dick may be the friend of Harry, but Tom may or may not be the friend of Harry. Other non-transitive relations are:

. . . cousin of . . .

. . . unequal to . . .

. . . talks to . . .

. . . incompatible with . . .

How do we know what properties a relation possesses? Some are simply consequences of the meaning the term has. That 'identical with' is symmetrical, reflexive, and transitive is true by definition. From the meaning of 'married to,' the relation can hardly be anything but symmetrical and irreflexive. We see that the possibilities for 'shoots' make it a non-symmetrical, non-reflexive, and non-transitive relation. Such relations as 'north of' are asymmetrical, irreflexive, and transitive, for anything else would be inconsistent with what the term means. We do not need to make empirical investigations to support the contention that 'sibling of' is symmetrical, irreflexive, and non-transitive.

But, in some cases, the determination of properties *is* based on empirical evidence. Indeed, for some relations, the determination is a matter of dispute. Above, the relation 'loves' was declared non-reflexive. That is, some beings love themselves (which means that it is not irreflexive), and some beings do not love themselves (which means that it is not reflexive). But a philosopher might argue that *all* beings, as part of their drive for survival, love themselves—in other words, 'love' is reflexive. A psychologist might marshal facts to show that 'acquainted with' is non-reflexive, while most of us believe that it is reflexive. An anthropologist might do research to show that 'talks to' is reflexive. Is the relation 'rules' reflexive, irreflexive, or non-reflexive? Is it transitive or non-transitive?

Not all empirical determinations are controversial. We know from experience that 'proud of' is non-symmetrical, for while 'Pab' and 'Pba' held for Alice and Bill, 'Pcd' and 'Pdc' did not hold for Charlie and Doris. We know that 'friendly toward' is non-transitive, not because it has to be but because in fact it has been observed to be. Abner is friendly toward Ben and Ben is friendly toward Calvin, and, as it happens, Abner is friendly toward Calvin. But, while Amy is friendly toward Betty and Betty is friendly toward Cindy, Amy is hateful toward Cindy. And we know too, from sad experience, that 'loves' is a non-symmetrical relation. But, happily, it is not an asymmetrical one.

Concluding Summary: Relations can be assigned qualities in terms of symmetry, reflexivity, and transitivity. Sometimes the assignment is analytic: It follows simply from the meaning of the relation. Sometimes the assignment is synthetic: It is based on actual fact. And sometimes we cannot make the assignment at all.

Relational Arguments

Using the techniques and rules presented in the first two sections of this chapter, we can construct formal proofs containing relational statements. Indeed, proofs for some simple deductions are impossible without also using the techniques of relational logic. For example: All deer are mammals; therefore, the antler of a deer is the antler of a mammal.

When the relational aspects of statements are not essential to the structure of the argument, it is not necessary to construe and to symbolize them as relational. In the interest of simplicity, we can use the basic quantificational technique. For example:

> All Frenchmen live near Paris
> All Gascons are Frenchmen
> ∴ All Gascons live near Paris

> **1.** **(x)(Fx→Nx)**   *premise*
> **2.** **(x)(Gx→Fx)**   *premise*   /∴ **(x)(Gx→Nx)**

There is no point in expressing the major premise as:

$(x)(Fx \rightarrow Nxp)$

The relation 'near to' is irrelevant to the argument. 'Near to Paris' can easily be construed as a simple predicate.

Where relational statements are used, it often is unnecessary to make any assumption about the property of the relation involved. For example:

> There is someone who is tormented by everyone. Therefore, there is someone who torments himself. Universe of discourse: *people*.

> **1.** **(∃x)(y)Tyx**   *premise*   /∴ **(∃x)Txx**
> **2.** **(y)Tya**   *1 (EI)*
> **3.** **Taa**   *2 (UI)*
> **4.** **(∃x)Txx**   *3 (EG)*

All of Tom's children are unemployed. Arthur is a son of Tom. Anyone who is a son of someone is also a child of that person. Arthur, therefore, is unemployed. Universe of discourse: *people*.

> **1.** **(x)(Cxt→ ~Ex)**   *premise*
> **2.** **Sat**   *premise*
> **3.** **(x)(y)(Sxy→Cxy)**   *premise*   /∴ **~Ea**
> **4.** **Cat→ ~Ea**   *1 (UI)*
> **5.** **(y)(Say→Cay)**   *3 (UI)*
> **6.** **Sat→Cat**   *5 (UI)*

7. Cat   *6, 2 (M.P.)*
8. ~Ea   *4, 7 (M.P.)*

Members of the Q-team distrust everyone they meet. And they plot against everyone they distrust. Therefore, they plot against everyone they meet. Universe of discourse: *people*.

1. (x)(y)[Qx→(Mxy→Dxy)]   *premise*
2. (x)(y)[Qx→(Dxy→Pxy)]   *premise*   /∴ (x)(y)[Qx→(Mxy→Pxy)]
3. | Qa   *assumption*
4. | (x)(y)[Qx→(Mxy→Dxy)]   *1 (Reit.)*
5. | (y)[Qa→(May→Day)]   *4 (UI)*
6. | Qa→(Mab→Dab)   *5 (UI)*
7. | Mab→Dab   *6, 3 (M.P.)*
8. | (x)(y)[Qx→(Dxy→Pxy)]   *2 (Reit.)*
9. | (y)[Qa→(Day→Pay)]   *8 (UI)*
10. | Qa→(Dab→Pab)   *9 (UI)*
11. | Dab→Pab   *10, 3 (M.P.)*
12. | Mab→Pab   *7, 11 (C.S.)*
13. Qa→(Mab→Pab)   *3–12 (C.P.)*
14. (y)[Qa→(May→Pay)]   *13 (UG)*
15. (x)(y)[Qx→(Mxy→Pxy)]   *14 (UG)*

Adam loves Eve. Adam does not love anyone who is unmarried. Therefore, Eve is married. Universe of discourse: *people*.

1. Lae   *premise*
2. (x)(~Mx→~Lax)   *premise*   /∴ Me
3. ~Me→~Lae   *2 (UI)*
4. ~~Me   *3, 1 (M.T.)*
5. Me   *4 (D.N.)*

All pies are desserts. Therefore, whatever consumes a pie consumes a dessert.

1. (x)(Px→Dx)   *premise*   /∴ (x)[(∃y)(Py & Cxy)→(∃z)
2. | (∃y)(Py & Cxy)   *assumption*
3. | Pa & Cxa   *2 (EI)*
4. | (x)(Px→Dx)   *1 (Reit.)*
5. | Pa→Da   *4 (UI)*
6. | Pa   *3 (Simp.)*
7. | Da   *5, 6 (M.P.)*
8. | Cxa   *3 (Simp.)*
9. | Da & Cxa   *7, 8 (C.A.)*
10. | (∃z)(Dz & Cxz)   *9 (EG)*

11. $(\exists y)(Py\ \&\ Cxy) \rightarrow (\exists z)(Dz\ \&\ Cxz)$ *2–10 (C.P.)*
12. $(x)[(\exists y)(Py\ \&\ Cxy) \rightarrow (\exists z)(Dz\ \&\ Cxz)]$ *11 (UG)*

But there are a great many arguments involving relations in which the validity depends upon the properties of the relations. Consider the following arguments:

(1)   Pericles rules Greece
      Aspasia rules Pericles
∴   Aspasia rules Greece

(2)   The Hancock Tower is taller than Union Station
      The Sears Tower is taller than the Hancock Tower
∴   The Sears Tower is taller than Union Station

(3)   St. Louis is south of Chicago
      Atlanta is south of St. Louis
∴   Atlanta is south of Chicago

(4)   There is one person who everybody likes
∴   There is one person who likes everybody

(5)   Jerome helps Sandra
∴   Sandra helps Jerome

(6)   The statement 'All roses are red' contradicts the statement 'Some roses are not red'
∴   The statement 'Some roses are not red' contradicts the statement 'All roses are red'

(7)   Audrey is the mother of Sarah
      Sarah is the mother of Robin
∴   Audrey is not the mother of Robin

'(1)' is valid only if 'rules' is a transitive relation—which it is not. '(2)' and '(3)' are valid, because 'taller than' and 'south of' are transitive relations. '(4)' and '(5)' are invalid, because 'likes' and 'helps' are non-symmetrical relations. '(6)' is valid, because we are willing to assume that 'contradicts' is a symmetrical relation. '(7)' is valid, because we are willing to assume that 'mother of' is an intransitive relation. We could eliminate all doubt in our proofs by including the property of the relation in the list of premises:

(2) *1.* **Thu**   *premise*
     2. **Tsh**   *premise*
     3. $(x)(y)(z)[(Txy\ \&\ Tyz) \rightarrow Txz]$ *premise*   /∴ **Tsu**

4. (y)(z)[(Tsy & Tyz)→Tsz]   *3 (UI)*
5. (z)[(Tsh & Thz)→Tsz]   *4 (UI)*
6. (Tsh & Thu)→Tsu   *5 (UI)*
7. Tsh & Thu   *2, 1 (C.A.)*
8. Tsu   *6, 7 (M.P.)*

(6) 1. Cab   *premise*
     2. (x)(y)(Cxy↔Cyx)   *premise /∴ Cba*
     3. (y)(Cay↔Cya)   *2 (UI)*
     4. Cab↔Cba   *3 (UI)*
     5. (Cab→Cba) & (Cba→Cab)   *4 (Bic.)*
     6. Cab→Cba   *5 (Simp.)*
     7. Cba   *6, 1 (M.P.)*

(7) 1. Mas   *premise*
     2. Msr   *premise*
     3. (x)(y)(z)[(Mxy & Myz)→~Mxz   *premise /∴ ~Mar*
     4. (y)(z)[(May & Myz)→~Maz   *3 (UI)*
     5. (z)[(Mas & Msz)→~Maz]   *4 (UI)*
     6. (Mas & Msr)→~Mar   *5 (UI)*
     7. Mas & Msr   *1, 2 (C.A.)*
     8. ~Mar   *6, 7 (M.P.)*

Following are examples of increasingly complex arguments where the *property* of the relation is crucial:

(1) Sophomores are more knowledgeable than any freshman. Therefore, no sophomore is a freshman. Universe of discourse: *people*.

1. (x)(y)[(Sx & Fy)→Mxy]   *premise*
2. (x)~Mxx   *premise /∴ (x)(Sx→~Fx)*
3. (y)[(Sa & Fy)→May]   *1 (UI)*
4. (Sa & Fa)→Maa   *3 (UI)*
5. ~Maa   *2 (UI)*
6. ~(Sa & Fa)   *4, 5 (M.T.)*
7. ~Sa v ~Fa   *6 (D.M.)*
8. Sa→~Fa   *7 (M.I.)*
9. (x)(Sx→~Fx)   *8 (UG)*

(2) Any forward can out-jump any guard. Therefore, no guard can out-jump any forward. Universe of discourse: *people*.

1. (x)(y)[(Fx & Gy)→Oxy]   *premise*
2. (x)(y)(Oxy→~Oyx)   *premise /∴ (x)(y)[(Gx & Fy)→~Oxy]*

3. $(x)(y)[(Gy \& Fx) \rightarrow Oxy]$ *1 (Comm.)*
4. $(y)[(Gy \& Fa) \rightarrow Oay]$ *3 (UI)*
5. $(Gb \& Fa) \rightarrow Oab$ *4 (UI)*
6. $(y)(Oay \rightarrow \sim Oya$ *2 (UI)*
7. $Oab \rightarrow \sim Oba$ *6 (UI)*
8. $(Gb \& Fa) \rightarrow \sim Oba$ *5, 7 (C.S.)*
9. $(y)[(Gb \& Fy) \rightarrow \sim Oby]$ *8 (UG)*
10. $(x)(y)[(Gx \& Fy) \rightarrow \sim Oxy]$ *9 (UG)*

(3) Agnes was a partner of Sam. Any partner of Agnes made a lot of money. Therefore, Sam made a lot of money. Universe of discourse: *people*.

1. Pas *premise*
2. $(x)(Pxa \rightarrow Mx)$ *premise*
3. $(x)(y)(Pxy \rightarrow Pyx)$ *premise* /∴ Ms
4. $(y)(Pay \rightarrow Pya)$ *3 (UI)*
5. $Pas \rightarrow Psa$ *4 (UI)*
6. $Psa \rightarrow Ms$ *2 (UI)*
7. $Pas \rightarrow Ms$ *5, 6 (C.S.)*
8. Ms *7, 1 (M.P.)*

The second premise in '(1)' states that the relation 'more knowledgeable' is irreflexive. The second premise in '(2)' states that the relation 'can out-jump' is asymmetrical. The third premise in '(3)' states that the relation 'partner of' is symmetrical. Their presence makes the derivation of the conclusions possible.

Concluding Summary: Relational statements can be incorporated into the systems of propositional and quantificational logic and serve as expressions in formal proofs. The properties of the relations are often irrelevant to the proof. But when a property is relevant, an additional premise should be supplied setting forth the property that is essential to the proof.

EXERCISES

Exercise 71

Symbolize each of the following relational statements, taking people *as the universe of discourse wherever possible:*

1. Arnold emulates Richard.
2. Brenda introduced Carla to Denise.
3. Rockefeller is richer than anyone.
4. Everyone is loved by someone or another.
5. Every cause precedes its effect.
6. There is a novel with which everyone is acquainted.

7. Nobody likes everybody.
8. Good writers always have people who imitate them.
9. Smart men never imitate others.
10. It is a crime for anyone to assault someone.

Exercise 72

For each of the following binary relations, indicate, where possible, its symmetry, reflexivity, *and* transitivity:

1. . . . precedes . . .
2. . . . coincides with . . .
3. . . . stands beside . . .
4. . . . hates . . .
5. . . . is as smart as . . .
6. . . . is not as smart as . . .
7. . . . is grandfather of . . .
8. . . . attracts . . .
9. . . . searches for . . .
10. . . . controls . . .

Exercise 73

Construct formal proofs for the following arguments, taking people *as the universe of discourse wherever possible:*

1. Every Republican detests liberals. Bruce is a Republican. Ann is a liberal. Therefore, Bruce detests Ann.
2. There is a painting that every connoisseur covets, but George does not covet it. Therefore, George is not a connoisseur.
3. Fred is either taller than Del or he is heavier. Anyone taller than Del is a six-footer. Fred is not a six-footer. Therefore, Fred is heavier than Del.
4. Only a madman would plot to kidnap one of Henry's children. An associate of Henry plotted to kidnap Sam. None of Henry's associates is a madman. Sam, therefore, is not a child of Henry.
5. It is a sin to cheat anyone. Overcharging is a case of cheating. Therefore, if Bill overcharged Sue, Bill committed a sin.

Exercise 74

Supply the missing premise and construct a formal proof:

1. Harold plays bridge with all the females who are life-masters. Harold is a life-master. Therefore, Harold is a male.
2. Abraham is older than Jacob. Methuselah is older than Abraham. Therefore, Methuselah is older than Jacob.
3. All cities on the lake are north of Akron. Cleveland is on the lake. Therefore, Akron is not north of Cleveland. Universe of discourse: *cities.*

4. Helen is the spouse of Richard. Anyone who is lucky should be grateful. Any spouse of Helen is a lucky person. Richard, therefore, should be grateful.

5. George is the grandchild of Arnold. Arnold is the grandchild of Robert. Anyone who is not a grandchild of Robert is disinherited. George, therefore, is disinherited.

Chapter 8

Induction: Generalization

PREVIEW

In this chapter we begin the study of induction. The most elementary kind of inductive inference is that of generalization about a whole class on the basis of an examination of part of that class. We are never sure we are right, but there are principles which, when heeded, will improve our chances. Arguments from analogy derive what force they possess from the plausibility of an underlying generalization. That is why they are discussed in the same chapter. What are you expected to learn in this chapter?

1. How to recognize an analogy.
2. What uses an analogy may be put to.
3. How to bring out the generalization underlying an argument from analogy.
4. How to meet an argument from analogy.
5. How to distinguish inductive from mathematical probability.
6. How to distinguish an inductive generalization from a generalized description.
7. What a ''fair sample'' consists of.
8. What a ''random sample'' consists of.
9. How to stratify a sample.
10. How to evaluate the soundness of an inductive generalization.

Here is a ''warm-up'' quiz:

1. Do you think that the comparison of the American Civil War with the Revolutionary War is a good analogy?
2. Does it follow that if the first was defensible, then the second was also?
3. Could you generalize plausibly about Pakistanis on the basis of having met two of them in your chemistry lab?
4. Could you generalize plausibly about Pakistanis on the basis of having con-

ducted interviews with 100 of them who had just completed majoring in chemistry at your university?

5. If you were polling students about their views on abortion, would a group of members of the Newman Foundation constitute a good sample?

6. Mathematical probability is often calculated on the basis of relative frequency. Where do these relative frequency statements come from?

7. Would a fair sample of voters ("cross-section") with respect to one political issue necessarily be a fair sample with respect to some other issue?

8. Does a researcher or pollster ever know for sure that he or she has acquired a fair sample?

ANALOGIES AND ARGUMENTS

The Nature and Uses of Analogy

An analogy is a figure of speech in which two things are asserted to be alike in many respects that are quite fundamental. Their structure, the relationships of their parts, or the essential purposes they serve are similar, although the two things are also greatly dissimilar. Roses and carnations are not analogous. They both have stems and leaves, and may both be red in color. But they exhibit these qualities in the same way; they are of the same genus. The comparison of the heart to a pump, however, is a genuine analogy. These are disparate things, but they share important qualities: mechanical apparatus, possession of valves, ability to increase and decrease pressures, and capacity to move fluids. And the heart and the pump exhibit these qualities in different ways and in different contexts.

In discussing a crowded city, we do not offer an analogy when we compare it with another city. We are *merely* making a comparison. But if we compare the crowded city to an ant colony, we are setting forth an analogy. The two cities are not analogs; the city and the ant colony are. A ship manned by officers and a crew and crossing a stormy sea is a common analogy for a political state passing through perilous times. This is a popular analogy, for it brings out the striking similarities between two things notably dissimilar.

Like all figures of speech, the analogy serves rhetorical purposes. It enlivens discourse and may be used to stir the emotions. An analogy may, in addition, serve the descriptive function of giving a concrete and vivid simile for a concept that is too abstract or remote from ordinary experience to be clearly grasped.

Science classrooms find analogies indispensable. Everyone is familiar with the model (or analog) provided for chemical atoms: a nucleus containing neutrons and protons with the proper amount of electrons racing around it in one or more orbits. Another favorite is the analogical description of the behavior of molecules in solids, liquids, and gases:

We can form a rough human picture of what is going on in the following way. In a solid, the molecules can be pictured as a crowd of men all doing physical exercises—'the daily dozen'—without moving from the spot where they stand. If they have taken up their positions at random, we have a so-called amorphous or non-crystalline solid, such as glass or glue; if they are neatly drawn up in rows by a drill instructor, we have a crystalline structure, such as quartz or rock salt or washing-soda. In a liquid the molecules can be pictured as a swarm of men gathered together in a hall at a crowded reception; they are tightly wedged, but each one works his way through the others, with many a push and apology, and we cannot expect the same two men to be near each other all through the evening. . . . For a gas we have to think of a large open space on which men are walking without looking where they are going; each man continues in a straight line until he bumps into someone else, when he abruptly starts off again in a different direction.[1]

Analogies have performed a second useful function, that of suggesting hypotheses which can then be tested. The familiar analog for society—that it is a type of biological organism, persons being its cells, and that it is subject to certain diseases before it grows old and dies—has suggested several more concrete theories to social scientists. The venerable analogy that compares new leadership to a new broom which sweeps cleanly has obvious implications that could be tested. The analogy between bats' use of reflected sounds and the mechanical device called sonar suggests a theory on how they can fly in dark caves without hitting obstacles. The analogy between deliberate selection by breeders of animals in order to get a superior strain and the kind of selection exercised by the environment on wildlife in the struggle for existence, suggested to Charles Darwin that better qualities and new species may evolve in nature as the result of natural selection. But note that the truth of theories is not *established* by the analogy. Confirmation of the theory must be acquired independently of the analogy that suggested it.

Concluding Summary: Analogies are extended similes holding between two disparate things. They are useful in illuminating obscure conceptions and in suggesting ideas for further investigation.

Argument from Analogy

The argument from analogy consists of concluding that two things, which are alike in several respects, will also be alike in some specified further respect. It is based on a genuine analogy or a simple comparison. Some similarities are observed; another is inferred. Someone may argue that the wars and animosities among modern states are like gang wars in our cities. In both there are injuries and deaths, shifting alliances, peace treaties, and stockpiling of weapons: Since the way to eliminate

[1] Edward Andrade, *The Atom* (Tonbridge, England: Ernest Benn, Ltd., 1927), p. 18. Quoted in L. Susan Stebbing, *Thinking to Some Purpose* (Harmondsworth, England: Penguin Books, 1948), pp. 108–109.

gang warfare is to break up the gangs, the way to eliminate international warfare is to break up the modern states. The form of the argument is:

X and Y both have attributes w, x, and y
X is found, in addition, to possess attribute z
∴ Y possesses attribute z

An example of an argument from analogy based on a comparison is this: Leaf X and leaf Y have the same shade of green, grow in shady places, and have similar odors. Leaf X, in addition, has been found to cause an itching skin rash. Leaf Y, therefore, will cause an itching skin rash.

The argument from analogy obviously is not a valid deductive argument. The conclusion does not follow necessarily. It is not already implicit in the premises. It is possible for the premises to be true and the conclusion false. It *is* an argument, so can we call it a case of induction? Perhaps. But if it is an inductive argument, it is a very poor one indeed. It rests simply on the dubious principle that things resembling one another in some respects will be found to resemble one another—not simply in a fourth, but in a *specified* fourth respect. Now, further resemblance is certainly a possibility, but that it is any more than this is doubtful. Such premises as these do not justify, even in inductive inference, our calling the conclusion "probable."

To point out that premises like these offer no support at all for the conclusion should be enough in meeting an argument from analogy. What, we may ask, is the connection? Where is the support? How is the truth of the premises relevant to the truth of the conclusion? If two things are alike in three respects, they might be dissimilar in the next *ten* respects. The things are, after all, only analogous to one another, so the similarities may stop anywhere.

But this may be too abstract. There are two other ways of meeting an argument from analogy, both more rhetorical than simply refusing to see the relevance of the

> *Look round the world. Contemplate the whole and every part of it: You will find it to be nothing but one great machine, subdivided into an infinite number of lesser machines, which again admit of subdivisions. . . . All these various machines, and even their most minute parts, are adjusted to each other with an accuracy, which ravishes into admiration all men, who have ever contemplated them. The curious adapting of means to ends, throughout all nature, resembles exactly, though it much exceeds, the production of human contrivance; of human thought, wisdom, and intelligence. Since therefore the effects resemble each other, we are led to infer, by all the rules of analogy, that the causes also resemble; and that the Author of nature is somewhat similar to the mind of man; though possessed of much larger faculties, proportioned to the grandeur of the work, which he has executed. By this argument . . . and by this argument alone, we do prove at once the existence of a Diety, and his similarity to human mind and intelligence.*
> —*David Hume*, Dialogues Concerning Natural Religion (Cleanthes)

premises to the truth of the conclusion. The first consists of questioning the assumed resemblances. This is always possible in an analogy, for the two things are not put forward as identical. One could point out in the first example above that the one group has atomic weapons and the other does not; that there are police forces that can intimidate gangs but nothing comparable for intimidating nations; that gangs are small while nations are large; that gangs do not have the history, language, tradition, and patriotism that nations do; and so forth. In the second argument, one could point out the differences in the size of the leaves and the configuration made with other leaves of the same plant. It is not long before the proponent of the argument throws up his hands in disgust, snarling, "It's only an *analogy!*" To which the critic cheerfully assents, "Exactly."

The second rhetorical way of meeting an argument from analogy is just the opposite of the first. Here we agree that the two things are very similar indeed. Then we proceed to make *other* inferences about *other* similarities that the second must be expected to have to the first. The more ridiculous, the better, for the strategy here is to cause the proponent of the argument to disavow the analogy altogether.

David Hume, eighteenth-century British philosopher, employed this method with great success in *Dialogues Concerning Natural Religion.* Cleanthes had compared organisms in nature to human contrivances. There are the same adjustment of means to end, the same marks of intelligent planning. If the elements that constitute a watch could not have come together by chance, then surely natural objects, nature itself, and the whole universe—all much more complicated than a watch—must be the product of designing wisdom. Philo, speaking for Hume, accepts the analogy asserted to hold between man/contrivances and God/nature, and extends it until it boomerangs. Perhaps God made several worlds, some more botched than others. This one, being imperfect, suggests an intelligence like man's: limited. Perhaps God has abandoned this world—as men abandoned some of their contrivances. Men often create their things jointly: Carpenters, masons, and plumbers work together in building a house. Then we should infer that a group of gods got together to create the universe. Philo's flight into anthropomorphism challenges all the traditional attributes of God: his providence, his omnipotence, his omniscience, his unity, and his uniqueness. But it is *Cleanthes'* analogy that leads to all these blasphemous things. Philo is just more consistent in its use than Cleanthes. The strategy here is to show what *else* the analogy leads to so that its proponent will abandon it.

Concluding Summary: The illegitimate use of analogy is to base an argument on it. Two things are observed to be analogous, so it is argued that, since one is like the other in some respects, it will be like it in some other specific respect. There is no cogency to such an argument. If its proponent will not agree, one may

---

Similes are like songs in love:
They must describe; they nothing prove.

—*Matthew Prior,* Alma

employ rhetorical devices against him or her: (1) Emphasize all the dissimilarities in the analogous objects. (2) Accept the similarities and claim some more, more than your opponent is willing to accept.

The Underlying Generalization

Despite the absence of force in the argument from analogy, it is very popular. Taking argument from analogy in the broadest sense, it seems almost impossible to refrain from employing it. It seems to be the most simple and natural way of learning from experience. And if we can't learn from experience, what can we learn from? We see a leaf like another leaf that gave us ivy poisoning. Can't we infer, inductively, that this leaf can give us ivy poisoning also? The child experiences fire and is burned. The next time he encounters a phenomenon similar to the first one, he stays away from it. We see a round object with twelve numbers and two hands. We infer on the basis of its similarities to other objects we have experienced that it was designed to tell time. Isn't all this the inductive method at its plainest and most useful?

This kind of reasoning has force only when made in the light of an implicit generalization. Our conclusion that this leaf will give us ivy poisoning could be derived from an unstated premise that *all* leaves with these characteristics produce ivy poisoning. Our conclusion that this fire will burn is not simply based on its resemblance to another fire which burned, but on an implied generalization that all fire burns. The conclusion is a *deductive* one from a general premise which itself was an inductive conclusion. The form of the reasoning is:

We really, then, are subsuming the particular event under a whole class of similar events rather than making an analogical comparison with one.

It is natural in refuting analogical arguments to bring out this underlying generalization for scrutiny. Someone says: "Stanley and Eugene are both Slobovians. Stanley is lazy, so Eugene is too." We instinctively retort, "Are you maintaining that *all* Slobovians are lazy?" Only thus can the conclusion have any force. Cleanthes' argument has force only if he is willing to generalize that all (or most) objects whose parts are related in such a way as to serve a useful function have been designed or created by an intelligent mind.

There is nothing in which an untrained mind shows itself more hopelessly incapable, than in drawing the proper conclusions from its own experience.
—John Stuart Mill, Inaugural Address at Saint Andrews

That the final inference is a deductive one should not obscure the fact that some induction took place before we arrived at it. Induction enabled us to get at the underlying generalization. If, on the basis of the evidence, we are confident that the generalization is true, we may repose the same degree of confidence in the truth of the conclusion we validly deduce from it. If we have reason to be doubtful of the truth of that generalization, we should be equally doubtful about the truth of anything we deduce from it. The real concern with an "analogical argument," then, should be with the soundness of the underlying generalization. And that is the topic of the next part of this chapter.

It should be noted here that the generalization does not have to be a universal generalization. Premises of the form 'All X are Y' and 'No A are B' do yield categorical conclusions, and we can be as sure of the truth of these conclusions as we are of that of the premises. But 'Most C's are D' and '76 percent of E's are F' are also generalizations from which consequences can be drawn. And here, as was shown in the last part of the sixth chapter, mathematical probability enters into the picture to take its place beside the inductive probability that is attached to the drawing of the generalization itself.

Concluding Summary: Many inductive arguments, although not really based upon analogies and often involving comparison of the thing concluded about with more than one entity, are called analogical arguments. Whatever strength such arguments possess derives from an underlying generalization. The generalization, whether backed by strong or weak inductive evidence, is then used as a premise for a deductive argument.

Judging Analogical Arguments

The various criteria offered for "appraising analogical arguments" are really criteria for judging the soundness of their underlying generalizations.

(1) The greater the resemblance between the things compared, the more likely the conclusion. This is also to say that the greater the dissimilarity between them, the less likely the conclusion. The better the analogy, the stronger the argument. What this principle does is to say that two things which share essential qualities are likely to be of the same species and thus instances of several generalizations. If two instances of liquid are of the same color, weight, temperature, volume, and chemical composition, they are so close to being identical that what is said about one could be said about the other. If this cup of water quenches thirst, then that one will too, for it seems to be the same substance. If differences are noted (for instance, this water has salt dissolved in it and that water does not), drawing the conclusion becomes more risky.

According to the first criterion, the evidence in argument 2 is better than that in argument 1:

1. *X* and *Y* have attributes *a, b,* and *c*
   X also has attribute *q*
   ∴ *Y* has attribute *q*

2. *X* and *Y* have attributes *a, b, c, d, e,* and *f*
   X also has attribute *q*
   ∴ *Y* has attribute *q*

In both arguments, what really makes the conclusion follow is the generalizations, respectively, that whatever has attributes *a, b,* and *c* also has *q,* and that whatever has attributes *a, b, c, d, e,* and *f* also has *q.*

Employing this criterion, we will be less worried about getting ivy poisoning if the leaves we touch grow in clusters of *five* instead of clusters of *three* (which was the case the last time we got ivy poisoning). We will be more confident of getting good service from a TV set that is of the same brand and model as one that gave us good service before than if we had switched. If the beef Stroganoff dinner was delicious last week, we expect the same if we order it again at the same restaurant on a night when the same chef is on duty and we have the same drinks beforehand.

(2) The greater the number of things compared, the more likely the conclusion. The importance of the underlying generalization is even more obvious in this criterion. Indeed, if the argument from analogy is still present, it is a strange one, for we are comparing more than two entities! The criterion is a legitimate one simply because it indicates that the generalization will be stronger if it is based on a greater number of entities. My generalization that all white blue-eyed tomcats are deaf is stronger if based upon the examination of sixteen such cats than if I had only examined one.

According to this criterion, the evidence in argument 2 is better than that in argument 1:

1. *X* and *Y* have attributes *a, b,* and *c*
   X also has attribute *q*
   ∴ *Y* has attribute *q*

2. *V, W, X,* and *Y* have attributes *a, b,* and *c*
   V, W, and *X* also have attribute *q*
   ∴ *Y* has attribute *q*

In both arguments, what really makes the conclusion follow is the underlying generalization that whatever has qualities *a, b,* and *c* also has the quality *q.* And we have a little more evidence for this generalization in 2 than in 1.

Employing this criterion, we are more willing to predict that the next crow will be black if we have seen two hundred black crows than if we had only seen two. If we have known three young, white film actresses and they were all conceited, we might predict that Eloise, a young, white film actress will be conceited also. But we would make this prediction with more confidence if we had known several dozen young, white film actresses, all conceited. If we know that a basketball player has made 98 out of 100 free throws, we are on firmer ground in predicting that he will make his next one than if we knew only that he had made his last one. In this case, 98 percent is stronger evidence than 100 percent.

(3) The greater the diversity among the things that the particular instance is compared with, the more likely the conclusion. This criterion, like the others, actually points to the unstated generalization. Is it based on examination of the many subclasses of the class in question? Does it take into account what may be a very heterogeneous group of entities? My prediction that Eloise will be conceited is better if I have knowledge of serious actresses as well as comic ones, leading ladies as well as supporting players, European as well as American. This is so because the generalization is made on the basis of a varied set of instances.

According to this criterion, the evidence in 2 is better than that in 1:

1. X_1, X_2, X_3, and Y have attributes a, b, and c
   X_1, X_2, X_3 also have attribute q
   ∴ Y has attribute q

2. V, W, X, and Y have attributes a, b, and c
   V, W, and X also have attribute q
   ∴ Y has attribute q

In both arguments, what really makes the conclusion follow is the underlying generalization that all or most of the class we are talking about has the attribute q. Its dissimilar members in 2 support the conclusion better than its similar members in 1.

We should be careful not to confuse criterion (1) with criterion (3). The first criterion tells us that dissimilarity between the thing concluded about and the things that we already have knowledge of *weakens* the argument. But the third criterion tells us that dissimilarities among the things we already have knowledge of *strengthens* the argument. If Chevrolets, Oldsmobiles, Buicks, and Cadillacs tend to have faulty cooling systems, we have more reason to believe that *this* General Motors car, which happens to be a Pontiac, has the same fault than if we had only examined Chevrolets.[2] If a filly has run well on wet tracks *and* dry tracks, we will have more confidence that she will do well next month than if we knew only that she had done well on dry tracks.

(4) The greater the scope of the entities compared with, relative to that of the thing concluded about, the more likely the conclusion. Suppose that Hayes University has won all its games by at least five touchdowns. We predict that it will win its next one by at least three points. This is more likely than that it will again win by five touchdowns.

---

[2] We are not in this example arguing from a comparison of *subclasses* of GM cars: we are arguing from a comparison of individuals that happen to be in different subclasses. From the supposed "facts" provided in the example, it would seem that a GM car is likely to have cooling problems *whatever* subclass it may belong to. This is, incidentally, only a contrived example; the author does not wish to assert *anything* about GM cars.

According to this criterion, the evidence in 2 better supports the conclusion than that in 1:

1. W, X, and Y have attributes a, b, and c
   $\underline{W \text{ and } X \text{ also have attribute } q \text{ (to a great degree)}}$
   $\therefore$ Y has attribute q (to a great degree)

2. W, X, and Y have attributes a, b, and c
   $\underline{W \text{ and } X \text{ also have attribute } q \text{ (to a great degree)}}$
   $\therefore$ Y has attribute q (to some degree or other)

In both arguments, what really makes a conclusion follow is the generalization that all or most of the things that have a, b, and c also have q to a great degree. From this it is a more modest inference that something else in this class will have the quality to at least *some* degree than that it will have it to a great degree. A safety margin is provided.

Employing this criterion, I will be more certain that the old bridge will support an automobile than another bus, more confident that Beatrice will at least pass her engineering course than that she will get her fifth straight 'A,' and more confident that I will get at least twenty miles per gallon on my next trip in the car that averaged thirty-five miles a gallon on previous trips than that I will get at least thirty miles per gallon.

Concluding Summary: The four criteria with which to evaluate the strength of analogical arguments all pertain to the degree of support that the data afford for the underlying generalization. The positive criteria for good analogical arguments are: (1) the number of respects in which the thing concluded about is similar to the other entities; (2) the number of other entities that the thing concluded about is compared with; (3) the number of dissimilarities among the entities that the thing concluded about is compared with; (4) the greater the scope of the entities relative to the scope of the thing concluded about.

A servant who was roasting a stork for his master was prevailed by his sweetheart to cut off a leg for her to eat. When the bird came upon the table, the master desired to know what had become of the other leg. The man answered that storks had never more than one leg. The master, very angry, but determined to strike his servant dumb before he punished him, took him next day into the fields where they saw storks, standing each on one leg, as storks do. The servant turned triumphantly to his master, on which the latter shouted and the birds put down their other legs and flew away. 'Ah sir,' said the servant. 'you did not shout to the stork at dinner yesterday; if you had done so, he would have shown his other leg too.'
    —De Morgan, quoted by Morris R. Cohen and Ernest Nagel, Logic and
Scientific Method

EXERCISES

Exercise 75

State whether the analogies in the passages are used to illuminate a concept, inspire a hypothesis, or serve as the basis of an argument:

1. "Eighteen hundred years ago, Marcus Aurelius, a great and wise Roman emperor, wrote these words: 'Do not be ashamed of being helped. It is incumbent upon you to do your appointed work, like a soldier in the breach. What if you are lame and cannot scale the battlement alone, but can with another's help?' This thought seems particularly applicable to the trained expectant mother. She, too, if she conscientiously does her 'appointed work' must feel no sense of inadequacy because she cannot do it alone; neither should she feel defeat if she does not attain the full goal which she has ambitiously set for herself." Herbert Thoms, *Understanding Natural Childbirth* (New York: McGraw-Hill Book Company, 1950), p. 6.

2. "Each sperm looks somewhat like a tiny tadpole, but it is even more microscopic than the egg. The sperm can wiggle along with a tadpolelike movement, traveling an inch or two per hour. After being deposited in the vagina, they immediately begin to travel under their own power to the place where the egg may be found." *Ibid.*, p. 18.

3. "The success of labor depends upon the mother grasping her reactions and feelings and realizing that labor calls for control and skill and, like other physical feats, is a character-building undertaking." Helen Heardman, quoted in *ibid.*, p. 45.

4. "An athlete in the excitement of contest is often unaware of injuries which otherwise would cause acute suffering. The athlete under these conditions may be tense about his part in the contest, but he is not tense about his own welfare. Thus, it is easy to understand why some women have more discomfort than others during labor. The anxious, tense woman in labor experiences more discomfort for the very reason that she is chiefly apprehensive about her own safety." *Ibid.*, p. 60.

5. "Nothing in the life of a man or a woman is going to be as important to themselves or to society as their parenthood. It seems reasonable, then, that prospective parents should apply at least as much intelligence and foresight to this as to designing a home, buying furniture, planning a vacation, or perhaps even choosing a career. Knowledge and thought can be applied to the production of a family with at least as much prospect of success as in the case of any other human activity." John Rock and David Loth, quoted in *ibid.*, p. 93.

Exercise 76

State whether the analogies in the following passages are used to illuminate a concept, inspire a hypothesis, or serve as the basis of an argument:

1. You want to know how I feel at income tax time? I feel like the stone crabs off the Florida coast. People like to eat their claws, so they catch the crabs, rip off one of their claws, and throw the mutilated animal back into the ocean. The stone crab is expected to survive and grow back its claw—before it's caught again. (Suggested by *Bloom County,* March 13, 1988.)

2. Paul Kennedy, in *The Rise and Fall of the Great Powers,* described powerful states of the past: the Spain of Philip II, the Russia of Nicholas II, the Germany of Hitler, and several others. These leaders made the ruinous mistake of permitting their economic base to deteriorate while increasing their military expenditures. They took on too much global responsibility and invested in the wrong things. I wonder whether there is a lesson for the United States here.

3. Running for President in this country is like competing in a marathon race. You have to train and get yourself in good shape. You have to be careful to husband your money, just as the racer must husband his energy. You've got to save something for a strong finish. You must resist all temptations to stray from the course you have set for yourself. It's a long and lonely ordeal. But at the end, when you stand in the winner's circle, you realize that all the work and discipline and pain were worth it.

4. Finding a man you want to marry is like choosing a car. You have to decide whether you want a new or "pre-owned" one. You have to figure out how much a spouse will cost you—in terms of money and freedom. Do you want a flashy and sporty model or a steady and dependable one? Do you want a domestic product or something exotic from Italy, Norway, or Japan? The parallels are endless. Therefore, you should be very careful: Look over the whole field and do not be swept off your feet by the first attractive man who offers you a good deal!

5. Learning to fly an airplane is like learning to ride a bike—although it may take a little longer. A certain speed is necessary before either bike or plane can maintain its course, and you have to learn what that speed is. You have to learn how steeply you can safely bank. You have to learn how to deal with variable wind conditions. The hardest thing of all is to master the technique of terminating things: the ride or the flight. For a bike, you have to come to a smooth halt without tipping over the vehicle, then safely alight. It's very similar for a plane. Both vehicles sail along gracefully, but tend to become awkward and unwieldly when the trip is over.

Exercise 77

Show how you would meet these arguments from analogy by either questioning the assumed resemblances or extending the analogy:

1. Human beings are much like dogs—some specimens are better than others and some strains are better than others. We can improve the quality of canine varieties by selective breeding, so we should do the same with human beings.

2. Sure, people get hurt and lives are ruined in a period of rapid economic growth. But this is unavoidable. You can't make an omelet without breaking eggs.

3. The reserve rule which operates in professional sports sets up a system of slavery. Players are bought and sold and sent from team to team and from league to league without consultation. Since slavery is wrong, the reserve clause in the contracts should be forbidden by law. Make the players free men so they can make their own deals. We need another emancipation proclamation!

4. Bridge partnerships are like marriages. You argue a lot and try to iron out differences. And it is very important that the partners trust one another. Since sexual infidelity damages a marriage, a bridge partner should never play with anyone else.

5. An objective study of various forms of animal life reveals that cooperation with members of the same species is characteristic of normal existence. Since man is so similar to the other animals, and since "mutual aid" works for them, mutual aid or socialism would be best for human beings.

Exercise 78

For each of the following analogical arguments, state the underlying generalization:

1. A man, like an ape, is a primate. Apes subsist largely on fruit and vegetables, so man should do so also.

2. Western countries were interlocked into complicated systems of alliances before World War I. Western nations again are entangled in complicated alliances. Since the first was followed by war, the present situation will also lead to war.

3. A nation is like a family in many ways. They are both groups of individuals related by blood or interest. A nation is best governed by elected, rather than hereditary, rulers. The same principle should apply in families. The father is not necessarily the best leader.

4. Bikes and cars are modes of transportation. You have to pass tests in order to get a license and operate a car. Therefore you should have to do the same in order to operate a bike.

5. "Anything Goes" has clever lyrics. So does "You're the Tops." And "I Get a Kick out of You," another Cole Porter song, has clever lyrics. I don't know the words to "Begin the Beguine," but I bet they're clever too.

6. Exercises 49, 51, and 53 in this book were easy. This is an odd-numbered exercise in the same book. So it is probably easy also.

Exercise 79

Indicate whether each change strengthens or weakens the analogical argument, and give the number of the criterion (as listed on p. 250) that applies.

1. You have bought medium-priced dress shirts at Armando's on three occasions. Each time they wore well. So you go back back again to buy medium-priced dress shirts, inferring that they too will wear well.
   (a) Suppose that you had bought shirts there on six occasions, rather than three, with the same results.
   (b) Suppose that you buy low-priced dress shirts this time.
   (c) Suppose that you infer that the shirts will wear fairly well.
   (d) Suppose that the sport shirts you had purchased also wore well.
2. The first book by Smythe that you read was set in Stuart England and was about a duke and a servant girl. The next one you read was about a count and a peasant girl in eighteenth-century France. And the third novel by Smythe was set in Renaissance Italy and told the story of a prince and a bondsmaid. You buy a fourth book, *Polish Passion,* expecting it to be a historical novel about a dashing nobleman and a poor but worthy young woman.
   (a) Suppose that this book, unlike the others, was written in Smythe's old age.
   (b) Suppose you found out by reading a review that an earlier book by Smythe had the same elements as those in the books you have read.
   (c) Suppose that this book was published by the same company as the others.
   (d) Suppose that you merely infer that this novel will have a European setting.
3. You have found a flint axe head on a hillside. It is similar in shape, size, and material to one possessed by the museum. You are told that the museum's axe head was made in the fifteenth century. So you conclude that yours was too.
   (a) Suppose that the museum's axe head was found in a river valley.
   (b) Suppose that the museum has six others of different shape, all of which are dated in the fifteenth century.
   (c) Suppose that the one you found was more like an arrowhead.
   (d) Suppose that both specimens were faintly striated.

DRAWING GENERALIZATIONS

Inductive Generalizations and Probability

Having seen the importance of generalization in so-called analogical reasoning, we should look more closely at the nature and types of generalization.

The basic distinction is that between *generalized description* and *inductive generalization*. A generalized description is one that is based on knowledge of every particular member of the class generalized about. The parent who says, "All of my children are boys," has made a generalized description (provided he knows all of his children).

The performer who counts the house and says, "Sixty-one percent of the audience were in formal attire," has made a generalized description. and so has the disappointed diver who, after completing his examination, says, "none of these oysters has a pearl in it." Such generalizations are arrived at by observation and calculation. They are sometimes called "pseudo-generalizations." Aristotle called them cases of "perfect induction"; by this he meant a *completed* examination or enumeration of all members of the class. But if there is inference involved in generalized description or "generalization by enumeration" (as it is sometimes called), it is deductive in nature.

The kind of generalization we are concerned with here is inductive. When we say something about the class as a whole on the basis of having examined only a part of it, we are stating an inductive generalization. Inductive generalization is resorted to when the class is so large or so scattered that it would be impossible or impractical to examine every member (grains of wheat in this elevator), or when the class is not complete during the investigators' lifetime (crows), or when the class, though manageable in size, is such that examination of its members consumes them (whether all or some percentage of the jelly beans are delicious). Examples of inductive generalizations are:

> All trees are less than two hundred feet tall.
> Seventy-five percent of all people are right-handed.
> No crows are chartreuse.
> Most houses are insulated.
> All these matches will light.

These are all inductive conclusions, so the best that can be said for them is that they are *probably* true. Deductive conclusions must be true whenever their premises are. But even if we grant the truth of all the premises for these *inductive* conclusions, we must still be uncertain about the truth of the conclusion. While the premises are true, the generalization *could* be false.

What are the premises (or evidence) for these inductive generalizations? Above, it was said that only part of the class was examined. Ordinarily the premises consist of singular statements attributing or denying the quality in questions to particular members of the class being generalized about:

> (1) This tree is less than two hundred feet tall
> That tree is less than two hundred feet tall
> That other tree is less than two hundred feet tall
> ∴ All trees are less than two hundred feet tall

> (2) Bill is right-handed
> Janet is right-handed
> Kathleen is left-handed
> Ann is right-handed
> ∴ Seventy-five percent of all people are right-handed

(3) This crow is not chartreuse
That crow is not chartreuse
That other crow is not chartreuse
∴ No crows are chartreuse

(4) My house is insulated
Your house is insulated
His house is insulated
∴ Most houses are insulated

(5) One hundred percent of the candies in the first box contains milk chocolate
One hundred percent of the candies in the second box contains milk chocolate
One hundred percent of the candies in the third box contain milk chocolate
∴ One hundred percent of the boxes contain candies one hundred percent of which contain milk chocolate

No attempt is made to get a complete account. On the basis of what is known about a part of the class, a conclusion is drawn about the class as a whole.

Like all inductive conclusions, generalizations are based on the facts but go *beyond* the facts. Some go too hastily beyond the facts. The inference is made without due caution. Some conclusions are more warranted than others. Any inductive argument could be conducted less well, in which case its conclusion would be less probable. And it can be carried out in a better manner also, in which case it would be more probable. The evidence offered in the premises can, in short, be weaker or stronger. Although we may not be able to assign a precise degree of probability, we do have more confidence in some conclusions than in others—and justifiably so.[3]

In all the arguments above there could have been more premises or instances. Three or four instances do not make a very large sample from which to generalize. If, in (2), five thousand people had been tested for right/left-handedness instead of just four, the conclusion would have been more probable. If, in (4), houses had been selected from different neighborhoods, the conclusion would have been more probable.

(5) seems to contradict the view that premises of inductive generalizations are always singular statements. Relative to the conclusion they are singular, for each is concerned about *one* of the boxes of candy that is the subject of the conclusion. If

> *Science, though it starts from observation of the particular, is not concerned with the particular, but with the general. A fact, in science, is not a mere fact, but an instance.*
>
> —*Bertrand Russell,* The Scientific Outlook

[3] For an attempt to assign degrees of probability to inductive conclusions, see Rudolf Carnap, "Statistical and Inductive Probability," in Edward H. Madden, *The Structure of Scientific Thought* (Boston: Houghton Mifflin Company, 1960), pp. 269–279.

the conclusion had been weaker in scope, it would have been more probable: 'All the boxes contain candies most of which contain milk chocolate' or 'Most of the boxes contain candies one hundred percent of which contain milk chocolate.'

The probability can be increased in many arguments by weakening the conclusion somewhat. No matter how careful we are in gathering evidence for the conclusion in (2), we can't believe that the percentage of right-handers in the world will *exactly* conform to the sample. But if we said that the percentage is *around* 75 percent, it would be more probable than to insist that it is exactly 75 percent. And if we are willing to say merely, as was done with houses in (4), that *most* people are right-handed, the probability would greatly increase.

We can also, although less easily, compare arguments about different things as to more or less probability. For example, if the generalization in (1) had been based on knowledge of millions of trees in every time period, geographic area, climate, and elevation, it would have been more probable than the conclusion drawn in argument (3).

The inductive probability of an inductive generalization is determined by the answer to this question: How confident are we that the sample we have examined is representative of the class as a whole? Whatever the answer is, it cannot easily be quantified. This holds for all inductive conclusions, whether generalizations, causal statements, or hypotheses in the narrow sense. If additional evidence is acquired which confirms an inductive conclusion, we tend to say it is more probably true. Evidence that supports a universal generalization increases its probability; evidence that is counter to that generalization destroys its probability. Evidence relevant to a generalization that is less than universal either confirms it or causes us to adjust the percentage. But, again, no precise degree can be assigned to inductive probability. Generalizations, unless they are simply calculations about what we have observed, possess in some vague sense *greater* or *less* inductive probability.

Mathematical probability, however, as we saw in the previous chapter, can be assigned degrees, for it is calculated from a priori possibilities and empirical frequencies. A statement expressing mathematical probability is deduced from these data and (in some cases) an additional assumption. Although the premise in such an argument may be a relative frequency statement which is an inductive generalization, the conclusion that expresses the mathematical probability of a particular event taking place is derived deductively. For example:

> Eighty-four percent of all women who have reached the age of thirty-five between the years of 1940 and 1970 have lived to see their forty-fifth birthday. (inductive generalization indicating relative frequency)
>
> The future will resemble the past (assumption)
> Helen is thirty-five years old
> ───────────────────────────
> ∴ The probability of Helen reaching forty-five is .84

How sure we are about the truth of the conclusion is relative to our confidence in the truth of our premises. If the first premise had been a generalized description instead of an inductive generalization, our doubt about the truth of the conclusion would be less. In any case, however, the conclusion follows deductively.

General statements often serve as premises of deductive arguments. Our confidence in the truth of the deductive conclusion is conditioned by our sense of confidence in the truth of these statements. Let us look at some examples of inductive conclusions (generalizations) and generalized descriptions serving as premises of deductive arguments:

(1) All phrenaxes are black
     Hubert is a phrenaxis
  ∴ Hubert is black

(2) No white blue-eyed tomcats can hear
     Reginald is a white blue-eyed tomcat
  ∴ Reginald cannot hear

(3) Seventy-five percent of all people are right-handed
     Susan is a person
  ∴ The probability of Susan being right-handed is .75

(4) Most houses are insulated
     The little house on the prairie is a house
  ∴ The little house on the prairie is probably insulated

(5) Fifty percent of the people in this room are right-handed
     Lou Boudreau is in this room
  ∴ The probability of Lou Boudreau being right-handed is .50

(6) Eighty-six percent of all people who have held power have been corrupted by it
     Suleiman the Magnificent held power
  ∴ Suleiman the Magnificent was probably corrupted by power

(7) Ninety-seven percent of all attempts of Legs Watson to steal a base have been successful
     Legs Watson is attempting to steal a base now
  ∴ The probability of Watson succeeding is .97

How sound was the inductive inference which gave us the major premise in (1)? If the inductive procedures were good, then its truth is probable, and since there is no doubt that Hubert is a phrenaxis, the deductive conclusion is probable. The probability of the conclusion is just as great as that of the major premise.

The major premise in (2) is also an inductive generalization. To the degree that it is probably true, to that degree can we be sure that Reginald is deaf, since it is certain that he is a white blue-eyed tomcat.

In (3) we again have inductive probability involved in the major premise. But the probability mentioned in the conclusion is mathematical probability. If the major premise was not drawn in the light of approved methods for good generalizing, the relative frequency claimed is erroneous, and the mathematical probability validly deduced from it erroneous as well. In any case, the certainty that Susan is right-handed is conditioned by two types of probability.

(4) is also a case of mathematical probability occurring along with inductive probability. How careful was the observer in ensuring that the sample was representative of the whole? If the major premise is probably true, the conclusion that the little house on the prairie has a mathematical probability of more than .50 of being insulated is probably true.

The major premise in (5) looks like a calculated (or generalized) description. So if we assume correct computation and the presence of Lou in the room, it is necessarily true that the mathematical probability of his being right-handed is .50.

The conclusion in (6) asserts that the mathematical probability of Suleiman being corrupted by power is more than .50. We can accept this mathematical probability to the degree that it is *inductively* probable that the major premise (an inductive generalization) is within 35 points or so of the truth.

The first premise in (7) is a generalized description expressing relative frequency. The conclusion is a statement of mathematical probability. We can be confident that it is true, provided that we are sure that the premises and the unstated assumption that the future resembles the past are true.

Concluding Summary: Inductive generalizations, in making assertions about a whole class, go beyond the evidence. They possess greater or less inductive probability, depending upon the relative strength of the evidence from which they are derived. Inductive probability cannot easily be assigned precise degrees, but comparisons can be made between stronger and weaker inductive arguments. When generalizations are employed as premises of deductive arguments, their strength or probability conditions the confidence that one may have in the truth of the deductive conclusion.

Size of the Sample

Since we cannot examine the entire class (as we do when we are making a generalized description), we are dependent on a sample of that class. And we hope that what we find to be true of the sample will also be true of the whole "population." If this is so, the sample is a fair sample. A *fair sample* is a section of a class which is representative of that whole class. It is the basis for a sound inductive generalization.

How do we know whether the sample is fair? We don't, for to know this we would have to know what the whole class is, and we would not *need* a sample. But there are deliberate steps we can take to increase the likelihood that the sample is not greatly unrepresentative. When we are oblivious to these concerns, we commit the inductive fallacy of "hasty generalization."

The first concern that should be heeded is this: Is the sample large enough? Have we examined enough of the population we are generalizing about? If we are generalizing about the television preferences of the American people, a sample of 36 seems to be too small, while 36,000,000 seems to be needlessly large. But it is difficult to say exactly how large the sample should be.

Size of sample cannot be expressed as a percentage, for who would know how many crows or swans there are in the world—past, present, and future? And if we don't know the total population, we could not calculate the proper size for the sample. More important, however, the required sample size varies with the nature of the population and the properties we are generalizing about. If the class or population is drops of water and we want to generalize about their reaction with sodium, we would be satisfied with a very small sample. Perhaps even one! But if we are dealing with the class of registered Democrats and want to know their views on the busing issue, we would want a larger sample. In the first case, a smaller sample will do, for the population is homogeneous. But when the population is heterogeneous, as in the second case, the sample must be larger. Kinsey in his study of sexual behavior was quite aware of the heterogeneity of the human populations he was studying. In his first "report," *Sexual Behavior in the Human Male,* Kinsey used a sample of 12,000. He thought it was large enough; many of his critics thought it was not.

Size is relative not only to the diversity of the population but also to the characteristics generalized about. Although drops of water seem to constitute a homogeneous population, we would have to get a fairly large sample if we wanted to find out how much of it in this lake, for instance, is below 70° F in temperature. Relative to chemical reactions, water drops are homogeneous; relative to its temperature, water drops in a lake are heterogeneous. If we are concerned with sexual behavior, the human male is a heterogeneous population. But relative, say, to how many ribs are possessed, the population seems quite homogeneous.

There is a hint of "begging the question" in this talk of homogeneity. It is true that the more we know beforehand about a population and the qualities of its members, the more effectively we can conduct our sampling procedures.

There is room in all this for honest difference of opinion. Producers of the television programs that have been canceled insist that the sample used by the Nielsen people is too small. Yet the television networks that pay dearly and pay often for the Nielsen reports apparently believe the sample is large enough. And the successful shows do not complain.

There is one way by which we can get some idea on whether the sample is large enough. It can be applied to many, but not all, problems of generalization. It is best expressed in terms of drawing jelly beans out of a very large jar.

Suppose we take several samples from the jar. We examine each sample, put the beans back in the jar, and shake the jar well. Suppose that the results are as follows:

Size of first sample: 10.
Composition: 3 red (30%), 5 white (50%), 2 blue (20%).

Size of second sample: 25.
Composition: 3 red (12%), 20 white (80%), 2 blue (8%).

Size of third sample: 50.
Composition: 12 red (24%), 30 white (60%), 8 blue (16%).

Size of fourth sample: 100.
Composition: 20 red (20%), 70 white (70%), 10 blue (10%).

Size of fifth sample: 150.
Composition: 29 red (19.3%), 106 white (70.7%), 15 blue (10%).

Size of sixth sample: 175.
Composition: 34 red (19.4%), 122 white (69.7%), 19 blue (10.9).

The last three draws have yielded similar results. There would seem to be no point in increasing the size of the sample. The errors brought in by samples that are too small have been eliminated. If large samples tend to repeat the composition found in smaller ones, we might just as well stop and save ourselves additional trouble. In the fourth try, we had apparently obtained a reasonably fair sample.

Concluding Summary: A fair sample is one that is representative of the whole population. For a sample to be fair, it must be large enough. The nature of the population and the traits we are generalizing about are relevant to the question of how large the sample should be. One practical way that is sometimes available for determining when to stop is to increase the size to that point where the results stabilize.

Randomness of the Sample

In conducting the examination of the jelly beans in the previous example we were careful to shake the jar thoroughly before removing the samples. We wanted every bean to have an equal chance of being selected. We did not want those beans which we had just put back to be on top and hence selected again.

It is an assumption in inductive generalization that the sample, if large enough, will be representative of the whole if pure chance or randomness is permitted to operate. If there are no factors at work to "load" the sample or distort it, it will be a fair one and thus the basis for a good generalization. If we had a card for each entity of the population and shuffled the cards well (as a data processing machine might do), those that are "dealt" would constitute a random sample.

If we are conducting a poll on attitudes toward the Equal Rights Amendment and choose our sample from among people shopping in grocery stores in midafternoon, we have interfered with randomness. Men would not be fairly represented, for there are not very many in grocery stores in midafternoon. They would not have an equal chance of being selected. Our sample is biased, for sexual differences are quite possibly linked to viewpoints on the proposed amendment.

We cannot generalize accurately about bird populations in Madison County if we observe only those birds on the shores of Dunlap Lake. If we are studying views about abortion, our sample is biased if it consists solely of Roman Catholic priests.

If we are trying to generalize about the quality of air over Akron, our sample has to include more than specimens taken from above the tire factory on South Main Street.

One of the greatest debacles in poll-taking history occurred in 1936 when the *Literary Digest* predicted that Alfred Landon would defeat President Franklin D. Roosevelt. The sample was enormous, almost two and one-half million. But the individuals polled were drawn from lists of automobile owners and telephone subscribers. This was not a random selection from American voters, for the people without cars or telephones (and in 1936 this was a sizable number) did not have an equal chance of being included in the sample. And, as it happened, this economic factor had direct bearing on political preferences. The great size of the sample was not enough to overcome its bias or lack of randomness. Roosevelt buried Landon in one of the greatest landslides in election history. And the *Literary Digest* went out of existence.

What may bias a sample with respect to one generalization might be irrelevant to another. If we are generalizing about the incidence of left-handedness, it would not be a serious flaw if it turned out to be the case that no people between the ages of thirty and thirty-nine were in the sample. This failure in randomness is not serious, for we cannot imagine how age would make any difference. But if we are generalizing about the incidence of marital infidelity and found that people in their thirties were missing from the sample, we would be upset, for being in this age group may well have a bearing on marital infidelity. This failure in randomness will almost certainly distort our results.

Concluding Summary: A random sample is one for which every individual of the population has an equal chance of being selected. It is believed that a random sample, if large enough, will be representative of the whole and thus be a fair sample.

Stratifying the Sample

If we are generalizing about all the swans or crows in the world, or about the American human male, or Caucasian females, or college graduates, we cannot make cards for each individual and put them in an automatic shuffler. We cannot, in other words, ensure randomness.

We can, as was shown above, try to eliminate conditions that might interfere with randomness and produce a biased sample. We will not limit our sample to Presbyterians if we are studying birth control. We will not exclude Cadillac owners if we are studying political views. We will not ignore Russian wolves when studying the predatory habits of wolves. We will not overlook Indians if we intend to talk about the religious preferences of Americans. But all this is preventive and negative.

Science is nothing but trained and organized common sense.
—*T. H. Huxley*. On the Educational Value of the Natural History Sciences

A more positive and deliberate way to ensure randomness is to stratify the population. If we were to buy a barrel of potatoes, wouldn't we want to examine some potatoes at the top, on the bottom, and in between? At every level or stratum? Stratification consists of constructing a sample such that every difference in the population that might *make* a difference in what we are generalizing about is represented in that sample.

If we are going to generalize about sexual behavior, for example, we make sure that individuals from all age groups are proportionately represented, for age is a factor that conditions sexual behavior. Religious conviction is also relevant, so major religious distinctions will be represented in the sample. Income level may also make a difference, so we get individuals from all levels into the sample. Race may or may not make a difference, but since we do not know that it doesn't, we take adequate care that all races in the population are represented in the sample. Age at onset of puberty might be a factor (Kinsey thought it was), so individuals with different histories in this area must be included. Indeed, if we list all the factors that may be relevant to sexual behavior and the various classes and subclasses they

"I'm just trying to get a fair sample."

create, we would have more subclasses than there are people in the world. Many of these classes would be sparsely populated or entirely empty. How many people (1) of Indian descent, (2) with an annual income over $100,000, (3) born in an urban area, (4) belonging to the Baptist Church, (5) who entered puberty at age eleven, (6) with an eighth-grade education, (7) whose occupation is college professor, and (8) whose age is over eighty years—how many such individuals *are* there? But each of these categories (and their corresponding ones) can be represented, although not all of their *combinations* can be.

The Nielsen ratings service seeks to have a cross section of the whole population of American television viewers in its small sample. All localities, income levels, religious affiliations, and educational backgrounds are represented. The Gallup and Harris pollsters create cross sections of the populations they generalize about. Where randomness cannot be left to chance, it must be induced by careful stratification.

Whether dealing with people, animals, or things, no stratification plan can serve all purposes. What categories we choose for stratification will be dependent on the population we are dealing with and the characteristic of that population we want to generalize about. Age of onset of puberty will be more relevant for human sexual behavior than for human political behavior. And it will be totally irrelevant (I think), if we are studying crows and the color of their feathers. If you were trying to determine which courses the students on this campus liked best, you would have a bad sample if you interviewed only those students you saw on the steps of the humanities building. You would want to talk to students leaving and entering *all* the academic buildings. But this type of stratification would not help you much if you wanted to find out students' views on the projected tuition hike. Here you would be more concerned to get a cross section of various economic classes than a cross section of academic interests. So you would try to ascertain students' income, the source of their tuition money, and their other financial responsibilities and see that these (and other) economic categories are represented.

What weight we would give each category might be hard to calculate. We would have to guess as best we could on the basis of what else we knew about the student population. Effective stratification depends on our knowledge of the population. We not only have to determine the categories we believe relevant for the particular generalization problem before us, but we also have to know how heavily to weight each subgroup. How *many* of the students, for example, receive no help from their parents? How *many* work? How *many* are badly in debt? This kind of information is hard to get—in this problem and in others.

It probably can be said that no sample is perfectly stratified. Which means that randomness is never perfectly achieved. But it can be more or less closely approached. Greater or less pains may be taken. We can be careful or careless. There are things we can do to strengthen the generalization which is our inductive conclusion. Its inductive probability derives from the effort we make to get a fair sample.

Round numbers are always false.
                    —*Samuel Johnson, quoted in Boswell's* Life of Dr. Johnson

Concluding Summary: A positive way to promote randomness in the sample is to stratify it. We choose proportionate representatives from every subclass of the population that might make a difference on what we are generalizing about. But our knowledge, both of the proportion and the relevance, is bound to be imperfect. So we can have only degrees of confidence that the sample is a fair one. No matter how much care we take, the drawing of a generalization remains an inductive inference.

EXERCISES

Exercise 80

For each of the following inductive arguments, (a) add a premise that would increase the probability of the inference, and (b) alter the conclusion in such a way as to increase the probability of the inference. Consider these alterations separately.

1. Donald quacks
   Daisy quacks
   Dewey quacks
   ∴ All ducks quack

2. My car has fouled plugs
   Your car has fouled plugs
   His car has fouled plugs
   Her car does not have fouled plugs
   ∴ At least 75 percent of all cars have fouled plugs

3. Fifty-eight percent of all Summit County high school graduates go on to college
   Sixty-two percent of all Portage County high school graduates go on to college
   Fifty-nine percent of all Wayne County high school graduates go on to college
   ∴ At least 58 percent of all Ohio county high school graduates go on to college

4. He is dishonest
   His wife is dishonest
   His son is honest
   ∴ Seventy-five percent of the family are dishonest

5. No African camels have two humps
   No European camels have two humps
   ∴ No camels have two humps

6. Steak at this restaurant is delicious
   Vegetables at this restaurant are delicious
   Dessert at this restaurant is delicious
   ∴ All dishes served at this restaurant are delicious

Exercise 81

Indicate what you think of the size of the sample in each of the following. Use this key: A = larger than necessary, B = too small, C = might be OK if random, D = can't say.

1. Population: American professors.
   Generalization: percentage possessing a doctorate.
   Size of sample: 300.
2. Population: visible stars in the Milky Way galaxy.
   Generalization: percentage that have ceased to exist.
   Size of sample: 10.
3. Population: quantities of hydrochloric acid.
   Generalization: percentage which, when added to sodium hydroxide, will produce salt and water.
   Size of sample: 10.
4. Population: London taxi drivers.
   Generalization: percentage who favor monarchy.
   Size of sample: 100.
5. Population: books in the Library of Congress.
   Generalization: percentage that have been checked out within the last year.
   Size of sample: 50.
6. Population: California human females.
   Generalization: percentage who favor trial marriage.
   Size of sample: 100.

Exercise 82

Why is each of the samples biased?

1. Population: American professors.
   Generalization: percentage possessing a doctorate.
   Sample consists of those who attended the last annual meeting of the American Association of University Professors.
2. Population: visible stars in the Milky Way galaxy.
   Generalization: percentage that have ceased to exist.
   Sample consists of those observed during the month of July.
3. Population: British taxi drivers.
   Generalization: percentage who favor monarchy.
   Sample consists of those who work in London's West End.
4. Population: books in the Library of Congress.
   Generalization: percentage that have been checked out within the last year.
   Sample consists of books published between the years of 1900 and 1914.
5. Population: California human females.
   Generalization: percentage who favor trial marriage.

Sample consists of women in attendance at a symphony concert in Orange County.

6. Population: American husbands.
   Generalization: percentage who subject their wives to physical abuse.
   Sample consists of subscribers to the *New York Review of Books*.

Exercise 83

For each problem, cite three sets of subgroups that should be represented in the sample.

1. Population: American college students.
   Generalization: their presidential preference.
2. Population: white blue-eyed tomcats.
   Generalization: their ability to hear.
3. Population: students who have had Mr. Pelf as a teacher.
   Generalization: what they think of him.
4. Population: movies of the last twenty-five years.
   Generalization: how many stress violence.
5. Population: British and American poems.
   Generalization: their length.
6. Population: American families.
   Generalization: percentage in which child abuse occurs.

Chapter 9

Induction: Causal Relations

PREVIEW

A generalization may tell us *that* all metals expand when heated. A causal statement may tell us *why* they expand when heated. A causal statement provides a more satisfying answer to our curiosity. How do we discover causal connections in the world around us? We believe that a genuine cause always precedes the effect, and that the effect cannot occur without it. And we believe that two phenomena that co-vary in degree may be causally related. In this chapter we will discuss the techniques that have long been employed in discovering causal connections. Since causal investigation is an inductive enterprise where probability is the best we can hope for, we must also note the limitations of these techniques or methods. What should you try to master in this material?

1. The various senses of 'cause.'
2. How to use the Method of Agreement.
3. What dangers or limitations to be alert to when using the Method of Agreement.
4. How to use the Method of Difference.
5. What dangers or limitations to be alert to when using the Method of Difference.
6. How to use the Method of Concomitant Variation.
7. What dangers or limitations to be alert to when using the Method of Concomitant Variation.
8. How to transpose what has been said about "finding the cause" to "finding the effect."

You do make causal inferences every day of your life, so you already know something about the matter. Test yourself:

1. Can you think of two causes for sleeplessness?
2. If there are at least two causes for sleeplessness, can either one be claimed as a "necessary condition" for sleeplessness?

268

3. Could you prevent an event by preventing one of its necessary conditions?
4. Could you prevent an event by preventing one of its sufficient conditions?
5. A gambler lost one day, won the next. He claimed a good-luck charm that he carried with him the second day made the difference. What is wrong with his reasoning?
6. Is the particular virus the whole cause of malaria?
7. An economist, in telling us what will happen, concludes by saying, "other things being equal." Are they ever "equal"?
8. If X has indeed caused Y in the past, may we be confident that it will in the future?

THE NATURE OF CAUSE

Causality and Generalizations

If qualities are found to possess a high degree of correlation, we might suspect that there is a causal link of some kind between them. Generalizations state such correlations:

All ruminants have horns.
All white blue-eyed tomcats are deaf.
Eighty-six percent of all people who contract lung cancer are heavy smokers.
No opera stars are humble.

We do not think that it is an accident that all animals who chew the cud also possess horns, and we would be very surprised to find one that did not. We may not know what the connection is between whiteness/blue-eyedness/tomcatness and deafness, but we think there is one. The high statistical correlation between smoking and lung cancer suggests that smoking causes lung cancer. And we think there is something about the qualities that make up an opera star that causally excludes the quality of humility.

Generalizing is the basic and most elementary form of inductive reasoning. And it is very important. It not only gives us major premises for deductive arguments, but suggestions for a deeper and more analytic investigation that could lead to results more satisfying. It is more satisfying to know *why* the tomcats are deaf than simply to know *that* they are deaf. Causal reasoning provides better explanation than simple generalization.

The qualities generalized about may be in direct causal relation (all heated metals expand) or in very indirect causal relation (73 percent of juvenile delinquents come from broken homes), or they may be causally related to some third thing or group of things (no dark-skinned people have blue eyes). Generalizations do not reveal causal connections; they only suggest that some may be present.

In the preceding chapter, we talked about the four criteria for evaluating the strength of analogical arguments. Each of these criteria is tied in with the strength of the underlying generalization. It is time now to state a fifth criterion: the *connection* between the observed similarities and the inferred similarity. Is the conjunction a purely accidental one, or are there causal laws linking the inferred similarity to the other(s)?

Let us compare two instances of analogical reasoning where the fifth criterion is crucial:

(1) Sandra purchased a frozen package of Mario's Pizza with sausage. It was in a red box. She found the pizza to be delicious. A few days later she bought Mario's Pizza with pepperoni. It came in a red box. She thought that this one was very tasty also. A week later she got a mushroom pizza, Mario's, which also came in a red box. She enjoyed it very much. Today she wants to try some pizza with anchovies. So, using the past as a guide, she purchases Borgia Pizza with anchovies, since it comes in a red box.

(2) Evelyn has had the same experience with pizza as Sandra. She also wants to try pizza with anchovies. She buys a package in a blue box made by Mario's Pizza and expects to enjoy it.

Evelyn obviously is reasoning better than Sandra. The observed resemblance she is banking on (the cook or company) is more relevant to the inferred resemblance (that the pizza will taste good) than the observed resemblance that Sandra is banking on (the color of the box). We can hardly imagine a causal connection between color of box and taste, although we can easily conceive of such a connection between the preparer of the food and the taste of the food.

The forms of the arguments are identical:

W, X, Y, and Z have the attribute x
W, X, and Y also have attribute q

∴ Z has attribute q

But in (1), x is the color red, and in (2), x is the name of the company. The underlying generalization in (1), 'All pizzas in red boxes are delicious,' is less plausible than that in (2), 'All pizzas made by Mario are delicious.'

Concluding Summary: Generalizations give us combinations of qualities; causal statements give us the connections. Generalizations order our experience by sorting things out. Causal statements tell us why such combinations are the case. Generalization shows us the distribution of qualities and suggests causal relations. When we have discovered the causal relations, we think we have found the reason for the correlation set forth in the generalization. The search for cause is the search for a deeper explanation.

To know truly is to know by causes.
                            —*Francis Bacon*, De Augmentis Scientiarum

Ideal Sense of 'Cause'

What do we mean when we say that X causes Y or that Y is the effect of X?

We mean, first of all, that whenever the conditions specified by 'X' are present, the event, Y, must occur. There is the element of necessity or compulsion. X inexorably produces Y. A cause suffices for the effect; it is the sufficient condition for that which it produces. We would not want to call X the cause of Y if it were possible for X to occur without being followed by Y.

A cause in this sense would have to be very complex, for it would have to include all the factors that, when given, necessarily produce the effect. It would not be enough to say that the Jonathan apples were the cause of the delicious apple pandowdy, for the apples alone could not have brought the dessert into existence. All the ingredients would have to be cited as well as the expertise of the cook and the condition of the oven.

Will all this guarantee the production of delicious apple pandowdy? Not quite. What if the electric power goes off when it is halfway cooked? What if a tornado comes along and blows cook and ingredients away? If cause really *is* a sufficient condition, everything that is needed to necessarily produce the effect is part of it. So a statement of a cause must include, explicitly or implicitly, the denial of certain intervening or counteracting events. We may call the injection of a certain protozoan into the bloodstream the cause of malaria, but we would have to specify that malaria would result only if the blood of the victim had not been immunized by Atabrine or other drugs. Thus the condition of the blood becomes part of the cause as well as the protozoan itself. Consumption of great quantities of apple pandowdy will cause obesity—provided the eater does not have a glandular or metabolic condition that burns off the calories. The statement of the cause, to be complete, must deny all the factors that might deflect it from its result. An easy but not always satisfactory way of getting around the problem of ruling out counteracting factors is to say, ''other things being equal. . . .''

It was noted above that generalizations suggest causal relations. It may be said here that statements asserting causal relations are generalizations. If X is the cause of Y, any X will produce Y. If the situation denoted by 'X' caused Y yesterday, then if the situation is exactly repeated tomorrow, Y will occur again. It is assumed that causal statements are universal in scope. The assumption is that nature is uniform, that history must repeat itself when circumstances are identical. That nature is indeed uniform cannot be established empirically or inductively. But it is the presupposition of causal reasoning. The contention that causal laws are universal follows from what we mean by 'cause.' That such laws exist follows from our assumption of the uniformity of nature.

The universality of causal laws rules out what is sometimes called ''the diversity of effects.'' If X is the cause of Y, Y will always follow X. P and Q will not. If hydrogen burns and bread nourishes (with the proper qualifications), they always, respectively, burn and nourish. If the golf ball, when struck a certain way by the driver, travels in a straight direction on a 300-yard arc, it will not someday hook to the left when struck in exactly the same way.

Ideally, we regard cause as *necessary* for the effect, as well as sufficient. If a certain event is observed to exist without having been preceded by Q, we do not regard Q as its cause. We want to be able to say that X always produces Y and that *Y cannot be produced in any other way.*

The phenomenon "plurality of causes" is thus ruled out. A, B, and C cannot be causes of Y. The cause of Y is X. This means that Y has but one cause (although, of course, it may be very complex). We are thus able to say, "Only if X, then Y."

Cause as sufficient condition enables us to infer one effect from the cause; cause as necessary condition enables us to infer one cause from the effect. A statement asserting that the causal relation holds between two events must, in this ideal sense of 'cause,' be expressed as a biconditional statement: 'If and only if X, then Y.'

The denial of the plurality of causes seems to be an affront to common sense. Aren't there several ways to cause death? It can be achieved through poison, strangulation, or a knife in the heart. Isn't each of these a sufficient condition for the effect, death? And if the intended effect (to go to something more pleasant) is to quench thirst, cannot this be done (or caused) in several different ways? We can drink water, guzzle beer, swallow milk, or consume iced tea. The ideal sense of 'cause,' however, is not *this or that* sufficient condition but what all the sufficient conditions have in common. It is the essence of the various sufficiencies. Whatever may be the medical definition of 'death,' there is only one set of circumstances that always produces it, and it is present in all of the murderous methods. And, in the other example, there is some quality present in all the beverages that produce the intended result.

Just as the ideal cause is not this or that sufficient condition, it is also not this or that necessary condition. For if it were *simply* a necessary condition, it would be *only* a necessary condition and fall short of sufficiency. Oxygen is a necessary condition for combustion, but not (ideally) the cause of it. But if, for any effect you specify *all* the necessary conditions, you have what is sufficient for that effect. And, if you do not have anything beyond those necessary conditions, you have what is necessary for that effect. And this is to say that *cause* in the ideal sense has been specified.

The ideal sense of cause assumes that any particular event is always and uniquely determined by one set of circumstances:

(1) $(a \ \& \ b \ \& \ c \ \& \ d) \rightarrow E$
(2) $\sim(a \ \& \ b \ \& \ c \ \& \ d) \rightarrow \sim E$

Which is to say:

(3) $(a \ \& \ b \ \& \ c \ \& \ d) \leftrightarrow E$

According to (2), the absence of any of these circumstances would result in the failure of the effect to occur. So a, b, c, and d are each necessary conditions for the effect. But they are the same circumstances which, when occurring *together* in (1) are *sufficient* to produce the effect.

> *Cause and effect, the chancellors of God.*
>   —*R. W. Emerson,* Essays: Self-Reliance

Concluding Summary: 'Cause,' in the ideal sense, is the sufficient and necessary condition for the effect. As the sufficient condition, it is the total of all those factors which will assuredly produce the effect and which will always produce the effect. As the necessary condition, it is that one and only set of factors which can produce the effect. 'Cause,' ideally, may be defined as 'that which all sufficient conditions have in common *but no more*' or 'the total of all the necessary conditions *but no more.*' This sense of 'cause' rules out diversity of effects and plurality of causes.[1]

Practical Senses of 'Cause'

Although the ideal sense of 'cause' has many theoretical applications and is the basis of ''Mill's Methods'' (to be discussed below), there are other senses of the word which are often more useful.

When we want to *produce* something, we may be satisfied with 'cause' in the sense of a *sufficient condition*. We may speak of several possible causes, and choose the one that is easiest to obtain. If our purpose is to destroy mice, what we want is an effective means. We will be satisfied with a sufficient condition: acquiring a good cat, putting down some strong poison, or setting traps. Without seeking the ideal cause, we will regard any one of these sufficient conditions as a cause of ridding the house of mice.

If you want to please your girlfriend, choose any one of the ''causes'' that will give her pleasure. Send her flowers, bring her candy, or compliment her reasoning ability. None of these is the cause in the strict sense, but, in the loose sense, we can say that the compliment *caused* her pleasant feeling.

How can I ''cause'' my earnings to go up? I can work longer. I can work better. I can get a better-paying job. It is more practical to set out on one of these sufficient conditions than to try to collect all those factors which always and only produce increased earnings.

Sometimes we may wish to *prevent* something. We do not need to eliminate the whole cause in order to prevent the effect from occurring. We do not even have to know what this ideal cause is. All we need to do is to eliminate *one* of the necessary conditions that constitute this ideal cause.

In a loose sense, we talk about ''the straw that broke the camel's back.'' This

---

[1] Much of this section is controversial. For a fuller discussion of some of its presuppositions, see H. W. B. Joseph, *Introduction to Logic,* Second Edition (Oxford: Oxford University Press, 1946), pp. 400–501. See also, Donald Davidson, ''Causal Relations,'' *The Journal of Philosophy,* 54:21 (November 9, 1967), pp. 691–703: J. L. Mackie, *The Cement of the Universe: A Study of Causation* (Oxford: The Clarendon Press, 1974).

straw, the 78,459th one we laid on his back, broke it! This one straw is the cause of his broken back! It is, of course, ridiculous to make that one straw the causal scapegoat for the unfortunate injury to the camel. But we can regard that straw as the necessary condition for the effect. And we could have prevented the effect if we had refrained from laying that one on his back. The 78,458 other straws are part of the cause too, but we could safely have piled them on.

A person may want to put out a fire. Oxygen "causes" fire in a sense, but it is really only a necessary condition for fire. But, if he wants to stop the fire, he can do so by removing this particular necessary condition for it. So he sprays it with liquid or smothers it with blankets. No oxygen→ no fire.

Sometimes there are factors that are neither ideal causes nor sufficient conditions nor necessary conditions, but it is natural and useful to call them causes. The bite of the anopheles mosquito does not suffice for malaria, since it does not always result in malaria. Nor is it necessary, since malaria may be produced by a hypodermic needle. But since malaria is *usually* preceded by anopheles mosquito bites, and since the bites *often* cause it, we take a major step against the disease by eliminating the anopheles mosquito bites. This may be done by killing the mosquitoes or by using protective netting and skin ointment. We may call the bite the cause, for, by removing the bite, we have, for all practical purposes, prevented the effect.

Strictly speaking, of course, a contributing factor is not the cause of an event. To call the factor the cause is to risk oversimplification. Ted Bundy, a convicted serial murderer who was executed in 1989, said that the cause of his actions was an addiction to pornography. This obviously is not a sufficient condition, for many people peruse pornography without killing young women. And it is not a necessary condition, because not all murderers are addicted to pornography. The most that could be said is that it contains (and perhaps conceals) a necessary condition.[2] Was it just an excuse that Bundy offered for himself, or was his use of pornography part of a complex set of factors that indeed influenced his dreadful actions in his own particular situation? It is possible that pornography, although not a necessary condition for the general act of rape or murder, could have been a necessary condition (or carrier thereof) in Bundy's case. That is, had this factor been absent from his background, he would not have done what he did. But it is also possible that, given his character and other factors he had been exposed to, he would have murdered whether or not he had ever perused pornographic materials. The project of causal analysis is an exceedingly difficult one. And whether we are looking for the whole cause, a "contributing factor," a sufficient condition, or a necessary condition, we can never be sure we have found it.

There is one more aspect of the causal problem to be noted. The more complete and dependable our description of the ideal cause becomes, the closer in time it

---

[2] It might be noted that neither the President's Commission on Obscenity and Pornography (1970) nor Attorney General Meese's Commission on Pornography (1986) could find any connection between nonviolent pornography and sexual violence.

moves to the effect. There is natural compression in time, for the cause must be universal and necessary; all chances of something going wrong or counteracting factors must be eliminated. We may argue that it is not the mosquito that causes the malaria, but the bite. Well, not the bite either, but the introduction of the protozoan into the bloodstream. Not that really, but the reaction that takes place between the protozoan and the blood. We tend to reach a point where a description of the cause is very similar to a description of the effect. Perhaps the most accurate description of a cause would be that of the condition of the universe in the very moment before the effect begins to exist! But this would not be very useful.

We may choose events or factors close to the effect (''proximate'') as the ''cause,'' or far away (''remote''). How remote or proximate they are depends upon the practical concern at hand. Casey Jones had an accident and ''took his farewell trip to the promised land.'' What was the ''cause''? Some possibilities, moving from proximate to remote, are:

(1) The speed of the train and its mass, in conjunction with the curve of the track. A physicist might be interested in this.
(2) The warning lights before the curve were not working. The safety engineer would be concerned with this.
(3) Casey had shoved the throttle forward and was not paying attention to signals anyway. The insurance adjuster might call this the cause.
(4) Casey was under great stress and had taken five snorts of rye whiskey before kissing ''his wife at the station door.'' A psychologist or physician might blame the accident on this.
(5) Casey was under great stress because he had been losing money on the stock market. An economist could blame the accident on the depression.

We can push this back indefinitely. Why was there a depression? Perhaps the ''ultimate'' cause of the accident was that William decided to invade England in 1066.

A necessity for one thing to happen because another has happened does not exist. There is only logical necessity.
                    —*Ludwig Wittgenstein*, Tractatus Logico-Philosophicus

---

Concluding Summary: Although sufficient conditions are not causes in the strict sense—being the vehicles for *the* cause—it is convenient, when our purpose is to produce something, to call them causes. And, while necessary conditions are not causes in the strict sense—being constituent elements of *the* cause—it is convenient, when our purpose is to prevent something, to call them causes. The cause (in the ideal sense) would occur very close in time to the effect, but we may select events several steps away from the effect and, if it suits our purpose, call them causes.

EXERCISES

Exercise 84

What possible causal connections does each of these generalizations suggest to you?

1. Most Disney movies make money.
2. There are no atheists in foxholes.
3. Drunkenness is involved in 71.8 percent of all automobile accidents.
4. Married people tend to live longer than single people.
5. All red-haired people have violent tempers.
6. Most candidates refuse to discuss the issues.
7. All great cities are on waterways.
8. Only 2.1 percent of all Tahitians ever experience hypertension.
9. Sixty-eight percent of all bowling champions are left-handed.
10. Wool sweaters are very warm.

Exercise 85

Indicate whether each of these "causes" is set forth as a sufficient condition or as a necessary condition:

1. Gray hair is caused by worrying a lot.
2. World War II was caused by Germany's attack on Poland.
3. The "grasshoppers" are so good because she used real ice cream.
4. The plane crash was caused by pilot error.
5. The patrons at Joe's Bar caused a great commotion.
6. Oliver graduated because he met the college's residence requirement.
7. His last tournament victory caused him to become the sixth million-dollar career winner.
8. I gained weight because I drank so many "grasshoppers."
9. Brock was a good base stealer because he studied the pitchers' moves.
10. The cause of tides is the gravitational influence of the moon.

MILL'S METHODS

Method of Agreement

These methods for finding the cause (or effect) of an event were formulated very carefully by John Stuart Mill in *A System of Logic: Ratiocinative and Inductive* (1843) and called "Methods of Experimental Enquiry." David Hume had set forth similar principles in *The Treatise of Human Nature* (1739), but it was Francis Bacon who first stated them in *Novum Organum* (1620).

Mill's formulation of the Method of Agreement is this: "If two or more instances of the phenomenon under investigation have only one circumstance in common, the circumstance in which alone all the instances agree, is the cause (or effect) of the given phenomenon.''

Suppose that we want to find out the cause of X. To use this method we would need at least two separate occurrences of X. Then we would check the antecedent circumstances for agreement.

ANTECEDENT CIRCUMSTANCES	THE EFFECT WHOSE CAUSE IS BEING INVESTIGATED
a b c d	X_1
d e f g	X_2

Since d is the only circumstance that the two occurrences of X have in common, it must be the cause of X.

Since, according to the ideal sense of 'cause,' it always precedes the event and is the only thing that always precedes the effect, the Method of Agreement will reveal it. The schematized example above assumes an experimental situation where the method works perfectly.

Sometimes, however, there is more than one circumstance in common among the factors antecedent to the occurrences of the effect:

ANTECEDENT CIRCUMSTANCES	THE EFFECT WHOSE CAUSE IS BEING INVESTIGATED
a b c d	X_1
c d e f	X_2

Here we cannot be sure that d is the cause, for c is also common to the positive occurrences of the effect. Circumstance d may be irrelevant—or maybe it is c that is irrelevant. Or perhaps the cause is a combination of c and d. What is clear in the problem, however, is that neither a, b, e, nor f is the cause of X, for X managed to occur without them. If a, b, e, and f are not necessary for the occurrence of X, they cannot be causes of X. So while we have not discovered the cause of X, we have eliminated some possibilities.

Suppose we find another occurrence of the effect and note the antecedent circumstances:

ANTECEDENT CIRCUMSTANCES	THE EFFECT WHOSE CAUSE IS BEING INVESTIGATED
d g h i	X_3

This not only eliminates c (since X_3 occurred without it), but leaves d as the only circumstance common among the antecedent factors. Of all the factors, only d is consistent with our notion of cause as both sufficient and necessary condition.

The Method of Agreement eliminates factors or circumstances. If two or more remain, more investigation is necessary. If one remains, that is the cause.

The Method of Agreement may effectively be used when there are several positive occurrences of the effect: cases of a disease, instances of an allergic reaction, cases of hitting a golf ball correctly, etc. Simply chart the antecedent factors and eliminate those that were not always present.

The actual workings of the method do not always yield results so neatly. We usually have to settle for causes not ideal and always with results that are at best probable.

Let us imagine that Stanley is trying to discover the cause of his hangovers. He keeps a careful record of what he drank the nights before four positive occurrences of the hangover:

ANTECEDENT CIRCUMSTANCES	THE EFFECT WHOSE CAUSE IS BEING INVESTIGATED
Scotch, soda	Hangover (January 1)
Bourbon, soda	Hangover (January 8)
Gin, soda	Hangover (January 15)
Brandy, soda	Hangover (January 22)

Using the Method of Agreement, he sees that soda is the only circumstance in common and concludes that soda is the cause of his hangovers.

We might point out to him that soda is not the only common circumstance, that the scotch, bourbon, gin, and brandy all contain alcohol, and that alcohol, therefore, is also a common circumstance. Stanley eliminated a possible cause when he threw out the various "vehicles" for alcohol. He failed to analyze the factors, to break them down into their ingredients.

But even if he does, he still does not know the cause, for there are now two common factors: soda and alcohol. He can make progress, using the same method, but he will need more instances and he will have to vary the factors. So, in the interests of science, he returns to his haunts:

ANTECEDENT CIRCUMSTANCES	THE EFFECT WHOSE CAUSE IS BEING INVESTIGATED
Alcohol, a, soda	Hangover (January 1)
Alcohol, b, soda	Hangover (January 8)
Alcohol, c, soda	Hangover (January 15)
Alcohol, d, soda	Hangover (January 22)
Alcohol, a, water	Hangover (January 29)
Alcohol, b, cola	Hangover (February 5)

As indicated in the chart, soda drops out and alcohol is the only common circumstance. Can Stanley now conclude with perfect confidence that alcohol causes his hangovers?

He is reluctant to do so. How can be be sure that his enumeration of possible circumstances is complete? Perhaps the alcohol has nothing to do with his hangovers. Looking back, he recalls that he smoked on every one of those drinking occasions. He needs to get more instances and to vary the factors still more. So he goes out drinking, but does not smoke. He still gets a hangover. Smoking has been eliminated, but what about the ice in the drinks? Maybe it is the late hours. It could be the people he drinks with that cause the hangovers. Perhaps the pretzels have something to do with the hangovers. Or maybe the cause is the combination of poor air and bad food. There is no end to the list of possible causes or relevant circumstances and their combinations. He could experiment for years and never be positive that all relevant circumstances but one have been eliminated.

Use of the Method of Agreement looks like a deductive process:

$$a \lor b \lor c \lor d \qquad \textit{(is the cause)}$$
$$\underline{\sim a \;\&\; \sim b \;\&\; \sim c} \qquad \textit{(because not present when the effect was)}$$
$$\therefore \qquad d \qquad\qquad \textit{(is the cause)}$$

But three questions arise: (1) Have we analyzed the circumstances sufficiently? Are we sure that a, b, c, and d do not all contain a common ingredient, x? Or that d is not contained in a, b, and c? (2) Have we included all the relevant circumstances? What about e, f, g, and h? (3) Have we adequately ruled out the possibility of combinations? Perhaps a and b could jointly have produced the effect but not separately. It is because of such uncertainties as these that finding the cause is an *inductive* enterprise.

Similar questions can be raised in connection with all the other methods. While finding the cause utilizes deduction, it mainly rests on induction. If the list of circumstances is erroneous, the disjunctive premise is false. If our rejection of circumstances (by whichever of Mills's Methods) is erroneous, the conjunctive premise is false. If we have reason to believe that these premises are only probably true, we can claim no more for the conclusion.

If we overcome the practical difficulties cited above, what sense of 'cause' do we end up with when we use the Method of Agreement? Surely not a *sufficient condition,* for it will not guarantee by itself the occurrence of the effect. At best it yields a factor which, *with other factors,* will cause the effect under investigation. If we do assume that drinking alcohol is the "cause" of the hangover, we would not want to say that it is the whole cause. It must be drunk in certain quantities, it must encounter a certain condition in the body that consumes it, and its dehydrating tendency must not be counteracted by the consumption of bland liquids in succeeding hours. Other factors must be cited to produce real sufficiency. Our "cause" produced the effect in the past because these other factors happened to be present also. They are taken for granted because it is too tedious to enumerate them.

Have we found, then, a *necessary condition?* Probably not. Our cause may be a "vehicle," containing more than is strictly necessary for the effect. Is it alcohol *per se* that causes hangovers or a particular quality of certain chemicals found in all alcoholic beverages?

Do we have a cause "in the ideal sense"? Obviously not. While the ideal sense of cause permitted us to eliminate possibilities through the use of the Method of Agreement, what we are left with is surely not a complex of all the necessary conditions and no others. What the method yields, then, is simply a condition which is in some loose sense both sufficient and necessary for the effect we are investigating.

Concluding Summary: The Method of Agreement utilizes two or more positive occurrences of the effect under investigation. It eliminates anything from among the antecedent circumstances that was not present when the effect was. If all but one circumstance can be eliminated in this way, then that circumstance may be said to be the cause. The most that can be claimed for the result is probability, for one never knows how far to carry the analysis of the circumstances or the list of possible circumstances. And he never can be sure that the factor he finally chooses is the only one that the positive instances have in common. In any case, the result will be incomplete, for a circumstance or a factor cannot be the whole cause.

Method of Difference

Mill's formulation of the Method of Difference is this: "If an instance in which the phenomenon under investigation occurs, and an instance in which it does not occur, have every circumstance in common save for one, that one occurring only in the former; the circumstance in which alone the two instances differ, is the effect, or cause, or an indispensable part of the cause, of the phenomenon."

The use of this method requires a positive and a negative instance, with antecedents differing in only one respect:

ANTECEDENT CIRCUMSTANCES	THE EFFECT WHOSE CAUSE IS BEING INVESTIGATED
a b c d	X *occurred*
a b c	X *did not occur*

Since the antecedent circumstances are the same in both instances in all respects but one, that one difference must be what made the difference. That is, *d* caused *X*.

If two rats are alike in all respects—age, size, health, maze-learning intelligence, and so forth—and are subjected to the same diet and other living conditions, we could deliberately introduce a difference: deprive Rat A of Vitamin B. If this rat does rather worse than Rat B in learning the next maze, we may attribute his backwardness to the only known difference: lack of Vitamin B.

The Method of Difference may be used with two *groups,* as well as two individuals.

The groups, then, must be kept as similar as possible, in order that the difference introduced in one group may plausibly be claimed as that which *made* the difference in that group. If two groups of men are quarantined and set off from everyone else in completely sterilized quarters, and if they (like the rats above) are subjected to the same living conditions with respect to food, temperature, humidity, and so forth, we have an experimental situation. We can release some infected anopheles mosquitoes in the living quarters of Group A ("experimental group"). If all the people who contracted malaria were in Group A, we have good evidence that the bite of the mosquito is a necessary condition for malaria.

The Method of Difference is sometimes called the laboratory method because the experimenter tries to control all the factors. He takes great pains to ensure that only one difference exists in the two individuals or the two groups he is working with. The more successful he is in controlling the situation in this way, the more confident he can be that the difference he introduces is what causes the difference in the observed effect.

If I use fertilizer Q on my front yard only and find that the grass prospers and is much greener and thicker than that in the back yard, I can attribute the difference to the fertilizer only if the stands of grass were alike to start with and were otherwise cared for in similar ways. Is the soil the same? Is the sunlight the same? Did both receive the same amount of moisture? Unless the answer to these and other similar questions is in the affirmative, it is quite possible that the grass in the front yard would have flourished *without* the fertilizer. Serums and pills, like fertilizer, can be deemed effective only by being tested in controlled situations.

The foolish and hasty use of the Method of Difference gives rise to what has been called the Post Hoc Ergo Propter Hoc Fallacy ("after this, therefore because of this"). Philip plays poker and loses. Philip takes his rabbit's foot to the next poker game and wins. He claims that the rabbit's foot did it for him. This would be good thinking only if the two games (cards, skill, players, stakes, and so forth) were alike in all respects but the presence in Philip's pocket of the rabbit's foot. This fallacy is the parent of superstition. A comet courses through the sky on the eve of the battle; the battle is won (or lost); so the comet caused the result. Joe Cronin says a prayer before coming to the plate and hits a home run; the prayer is responsible. A black cat crossed my path while I was on my way to take my second chemistry test. I failed the test. Since I had not failed the first one, I claim to have been jinxed by the black cat.

But the difference between foolish reasoning like this and wise use of the Method of Difference is only a difference of degree. This is an important difference. But no matter how cautiously we approach the problem, no matter how carefully we apply the Method of Difference, we can never be completely satisfied that only one difference is present. The nervous systems of Rats A and B are different. The ages of the men in the malaria test are different. I may, in the laboratory, wash my equipment thoroughly, but a fraction of a gram of a certain invisible chemical may be wafted through the air and drop into the beaker. This is the aspect of the Method of Difference that makes its use an *inductive* procedure.

"See what I just caused to happen!"

The second limitation of the Method of Difference is that it yields at best only a necessary condition. This is important to have, provided we want to *prevent* something, but we cannot expect to *produce* the effect with it. We may call the fertilizer the "cause" of the improved grass, the Vitamin B the "cause" of learning the maze, and the mosquito the "cause" of the malaria, but none of these circumstances is sufficient in itself for the intended effect. While oxygen is necessary for combustion, it does not suffice for combustion.

Actually, the Method of Difference does not always yield a necessary condition. In the previous malaria example, we can compare two men, X and Y, who were living under the same conditions. X is bitten by a mosquito, Y is not. X gets malaria, Y does not. But to say that the mosquito bite was *necessary* for malaria is just not so. For we happen to know that malaria can be contracted *independently* of mosquitoes—by injecting some blood of an infected person into the veins of an uninfected person. It would be accurate to say that the method gives us a circumstance which *is* a necessary condition (such as oxygen for combustion) or which *contains* a necessary condition (such as the introduction of the malaria bacillus into the bloodstream).

The Method of Difference may be used to supplement the information gained from the Method of Agreement or to confirm its results. On the basis of the Method of Agreement, we may conclude that alcohol in a specified quantity "causes" hangovers, for it always precedes hangovers. We may carry out an experiment and spend an evening in exactly the same way we did on an occasion preceding a hangover. We eat the same things, smoke the same number of cigarettes, retire at the same hour, and so forth. The only difference is that we do not consume any alcohol. If we find there is no hangover the next morning, we have a positive and a negative instance. So, using the Method of Difference, we can conclude that alcohol is the cause, or a necessary part of the cause, of our hangovers.

The Method of Agreement may be used to confirm the results obtained through use of the Method of Difference. If we give several rats of varying condition lots of Vitamin B and find that they all learn the maze easily, it is more probable that Vitamin B is causally connected with learning mazes. If use of the Method of Difference leads us to believe that the saliva from the anopheles mosquito causes malaria, we might expose several people to bites from these mosquitoes and see whether they contract malaria. The superstitious baseball player who thought the prayer caused his home run might pray the next time he comes to the plate and see what the results are.

Concluding Summary: The Method of Difference employs a positive and negative instance of the effect. If the two sets of antecedent factors are so controlled that there is only one difference between them, this difference may be said to be what caused the difference in the results. One cannot be absolutely certain of his or her results, for he or she can never be sure that the observed difference in the sets of antecedents is the only difference. Furthermore, the circumstance singled out is not the *full* cause. It can only be (or contain) a necessary *part* of the cause.

Joint Method of Agreement and Difference

Sometimes it is possible to use the two methods simultaneously rather than supplementing or checking the results of one by use of the other. The case of two groups of men—one subjected to the bite of the mosquitoes, the other group protected from such bites—lends itself to such an approach. If all the men who were bitten get malaria and all of the men who were not bitten fail to get malaria, it can be inferred with some probability that there is a causal connection between the bite of anopheles mosquitoes and malaria. The method used is the Joint Method of Agreement and Difference.

We need several positive instances of the effect (as the Method of Agreement does) and several negative instances of the effect (suggestive of the Method of Difference). If among the antecedent circumstances there is only one that is common to all the positive instances (agreement) and absent from all the negative instances (difference), there is good reason to believe that that circumstance is the cause of the effect. This would be a perfect situation for the Joint Method of Agreement and Difference:

ANTECEDENT CIRCUMSTANCES	THE EFFECT WHOSE CAUSE IS BEING INVESTIGATED
a c g	X *occurred*
b c g	X *occurred*
c d g	X *occurred*
c e g	X *occurred*
c f g	X *occurred*
x y z	X *did not occur*
u v w	X *did not occur*
x y c	X *did not occur*

The Method of Agreement alone would not have given us an answer from the above data, for there is more than one factor common to the positive occurrences: *c* and *g*. The Method of Difference alone would also have failed to yield an answer, for there are not two instances, one positive and the other negative, in which the antecedent circumstances are alike in all respects but one. By using the methods jointly, however, we get a good result: *g* is the only factor that is common to all the positive instances *and* absent from all the negative instances.

This method has another advantage. We do not have to control the situation as carefully as when we are using the Method of Difference. This is an advantage because some situations cannot *be* controlled, or can be controlled only with great difficulty, or (as in the malaria example) can only be partially controlled. That there are several differences between the positive and negative instances is not so bad if we have several positive and negative instances: irrelevances cancel out.

But even a "perfect" situation like that set forth above may obscure some important truths. It is possible that *g* has nothing to do with the effect. The circumstances, *a*, *b*, *d*, *e*, and *f*, may all be sufficient conditions for X, but eliminated because they are unanalyzed. To rule out this possibility, we would have to contrive some negative instances in which *a*, *b*, *d*, *e*, and *f*, respectively, are present.

Suppose a medical researcher believes that he has discovered a serum that will cure and prevent a certain plague. The plague breaks out on a Pacific island, so he flies to the island, intending to test his serum. As a good humanitarian he decides to administer the serum to all the inhabitants. Suppose they all got well. Can he claim that his serum, being the only difference, was what made the difference? No, for the epidemic may have run its course, or the wind may have shifted, or a natural enemy of the plague may have developed and killed the plague bacillus. The presence of his serum on the island may have been simply coincidental to the plague's disappearance. Nor can the researcher claim anything for his serum by means of the Method of Agreement. Everyone got well (positive instances), but was his serum the only antecedent factor these positive instances had in common? Certainly not.

But if he had given the serum to half the people and withheld it from the other half, while keeping good records, he may acquire some evidence for the efficacy of his serum. If it should happily turn out that everyone who did not get the serum died and that everyone who did get it survived, the researcher would have a very strong case for his serum, based on the Joint Method of Agreement and Difference.

In actual life, of course, things seldom work out so neatly. A few who received the serum may have died, and some who did not receive it may have survived. Evidence would be acquired, but it might not be as conclusive as one would like. One shortcoming of the Joint Method is that it is difficult to find or induce a situation in which there is one factor and only one that behaves as the method says it must. And, if the investigator thinks that he has found one, he may be deceived by a concidence while the real cause has not even been recognized as an "antecedent circumstance."

The method did supply a neat solution to the "red sweat" mystery that bedevilled Eastern Airlines for several months. Ninety-five flight attendants had broken out in a red rash or perspiration on New York to South Florida flights. The phenomenon usually occurred on the new A300 airliners, although not when these planes were used on other routes. After an intensive investigation by Eastern, the Centers for Disease Control, and the National Institute of Occupational Safety and Health, it was announced on March 19, 1980, that the cause was the red letters ("Demo Only") stenciled on the demonstrator life vests used by the attendants. This was the only thing common to the positive occurrences of the rash. The new planes carried new vests with fresh ink. Although the new vests were present in other flights, they were not demonstrated, for the flights did not go over water. So demonstration of the new vests was absent in every case where the effect did not occur. Sophisticated tests involving atomic electromagnetic spectrographic analysis yielded no clue, but a simple application of the Joint Method of Agreement and Difference solved the mystery.

We deal with the limitations and the pitfalls of the Joint Method as we do with those of the other methods: Analyze, extend, and vary the factors as much as is practicable; do additional experiments using the same method; and do additional experiments using different methods. The additional evidence acquired increases the probability of the conclusion that p is the cause of q. But recalling that the complete cause of an event is complex and never simple, the investigator will say that p is or contains an important part of the cause. He may or may not (depending upon his purposes) seek some of the other parts of that causal combination.

Concluding Summary: The Joint Method of Agreement and Difference either utilizes or sets up a situation in which there are both positive and negative instances of the effect under investigation. If there is an antecedent circumstance common to the former and absent from the latter, that circumstance is the cause. While the method has many of the same shortcomings that the other methods do, it has the advantage of being able to deal with instances in such quantity as to compensate for the deficiencies in the matter of control.

Method of Concomitant Variation

There are situations in which neither the Method of Agreement nor the Method of Difference can be used. The Method of Agreement cannot be used because there are not several positive occurrences of the effect, but one continuous occurrence of it. And the Method of Difference cannot be used, because it is impossible to get a negative occurrence. How would we find the cause of unemployment, of human blood pressure, of ice at the north pole?

Actually, we are not so much concerned to account for the fact that *there is* unemployment, human blood pressure, and ice at the north pole. What is of more interest is the *degree* of these things and the changes in the degree. Why is there more unemployment now than in 1960? Why does Bertrand's blood pressure fluctuate? Will there be more or less of the world's water frozen as ice at the north pole in 1995 than in 1990?

For finding the cause of phenomena that change in degree, Mill offers us the Method of Concomitant Variation: "Whatever phenomenon varies in any manner whenever another phenomenon varies in some particular manner, is either a cause or an effect of that phenomenon, or is connected with it through some fact of causation." Note that this method seeks not merely the cause of the variation, but of the phenomenon itself. When two events co-vary in intensity, the one may be the cause of the existence of the other.

Although this is a distinctly different method, it may be used in ways similar to two others. Where the antecedent circumstances cannot be controlled very well, we may view it as similar to the Method of Agreement:

ANTECEDENT CIRCUMSTANCES	THE EFFECT WHOSE CAUSE IS BEING INVESTIGATED
a b c^2 d	X *to* n *degree*
a^2 c d e	X *to* n + 1 *degree*
a^3 b c d	X *to* n + 2 *degree*

The circumstance *a* is not the only common antecedent, but it is the only one that co-varies with *X*. The more alcohol Stanley consumes, the more intense is his hangover.

Where the antecedent factors can be controlled, the Method of Concomitant Variation looks like the Method of Difference:

ANTECEDENT CIRCUMSTANCES	THE EFFECT WHOSE CAUSE IS BEING INVESTIGATED
a b c d	X *to* n *degree*
a^2 b c d	X *to* n + 1 *degree*
a^3 b c d	X *to* n + 2 *degree*

The only difference, the amount of *a,* must be what made the difference in the amount of *X.* The more Patricia exposes her skin to the sun, the darker her tan becomes.

Circumstances do not have to co-vary with the effect in *direct* proportion (as is the case in the examples above). If their co-variation is in *inverse* proportion, there is equal reason to suspect a causal connection. The years of schooling may vary directly with size of income, but inversely with amount of television watching. In either event, we may suspect a causal connection.

The difficulties in the use of this method are familiar. When it is used like the Method of Agreement, there may be more than one factor co-varying. While the stock market is going up, building activity is going up and interest rates are going down. Which is the causal factor? Or, if there is only one factor co-varying, it may be accidental, while the real causal factor is not even listed. Some people attribute various kinds of fluctuating phenomena to sunspot activity. A coach may argue that the more wind sprints his football team runs in practice, the higher their scores in actual games; but the fact is that their opposition is becoming weaker each week. When the Method of Concomitant Variation is used like the Method of Difference, there may be differences other than the co-varying circumstance that has been singled out, and the real causal factor is contained in these unknown differences. The more fertilizer I use on one side of my yard, the more it flourishes. But this is not the only difference between this side of the yard and the other ("control") side, since I always water the "experimental" side after fertilizing it. So the additional moisture is *another* difference that might on its own (or partly) account for the different results. And, in both cases, the investigator has to avoid mistaking what is probably only a part of the cause for the whole cause.

In addition to these familiar problems, the Method of Concomitant Variation has some that are peculiar to itself.

(1) What are the boundaries of co-variation? Exercise may build stronger bodies. Fertilizer may produce greener grass. Decreased interest rates may push up the stock market. But in all these there is a point of diminishing returns. There is a limit to the strength that increased exercise can produce. Fertilizer may be applied in an amount that will kill the grass. And loans may become so easy to get that the stock market crashes. Many things that co-vary do not co-vary indefinitely.

(2) Which is cause and which is effect? Two factors may co-vary with startling consistency, but we may be uncertain as to which is exerting the causal pressure and which is receiving it. A child noticed that the higher the mercury in the thermometer outside, the higher the temperature of the air. So on a cold day she rattled the thermometer, believing that if she could get the mercury to go up, she could improve the weather. Does Bertha overeat because she's unpopular, or is Bertha unpopular

---

The causes of events are always more interesting than the events themselves.
—*Cicero,* Ad Atticum

because she overeats? Does the increased building stimulate the stock market, or does the rising market stimulate building? Does the increased temperature of a gas increase the pressure, or does the increased pressure increase the temperature? About all we know for sure is that the cause *precedes* the effect in time.

Some co-varying factors may reciprocally affect one another. The rise of the stock market on Monday, for example, may stimulate increased building on Tuesday, which in turn stimulates the further rise of the market on Wednesday, which gives another boost to building on Thursday, and so on. Events of both types (rising stock market and increased building) may be causes of events of the other type. Causal efficacy operates, then, in both directions.

(3) Is there a third factor? That two co-varying factors are causally related does not mean that they are related to one another. They may be effects of a third factor. They co-vary with one another only because each of them co-varies with a third factor. People who enjoy smoking cannot but be impressed with its correlation with lung cancer. One such smoker denied the direct connection, claiming that the desire to smoke and the tendency to get lung cancer are effects of a common cause, as yet undiscovered. A decathlon performer finds that his speed and his strength are increasing at similar rates. He does not assert a causal connection between them, but sees them both as effects of an expanded program of a special exercise.

Concluding Summary: The Method of Concomitant Variation may be used to supplement the other methods or may be used when the others cannot be used. When the amount or degree of the effect varies directly or inversely with the amount or degree of an antecedent circumstance, the two may be causally related. It is natural to suspect a causal connection wherever co-variation is observed, but many cases of co-variation are merely accidents and coincidences. The Method of Concomitant Variation has most of the problems that the other methods have, as well as some that are unique to itself.

Finding the Effect

We have discussed how Mill's Methods are used to find the cause of events. As his own formulation of the methods indicates, they are equally useful in finding the effect.

The methods are predicated on the ideal sense of cause in which a biconditional relationship holds between cause and effect. The cause occurs before the effect in time, and the causal productiveness flows from cause to effect. But, whatever can be said about the cause can be said methodologically about the effect also, for the conditional arrow points both ways.

$$\left. \begin{array}{c} C \rightarrow E \\ E \rightarrow C \end{array} \right\} = C \leftrightarrow E$$

'C' is the necessary and sufficient condition for 'E,' and 'E' is the necessary and sufficient condition for 'C.'

We can thus employ the Method of Agreement to find the effect in much the same way that we employ it to find the cause. Instead of talking about "antecedent circumstances," however, we will talk about "consequent circumstances":

THE CAUSE WHOSE EFFECT IS BEING INVESTIGATED	CONSEQUENT CIRCUMSTANCES
X_1	a b c d
X_2	d e f g
X_3	x y z d

Since d is the only circumstance common to all the consequences of X, it must be the effect of X. The effect of drinking the cranberry juice was the skin rash, for that always followed it and was the only thing that did.

Similar cautions are in order: Have we by chance eliminated different factors (say, a, e, and x) that contain the same ingredient which *really* is the effect of X? *Is d* the only thing common in the consequent circumstances? Can we ever be sure that what we have is the only common consequent? *Whatever* we select, is it the whole effect of X or only a part of that effect?

We can employ the Method of Difference to find the effect just as we used it to find the cause:

THE CAUSE WHOSE EFFECT IS BEING INVESTIGATED	CONSEQUENT CIRCUMSTANCES
X occurred	a b c d
X did not occur	a b c

Since the consequent circumstances are the same in both instances in all respects but one, that one difference must have been the effect of the cause. That is, d is the effect of X. In the first instance, a blue precipitate was formed when H_2SO_4 was placed in the test tube. In the second, there was no H_2SO_4 and no blue precipitate. So the precipitate was the effect of H_2SO_4.

> *Nature is not governed except by obeying her.*
> —*Francis Bacon*, De Augmentis Scientiarum

Similar cautions are in order: *Is* the observed difference in the consequents the only difference? Is *d* the whole effect, more than the effect, or less than the effect? Exactly what two complexes of circumstances is the causal relation supposed to connect?

The Joint Method of Agreement and Difference may be employed to find the effect if the data can be ordered in this way:

THE CAUSE WHOSE EFFECT IS BEING INVESTIGATED	CONSEQUENT CIRCUMSTANCES
X occurred	a b c
X occurred	a c d
X did not occur	a b x
X did not occur	d x y

Since *c* is the only factor always present when the cause occurs and always absent when the cause does not occur, *c* must be the effect we are seeking. If rickets is the only thing that always is conjoined with a deficiency of Vitamin D and absent when there is no deficiency, then rickets assuredly is the effect of a deficiency of Vitamin D.

Finally we may note that the Method of Concomitant Variation may be employed for finding the effect. It may take this form:

THE CAUSE WHOSE EFFECT IS BEING INVESTIGATED	CONSEQUENT CIRCUMSTANCES
X *to* n degree	a b c^2 d
X *to* n + 1 degree	a^2 c d e
X *to* n + 2 degree	a^3 b c^3 e

Or this form:

THE CAUSE WHOSE EFFECT IS BEING INVESTIGATED	CONSEQUENT CIRCUMSTANCES
X *to* n degree	a b c d
X *to* n + 1 degree	a^2 b c d
X *to* n + 2 degree	a^3 b c d

This method most obviously goes both ways, for it looks for variation, direct or inverse, between any two factors. The one that precedes the other in time is called the cause.

Concluding Summary: Since the conception of the cause/effect relation that Mill's Methods are based upon is a biconditional one, the methods may be used to find the effect as well as to find the cause. Whatever logical relations hold for the cause also hold for the effect.

EXERCISES

Exercise 86

Critically examine each of these uses of the Method of Agreement:

1. Three times I've flown across the Atlantic Ocean, and three times I've made a contribution at the shrine of Apollo just before taking off. Since I plan to go to London next month, I must not forget this safety measure!
2. When Woodrow Wilson, a Democrat, was President, the United States got into World War I. When Franklin Roosevelt and the other Democrats were running the country, we got into World War II. Harry Truman, another Democrat, got us into the Korean War. A Democrat, John F. Kennedy, was President when American troops were sent to Vietnam. The conclusion is obvious: American wars are caused by Democratic administrations.
3. Dew, the deposit of moisture on the outside of a cold glass, and the condensation of steam on the inside of a teacup all have one thing in common: air containing moisture is cooled to the point where it can no longer contain it all. This, then, is the cause of the phenomena: temperature dropping below the point of supersaturation.
4. Steady Eddie rode five winners at Fairmount yesterday. Two were favorites, two were long shots, and one was 8 to 1. The races were run at two distances. Two of the horses were fillies. It rained after the first two races. The only common thing about the races was the jockey. Steady Eddie was the cause of those five winners.
5. I did very well on my astronomy exam again. What makes me such a good student? Before the first exam I had a good breakfast of pancakes, eggs, and sausage and rode my bike to school. Before the second exam, I also studied a lot, but I overslept and, after a quick cup of coffee, drove my VW to the classroom building. The last time was different. I got up at the crack of dawn and studied until ten minutes before the exam, when my sister dropped me off. I don't know whether I ate anything or not. The cause of my success is simple: study!

Exercise 87

Critically examine each of these uses of the Method of Difference:

1. The city streets commissioner wishes to test two brands of highway paint. He used Brand A to mark white lines on Elm Street where the library is. On Maple Street, near Wilma's Tavern, he used Brand B to mark white

lines. He used the same amount of paint in each instance and the streets were of the same composition. At the end of the year he found that Brand B had almost worn away, while Brand A was still bright and clear. Conclusion: Brand A wears better than Brand B.

2. Judith and Janice are identical twins. They both use water from the same city when they wash dishes, and they both wash the same number of times a week. Judith uses Mystic Detergent, while Janice uses Sandstone Soapflakes. Judith's hands are soft and nice; Janice's are red and ugly. The cause of this difference is the different soaps.

3. Chester Wadsworth visited the shrine before his transoceanic flight. The late Horace Claiborne did not. Mr. Wadsworth made the trip safely. See?

4. Oscar drank a beer after his first nine holes of golf on a hot and humid day. When he completed the second nine, he gulped down a glass of ice water—and passed out. If he had stuck to beer, he would have been OK.

5. I have two African violets. Two weeks ago they were the same size and color and in the same state of health. They are in the same room where they get the same light. I feed, water, and spray them in exactly the same ways. The only difference is that I speak kindly to the one on the left, while pointedly ignoring the other one. Well, the one I talk to has grown eleven inches, while the other one droops dejectedly, a foot shorter. This proves to me that it works to talk to your plants!

6. A recent study showed that married males lived, on the average, almost ten years longer than unmarried males. After reading this, Clarence decided to look for a wife.

7. In 1988 the United States indicted Ferdinand Marcos and his wife, Imelda, for embezzling more than $100 million from the Philippine government. A few days later, the Philippine government agreed to extend the lease of military bases to the United States. The indictment obviously is what made the agreement possible.

8. From a chain letter: "Do not break the chain! Dire things have happened to those who do. Thomas G., in Charlotte, failed to send out copies on time and experienced an automobile accident demolishing his Buick. Mildred W. of Portland, ignored the warnings and had a miscarriage. William T. of Utica, on the other hand, who promptly mailed the copies, learned later in the same week that he was a big lottery winner. The most interesting case is that of Abner D. He was late mailing the copies and had a big elm tree blow down smashing his sun porch. When he did mail the copies, he was informed by his doctor that his case of cancer was now in remission."

Exercise 88

Critically examine each of these uses of the Method of Concomitant Variation:

1. In 1975, the city of North Snowshoe spent $40,000 to enforce the law. A total of thirty-two crimes were reported. In 1976, the city spent $59,000 to

fight crime. Forty-eight crimes were reported. In 1977, the budget for law enforcement was raised to $75,000. But the figure for law violations that year was sixty-three. So the town fathers, in an attempt to reduce crime, voted only $15,000 for law enforcement in 1978.

2. There is a close correlation between the amount of gasoline sold in a year and the number of traffic accidents. The more gasoline sold, the more annual accidents. This holds true for the last twenty-five years. So if we ration gasoline, we might find that we are also rationing automobile accidents!

3. Mrs. Jones baked three cakes on three separate days. She used the same basic ingredients in all cases and baked the cakes in the same oven. In the batter for the first cake, she placed a few drops of rum. She put a teaspoon of rum in the second cake and used three tablespoons in the third. Mr. Jones' remarks on being served pieces from each of these cakes were: (1) ''The cake is good, dear.'' (2) ''The cake is especially good tonight!'' (3) ''Delicious, honey! Give me another piece.'' Conclusion: Mr. Jones' reactions were caused by the rum.

4. Four years ago the Hornets finished in fifth place and were last in the league in attendance. Three years ago they got up to third; attendance improved also. Two years ago they came in second and had excellent attendance. Last year they won the championship and played to capacity crowds. The management has improved the parking, provided fancy uniforms, and tried several promotions, but the figures tell the story: winning teams bring out the fans.

Exercise 89

Briefly indicate what method you would first use and how you would proceed in order to find:

1. The cause of your headaches.
2. The cause of truancy in children.
3. The effect of smoking marijuana on sexual performance.
4. The cause of poets' popularity during their own lifetime.
5. The effect of weightlessness on human consciousness.

Chapter 10

Induction: Hypotheses

PREVIEW

All inductive conclusions are hypotheses. While based on the facts, they all go beyond the facts. This chapter deals with hypotheses that go further than generalizations and causal statements in imposing patterns on the facts and thus explaining them. Some of these hypotheses may be very specific: Billy the Kid murdered a homesteader named Wilson in 1875; there is a leak in the car's cooling system. Some hypotheses can be very comprehensive: Complex forms of life have evolved from simpler forms of life, e = mc², for example. What do you need to know about hypotheses?

1. Exactly what it means to say that hypotheses *explain* the facts.
2. How hypotheses are tested.
3. The importance of testability.
4. The nature of confirmation, verification, and disconfirmation.
5. The use of *auxiliary assumptions* in explaining and predicting facts.
6. The use of deduction in hypothetical reasoning.
7. How *likelihood* may be used in choosing from among rival hypotheses.
8. How *simplicity* may be used in choosing from among rival hypotheses.

Test yourself with these relevant questions:

1. Has the theory of evolution been proved?
2. Has it been proved that Socrates drank the hemlock?
3. Let's suppose that the stock market drops sharply today. Can you think of two hypotheses to explain this fact?
4. Is it true that a theory that leads us truly is necessarily true?
5. Which is more likely: (1) The student attended the funerals of four grandparents during the semester. (2) The student skipped the scheduled exams because he was unprepared.
6. If you were on a jury, would you tend to believe a very complicated account

of the movements of the accused on the day of the murder or a very simple account?

7. What hypothesis would you formulate to explain the presence of a Girl Scout with circulars and order blanks at your door?

8. True or false: A hypothesis must have observable consequences; it must make a difference in what is to be expected in the future.

THE NATURE OF HYPOTHESES

Fact and Theory

The content of inductive premises is fact. The most indubitable facts are those of direct sense observation:

(1) The wall of this room is green.
(2) The precipitate in the test tube is red.
(3) The pointer hovers between four and five.
(4) Light is seen on the cross hairs at 10:48:33 P.M. at such-and-such an altitude and azimuth.
(5) The thighbone is connected with the hipbone.
(6) The stone is covered with moss.

Although we may be sure of the truth of such facts, they are not very interesting. Simply as facts, they exhibit no pattern, they proclaim no relationships. No one will understand anything, nature or society, by amassing facts. He who goes around collecting facts will remain at a very low level of knowledge. As Poincaré said, "Science is built up of facts, as a house is built up with stones; but an accumulation of facts is no more a science than a heap of stones is a house." Unconnected facts are true but lead nowhere.

For facts to be meaningful, imagination is necessary. Something *beyond* the facts must be conceived. This is where the inductive conclusion comes in. It relates the facts and makes them meaningful. It imposes a pattern. The drawing of an inductive conclusion effects a happy marriage between fact and imagination. Facts without theory are blind; theory without facts is empty.

It should not be assumed that there is a clear dividing line between factual statements and theoretical statements. (1), above, seems to be less theoretical than

> *I mean by 'hard' data those which resist the solvent influence of critical reflection, and by 'soft' data those which, under the operation of this process, become to our minds more or less doubtful. The hardest of hard data are of two sorts: . . . The facts of sense (i.e., of* our own *sense-data) and the laws of logic. . . . The problem really is: Can the existence of anything other than our own hard data be inferred from the existence of those data?*
> —*Bertrand Russell,* Our Knowledge of the External World

(4), for the latter assumes a great deal about chronometers and telescopes, but (1) is not without some theoretical cargo also. That the color perceived is the surface of a *wall* is not itself given in the experience of the speaker. It may be a ceiling, a reflection, or even a hallucination. Is the "precipitate" in (2) really a precipitate, or is it the *solution* that is red? It is difficult to doubt (3), but, conceivably, in a split second, while we blinked, the pointer could have jumped to seven and back. Are we sure that (5) is always true? And in (6), is it the stone that is covered with moss or is it a plaster-of-Paris reproduction?

Relative to the conclusion, the premises of an inductive argument are factual. And relative to the premises, the conclusion is hypothetical. Unless the inductive reasoner is to restrict himself to such data as 'red here now' and 'pain now,' he will have to employ premises that are not entirely indisputable. They will be much *less* indisputable, however, than the conclusion.

For our generalization 'all white blue-eyed tomcats are deaf,' we examined Reggie and Clarence. When we pronounced Reggie deaf and used 'Reggie is deaf' as a premise, we had something we could be confident was true, but it is *possible* that Reggie only pretended to be deaf. At any rate, the generalization, the inductive conclusion, is much more hypothetical. It will be recalled that in deduction we do not encounter any loss of certainty when we go from premises to conclusion. Where the argument is valid, the conclusion will enjoy the same degree of certainty as the premises. But in induction we move beyond the scope of the premises.

Since all inductive conclusions, relative to their premises, are hypothetical, we may call them all *hypotheses*. Generalizations, statements of causal relations, and hypotheses in the narrow sense impose a pattern on facts. They relate them and make them meaningful. The generalization, 'all ruminants have horns,' introduces some order to a host of facts about deer, cattle, and sheep. The causal statement, 'if the blossoms are frozen, the tree bears no fruit,' sheds some light on our unhappy experience with peach trees last spring. The hypothesis (in the narrow sense) that Bruno Hauptmann kidnapped the Lindbergh child makes meaningful the facts that he spoke with an accent and was in possession of the ransom money.

The hypotheses illuminate the facts, while the facts support the hypothesis.

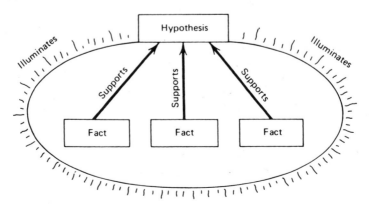

The hypothesis is an effort to understand the facts, while the facts stand as evidence for the hypothesis. The hypothesis is created; the facts are found.

Concluding Summary: All inductive conclusions are hypotheses. A hypothesis goes beyond the "factual" premises. By imposing a pattern on the facts, it makes them meaningful. The truth of the hypothesis, while not proved, is supported by the facts it illuminates.

What is now proved was once only imagined.

William Blake, Proverbs of Hell

Explaining the Facts

What does it mean to "illuminate the facts"? A hypothesis illuminates the facts when it tells us why these facts are the case instead of some other facts, when it accounts for the facts, when it *explains* the facts. A hypothesis explains the facts in the sense that once we assume that it (the hypothesis) is true, the facts are just about what one would expect to find. The facts are no longer strange and baffling, external to our comprehension.

Ordinarily we take the facts for granted. We do not bother to illuminate them. We are not scientists who seek to answer such questions as: "Why does the Nile overflow its banks?" "Why does the sun 'rise' in the morning?" "What is the significance of this fossil discovered in the mound?" We are not detectives who try to formulate a theory to account for the cartridge shell found in the dining room and the mysterious behavior of the butler. We are not newspaper reporters who try to account for the fact that great sums of money were transferred four times in one day in Miami banks. But when facts are strange or fall within our own experience, we are often moved to account for them, to explain them, to answer the question, *why?*

Suppose Alfred returns home late one night. When he approaches the door he finds that the lock has been broken. He enters the house and turns on the light. Muddy footprints are on the floor. While pondering these unusual phenomena he begins to prepare for himself a midnight snack. He finds to his dismay that the silverware is gone. The factual situation has now become a problem for him. He wants to know what happened; he wants to account for the strange facts; he wants to understand them.

To explain the facts Alfred must go *beyond* the facts; he must theorize. He must formulate a hypothesis. Taking the observed facts as premises or evidence, he must draw an inductive conclusion.

The obvious one, the one that occurs to him first, is that the place has been burglarized. His "argument" takes this form:

Premises or Evidence {
The lock on the door has been broken (observed fact 1)
There are muddy footprints on the floor (observed fact 2)
The silverware is gone (observed fact 3)

Conclusion: The place has been burglarized (hypothesis)

This inductive conclusion does indeed explain the facts. In view of a burglary having taken place, these facts are quite appropriate. Alfred's thought has found a place to rest; his curiosity is satisfied. Although the facts are still disturbing, they are not so *intellectually* disturbing, for Alfred now has an *explanation* for them.

If the place had been burglarized, the facts would seem to follow. Entry would have had to be forced at some point. It was. Signs of a stranger's presence might be found. They were. Something of value would be missing. It was. With the formulation of the hypothesis, these facts, though inconvenient, are no longer absurd creatures outside human comprehension.

A more exact way of stating how a hypothesis explains the facts is this: The hypothesis, together with auxiliary assumptions, can serve as premises in deductive arguments of which the facts are conclusions. The facts are explained by the hypothesis from which they can be deduced. The hypothesis remains an inductive conclusion. It is its *explanatory* function that is indicated by its capacity to serve as a premise (along with auxiliary assumptions) from which the observed facts can be deduced.

Deductive {
The place has been burglarized (hypothesis)
If the place has been burglarized, everything of obvious value will be missing (auxiliary assumption)
The silverware is of obvious value (auxiliary assumption)

∴ The silverware is missing (observed fact 3)

When an inductive argument can be turned upside-down to make (with the addition of some auxiliary assumptions) a deductive argument, the facts have been explained.

The generalization (an inductive conclusion) that all ravens are black explains the fact that the visitor to Poe's study was black, for the latter can be deduced from the former and the auxiliary assumption that Poe's visitor that evening was a raven. The causal statement (an inductive conclusion) that alcohol causes hangovers explains the fact that Stanley got hangovers after every evening of drinking, for the latter can be deduced from the former and the auxiliary assumption that alcohol was present in his drinks. The hypothesis (an inductive conclusion) that Hauptmann kidnapped the Lindbergh child explains the fact that the kidnapper had a distinctive accent, for the latter can be deduced from the former and the auxiliary assumption that Hauptmann was a German immigrant.

Even statistical generalization may be said to provide explanations. The observed fact that Rita prefers Nacelle Bras is explained by the statistical generalization that 88 percent of all Las Vegas showgirls prefer Nacelle Bras. But the logic is a little different. The fact cannot itself be deduced from the generalization and the auxiliary assumption that Rita is a Las Vegas showgirl. The most that can be deduced is that there is a probability of .88 that she prefers the brand.

If a statement does not explain the facts in some such way as above described, it is not a hypothesis. And, since all inductive conclusions are hypotheses (in the broad sense), a statement that does not explain the facts cannot be an inductive conclusion from those facts.

Concluding Summary: All inductive conclusions or hypotheses must explain the facts from which they are derived. If a hypothesis and auxiliary assumptions can serve as premises in an argument from which a particular fact can be deduced, that fact may be said to be explained by that hypothesis.

Testability

Since inductive conclusions are at best only probable, they should be drawn in a spirit of tentativeness. That *this* hypothesis explains very well a set of facts does not mean that it is true. Some other hypothesis might explain them just as well. For any set of facts, more than one explanation (or hypothesis) is possible.

In the burglary example, it may indeed be the case that no burglary took place. The lock may have been broken by Alfred's wife—who was angry at losing her key. The footprints may have been left by the plumber who fixed the dishwasher that afternoon. And the silverware may have been sent out for cleaning. The burglary hypothesis is a good one, but not the only one possible. It adequately explains the facts but is not the only explanation available.

Modern science is an inductive enterprise. It employs hypotheses to explain the facts. Its theories explain many facts, but they are hypotheses and are not, therefore, absolutely certain. The laws of gravity account for the motion and velocity of millions of particles. The theories of historians account for letters, records, and artifacts from ancient society. The anthropologists have theories about bone fragments and fossils that tell us about the nature of prehistoric man. But all these are hypotheses. They are explanations of sets of facts that can have other explanations.

Those theories in which we have most confidence are theories which have been *tested* and have passed the tests. Rival theories have been tested and have failed the tests.

A hypothesis is tested by deducing *other* observable facts from it (and auxiliary assumptions). One asks: What *else* should we expect to be the case if the hypothesis is true? A hypothesis not only explains the present. It must also look to the future. It must make a difference in what will be observed. It is through tests that one comes to prefer one hypothesis over another and that one accumulates additional evidence for some hypotheses. Did Hypothesis A lead us rightly? If so, it is confirmed. If not, it is disconfirmed.

Since tests are resorted to in order to choose from among rival hypotheses and to acquire additional evidence for a successful hypothesis, it is important that statements that purport to be hypotheses are indeed, at least in principle, testable.

It is the mark of stubborn and dogmatic persons to be oblivous to the need either to test their own beliefs or to recognize the successful tests that opposing beliefs have undergone. Copernicus caused widespread consternation when he suggested that the earth revolved around the sun. Though he had impressive evidence for this theory, it was received in ill humor by most religious groups. Martin Luther complained: "People give ear to an upstart astrologer who strove to show that the earth revolved, not the heavens or the firmament, the sun and the moon. . . . This fool wishes to reverse the entire science of astronomy; but the sacred Scripture tells us that Joshua commanded the sun to stand still and not the earth." And John Calvin exclaimed: "Who will venture to place the authority of Copernicus above that of the Holy Spirit?" Somewhat later, Galileo, who was to be persecuted by the Roman Catholic Church, could not even persuade the professors at Padua to examine the evidence for his contention that the planet Jupiter had satellites. One professor refused to look through the telescope, for he knew that there had to be exactly seven heavenly bodies, no more, no less. What "reason" did he give? "There are seven windows given to animals in the domicile of the head. . . . From this and many other similarities in nature, such as the seven metals, etc., which it were tedious to enumerate, we gather that the number of planets is necessarily seven. Moreover these alleged satellites of Jupiter are invisible to the naked eye, and therefore can exercise no influence on the earth, and therefore would be useless, and therefore do not exist. Besides, from the earliest times men have adopted the division of the week into seven days, and have named them after the seven planets. Now if we increase the number of planets, this whole and beautiful system falls to the ground."

A statement must make a specific difference in what is to be observed if it is to be regarded as a genuine hypothesis. The statement, "everything that happens is eventually for the best," is not a hypothesis because on its basis nothing definite can be predicted for any specified time in the future. A statement to the effect that a German invasion of the United States had been prevented by thought waves emanating from the meetings of the "I Am" cult of California is also untestable. If there are no possible ways to overthrow a statement, it is not a hypothesis. And there is no way to overthrow a theoretical statement except to show that it has erred in its prediction. The statement, 'Gold was mined in Central City,' is testable. If we assume it for a moment, we can expect to find abandoned mines there, a certain type of geological formation, and records in the old newspapers. If these predictions come true, we have gotten confirmation for the hypothesis; if they do not, we have discon-

---

It has been said that the mandate issued to the age of Plato and Aristotle was Bring your beliefs into harmony with one another; *that the mandate of the Mediaeval Spirit was* Bring your beliefs into harmony with dogma; *and that the mandate of the new spirit which rebelled against the authority of the Church was* Bring your beliefs into harmony with fact.

—*H. W. B. Joseph,* An Introduction to Logic

firmed it. Astronomical theories are legitimate hypotheses also. On their basis, very specific predictions are made as to what we will see through a telescope at a certain angle at a certain time. A genuine hypothesis commits itself to the future; a phony one does not.

A Pan Am 747 jet crashed in Scotland in December 1988, killing 259 people. The plane had been cruising at an altitude of about 31,000 feet with no indication of trouble when it suddenly disappeared from the control tower's radar screen. Wreckage was found scattered over several miles. What is the explanation? From the beginning of the investigation FAA officials were quite sure that the mystery could be solved. One hypothesis (A) held that the cause of the crash was a bomb explosion. Another (B) held that the cause was a series of structural failures. Both are testable. If A is true, a thorough examination of wreckage bits should turn up evidence of a chemical residue. If B is true, wreckage pieces should show signs of metal fatigue. On the basis of A, jagged holes should be found; on the basis of B, breakage should be spotted along the seams of the aircraft's body. On the basis of A, pieces would be bent and tangled, as well as singed; this would not be so on the basis of B. The sounds of a bomb explosion are different from those of a structural disintegration. Recovery of the cockpit recorder was expected to support one or the other of the hypotheses. Within about a week, authorities were quite sure that the crash was caused by a bomb. All the implications of Hypothesis A turned out to be true, while none of the implications of Hypothesis B were true. Although chemical analysis of pieces of the wreckage continued, authorities believed that the evidence for the detonation of a powerful explosive on board the aircraft is "conclusive."

It should be understood in the foregoing examples that the statements themselves, in isolation, cannot be expected to suffice for the prediction of observational consequences. Choice of appropriate auxiliary assumptions is also required. It is when consequences cannot be derived from the statement in conjunction with auxiliary assumptions which could not have been derived from the auxiliary assumptions alone that the statement fails to qualify as a genuine hypothesis. In the case of the Pan Am jet, the auxiliary assumptions embody knowledge about chemical residue from bombs, results of explosions and structural collapse of metal, typical sounds of explosions and disintegrations, and so on. The facts, observed and unobserved, were logical consequences of these assumptions (known independently of the occasion of the crash) in conjunction with the two hypotheses.

One of the greatest blocks against testability in hypotheses is the presence of key terms whose meanings are not clearly known. If we do not clearly know what the hypothesis means, we will be uncertain as to what consequences follow from it. We don't know how to set about to test it. How do we deal with the "hypothesis" that the great wars in our time are symptomatic of "the fatal spirit of modern civilization"? A statement expressed so indefinitely that we cannot be sure what its consequences are is no hypothesis at all; it is a pseudo-hypothesis.

The presence of vague terms discredits the "hypothesis" in which they occur, for we will not know which consequences clearly count *for* the hypothesis and which

> *Whereof one cannot speak, thereof one must be silent.*
> *—Ludwig Wittgenstein,* Tractatus Logico-Philosophicus

count clearly *against* it. The Marxian hypothesis that economic factors determine every major event in history contains at least three vague terms. How much of a certain kind of activity has to be present before a factor can be called "economic"? How unimportant does an event have to be for it not to be "major"? How influential or proximate does a factor have to be to be "determinate"? If we can agree that an event is major and go back in time until we find something that is in some sense "economic" and in some sense "determinate," have we clearly confirmed the hypothesis? There seems to be very little chance of *dis*confirming it! A statement expressed in such a way that there is very little chance of disconfirming it, is not a satisfactory hypothesis. If a philosopher or scientist takes no risk in what he claims, he cannot be claiming much.

Genuine hypotheses are not necessarily true hypotheses; many turn out to be false. But hypotheses that have been disproved have performed a real function. They have stimulated research, have guided inquiry, and have led to some important observations that would not otherwise have been made. De Morgan remarked, "Wrong hypotheses, rightly worked, have produced more useful results than unguided observation." In fact, at the beginning of an investigation we can adopt "working hypotheses" on the basis of rather slender evidence. The important thing is to get started. We learn through error. Our collection of facts becomes meaningful only when we have a hypothesis in mind. Without it, we wouldn't even know what kind of facts, out of the billions we are confronted with, to look for. Darwin said that observation, to mean anything, must be for or against some view. And Einstein told an interviewer: "I think and think, for months, for years. Ninety-nine times the conclusion is false. The hundredth time I am right." But an untestable proposition really ventures nothing. Anyone can think them up and run no risk of being shown wrong. But the old maxim is correct. "Nothing ventured, nothing gained."

Concluding Summary: In light of the facts they explain, hypotheses are more or less probable. But, since any set of facts has several possible explanations or hypotheses, we need a criterion for choosing from among them. The best criterion is the capacity to pass tests. Statements that are not testable are not hypotheses. A statement is testable if on its basis predictions can be made about the future. It commits itself on what will be observed under given conditions. As a result of the test, the hypothesis is either confirmed or disconfirmed.

> *That fellow seems to me to possess but one idea, and that is a wrong one.*
> *—Samuel Johnson, Boswell's* Life of Johnson

EXERCISES

Exercise 90

Formulate hypotheses to explain each of the following sets of facts:

1. (a) Herbert is drinking heavily, by himself.
   (b) It is Friday night—when he usually is out with Helen.
   (c) He snarled when someone asked about Helen.
2. (a) The campsite is a mess.
   (b) Food containers have been opened and garbage is strewn around.
   (c) Cameras and other valuable pieces of equipment have not been taken.
   (d) The tent has been torn.
3. (a) Giles has not returned home from India.
   (b) His Indian visa has expired.
   (c) His family has had no word from him.
4. (a) Millicent no longer takes babysitting jobs on weekends.
   (b) She is taking much more care about her personal appearance.
   (c) She seems to be in a happier frame of mind.
   (d) She has not been home the last four Saturday nights I've phoned her.
5. (a) A derelict ship was found drifting in the Atlantic.
   (b) No one was on board.
   (c) The cargo was intact.
   (d) There were no signs of violence.
   (e) Chronometer, sextant, and lifeboat were gone.
   (f) There was no mention of any trouble in the ship's log.

Exercise 91

THE STORY OF THE DESERTED PICNIC

"A man walking in the country one fine summer evening came upon a tablecloth spread upon the ground. Four places were laid, as if for a meal. The food on three of the plates had been almost entirely consumed, while the food on the fourth plate seemed to be untasted. Some of the food was still warm to the touch, and a fire was still burning, though the logs had been scattered. Articles of clothing and other personal belongings had been left, but no signs of disorder were visible. Further observation showed two facts that seemed to deserve attention. The fourth (untouched) plate had very little food upon it, and no knife seemed to have been provided for the person who was to eat from it. A piece of paper large enough to hold a pound of butter still showed traces of butter, but no butter was anywhere in sight. There were no people to be seen anywhere in the neighborhood."[1]

What is the explanation?

[1] Max Black, *Critical Thinking* (New York: Prentice-Hall, 1946), p. 262.

CHOOSING FROM AMONG HYPOTHESES

Confirmation and Disconfirmation

A hypothesis is tested by drawing out its consequences. Descriptions of future events are deduced from the hypothesis (and auxiliary assumptions). Predictions are made. If the consequences are the case, if the predictions come true, if, in other words, the hypothesis has led us truly, it is said to be confirmed. The additional evidence that was thus turned up in the testing process now serves as additional "premises," strengthening an inductive argument of which the confirmed theory is the conclusion. The conclusion has not been proved, but it has been made more probable. If the consequences are not the case, if the predictions do not come true, if the hypothesis has led us falsely, it is said to be disconfirmed. It is thus discarded as an adequate explanation for the facts.

The best principle for choosing among rival hypotheses is to discard the ones that are disconfirmed and to accept with increasing confidence those that are confirmed.

Suppose we have a problem with a baby. The baby is crying. One hypothesis to account for his behavior is that he has gas on his stomach. This does explain the fact that he is crying. Gas on the stomach creates pain (auxiliary assumption), and babies cry when they are in pain (auxiliary assumption). But we know that this is not the only hypothesis to explain the crying. So we formulate another one: The baby feels neglected and wants attention. This too explains the fact, for feeling neglected is distressing and productive of crying (auxiliary assumption).

We now have rival hypotheses. On what basis can we select one or eliminate the other? How do we choose between them? We test them. If one fails the test, we throw it out and "go along with" the other. If both fail, we look for a third hypothesis. If they both pass, we look for other tests.

To test any hypothesis we ask: What *other* facts should be observed if the hypothesis is true? With respect to the first hypothesis, we would expect the crying to cease if the gas on the stomach could be eliminated. Assuming that this particular medicine will eliminate gas, we administer it to the baby and predict that he will stop crying. If he does, the gas hypothesis is confirmed. If he does not, it has been disconfirmed. We can test the second hypothesis by holding and cuddling the baby, and making soothing sounds. On the basis of what we know about child psychology, we predict that he will stop crying. If he does, the neglect hypothesis is confirmed. If he does not, it has been disconfirmed. It is hoped that from a list of rival hypotheses one will survive and the others will be eliminated.

It is sometimes possible to confirm a hypothesis and disconfirm its chief rival with the same test. Such a test (or experiment) is called a "crucial" one. A very dramatic instance of this occurred some years ago when the truth of the Newtonian and Einsteinian theories was being debated. According to Newtonian science, a telescope raised to a specified altitude and set at a specified azimuth would at a specified date and time *not* reveal light. According to Einsteinian science, the telescope *would* reveal light. Whether the light was observed or not was a definite consequence of each theory. From the Newton hypothesis the deduction was: no light. From the Einstein hypothesis the deduction was: light. At the appointed time, the scientists were at the telescope. When the chronometer indicated the prescribed split second, the light was observed on the cross hairs. Einstein's theory was confirmed—it had successfully predicted the new fact. Newton's theory was disconfirmed—it had predicted what in fact had *not* occurred. That which leads us truly becomes more probably true. That which leads us falsely is false.

Strictly speaking, we cannot ever say that a theory or hypothesis is *proved*. No matter how much additional evidence is piled up by successful prediction, no matter how many times a theory is confirmed, it is still only probable. You may be virtually certain that Julius Caesar crossed the Rubicon, but you did not see him do it. You may be quite confident that the silverware was stolen after a felon confessed to the deed and the silverware was found under his mattress. But the silverware *may* have been given to him by Alfred's wife, who wanted to collect some insurance. We may feel that it was gas that bothered the baby—he did stop crying after taking the medicine—but he may have been crying for something to drink.

There is one possible exception to all this. If a hypothesis is about something that can be verified by direct inspection, it may be established with certainty. If my hypothesis is that the path leads to the river, it may be verified. The hypotheses that there is a cross at the top of the mountain or a unicorn in the garden can be verified. A hypothesis that has been verified is no longer a hypothesis. It is a statement of fact. But most hypotheses are about matters that cannot be verified by direct inspection. Such hypotheses can be confirmed but not proved.

To say that confirmation *proves* the theory would be to commit the fallacy of "affirming the consequent," for the confirming evidence is nothing but the consequent of the theory, and there is no assurance that it is the only theory that would have this consequent.

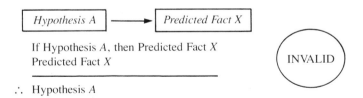

If Hypothesis *A*, then Predicted Fact *X*
Predicted Fact *X*
_____
∴ Hypothesis *A*

Some people have argued that although we cannot *prove* a theory, we can disprove a theory. This is quite plausible, for it is not fallacious to argue: If *A*, then *X*. Not-*X*. Therefore, Not-*A*. It is then claimed that one can deal with hypotheses through the method of elimination (which is indeed what Mill's Methods do). When we have several hypotheses clamoring for recognition, all we have to do is test them, disprove all but one, and take the remaining one as probably true. This is a good method and is widely used in science and common sense.

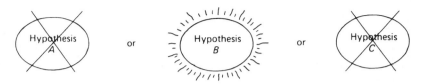

There are, however, three difficulties with this view.

The first is an obvious one. We can never be sure that we have considered all the possible hypotheses. Perhaps there is a Hypothesis *D* which is really better than all the others. Simply because we have overlooked it, we're stuck with *B*.

Secondly, it may not be practicably possible to eliminate all but one hypothesis. It was not possible to disprove the Ptolemaic (geocentric) theory until many years after Copernicus' (heliocentric) theory challenged it—and some people still insist that the geocentric theory has not been disproved. The wave theory and the corpuscular theory of light contended for many years without a crucial test to make the determination; they have both been supplanted by modern quantum theory which incorporates features of each. And how can we presently test whether Nixon did or did not know in advance of the Watergate break-in?

The third difficulty is that disconfirmation is not always clear and indisputable. If the predicted fact followed from the hypothesis *alone,* then a bad prediction would mean that the hypothesis was false. But scientific and ordinary hypothetical reasoning seldom depends on the hypothesis alone. When we deduce something from the hypothesis, we usually employ (covertly or openly) some *auxiliary assumptions.* These generally are, or should be, propositions whose truth is really not in question. But, if they are themselves hypotheses (sometimes called ''collateral hypotheses''), they are not indisputably true. The detective who concludes that Spike is not guilty employed auxiliary assumptions having to do with fingerprints. The mother who concludes that the baby did not have gas on his stomach utilized assumptions about alkalinity, acidity, and curative powers of certain medicines. The partisans of Einstein depended upon certain assumed truths about the time of day and the mechanical functions of the telescope. We never deal with a hypothesis in isolation from other propositions believed to be true. We should be careful that these other assumptions be credible, but we can never *guarantee* their truth.

If it is the case that consequences or predicted facts are deduced from the hypothesis that is to be tested *and* auxiliary assumptions, the process of testing should be represented as follows:

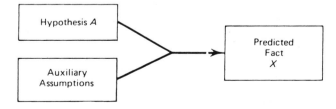

If (Hypothesis A and auxiliary assumptions), then Predicted Fact X.

If the predicted fact is indeed observed, the hypothesis has been confirmed (provided that the fact could not have been deducted from the auxiliary assumptions alone). If the predicted fact is not observed, one can conclude that it is not the case that *both* the hypothesis and the auxiliary assumptions are true. That is, either the hypothesis is false or the auxiliary assumptions are false. It is only to the degree that one is sure of the truth of his auxiliary assumptions that he can say that the hypothesis has been disproved.

Concluding Summary: Hypotheses are confirmed by making successful predictions. They are disconfirmed by making unsuccessful predictions. These predictions are deductive consequences of the hypotheses and auxiliary assumptions. Confirmation increases the probability of a hypothesis being true, while disconfirmation reduces its probability drastically. While it is easier to eliminate hypotheses than to establish them, categorical denial of the truth of a hypothesis requires absolute confidence in the auxiliary assumptions used with it.

> *That the sun will rise to-morrow, is an hypothesis; and that means that we do not* know *whether it will rise.*
> —*Ludwig Wittgenstein,* Tractatus Logico-Philosophicus

Likelihood

Suppose that two rival hypotheses both account for the very same facts, and there seems to be little chance to disprove one of them in the immediate future. In such a case, one is advised to choose the hypothesis with the greater *likelihood.*

Likelihood is a vague criterion, but it seems to mean coherence with other well-tested hypotheses. If one hypothesis coheres better with other more-or-less-established theories in other fields, it is regarded as more likely. One should not go against the findings of other branches of science merely to formulate hypotheses in his own. In history, for example, one might be tempted to explain the famous escape of Promanthodorus thus: "With one heave of his mighty muscles he burst the chains, drove away the crocodiles with his bare hands, and flew away." One should be suspicious of such a hypothesis. Though it explains the facts, in view of established theories about human strength and faculties, it does not seem likely.

> *Our direct perceptions of truth are so limited.—we know so few things by immediate intuition, or, as it used to be called, by simple apprehension.— that we depend, for almost all our valuable knowledge, on evidence external to itself; and most of us are very unsafe hands at estimating evidence. . . .*
> —*John Stuart Mill,* Inaugural Address at Saint Andrews

Consider the following account:

> I'd had this terrible pain in my back for years. Most days I couldn't even stand up straight. I've gone to chiropractors, osteopaths, and regular doctors. I've tried exercise, liniments, and pills. Nothing seems to help. Last week the doctor put me on some new expensive pill that had just been developed at some medical center in Cleveland. But that didn't help either. Well, two days ago I went to an evangelistic meeting that had a faith healer. I was desperate. There was preaching and singing, and then some of us afflicted people came forward to see if we could be helped. The faith healer touched my back and called for divine aid. From that moment I began to feel better. And today there's no pain at all and I can stand up like I used to. I'll finish taking the pills—after all, I paid for them—but I know what cured me. It was the Holy Spirit, not doctors!

The hypothesis that the man was healed by divine intervention is less likely than the obvious hypothesis that the medication had begun to have its cumulative effect. It coheres much better with medical science.

Likelihood can also be understood in terms of frequency. The one hundred dollar bill I found on the floor of the baggage area of the San Francisco air terminal may be explained in various ways:

(1) It was dropped accidentally by someone who had just left the nearby car-rental counter.
(2) It was thrown away by someone who thought it was a used ticket or boarding pass.
(3) It was deliberately placed near me to test my honesty.

In terms of frequency, the first hypothesis is best (most likely), and the third hypothesis is worst (least likely).

The hypothesis that a person last seen swimming by himself in a lake has drowned is more likely than the hypothesis that he has pretended to drown to escape his creditors. The hypothesis that someone leaving Vanzo's saw a Martian is less likely than the hypothesis that he (the "observer") was drunk.

The criterion of likelihood directs us to examine the auxiliary assumptions that are used along with the hypothesis to account for the facts. If we have to assume that Promanthodorus was capable of unaided flight to account for his escape, then the hypothesis, as indicated above, is unlikely. If we have to assume that divine power will respond to the singing and shouting of the revival services, the hypothesis that a person was healed by faith is unlikely. If we have to assume that travelers' honesty is often tested by strewing one hundred dollar bills before them, the hypothesis that describes such a thing is unlikely. If we have to assume that Roger Rumpot

---

Coherence is our only source of truth.
                                        —*Brand Blanshard,* The Nature of Thought

was sane and sober the night he reported seeing the Martian, the hypothesis that a Martian was present is unlikely.

If no concern is paid to auxiliary assumptions, just about any hypothesis will have equal claim, in terms of likelihood, to explain the facts. The hypothesis, "the moon is made of green cheese," can be shown to explain the fact that two people are absent from class today—*provided that* we have perfect freedom in our choice of auxiliary assumptions. From these assumptions and the green cheese hypothesis, we can indeed deduce that John and Mary are absent. For example:

> *The Moon Is Made of Green Cheese.* (Hypothesis)
>
> John has a strange neurological constitution which makes him seek a dry and hot climate under certain conditions. (auxiliary assumption)
>
> So does Mary. (auxiliary assumption)
>
> When the earth and moon are in a certain relationship, the green cheese in the moon emits a certain vapor which is experienced in a particular town in Illinois. (auxiliary assumption)
>
> This vapor, on the morning in question, aggravated John's and Mary's neurological state and produced an overpowering urge to go to Arizona. (auxiliary assumption)
>
> They succumbed to this urge immediately. (auxiliary assumption)
>
> *John and Mary Are Absent.* (observed fact)

Because the auxiliary assumptions make too great a strain on our credulity, we rightly reject the hypothesis that relies on them. It is possible, but *most unlikely.*

Concluding Summary: When the choice from among rival hypotheses cannot be made on the basis of confirmation/disconfirmation, we may appeal to the criterion of likelihood. Likelihood has to do with how the hypothesis coheres with well-founded scientific principles and with the relative frequency of the type of thing set forth in the hypothesis. The plausibility of the auxiliary assumptions one needs to use with the hypothesis is a good indicator of how likely that hypothesis is.

Simplicity

Another criterion is appealed to when one is trying to choose between rival hypotheses. It is the principle of *simplicity.* If two rival hypotheses explain the same facts, are equally likely, and no tests have been devised for eliminating one of them, we should choose the simpler one.

There is no rationale for this procedure. There is no reason why nature should choose the shorter route. The long and complicated hypothesis is ruled out, if not for unlikelihood, merely because it *is* long and complicated. For the sake of convenience, the simpler one is chosen, though, so far as we know, nature is not concerned to make things convenient for man.

The ancient geocentric theory of Ptolemy explained the same facts as the heliocentric theory of Copernicus. And predictions were equally reliable in both theories. The chief difference was that, for Ptolemy, the earth was the center of things and, for Copernicus, the sun was. But the latter theory was preferred because Copernicus' orbits were somewhat easier to work with than Ptolemy's complicated chart of epicycles and epicycles in epicycles. And with the discoveries by Kepler and Newton, the heliocentric theory became vastly simpler than the geocentric theory.

Astronomers make observations, plot them on a chart, and draw lines between them which are supposed to represent the paths of celestial bodies. Physicians make graphs representing changes in the temperature or blood pressure of their patients. A man on a diet weighs himself every week and illustrates his progress on a graph. But why are these people justified in connecting the observed points by straight or gracefully curving lines? Perhaps the actual course of events would be more accurately represented by an irregular line:

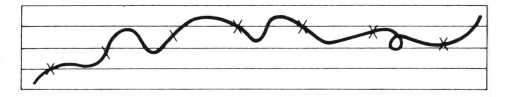

But, on grounds of simplicity, we prefer to say that this line is more representative:

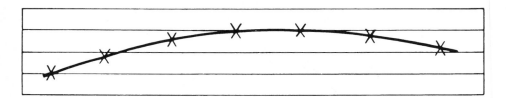

And no matter how many observations we make, there is still the possibility of erratic movement between the points observed![2]

A somewhat different sense of simplicity is expressed in the principle of *parsimony:* "Entia non sunt multiplicanda praeter necessitatem." This principle was expressed by the medieval philosopher. William of Ockham, and is called "Ockham's razor."

---

[2] The use of these graphs was suggested by a similar approach by Howard Kahane in *Logic and Philosophy,* Second Edition (Belmont, Calif.: Wadsworth Publishing Company, Inc., 1973), p. 289.

An example of its use is the fate of the concept *ether* as the medium through which light travels in interplanetary space. When scientists recognized that theories which employed the concept could explain no more than theories which did not, the concept was abandoned. "Entities should not be multiplied beyond necessity."

A third sense of simplicity is illustrated in the case of Harry Fletcher. He has been accused of murder. His fingerprints are on the gun, he had threatened the victim, he was seen in the victim's residential area the night of the murder. It looks bad for Harry, but Harry can formulate a hypothesis of his own which will explain the facts. He had threatened the victim, not really intending to do him any bodily harm. He just wanted to frighten him into paying off an old gambling debt. He was in the neighborhood because he likes to jog in different neighborhoods each night, and he hadn't visited that one yet. His fingerprints were on the gun because he had owned it once, had sold it to a shady character, and had shown him how to aim it. And so forth and so forth. The more complicated his explanation becomes, the more preferable becomes the obvious hypothesis: that he did the murder. This is the simpler one. And when Harry's "friendship" with the victim's wife was discovered, it was the one that sent him to prison.

This sense of simplicity seems to be similar to the "frequency" sense of likelihood. The parts of the complicated theory may not be especially unlikely in themselves, but their composite constitutes a total picture that is. When too much has to be granted to coincidence, we are properly suspicious. Still, coincidences themselves abound in the world, and every set of facts is, in the literal sense, a "coincidence" of events with diverse causes. While this sense of simplicity has more theoretical reason to recommend it than the other two, it must be admitted that the complicated explanation may be the true one, and the reason we discard it in favor of a simpler one is practical as well as theoretical.

Concluding Summary: If two hypotheses explain the same set of facts, receive equivalent confirmation, and seem equally likely, we may, for practical reasons, choose the one that contains briefer descriptions or posits fewer entities. But why the simpler theory has a better claim to truth than the more complicated one, I cannot say.

EXERCISES

Exercise 92

How would you go about testing each of these hypotheses? State at least one auxiliary assumption that would be employed in the text.

1. The path is a trace of an old interurban (railway) line.
2. She (or he) is in love with you.
3. Helmut is an ex-Nazi gestapo agent.
4. That movie was directed by Alfred Hitchcock.

5. Professor Jones is being interviewed on another campus for an administrative post.

Exercise 93

True or false?

1. When a hypothesis has been confirmed a great many times, it may be said to be proved.
2. A skillful investigator can usually find a way to verify a hypothesis.
3. If a hypothesis is disconfirmed, it is necessarily false.
4. All genuine hypotheses are true.
5. If the prediction is false, either the hypothesis or an auxiliary assumption is false.
6. If a statement is not testable, it is false.
7. If a statement is not testable, it is meaningless.
8. If a statement is not testable, it is not a hypothesis.
9. The observable facts that a confirmed hypothesis predicts constitute additional evidence for the truth of that hypothesis.
10. Scientists are interested in fact, not theory.

Exercise 94

What do you suspect might be wrong with each of these "hypotheses"? Use this key: A = Untestable; B = Unlikely; C = Too complicated.

1. Frank missed the final examination because he got a late start when his alarm clock failed to go off, and he ran out of gas when he tried to take a shortcut and got lost driving to school.
2. Good people go to heaven when they die.
3. There was no poverty on the lost continent of Atlantis.
4. The politician may have lost some votes by his answer, but his sole motive was to tell the truth.
5. Everything is either mind or states of mind.
6. The footprints, going from the front to the back door, were made by a person walking backward from the back to the front door.
7. He goes to church regularly and over the years has built a reputation for honesty. Apparently he is on the verge of perpetrating a great swindle at the bank where he works.
8. Human beings have freedom of will.
9. The magician caused three rabbits to materialize in his hat, just by saying the proper words.
10. He has dealt himself a royal flush the last three times. What luck!
11. Television evangelists Jim Bakker and Jimmy Swaggart have offered identical explanations for their scandalous behavior: "The devil made me do it."

EXAMPLES OF HYPOTHETICAL REASONING

Bats

"Since ancient times the bat has been an object of interest to biologists and laymen alike. The bat flies at night, and this fact has appealed both to mystics, who saw in its nocturnal wanderings collusion with the powers of evil, and to naturalists, who speculated on how the animal directs itself under conditions where its eyes can be of little or no use."[3] Bats live in dark and twisting caves, but are able to navigate swiftly and surely.

The problem is: How are bats able to avoid obstacles in the darkness? It was an Italian investigator named Lazzarro Spallanzani who in the late eighteenth century made the first scientific attempt to solve it.

Spallanzani knew that human beings use their sense organs to avoid obstacles— sight, touch, hearing. Perhaps the bats did too. So he proceeded to test several hypotheses based on the assumption that one or more of their sense organs was involved in their mysterious ability to fly in the dark.

Hypothesis A: Bats have extraordinarily acute vision which enables them to see in almost total darkness. After capturing some bats, Spallanzani was ready to test the hypothesis. He destroyed their vision and released them in the darkness. The consequence of the hypothesis (and the auxiliary assumptions about the eyes and their role in vision) is that the bats would be unable to avoid the obstacles. This is the prediction. But the prediction did not come true. The blind bats did just as well as the others. So Hypothesis A, having failed the test, was rejected.

Hypothesis B: Bats have an extraordinarily acute sense of touch which enables them to respond to subtle air disturbances near obstacles. To test this hypothesis, Spallanzani painted a bat with a thick coat of varnish and released him. Contrary to the prediction, the bat's facility for flying around obstacles was unimpaired. So Hypothesis B was rejected.

Hypothesis C: Bats utilize the sense of taste. This is unlikely, since the auxiliary assumptions we would have to make to link it with the facts to be explained are very questionable. Spallanzani tested it anyway. The bat whose tongue had been cut out retained the ability to fly around without hitting obstacles. So Hypothesis C was eliminated.

Hypothesis D: Bats depend on the sense of smell. The investigator tested this hypothesis by plugging the noses of several bats. Failure to navigate well would confirm the hypothesis; continued ability to navigate well would disconfirm it. The results were not clear-cut. Some bats were disabled, and some were not. But since some still flew without collision, Spallanzani attributed the failure of the others to difficulty in breathing. So the smell hypothesis was eliminated.

Hypothesis E: Bats utilize the sense of hearing in some way to avoid obstacles.

---

[3] Robert Galambos, quoted in Lewis White Beck, *Philosophic Inquiry* (New York: Prentice-Hall, Inc., 1952), pp. 109–110. The account given here is based on Professor Beck's account, pp. 109–115.

He tested this by plugging up the ears of eleven bats. Ten of them still flew successfully, counter to the prediction. One bat did have trouble, but Spallanzani discounted this "renegade instance" and rejected the hearing hypothesis.

Hypothesis F: Bats depend on a combination of two or more sense organs. Another investigator tested this by covering all the head organs of several bats with hoods. The prediction was that they would be unable to fly and avoid obstacles. This prediction did prove to be correct, so Hypothesis F was confirmed: two or more organs are involved. Spallanzani did not think very highly of it, however, for no *single* sense organ had turned out to be necessary for guided flight.

Hypothesis G: Bats depend on sixth sense. Strictly speaking, this may not be a hypothesis at all, for there are no obvious ways by which it can be tested. If it is simply a way of saying that bats have a mysterious faculty that humans know nothing of, it is not a hypothesis.

Several hypotheses had been rejected, some (D and E) not conclusively. One had been confirmed (F), and one (G) was untestable. Spallanzani had not solved the problem but he had acquired knowledge.

It was only after a century and a half that another hypothesis was formulated and tested. It was suggested as an analog for submarine-detecting devices used in World War I: Ships, sending sound vibrations into water, receive echoes when the vibrations hit a submarine; on the basis of the directions from which the echoes come and the time it takes them to get back to the ship, the location of the submarine can be calculated.

Hypothesis H: Bats send out sounds and determine the bearings and distances of obstacles by means of the echoes from these sounds. This hypothesis accounts for all the facts, including the mixed results in D and E. The noses of the bats are involved in sending out the signals (D) and the ears in picking up their echoes (E). It is a simpler explanation than F, for we now have two specific faculties (sound making and hearing) involved instead of "two or more organs." There are, however, three difficulties with this hypothesis: (1) Why were so many of the bats with plugged noses able to navigate? (2) Why were so many of the bats with plugged ears able to navigate? (3) Flying bats are silent!

The first one was met by conducting another experiment. This time the snouts of the bats were so snugly tied that they could not possibly emit sounds. Prediction: inability to navigate. Results: inability to navigate. Hypothesis H is confirmed.

The second difficulty was cleared up by conducting another experiment with other bats. This time the ears were so tightly plugged that they could not possibly hear sounds. The prediction that the bats would be unable to get around without hitting obstacles was borne out, so the hypothesis again was confirmed.

The third difficulty was met by setting up a machine that converted ultrasonic frequencies into audible ones. If the bats indeed were emitting high-frequency sounds while flying, this machine would detect them. This test could only be conducted in conjunction with a great many auxiliary assumptions about the machine and the basic principles of the theory of sound. When the test was carried out, involving one hundred bats of several species, the bats were found to be emitting sounds in flight. Hypotheses H was thus again confirmed.

Concluding Summary: Hypothesis H is the only hypothesis that has passed all tests. It accounts for all the original facts and was instrumental in predicting new ones. While it is not proved, we have very good reasons for believing that it is true.

Vikings

THE KENSINGTON STONE

In 1898 a Swedish farmer who was clearing some land on the edge of a swamp near Kensington, Minnesota, found a curious stone under and between the roots of a tree. It was a rectangular piece of hard stone, six by sixteen by thirty-one inches, weighing 202 pounds, and carved in runic letters. Professor Breda, at the University of Minnesota, was able to translate most of the inscription, though not the numerals. It reads:

> We are . . . Goths Swedes and . . . Norwegians on an exploration journey from Vinland through the West. We camped by a lake with . . . rocky islands, a day's journey north from this stone. We fished one day. When we returned, we found . . . of our men red with blood and dead. Ave Maria, save us from evil. We have . . . men by the sea to look after our ships . . . days' journey from this island. Year. . . .

Professor Breda was convinced that the inscription was a hoax, and this was generally believed for many years. In the twelfth century there was a Norse colony in Greenland, and there is evidence that some of the Norsemen reached, and settled, 'Vinland,' on the New England coast. But it was impossible for a twelfth-century Viking to have carved the Kensington stone. Scholars pointed out that the language of the stone was a mixture of Norwegian, Swedish, and Old English, but in those days the Swedes and Norwegians (who were united into one kingdom in 1319) were bitter enemies: unlikely partners for an expedition. The letters 'AVM' (for 'Ave Maria') were Latin, not runic, and the Roman alphabet was not introduced into Scandinavia until after the twelfth century.

For nine years the stone was used as a door-step. Then Hjalmar J. Holand (later curator of archives of the Norwegian Society of Ephraim, Wisconsin), a student of Scandinavian antiquities, became interested in the question and studied the inscription. He was able to interpret the numerals, and complete the translation. He found that the inscription spoke of 8 Goths, 22 Norwegians, 10 men massacred by a lake with 2 rock islands, one 'day's journey' (a technical unit of measurement meaning about 75 miles), and 10 men left with the ships 14 days' journey from the stone. The year was 1362.

The facts that had counted most heavily against the authenticity of the stone now counted in its favor. The special runes employed date the stone as belonging to the fourteenth century. At that time the Latin alphabet had been introduced into Scandinavia, and its letters were often combined with runes.

Then, in the royal library at Copenhagen, there was found an order of 'Magnus, King of Norway, Sweden, and Skaane,' commissioning 'Paul Knutson,' a young nobleman of the court, to take a party on an expedition to the Norse colonies on Greenland. The Scandinavians had been out of touch with these colonies, and the King feared that they were weakening in their religious faith. The order was dated 1354.

Holand was now able to set forth a possible explanation of the Kensington stone. If Knutson made the expedition, he may have gone to Greenland, and from there on to Vinland, sailing around into Hudson Bay, and making his way up the rivers into Minnesota. For several years, Holand investigated the question, with the help of a growing number of other scholars, and together they have been able to amass a considerable amount of supporting evidence. For example, the weathering of the Kensington stone shows that it had been in the earth for centuries, and the tree under which it was found must have been at least 70 years old in 1898. But before 1860 that part of Minnesota had not yet been settled, and was in the territory of the savage Sioux. Geological evidence shows that the spot where the stone was found was almost surely an island in 1362.

It was further discovered that Cormorant Lake, about 75 miles north of Kensington, has two rocky islands. And at one point on its shore were found glacial boulders, drilled with triangular holes—a common 14th-century device for mooring boats in Norway. Other and exactly similar mooring stones were found along what might have been the course of the expedition. In various parts of Minnesota various implements (battle axes, fire steel, a sword, a spearhead) have also turned up.

In 1948 the Kensington stone was accepted by the Smithsonian Institution in Washington as an authentic historical record.[4]

The original observed facts are the stone's size and weight and its place and time of discovery. They occur in a problematic situation. The problem is: Where did the stone come from?

Is the translation of the stone also factual? This is difficult to answer. The runic language is fairly well known by scholars, but no one speaks the language today. The understanding and mastery of a dead language involves a lot of hypothetical reasoning, because its natural users are not alive to verify our theories about its vocabulary and syntax. Few facts are absolutely free from hypothetical elements.

---

[4] This account of the Kensington Stone is from Monroe C. Beardsley's *Practical Logic*, pp. 548–549. Beardsley himself is indebted to Hjalmar J. Holand, *Westward from Vinland* (New York: Duell, Sloan and Pearce, 1940).

Factualness is a relative matter. Relative to the problem of the stone's origin, then, let us regard the translation as factual. The marks on the stone are accurately translated.

In the third paragraph, one hypothesis is implied and another one is stated. We will call the first:

Hypothesis A: *The stone was carved by twelfth-century Vikings.* This hypothesis was suggested by the widely accepted belief that Vikings were in the New World at that time. Hypothesis A, though new and specific, was formulated in the context of other knowledge about Vikings. Hypotheses are seldom drawn in isolation from established knowledge, and this established knowledge can serve as useful auxiliary assumptions to be used in conjunction with the hypotheses.

But the trouble with Hypothesis A is that it does not quite account for all the facts. One fact is that the stone speaks of an expedition of Swedes and Norwegians. The hypothesis would not *yield* this fact, for if an expedition set out in the twelfth century, it would *not* be composed of enemies like the Swedes and Norwegians (auxiliary assumption). The other fact is the presence of the Latin expression "AVM." Auxiliary assumptions about the date of the introduction of Latin into Scandinavia, when used with the hypothesis itself, would indicate that there would *not* be Latin in any message left by the Vikings.

Hypothesis A, having been rejected because it did not account for all the facts, is replaced by:

Hypothesis B: *The inscribed stone is a hoax.* This is a vague hypothesis, but not entirely unlikely. People have often tried to embarrass scholars by "planting" unusual evidence. The "Piltdown Man" was a hoax but for years was believed to be genuine. There are many people in the world who enjoy seeing scholars make fools of themselves. The hypothesis prevailed for nine years—until Holand arrived on the scene.

Holand was dissatisfied with the hoax hypothesis because no additional evidence for it had been forthcoming. He managed to complete the translation, filling in the missing numbers. The factual basis has now become enlarged.

The fifth paragraph suggests another hypothesis:

Hypothesis C: *The stone was carved by fourteenth-century Vikings.* This hypothesis explains very nicely the facts that proved to be so troublesome to Hypothesis A. Our auxiliary assumptions about the relationship of the Swedes and Norwegians and the introduction of Latin to their countries make the possibility of a combined expedition and a runic message using Latin quite plausible. The facts of the inscription's meaning are very well explained by the new hypothesis. They indeed are just what one would expect to find in such a message.

Holand next had to get some *additional* evidence for his theory. With his hypothesis in mind, he searched the ancient records for some indications of a long westward trip around 1360. *"If* the hypothesis is true," he reasoned, "then I ought to find some reference to the expedition in the old records." Had he not been looking for such data *in order to test a particular hypothesis,* he probably would not have found them. These predicted facts now take their place as additional support for Hypothesis C.

The seventh paragraph is a refinement of his hypothesis. It now includes the route that Knutson and his men took from Scandinavia. We may call this Hypothesis C′. Holand tested this theory by looking for mooring stones and medieval implements along the hypothesized route of the expedition—and he found them. He found a lake at the proper distance; it contained two rocky islands, and there were the typical Viking triangular-shaped holes in the glacial boulders. The evidence for Hypothesis C′ is now very impressive.

What about the hoax theory, Hypothesis B? It was never disproved, and some people still adhere to it. But there are additional facts that are not consistent with B but which are consistent with C: the time the stone had been in the ground, the age of the tree, the fact that the area in which the stone had been found was an island in 1362. If B is correct, these "facts" would in all likelihood have been otherwise. If C is correct, these "facts" flow from it through the use of quite acceptable auxiliary assumptions. If the facts are as alleged, Hypothesis B is very unlikely. It would require the hoaxer to have carried the stone into territory occupied by hostile Indians, transported it to an island, and to have buried it around 1828. He would have had to have a good grasp of the runic language and Scandinavian history. And he would have to have been willing to carry his secret with him to the grave.

No one alive today could have seen the stone actually being carved, but on the basis of the evidence many people are more inclined to attribute it to fourteenth-century Vikings than to some brilliant and courageous hoaxer.

The analysis above is based upon Beardsley's summary of Holand's book. It should be noted that the great historian, Samuel Eliot Morison, believes that the stone is a hoax. He calls the Viking theory "preposterous" and blames the whole thing on Holand, a gullible local furniture salesman, Vogelblad, a joker who was a runologist and a local schoolteacher, and the farmer, Ohman. There is, then, positive evidence for the hoax hypothesis. Morison also offers considerations against the likelihood of the Vikings hypothesis, such as the auxiliary assumption that they were not interested in land exploration. But the most effective part of Morison's case is his challenge of material that we accepted as factual data. The inscription is *not* authentic medieval Scandinavian. The stone is old, but the carving is not. And what about the artifacts turned up along the route? "The halberds turned out to be tobacco cutters manufactured by the Rogers Iron Company of Springfield, Ohio, and the battle-axes were premiums given to collectors of labels from Battle-Axe Plug, a popular chewing tobacco around the turn of the century."[5]

Concluding Summary: The debate over the authenticity of the stone testifies to the importance of auxiliary assumptions. Where were the Vikings in the fourteenth century? What was their written language? What were their interests? The debate also shows the importance of agreement on "basic facts." It is sometimes difficult to get these established. Since "facts" sometimes have a hypothetical component,

---

[5] See Samuel Eliot Morison, *The European Discovery of America: The Northern Voyages* (New York: Oxford University Press, 1971), pp. 74–78.

auxiliary assumptions in a great many fields may be relevant also in determining exactly what the facts *are* that need explanation. *Had the stone been carved before or after it had been taken from the ground?*

[Sherlock Holmes] shook his head with a smile as he noticed my questioning glances. 'Beyond the obvious facts that he has at some time done manual labor, that he takes snuff; that he is a Freemason, that he has been in China, and that he has done a considerable amount of writing lately, I can deduce nothing else.'

—*A. Conan Doyle,* ''The Red-Headed League''

EXERCISES

Exercise 95

You have been very listless for the past two weeks. You don't have much of an appetite. Your friends bore you, and you can't seem to get very interested in anything. Your grades are beginning to go down.

Formulate three hypotheses to account for the situation and show how you would test each of them, indicating the predictions you would make.

Chapter 11

Seduction: Emotional Appeals

PREVIEW

We have seen how it is possible to present a convincing argument based on the logical principles of deduction and induction. Is it possible to present a persuasive appeal which is neither deductive, inductive—or even logical? Unfortunately, it is. Although such appeals are fallacious, they are effective. Your main objective in this chapter is quite obvious: to develop the ability to recognize these appeals for what they are worth: nothing. You will thus reject them in your own thinking and in that of others. More specific objectives are:

1. Learn to identify the various forms that "fallacies of relevance" can take.
2. Learn something about the psychology that makes them work.
3. Learn how to "answer back" to someone who seeks to seduce you with an emotional appeal.

You already know a lot about emotional appeals and their worthlessness. Otherwise you would have been victimized by every "con artist" who crossed your path! Here is a little test:

1. Does the fact that a product has been endorsed by famous people make it good?
2. If you found out that Rousseau had been quite unethical in his personal life, would you become skeptical of his moral philosophy?
3. Name two situations in which a person's moral character is *not* irrelevant.
4. Does the fact that a viewpoint cannot be refuted prove that it is true?
5. Can the appeal to hope be used to sell cosmetics?
6. Can the appeal to fear be used to win elections?
7. When is thought more effective: When it is passionate or when it is dispassionate?

8. Can you think of an example in which an advertiser tries to sell a product by arousing sexual feelings?
9. Are we easier targets when we have been placed in a good mood?
10. What do you think of the expression, "flattery will get you nowhere"?

THE NATURE OF EMOTIONAL APPEALS

Relevance: *Ignoratio Elenchi*

Having discussed deductive and inductive arguments, as well as the statements and words that make them up, we would appear to be at the end of the journey. But there is yet another topic that should be discussed: emotional appeals. Strictly speaking, this topic does not belong in a logic book at all, for emotional appeals are neither logical nor illogical. They are non-logical. Emotional appeals are not arguments; they are substitutes for argument. They are not cases of good thinking or bad thinking; they are attempts to induce a state of *no* thinking.

Although most of these appeals have been called "fallacies," they are unlike any of the other fallacies we have discussed. They do not result from inattentiveness to shifts of meaning, failure to adhere to the rules of distribution, inconsistent use of words like 'if' and 'or,' obliviousness to the limitations of one of Mill's Methods, haste in drawing generalizations, or poor judgment in evaluating evidence. The fallacies we are familiar with occur in the course of thought. They are lapses in good thinking, blemishes on the face of a rational countenance. Although they may be committed in bad faith, dishonestly, in order to deceive an opponent, they exist in the lap of reason and are unfortunate or undesirable aberrations of the rational faculty. The "fallacies" that are based on emotional appeals, however, are totally removed from serious thought and bear no resemblance to it. Bad argument has certain similarities to good argument, but emotional appeals do not. It is only by an act of grace that we can dignify these appeals by calling them "fallacies." To deal with them we have to enter the underworld of logic.

Many of these appeals were discovered and named by the ancient Greeks and Romans. Traditionally they have been called "fallacies of relevance." They might better be called "fallacies of irrelevance," for the appeals (we will not call them arguments) are utterly irrelevant to the particular question at issue. What does the sexual life of John M. Keynes have to do with the truth of his economic theories? What does the fact that his wife and children were unhappy have to do with the guilt or innocence of Socrates? Emotional appeals present considerations that are not germane. They seek to create an emotional mood that will make one disdainful of mere logic. If they are concerned with fact at all, it is to induce the listener to *keep out* fact (and thus oversimplify) or to bring in *irrelevant* fact (and thus be distracted).

There is a particular fallacy called *"ignoratio elenchi,"* which means "ignorance of the refutation" (or "missing the opponent's point"). A speaker may be saying a

> *Passion overcometh sober thought;*
> *And this is the cause of direst ills to man.*
>
> —*Euripides*, Medea

lot of things, but they just don't seem to have any bearing on what is at issue. The issue may, for example, be whether the city should build a swimming pool. A person who discoursed on poolside safety and the importance of acquiring competent lifeguards would be guilty of this fallacy. There is nothing in what he says that makes building a swimming pool more or less advisable. If the question is whether the city can *afford* to build a pool, the person who holds forth on how badly the city *needs* one is also committing an *ignoratio elenchi.*

The fallacy is also called that of ''irrelevant conclusion.'' Much of the speech of the presidential candidates during the televised debates in the fall of 1980 was a case of *ignoratio elenchi.* The candidates did not speak to the issues raised by the questioners but argued earnestly for conclusions that were irrelevant to those issues. Commission of the fallacy may sometimes be forgiven. When a discussion on an issue is prolonged, the disputants, grown tired, may simply *forget* what the question is. Our presidential candidates, however, were determined from the beginning to present their arguments and conclusions whether they were asked for or not. Arguing one's *own* ''issue'' is a way to seem to be winning.

In the broad sense of the term, all the emotional appeals discussed below are forms of the *ignoratio elenchi* fallacy. They all engage in bringing in material that has no apparent bearing on the truth or falsity of the question at issue. If Congress is discussing a proposal to take the United States out of the United Nations, and a senator presents a case for the conclusion that there is life on Mars, he has committed the *ignoratio elenchi* fallacy. The arguments to be discussed below are often just as wide of the mark as this!

Concluding Summary: Emotional appeals are part of the logic of neither deduction nor induction. They operate more like seduction, where reason is absent. These appeals present nothing that is relevant to the question at issue, so may be considered as variations of the fallacy of *ignoratio elenchi.*

Coercion: Ad Baculum

There is another ancient fallacy called *''argumentum ad baculum.''* This is the appeal to the club. If your opponent does not see the wisdom of your point of view, you beat him into submission. Automatic pistols have been called ''persuaders'' by underworld characters.

In the comic strip, *Lolly* (8/11/75), this conversation took place between Junior and Liz:

"Of course not, Liz. You can't be on the men's office bowling team."

"But I think you should let me on."

"Just tell me why I should let a gal on our bowling team."

"Because if you don't I'll break every bone in your crummy body."

"Well, yes, that is a rather good reason."

"I knew you'd listen to reason."

Suppose a parent wants his child to eat her spinach, and the child wants to know why she should. The parent might try to convince her on the basis of the nutritional qualities of the spinach, but if this fails, he may resort to "persuasion": "If you want some banana-cream pie for desert, you'd better eat your spinach!"

It does seem strange to call these appeals *arguments*. To threaten harm or violence is not to give reasons. To force a point of view on someone is not to convince him that it is true. No matter how effective power is in this world, might does not, in fact, make right. Galileo was forced to recant, but the strenuous efforts of his persecutors did not alter the fact that it was the earth that moved and not the sun. That people are willing to fight for a viewpoint is not a reason for the *truth* of that viewpoint.

As absurd and as sad as it is that people are sometimes forced to give lip service to beliefs they do not hold, there is one thing worse: to get them to actually *believe* that to which their reason cannot give assent. "Brainwashing" is the *ad baculum* carried to the final degree. Here the person is forced not merely to *espouse* a particular viewpoint, but to subscribe to it as well. In *1984*, it was not enough for Winston to *say* that 2 + 2 = 5; he had to be *convinced* that it was. This marks the kind of destruction of the rational person that the "argumentum" *ad baculum* aims at.

Any attempt to deal with human beings as things, to find the causes and cues that will work in producing the desired actions and beliefs on their part, their rational faculties dulled, deflected, or bypassed, is a kind of *ad baculum* appeal. It is *ad baculum* because the resort is to a kind of force instead of to reason. The attempt is to create pressure that the person cannot withstand, that will prevail in the end. Stalin called his propagandists "engineers of the human mind": They could construct any point of view prescribed. *Ad baculum* appeals produce belief; they do not establish truth.

The number of emotional appeals discussed below is eleven. But this list is not complete. *Any* emotion may be exploited to make a conclusion seem to follow when it does not.

> *Numberless . . . are the ways, and sometimes imperceptible, in which the affections colour and infect the understanding.*
> —*Francis Bacon*, Novum Organum

Concluding Summary: The essential human quality is to be rational. Beliefs characteristically are based upon reasons. To compel belief or agreement from a person through non-rational means is to do violence to him and to his deepest nature.

It is to use force where enlightenment is called for. Emotional appeals, then, being devoid of logical substance, are forms of the fallacy of *ad baculum*.

SPECIFIC EMOTIONAL APPEALS

Argumentum ad Hominem

This "argument" consist of attacking one's opponent instead of his argument. If he can be made to look bad, third parties will, it is hoped, transfer their derogatory attitude to his argument. An alternative term for the appeal, "poisoning the well," suggests the strategy. If the well is thought to be bad, any water taken from it will be unfit for use.

In a *Peanuts* cartoon several years ago, Lucy was losing an argument. Her contention that snow comes up through the ground had been effectively refuted by Charlie Brown. Lucy is silent for one panel and in the last one says, "Boy, have you ever got a funny-looking face!" Chuck Norman of the country music station WGNU quoted Stan Kenton's comments on country music: "a national disgrace . . . ignorant . . . lowest form of contemporary music . . . no charm whatsoever." Norman's defense consisted of this: "Stan's mad because nobody buys his records anymore (if they ever did)." It should be obvious that the appearance of Charlie's face has nothing to do with the question of the origin of snow and that Stan's record sales have nothing to do with the soundness of his comments on country music. To argue as if there is a connection is to commit the *ad hominem* fallacy.

The fallacy may operate in a more subtle way. The speaker does not directly attack his opponent but points out the *circumstances* that his opponent is in and suggests that his views are a product of those circumstances. A schoolteacher argues for increased pay for schoolteachers. Someone may say, "Sure! It's easy to see why *you're* in favor of a raise!" Such a person who ignores the argument in order to emphasize the circumstances is committing the *ad hominem* fallacy. He is suggesting that the teacher's point of view is simple bias instead of the conclusion of a reasoned argument. If I reject the views of Schopenhauer on women because I happen to know that he was disliked by his mother, I have committed the fallacy. If my criticism of Armistead's defense of England's policies in America in the eighteenth century consists in pointing out that he was an Englishman, I again commit the *ad hominem* fallacy. The only *relevant* response to the teacher's argument, Schopenhauer's philosophy, or Armistead's theory consists of showing that their premises are false or that their inferences are unsound.

William Rusher, syndicated columnist, in defending the appointment of Robert Bork to the Supreme Court, cited in his column "four Senatorial sleazeballs" who are leading the attack on him: Joseph Biden, "pathological liar"; Edward Kennedy, "notorious skirt-chaser"; Howard Metzenbaum, who had illegitimately accepted a "finder's fee" in a business transaction; and Patrick Leahy, who had "apparently" leaked classified information to the press. "These are the paragons who are leading the battle for the proposition that Robert Bork is unqualified to sit on the Supreme Court.''[1] Even William Buckley conceded that it was difficult to defend Bork ''without going into the disqualifications of the anti-Bork figures.''[2] Surely the *character* of Bork's backers (or supporters) is irrelevant in this debate. What *is* relevant are the qualifications of Bork and the arguments employed against him and on his behalf.

In disputation, the *argument* is the thing, not the characteristics or circumstances of the people involved. Arguments must be evaluated on their own merits. That our opponents beat their wives has no bearing on the question at issue. Scoundrels can espouse great truths and ''nice guys'' can be hopelessly confused.

The only way to deal with the fallacy is to insist that the speaker confine his remarks to matters germane to the question, that he be *relevant*. One should *not* go on the defense when his opponent perpetrates an *ad hominem*. The latter is probably losing the argument on its own merits and would just as soon see it distracted into another channel. No defense of the *person* of Charlie Brown, Stan Kenton, the teacher, Schopenhauer, or Armistead is needed, for the person was not the point at issue in the first place!

This is not to say that personal qualities are always irrelevant. If we want to know whether to vote for a candidate, his circumstances and values are relevant. If we want to know whether to accept the testimony of a witness, his sobriety and honesty become relevant. If we want to know whether to propose marriage to someone, his or her personal qualities are surely relevant. But when one's position on an issue or the strength of an argument is to be evaluated, personal characteristics are utterly irrelevant.

Concluding Summary: It is fallacious to attack the person instead of the position or argument, for the truth of a position and the strength of an argument must be examined on their own grounds. Personal qualities and circumstances are utterly irrelevant to such an examination.

Argumentum ad Verecundiam

This ''argument'' consists of associating the speaker's point of view with a great respected person. The feeling of reverence felt toward this personage seems to give a blessing to what is being said. Who could be critical of a particular coffeemaker when Joe DiMaggio himself praises it!

The argument is sometimes called ''appeal to illegitimate authority.'' It is a fallacy to try to transfer the respect we feel toward a person in one area to the pronouncements that he makes in some other area. If ''Joltin' Joe'' were to tell us how to hit a curve ball or how to play center field, we ought to listen. But what special competence does he have in the field of coffeemakers? None!

[1] See *St. Louis Post-Dispatch*, October 5, 1987, p. 3D.
[2] See *St. Louis Post-Dispatch*, October 2, 1987, p. 3C.

> *I am not disposed to approve the practice traditionally ascribed to the Pythago-*
> *reans, who, when questioned as to the grounds of any assertion that they*
> *advanced in debate, are said to have been accustomed to reply, 'He himself*
> *said so' . . . 'he himself' being Pythagoras.*
>
> —*Cicero*, De Natura Deorum

This appeal, so obviously fallacious, must be very effective, for great sums of money are spent to foster it. Athletes and movie stars, all highly regarded by the people, are paid well to endorse all kinds of products. Karl Malden's opinion on travelers' checks is irrelevant to the question whether they should be purchased. Bill Russell is no authority on telephone calls. And what is Joe Namath's special competence in popcorn poppers or pantyhose? Jim Lovell, ex-astronaut, is paid to endorse a life insurance company! The strangest instance of this fallacy occurred in an advertisement extolling the merits of a recording tape. The "authority" appealed to is dead and was dead before tapes were even invented, yet: "If Beethoven were alive today, he'd be recording on 'Scotch' brand recording tape." The ad goes on to say that Beethoven was a genius. "But he was even more than that. He was a pro." Like Russell and Namath, presumably.

In March, 1980, Joe Frazier, Mickey Mantle, and Nick Buoniconti, who had been appearing in TV commercials praising Miller Lite beer, made a historic switch. They now maintain that Anheuser-Busch Natural Light is the best tasting light beer. Norm Crosby expressed surprise: "I thought you were enameled with that other light beer." But there was nothing illegal in their switch: Their contracts with Miller had expired.

There are, of course, occasions when we are constrained to accept things on authority. We cannot check out every proposition, test it, and prove it to a logician's satisfaction. But there are two stipulations that any person of common sense would want to make: (1) Choose the authority from the field in which the opinion or point of view is asserted. Ask Einstein about physics, not religion. Pay attention to Yogi Berra when he's talking about hitting, not shaving. Consult J. P. Morgan on principles of banking instead of principles of ethics. Read what Johnny Miller says about hitting a golf ball, not about selecting shirts. Take seriously what a physician says about blood pressure, discounting what he says about politics. (2) Ignore any "authority" whose testimony has been purchased in order to sell a product, whether it is in his field of competence or not. Where fact and argument are offered, they can be evaluated. But unsupported opinion is worthless if the name and opinion have been purchased for ulterior purposes.

There is a somewhat different manner in which this appeal can be employed. It consists not of an appeal to a specific "authority" but to the general one of custom or tradition. We should be wary when we hear:

"Everyone knows that . . ."
"It is a well-known fact that . . ."

"They say that . . ."

"It has long been known that . . ."

When a viewpoint has been around a long time and has been held by a lot of people, it becomes respectable. Those of us who respect age tend also to respect old ideas. Since they have had every opportunity to be refuted and they are still with us, they must be true! False views, we think, would surely not have lasted so long! So the appeal to conventional "wisdom" may make independent fact-finding and argument seem to be unnecessary.

It is because of our emotional tendency to respect customary beliefs as authoritative that many of us still believe such falsities as these:

Lincoln wrote the "Gettysburg Address" on the back of an envelope while riding a train to the battlefield.

Robert Fulton invented the steamboat.

W. C. Fields said that anyone who hated children and dogs couldn't be all bad.

"The Spirit of '76" was painted during colonial times.

The Chicago Fire started when Mrs. O'Leary's cow kicked over the lantern.

Hitler's real name was 'Schicklgruber.'

The Battle of Bunker Hill was fought on Bunker Hill.

Lightning never strikes twice in the same place.[3]

Despite what we were brought up to believe, Sherlock Holmes never said, "Elementary, my dear Watson," and Greta Garbo never said, "I vant to be alone." The Pennsylvania Dutch are not descendents of the Dutch, and mustard gas neither is a gas nor is it derived from mustard.

Concluding Summary: It is reasonable to consult authorities when they are speaking in their own fields of competence and are not being bribed. It is unreasonable to accept the views of revered people when they speak outside their fields or accept bribes. The views of such people are utterly irrelevant, and to appeal to them is to commit the fallacy of illegitimate authority. Custom, being erroneous, is not a legitimate authority.

Argumentum ad Populum

In the broad sense, any "argument" that is designed to appeal to the multitude, to arouse the feelings of the masses, could be called an *"argumentum ad populum."*

---

[3] These and many other errors are discussed in Tom Burnam, *The Dictionary of Misinformation* (New York: Thomas Y. Crowell Company, 1975).

In this sense, just about any appeal on our list could qualify if addressed to enough people. For they all discount the ability of people to think.

We shall, however, take the term in a narrower sense here and call the *argumentum ad populum* an attempt to create a "bandwagon" effect. This appeal works when addressed to timid people who do not want to be separated from the great majority, to people who derive comfort from being part of the crowd. Such people will take up backgammon (or anything else)—if that is what everyone else is doing. They will read Jacqueline Susann's latest book—if it is a best seller. They are sure that 50,000 Frenchmen can't be wrong—unless 60,000 Frenchmen feel differently. They tend to identify with masses of people, perhaps proud of the fact that they are members of the "Pepsi generation." If a bandwagon is building up, they would rather be riding on it than trudging off alone in a different direction.

Merchandisers sell millions of products by means of popular appeals. A few summers ago they persuaded millions of men to buy white shoes and white belts. One would really be a social outcast without them. Men have to change the width of their neckties every few years. Women, too, are conditioned to respond faithfully to the dictation of changing fashions. Commodities are praised for being at or near the top in number of sales, and Madison Avenue has trained many of us to believe that "popular" means "good," that quantity means quality. An advertisement tells us: "Gordon's Gin. Largest seller in England, America, the world." What, exactly, are we supposed to infer from that?

Politicians always talk about how big they are winning, knowing that many voters want to be identified with a large group of people on a winning side. Preachers like "crusades," large movements away from sin and toward salvation. Let a few repentant sinners come forward in a revival service and several more will be sure to follow.

The United States government, one of the three or four biggest advertisers in the nation, bought a double-page ad in at least one popular magazine (*Newsweek*) to stimulate enlistment in the army. Several rows of healthy, vigorous, and smiling young soldiers (minorities properly represented) are shown running towards us. Above the picture (in part): "Since the end of the draft a lot of young people are discovering a good place to invest their time. The Army. They've come, over 250,000 strong. . . ." Below the picture is this injunction in huge letters: "Join the people who've joined the Army."

Why the *ad populum* argument is fallacious is almost too obvious to explain. That many people *believe* something to be true has no bearing whatever on whether

> *Public debate is necessarily only a matter of giving unity and morale to organizations. It is ceremonial and designed to create enthusiasms, to increase faith and quiet doubt. It can have nothing to do with the actual practical analysis of facts.*
>
> —*Thurman Arnold*, The Folklore of Capitalism

it *is* true. We do not establish propositions by counting their adherents. We establish them by formulating true premises and drawing valid inferences!

Concluding Summary: It is reasonable to count opinions when conducting a poll. It is unreasonable to do so when pursuing truth. To seek support for a conclusion by appealing to popular opinion is to commit the *ad populum* fallacy.

Appeal to Flattery

An independent thinker whose standards are his own and not those of the populace will not be vulnerable to the *argumentum ad populum,* but he may be a pushover for the appeal to flattery. Discourses that claim to be aimed at the *discriminating* smoker, the *conscientious* parent, the *independent* voter, or the *fastidious* dresser have half won the battle by means of flattery. If Gordon's Gin is the big seller, then House of Lords is used for the *gentleman's* martini and Beefeaters by those who spare no expense. Those who want to "rally 'round the fun with young America" will flock to Harley Davidson, while the *connoisseur* will select a Ducati.

One ad tells us about the cigarette "with the thinking-man's filter." Another one begins: "The active ingredient in Mon Triomphe is you. There is no one quite like you. You've got your own personality. Your own chemistry. And that's the active ingredient in Mon Triomphe cologne." More subtle is the campaign on behalf of Toyota: "You asked for it. You got it."

Why does the appeal to flattery, so obviously irrelevant to the issue, work? In the first place, people like to be flattered. Most of us are not praised enough. Rodney Dangerfield complains (on behalf of us all), "I don't get no respect!" The reader may wish to test the capacity of people to accept flattery. Heap it on by the ton. Some people may discount it a little, but most will accept the most outrageous compliments as their due. If someone's hair is messed up, praise his or her "windblown freshness"; if it is not messed up, comment on how neat and well-groomed he or she is. In the second place, the recipient of flattery will give the flatterer high marks for perspicacity. At last, someone who recognizes my good qualities! The flatterer has instantly established his own intelligence. His argument will not be looked at so critically now. In the third place, the flatterer has established his goodness. How kind of him to speak out and express his true feelings! It would be churlish to attack or even question the argument or viewpoint of such a nice person. A generous and truthful person should be *believed!*

Appeal to flattery is indispensable for politicians of all persuasions. Hitler praised the history, strength, spirit, and blood of the German *volk* in extravagant terms. The millions who believed him voted for him. Presidential candidates in *this* country tell Americans how wise they are and how accurate their judgment is. One candidate repeatedly said that he only wanted to give the people a government that was as good as they (the people) are. The obvious irony in all this is that the appeal to

flattery is an insult to the rational faculties of those who are flattered; it consists of offering irrelevancies instead of argument.

Related to the appeal to flattery is the rhetorical device called "identification with the audience." Politicians begin their remarks with, "Fellow Americans. . . ." A university chancellor begins his speeches to the faculty with the salutation, "Colleagues. . . ." Someone may affect the language of his listeners and try to show that he shares their feelings and prejudices. He wants to be *like* them—a form of flattery. If he can get himself accepted as one of them, he will be regarded as "OK" and what he has to say will be viewed less critically. Examples of this basically dishonest ploy are: teachers who talk, shave, and dress like students; whites who employ the slang and handshakes of blacks; priests who swear a little; presidents who serve inexpensive casseroles during recessions; and nurses who ask us how we are feeling this morning.

There is nothing wrong or illogical in wanting to be accepted by others. But if a person seeks acceptability in order to make it easier to palm off a bad or counterfeit argument, he or she is committing a fallacy. That a person may be "one of the boys'' (or ''girls'') is irrelevant to the soundness of his or her argument. It must be examined on its own merits.

Concluding Summary: The flatterer may be a generous and even truthful person, but that he thinks you are a fine person has nothing to do with the issue. He or she should be thanked and asked to get back on the subject. And the individual who succeeds in identifying himself or herself with his or her audience is still responsible for relevant fact and inference.

Argumentum ad Ignorantiam

This is an appeal based on ignorance. That something cannot be proved does not mean that it is false; and that something cannot be disproved does not mean that it is true. Both are simply cases of uncertainty. The wise person should incline his or her belief in the direction where the evidence may be greater or suspend judgment entirely.

A seventeenth-century French mathematician named Fermat had noticed that many squares could be separated into two squares:

$$5^2 = 3^2 + 4^2$$
$$10^2 = 6^2 + 8^2$$
$$13^2 = 5^2 + 12^2$$

But could this be done with numbers the exponents of which are greater than two? After Fermat's death in 1665, this marginal note was found on one of his papers: ''It is impossible to separate a cube into two cubes, a fourth power into two powers of the same degree. I have discovered a truly marvelous demonstration which this margin is too narrow to contain.'' The proof for this, ''Fermat's last theorem,'' was never found, and to this day no one has been able to prove (or disprove) it. One may say it is true because unrefuted, or that it is false because unproved, but to do either would be to commit the *ad ignorantiam* fallacy.

It is a fallacy because what we happen to be ignorant of is irrelevant to the truth of a proposition. What is unknown today *may* be known tomorrow. The fallacy works because a person who is aware of his own inability to disprove a particular proposition sometimes feels that he has to accept an assertion put forth with confidence by someone else.

It is presumptuous to say that a claim is false because unproved or that a claim is true because not disproved. Is this presumption ever justified? It is sometimes said that such presumption is properly made in courts of law: if a person's guilt cannot be proved, he is presumed innocent. This presumption, however, is made possible by a special legal principle and establishes the fiction that the defendant is innocent. Failure to prove guilt does *not* mean that the person is innocent; it only means that society is directed by law to treat him *as if* he were innocent.

The *ad ignorantiam* appeal is similar to an appeal called ''the fallacy of fake refutation.'' Since the two requirements of a good argument are true premises and valid inference, an argument can be refuted by successful challenge of the truth of a premise or the validity of the inference. After doing this, one is sometimes tempted to say that the conclusion, therefore, is false. But this, of course, would be wrong. All that can be said is that it has not been *established*. That there is ignorance here on how to establish the conclusion does not mean that the conclusion is false.

The pervasive practice among passionate persuaders to make unsupported claims is a species of the *ad ignorantiam* fallacy. When the advertiser claims that his product is ''the best,'' ''the greatest,'' or ''the most delicious,'' we lack the means quickly to refute him. In the disadvantage of our ignorance, we tend to accept the claim—at least in part. If a politician boasts of his excellent record in the Senate, his leadership and sponsorship of important bills, we may suspect some exaggeration, but we tend to take him at his word. We do not, after all, read the *Congressional Record* every week. How can we dispute Scott's claim that its equipment provides ''the optimum combination of price and performance'' or Chrysler's claim that the owners of its New Yorker model ''put it in a class with Cadillac or Lincoln''? But the point is that we do not have to refute a claim in order to *decline to accept it*.

Concluding Summary: It is fallacious to make an inference from ignorance, for ignorance means quite literally that something is not (yet) known. Subjective doubt cannot be made the basis of a claim to objective knowledge. It cannot function as a premise.

Argumentum ad Misericordiam

The appeal to pity is resorted to when the speaker wants the hard, cold, and critical attitude of his listener to be suffused by feelings of warm concern. People do have difficulty in being dispassionate for very long; their humane and sympathetic impulses can be easily aroused. If a lawyer can induce the members of the jury to feel pity for the defendant, they may not be so receptive to the prosecutor's argument against her.

There are times, of course, when appeals to sad circumstances are not entirely irrelevant. One may argue against a proposed tuition increase by citing poverty-stricken students who just barely get by at the *present* rate. That there are some students who could not pay more or could do so only at great hardship is relevant to the issue whether tuition should be raised. The appeal to their plight becomes fallacious in the *ad misericordiam* manner only if it is presented as the *only* relevant fact and in such a way as to generate a lot of emotion. When pity is aroused in order to produce some kind of passionate oversimplification, a fallacy is present.

One of the most famous instances in literature of the appeal to pity is Mark Anthony's funeral oration in Shakespeare's *Julius Caesar:*

If you have tears, prepare to shed them now.
You all do know this mantle: I remember

The first time ever Caesar put it on;
Twas on a summer's evening, in his tent,
That day he overcame the Nervii:
Look, in this place ran Cassius' dagger through:
See what a rent the envious Casca made:
Through this the well-beloved Brutus stabb'd;
And as he pluck'd his cursed steel away,
Mark how the blood of Caesar follow'd it,
As rushing out of doors, to be resolved
If Brutus so unkindly knock'd, or no;
For Brutus, as you know, was Caesar's angel:
Judge, O you Gods, how dearly Caesar loved him!
This was the most unkindest cut of all.

This speech not only turned the crowd against Brutus and the conspirators in the context of the play, but turns the readers against them also. It is so effective that we tend to forget that Brutus is a man of high principles, the hero of the play, "the noblest Roman of them all."

Another successful and famous use of the appeal to pity took place on September 23, 1952, when Richard M. Nixon, vice-presidential nominee, appeared on television to defend himself against charges of financial impropriety. While millions watched, including Dwight D. Eisenhower, the presidential nominee, Nixon presented such irrelevancies as these:

I owe $3,500 to my parents, and the interest on that loan, which I pay regularly, because it is a part of the savings they made through the years they were working hard—I pay regularly four percent interest. And then I have a $500 loan, which I have on my life insurance. Well, that's about it. That's what we have. [Nixon had listed his property holdings] And that's what we owe. It isn't very much. But Pat and I have the satisfaction that every dime we have got is honestly ours. I should say this, that Pat doesn't have a mink coat. But she does have a respectable Republican cloth coat, and I always tell her that she would look good in anything. One other thing I probably should tell you, because if I don't they will probably be saying this about me, too. We did get something, a gift, after the election. A man down in Texas heard Pat on the radio mention that our two youngsters would like to have a dog, and, believe it or not, the day before we left on this campaign trip we got a message from Union Station in Baltimore, saying they had a package for us. We went down to get it. You know what it was? It was a little cocker spaniel dog, in a crate that he had sent all the way from Texas, black and white spotted, and our little girl (Tricia), the six-year-old, named it Checkers. And, you know the kids, like all kids, loved the dog, and I just want to say this, right now, that regardless of what they say about it, we are going to keep it.

It isn't easy to come before a nationwide audience and bare your life, as I have done.

The speech was a masterpiece of its kind. Most of the voters were satisfied, and Nixon's running mate pronounced him "clean as a hound's tooth." But he had not said anything to refute the charges.

Concluding Summary: The fallacious appeal to pity seeks to create sympathetic feelings in order to offset detached logical scrutiny. Offering little that is relevant, it aims at evasion or oversimplification.

Appeal to Fear

Human beings are also susceptible to the emotion of fear. Indeed, we can feel fear at the very moment when our rational faculties tell us there is nothing to be afraid of. A good storyteller can make us afraid of ghosts, though we don't believe in ghosts. A well-made movie chiller can terrify us, though we know we are watching nothing but shadows on a screen.

The strategy of this appeal is simple. Frightened people look for immediate relief, for "solutions." If they're scared enough, they will be desperate. Instead of saying, "Show me first that there is something that actually threatens me and then convince me that you have the best remedy for it," they will say, "What must I do to be saved?"

The cosmetics industry has made millions of dollars from appeals to fear. Are you safe or only half safe? Do you have a dry and itchy scalp? Can your makeup pass the close-up test? Do you have an affliction that not even your best friends will tell you about? Do people notice your broken fingernails? Are they turned off by skin blemishes or unsightly body hair? On such profound matters as these, we can't take chances. So we buy liquids, pastes, and sprays in order to be *sure*.

Geritol, which contains iron, began an ad campaign forty years ago scaring people with the assertion that they may have "tired blood." Recently its ads have referred to "iron-poor blood" and have asserted that "Geritol's iron will actually build your blood back to normal." Most people get sufficient iron in their daily diet, and if they do not, a dose of Geritol probably won't help. As the Consumers Union points out, "Anyone whose blood is not 'normal' should be under a physician's care, not under the care of commercial hucksters."[4]

Fear is used to sell insurance (fires and accidents occur), automobile tires (cars go out of control), and travelers' checks (money is lost or stolen). It is used to sell soap: Do you have "pink toothbrush" or "ring around the collar"? A mail advertisement read as follows:

The national health crisis we're in is real and extreme. . . . Horrible as all the stories are about AIDS, herpes, influenza (and the list goes on and on), the whole story hasn't yet been told! A frightening report issued by the U.S. surgeon

---

[4] *The Medicine Show* (Mount Vernon, New York: Consumers Union, 1983), p. 139.

general says that 1,300 doctors and health professionals from around the world call AIDS "the biological equivalent of the nuclear bomb," which is all that is needed to "render the human race extinct within 50 years." The AIDS virus may have contaminated the surfaces of everything you and your family come in contact with daily! Public toilet seats, telephones, restaurant tables, silverware and doorknobs. We now offer you a brand-new way to protect yourself from AIDS. A disposable, specially treated paper towelette which will destroy the AIDS virus! Use it on your hands, and all surfaces that may be contaminated. . . . Just fill in the form and enclose check or money order. . . ."[5]

Fear is also used to win elections. The results of your opponent winning are always fearful. Democrats remind us of the Depression, Hoovervilles, and breadlines. Republicans warn us of wars and fiscal irresponsibility. Conservatives dramatize the communist menace internationally and domestically, while alerting us to the growth of socialism (creeping or galloping) in America.

A successful attack on Barry Goldwater in the 1964 presidential election consisted of suggestions by the Democrats that Goldwater was "trigger-happy" and would unleash a nuclear war. The Republicans in later elections mounted "law and order" campaigns. The head of communications of the Republican National Committee (G. Norman Bishop) tested two 60-second commercials to see which would arouse more fear. One of them showed an attractive young woman walking down a dark street. There is the sound of ominous footsteps coming closer and closer.

Fear flashes over her face as she breaks into a run. In the distance drums beat, setting a mood for impending doom. The action stops with a closeup of the panic-stricken woman and a voice from off-camera says, 'Americans should be able to walk down any street anywhere without fear of violent crime. We can't do this. We need to elect men and women who are dedicated to stronger laws and assure longer jail terms—who will put teeth into our law enforcement. . . . Elect a Republican Congress in November.'[6]

"Law and order" is usually a fake issue, drummed up to displace other issues. Nixon used it successfully in 1970 and 1972. We will not soon forget the "mileage" that 1988 Republican candidate George Bush got out of Willie Horton in 1988: A

State Senator John McNaboe of New York bitterly opposed a bill for the control of syphilis in May, 1937, because 'the innocence of children might be corrupted by a widespread use of the term. . . . This particular word creates a shudder in every decent woman and decent man.'
    —Stuart Chase, The Tyranny of Words (quoted in S. I. Hayakawa, Language in Thought and Action)

---

[5] See Abigail van Buren, St. Louis Post-Dispatch, March 23, 1988, p. 2F.
[6] See Mitchell E. Cohen, St. Louis Globe-Democrat, April 23, 1976.

vote for Dukakis was a vote in favor of turning murderers and rapists loose on the American people!

Hitler was adept at arousing feelings of fear. The Jews are to be feared, he said, for they have loyalties "higher" than to the fatherland. They are also part of the international conspiracy of bankers. Those Jews who are not part of this international conspiracy are members of another one: Communism. Communists have long plotted against German institutions, and all left-wingers are Communists, Communist-sympathizers, crypto-Communists, or dupes of Communists. Since only Hitler recognizes these dangers so clearly and experiences the danger to Germany so deeply, he should be given full power to deal with them. The danger is so great, he argued, that vigorous and decisive action is necessary *now*. The German people agreed with him.

And many Americans agreed with John Kennedy when he spoke of the (non-existent) missile gap during the 1960 presidential campaign.

Concluding Summary: One's critical and rational faculties do not work so well when he is in a state of fear. The appeal to fear attempts to create this state in order to exploit it.

Appeal to Hate and Indignation

Just as the feeling of fear can be induced in a person without giving that person any grounds for believing that the object of the fear exists, so too can the feelings of hate and indignation. We may be led to hate or to feel indignation toward something without being given any facts to show that it really *is* hateful or contemptible.

The emotions of hate and indignation are often employed in conjunction with that fear. We can easily be made to feel these emotions toward that which we fear. Hitler, again, aroused the feeling of hate when he talked about the Jews. And he used the emotion of indignation when he talked about the western democracies, the Versailles Treaty, and the millions of good Germans suffering oppression in Poland, Austria, and Czechoslovakia. The Ku Klux Klan utilizes all these emotions against the blacks. One especially effective use of fear/hate/indignation is the group's insistence that the blacks will mongrelize the race by intermarriage with whites, and that black males think of little else than how to rape white females. In the grip of these emotions, people are expected to suspend their rationality, to look for immediate and forceful action, and to be uncritical of criminal and depraved methods.

Mike Royko had an amusing but instructive column on a campaign to impeach one Michael G. Milsap:

> "Shouldn't that louse, Michael G. Milsap, be impeached for the way he has stolen and squandered the taxpayers' money?"

> That was the question recently put to people at three suburban shopping centers. The people were stopped, shown some printed material on Milsap's loathsome behavior, and asked to sign petitions that would bring about his impeachment.

The anti-Milsap literature said:

"YOU'VE ALL READ ABOUT IT—NOW HERE'S YOUR CHANCE TO DO SOMETHING ABOUT IT.

"Michael Gordon Milsap is a name that has caused grief in our county government.

"The Department of Public Aid has within its ranks many appointed officials over whom we, the people of Cook County, have little say. But thanks to recent legislation, one elected office has been formed. That position is known as Executive Economic Administrator. Michael G. Milsap is the current holder of this office.

"Michael G. Milsap is a thief."

The literature goes on to say that Milsap manages to live like a jet setter on a modest salary because he has committed the following scurrilous acts:

". . . Removed funds earmarked for Mayor (Richard J.) Daley's Youth Foundation.

". . . Charged with embezzlement of county monies for personal gain.

". . . Appropriated a part of the county budget to help Du Page County initiate its mosquito abatement plan.

". . . Picks pickled peppers by the lakeshore.

" . . Sunk county money into the establishment of the now defunct Chicago Fire and Chicago Cougars.

". . . No one has fired Milsap yet. But WE can impeach him NOW.

"Cook County needs your support—Impeach Milsap."

More than one-third of the people who read the literature were so outraged by Milsap's behavior that they signed the petitions. And Milsap might be worried today—if he existed.

But he doesn't. He and his crimes were dreamed up by a group of Northwestern University students who are taking a course in how people can be manipulated. They decided to see whether they could do it. They set up tables in suburban Morton Grove, Lincolnwood, and Wilmette and told people about Milsap.

They were surprised by how many people were eager to get Milsap and how many already knew about him.

One young man said: "Oh sure, we learned about this guy in political science class."

Another said: "Yes, I heard about that on the news this morning."

One woman refused to sign and gave this as her reason: "You won't believe this, but he lives two doors away from me. How would it look if he saw his neighbor's name on a petition?"

Other signers said things like: "We don't want any more crooks," or "I don't have anything better to do."

Only twelve people noticed that among Milsap's alleged sins was that he "picks pickled peppers by the lakeshore." And nine of the twelve signed anyway after it was explained that the sentence was put there just to test their alertness.[7]

The people's sense of indignation was real, although its object, Milsap, was not. The feeling itself was enough to make them sign the petition demanding his impeachment. Facts were unnecessary; the feeling was enough. Many of the signers could probably have been persuaded to contribute money to support the cause!

The object of the fear, hate, or indignation aroused *may* be real, but there is no attempt to show how the "solution" suggested for it will work. Crime is real, but will this legislation or this candidate reduce it? Corruption is real, but will this office seeker reduce it? Unemployment is real, but will this measure effectively deal with it? If the feelings are strong enough, further explanation may not be necessary.

Concluding Summary: One's critical and rational faculties do not work so well when he is feeling hate or indignation. These feelings are often aroused (along with that of fear) to secure support for prompt and vigorous action. When appeals to such emotions are successful, there is no need to show that there really is something to hate or to be indignant about, or that the suggested course of action will be efficacious against it.

Passion and prejudice govern the world; only under the name of reason.
—*John Wesley,* Letter to Joseph Benson

Appeal to Sex

Sexual emotions are easily aroused, and the more strongly one feels them, the greater the danger is that he will fail to conduct himself rationally. Reason is sometimes called on to perform herculean tasks when *this* particular passion is loose!

St. Augustine's lifelong obsession with lust is a product of the difficulties he had in controlling the sexual passion. If x loves y, or lusts for y, he can manufacture a dozen rationalizations for having y. Feelings get in the way of good thinking and blur his or her judgment. Spinoza entitled a chapter of his book, *Ethics,* "Of Human Bondage," and Somerset Maugham wrote a novel with the same title. The worst kind of slavery is slavery to oneself, to one's own passions. Especially the sexual

---

[7] Mike Royko, "Manipulated by Milsap," *St. Louis Post-Dispatch,* January 11, 1976, p. 3M. Royko concludes his column by pointing out that the two-thirds who did not sign showed good sense. The other third showed some good sense, for such things can happen in Cook County. But his last statement is not so sanguine: "If there were a real Michael G. Milsap, he would probably be swept back into office."

passion. In Maugham's novel, Philip realized that Millie was destroying him. He was clearly aware of a hundred good reasons for leaving her alone, but he could not. Love and lust have inspired great deeds, but are also responsible for a lot of foolishness. Could Samson be logical in the presence of Delilah? Ingrid Bergman in the presence of Roberto Rossellini?

The imagined possibility or the prospect of sexual intimacy is enough to arouse many people. The appeal to sex exploits this human propensity.

It is difficult to find a vacation brochure or pamphlet that does not offer sex in some guise as an inducement. The scantily clad beautiful young woman (or handsome young man) smiles at us and beckons from nearly every page. Billboards, heedless of highway safety, offer us physical beauty on a grand scale. The presence of shapely young ladies beside new cars is virtually obligatory in ads—as if one came with every car (standard equipment). One ad showed a cute little blonde perched on the hood of an Austin Healey Sprite. "You can buy a Sprite," said the caption, "for less than two grand." (This was in 1966. Sprites are no longer manufactured.)

National Airlines, after a four-year period of advertising based on FLY ME, recently abandoned the slogan. The campaign had been widely criticized as sexist. The company then announced a new slogan: TAKE ME. But so long as attractive stewardesses were pictured in its ads, the new slogan was no improvement.

> *Give me that man*
> *That is not passion's slave, and I will wear him*
> *In my heart's core, in my heart of heart.*
>
> —*Shakespeare*, Hamlet

Concluding Summary: The appeal to sex is fallacious, for it is used to lure one into decisions and actions that his or her reasons cannot defend. Either sexual gratification is obtained or it is not. If it is, it may have been purchased at too great a price. If it is not, the person has been cheated; the "promise" was not kept.

Appeal to Hope

"Hope springs eternal in the human breast." Well, hope can be a foul and deceitful thing too. Our hopes can be deliberately aroused, and we can be most deceived when our hope burns brightest.

This appeal may be utilized along with the appeal to sex. Such a combination could be very strong. The appeal to *hope of sex* arouses and exploits *two* emotions. A person might be induced to buy a Caribbean cruise after reading an ad that arouses his or her hope for a sexual encounter. The sale of some lines of clothing is promoted through the appeal to hope for sex.

But sex does not have to be involved. A man may agree to go sky diving if his hope for adventure or novelty is aroused. I may go to Las Vegas if my hope for overnight wealth is properly exploited. "Turn yourself into a learning machine," says Executive Research Institute, Inc., to hopeful and ambitious young men. "I take old bodies and turn out new ones," says a superbly muscled Charles Atlas. Things work out just fine—in hopeful imaginations.

In a state of hope, one doesn't ask the right questions. One is in a hurry to embark, to realize one's hopes before the opportunity is snatched away. A possibility is converted mentally to a probability, and a probability into a virtual certainty.

There is quite a large and busy swarm of vultures growing fat on the hopes of others. The hopes of adolescents to be attractive and popular are cultivated by various merchandisers and, for a price, "satisfied." If the young want to look mature, the mature hope to remain young. "A woman faces so many things," says Helena Rubinstein. "Why should looking her age be one of them?" The hopes of afflicted persons for cures or relief are "met" by medical and religious quacks. The hopes of old people for a serene retirement are "looked after" by real estate agents and housing developers. The hopes of all of us for intelligent and honest government are played upon by politicians who will say anything to get votes. So long as people are hopeful, they are vulnerable.

Two great problems of our day are inflation and energy. Politicians and merchandisers enlist us in the struggle to solve these problems, a struggle in which they have been laboring valiantly for a long time. We all hope to make headway against these twin evils. So we are persuaded to follow the confident politicians who have plans, no matter how fuzzy, to deal with them. We are persuaded to buy products that "attack inflation" by being terribly inexpensive or incredibly durable. It is indeed marvelous that we can be induced to believe we are extinguishing inflation at the very moment we are feeding its fire! We are persuaded to buy other products in the hope that we are contributing to a solution of the energy problem: insulation, thick window-glass, electric blankets, fireplaces, etc. Oil companies, in defending their high prices, assure us that they are seeking new domestic wells in order to beat OPEC prices; and automobiles, virtually all models, boast that their MPG is the best of its class.

> Hope! of all ills that men endure,
> The only cheap and universal cure.

So wrote the English poet, Abraham Cowley, in the seventeenth century.

It is perhaps the spirit of hope that makes us respond to the "sales" that many stores proclaim every week. There is a back-to-school sale, a pre-Thanksgiving sale, a Thanksgiving sale, a post-Thanksgiving sale, and then the various Christmas sales, to be followed by a post-holiday sale. There are sales for every season, for every anniversary, for every occasion. Each sale is built up as "the big one," the "sale of sales." Prices are reduced by 15 percent or 30 percent, or even 60 percent. Sale prices are ten, twenty, or five hundred dollars below the "regular" price—with perhaps a cash rebate thrown in as well. Are we really getting a bargain? It is hard to say. In a few cases we are; in many we are not. But we *hope* that we are, for our hopes have been kindled. In this hopeful spirit, we believe that we are *saving* at the very moment we are *spending!*

Concluding Summary: It is unreasonable to be stampeded into a conclusion or decision because your hopes have been aroused. While we all try to fulfill our hopes, we need to know on the basis of good thinking whether and how this or that proposal will serve our purpose. Our hopes cannot in themselves change the facts. It is *not* the case that, if one hopes for something strongly enough, his wish will come true!

> *Advertising persuades people to buy things they don't need with money they ain't got.*
>
> —*Will Rogers*

Appeal to Humor

To be amused is to experience an emotion. This emotion, like others, makes life interesting and is often harmless. But it can get in the way of good thinking.

One use of humor can be a form of the *ad hominem* appeal. If a speaker can be funny at the expense of his rival, he may weaken him in the eyes of the audience. If the humor is mean and scornful, it may humiliate the rival to the point where he is unable to continue effectively. The humorous "put-down" is seldom relevant to the issue under discussion, but it is an effective stopper. The person who suffers it may make the mistake of defending himself—which is permitting himself to be drawn off the subject. Or he may try to respond in kind—the success of which requires a quick wit and a lot of luck. In any case, he has allowed himself to be drawn into irrelevancies.

To be able to squelch your opponent is not the same thing as to defeat him in an argument, although it may seem to be. And because it only *seems* to be, it is a fallacy.

Two discussants, Pat and Mike, differed on how David Hume's theory of religion should be interpreted. Pat, who was losing the argument, tried to conclude the discussion (and gain a tie) by suggesting that when he died and went to heaven he would ask Hume what he really meant.

Mike: "What if Hume isn't *in* heaven?"

Pat: "Then *you* ask him."

Pat had the last laugh on Mike—and this is what people remembered, although Mike's argument on the correct interpretation of Hume's theory may have been as good as Pat's.

The controversy over Darwin's theory in the nineteenth century produced many irrelevant but humorous "arguments." A famous exchange took place at a meeting of the British Association for the Advancement of Science in Oxford in 1860. Bishop Samuel Wilberforce ("Soapy Sam") and Thomas Huxley ("Darwin's bulldog") were on the program. Wilberforce spoke first and was eloquent, unfair, entertaining, and sarcastic. Finally he turned to Huxley and asked whether it was through his grandfather or grandmother that he claimed to be descended from a monkey. The crowd roared. Huxley bided his time, and when it was his turn to speak he stated that he would rather have an ape for an ancestor than an intellectual prostitute like Wilberforce. Neither of these sallies, of course, had any bearing on the question of evolution.

It is not necessary to ridicule your opponent to draw attention away from the issues. The humor does not have to be directed at a participant to destroy an argument or prevent its being seriously pursued. At one time it was very difficult to discuss the issue of political and economic equality between the sexes with any seriousness. There would always be jokes and "witticisms" (mostly predictable). At a midwestern college, discussion by a committee on whether to approve a new course called "Death and Dying" became so silly that a decision had to be postponed until the next meeting. (There were questions about prerequisites, follow-up courses, and whether "death and dying" was being proposed as a graduation requirement.)

John Dewey became quite impatient during a meeting of professional educators. They had been discussing various ways of measuring intelligence. Dewey said that their tests reminded him of how the farmers in New Hampshire figured out how much their pigs weighed. "You lay a plank across a fence. On one end you place the pig. On the other end you pile rocks until the plank balances. Then you guess the weight of the rocks."

A serious discussion of excessive drinking degenerated into something else when a friend asked a woman whether her intemperate husband had ever tried Alcoholics Anonymous. "I suppose he has," she said. "That man will drink anything."

Finally, a story may be so amusing and apt that it seems to simplify things and win the argument. Norbert Wiener was part of a group discussing the problem of storage and retrieval of information. He conjectured about the old puzzle of the monkeys, whether, if given typewriters, plenty of paper, and enough time, they would type out the text of *Hamlet*. Wiener thought that it might be possible. "But how," he asked, "would we ever *find* the play in the mountainous pile of paper? There is a moral here. It is this: We've got to keep the monkeys away from the typewriter."

Advertisements sometimes use humor effectively to win people to the product they are selling. Burma Shave was a pioneer with its roadside signs. Alka Seltzer got a lot of mileage from its punchline, "I can't believe I ate the whole thing!" Volkswagen has had many amusing ads. One pictured the VW as a police car. "Don't laugh!" said the caption disingenuously. Jack-in-the-Box ads recount the story of a spouse who sneaks out at night to get a hamburger. Goodrich and National Car Rental have had some funny ads involving "the other guys," the former claiming the term for itself, the latter using it for its competitors. The Stiller and Meara commercials for Blue Nun are classics. Humor seems to be the basis for most low-calorie beer commercials. Products involved in such good fun must be OK!

Wit is the salt of conversation, not the food.
                    —*Hazlitt*, Lectures on the English Comic Writers

Concluding Summary: Humor engages our feelings and may get in the way of good thinking. It may be used to discredit a person (and thereby his point of view) or the point of view itself. Finally, humor may distract us from the issues or cause us to oversimplify them.

Enthusiasm is not necessarily an enemy of thinking clearly, whilst it is indispensable for achieving great and difficult ends. The danger arises from the feeling that the passionateness of a belief provides any guarantee of its truth. Our safeguards lies in an ability to ask the question: 'How did I come to believe this?'

—*L. Susan Stebbing,* Thinking to Some Purpose

CONCLUSION

It must not be thought that emotions are being derogated in this chapter. To reiterate, emotions are fine and wondrous things and without them life is not worth living. People *should* have hopes, high hopes. The sexual feeling, it is said, is delightful. The ability to feel pity is an essential human characteristic. Reverence and fear have their places, and occasional compliments should be given and received. It is not recommended that the human being be converted into a thinking machine, with all the passionate guts ripped out and replaced by wires and batteries.

The point is simply that emotions, when truth is the object, are out of place. Of what use is flattery when we are trying to come to terms with a serious issue? Of pity when we're trying to solve a complex problem? Of sex when we're trying to understand an involved situation? Of fear when we're trying to settle a difficult question? The passions, suspended while cogitation takes place, can return to the field afterwards. The field, better understood and furnished too, may afford passions a better opportunity to disport! The expression of a person's emotions will be more satisfying if he or she has an accurate conception of the realities and possibilities.

The emotions not only are out of place when truth is the object, they get in the way and thwart our efforts to understand. They close our minds to pertinent facts (oversimplification); they lead our minds to irrelevant facts (distraction); and they cause us to believe what we want to be true (rationalization). One must, if he wants to evade deception, listen to his mind and not his heart.

What is needed for *good feeling* may be left for other books to state. What is needed for *good thinking* is the ability to make reasonable inferences from given premises. This requires an understanding of the meaning of meaning, the structure of statements, the relationships between statements, and the nature of deductive and inductive inference. Anything else is superfluous.

If this sounds as if we are making an artificial bifurcation of human nature or digging a chasm between man's intellectual and affective natures, we can only say that thought and feeling, though they continually influence one another, are *two*

> *If we think of a fallacy as a deception, we are too likely to take it for granted that we need to be cautious in looking out for fallacies only when other people are arguing with us.*
> —*L. Susan Stebbing,* Thinking to Some Purpose

different functions of our nature. To even begin to understand them, we must separate them in our thought. And when we do, we find that the only emotions that serve the quest for truth are those that move us to use of the mind: the desire for accuracy, the hatred of deception, and the passion for knowledge.

EXERCISES

Exercise 96

Identify the fallacy:

1. I don't think you should pay any attention to what this man says about Shakespeare. After all, you know, he has a police record.
2. My client is the sole support of his aged parents. If he is sent to prison, it will break their hearts, and they will be left homeless and penniless. You surely cannot find it in your hearts to reach any other verdict than "not guilty."
3. Rheumatism sufferers: Are you sure you're getting maximum pain relief with your present medication? You might find that Patton's Pills will do more!
4. Transcendental meditation must be a very rewarding discipline. More and more people are taking it up.
5. No one has proved that there is no pot of gold at the end of the rainbow. So I am perfectly justified in believing that there is.
6. Shape up or ship out!
7. The ad says that Sammy Scatback himself wears this brand of socks! They must be good!
8. Are you slowly but surely losing your hair? Can you see yourself bald in five years? Don't let it happen to you! Send for a dozen bottles of Hairon today!
9. You've come a long way, fella! Sit back and enjoy a Stokey Stogie. These cigars have a flavor that successful executives like to savor.
10. Get on the bandwagon! Buy a Belchfire-8 this year! Everyone else is!

Exercise 97

Identify the fallacy:

1. If government tried to control the price of gasoline, we'd really be in trouble. There would be no money to search for new supplies. Sure, gasoline would still be at 50¢ a gallon, but the pumps would be dry!

2. Do you feel uninformed and inadequate when the conversation turns to serious topics? Subscribe to Newton's Newsletter and be in the know!

3. The committee report is worthless. It has to be, because the committee is composed of a bunch of crackpots.

4. "Well, I guess the paper is graded accurately," said the student, "but a 71 will give me a 'C' in the course, and I desperately need a 'B.' I've worked very hard for over three years, and it would be terrible to be turned down by medical school now. Couldn't you raise the exam to a nice, round 80?"

5. I will continue to torture him until he admits that the allegations against him are true. He'll finally decide to confess!

6. Objects do not exist when they are not perceived. Just try to prove that table is still there when no one is looking at it!

7. It's important to put your best foot forward. And that's not all. Our customers have reported an average bustline increase of two inches. A complete Bosom Beauty kit is yours for only $25.00.

8. Why do I patronize Weary Wanderer Motels? They're recommended by my favorite television comedian, and that's good enough for me.

9. I would like to believe what you say about the inadvisability of the tuition raise. But I happen to know that you are a student.

10. Psychology 301 must be a good course. Look at all the people taking it!

Exercise 98

Identify the fallacy:

1. Think of the poor, unmarried girl who finds herself pregnant! Why should she suffer pain and dishonor? Abortion should continue to be a legal alternative to bearing the child.

2. Councilman Jones has presented a very plausible plan for zoning. Since, however, he is a businessman himself and is doubtless looking after his own interests, we should reject it.

3. Smoking can be fun again. The clean, fresh taste of Altair makes good times just a little better!

4. Hey, man, is there someone in your life who would look good in a negligee like this? Just imagine her in these filmy things from Larry's of Las Vegas— and how she would show her appreciation!

5. When you give a dinner party and set out your finest crystal, it's spotless, isn't it? Are you sure? Are you *really* sure? (Adv. for a dishwashing detergent.)

6. Could your kids be doing better in school? Have you ever considered having a set of Encyclopedia Europa in your own home?

7. You're intelligent. You know how important it is to look your best while working in the office or dining in a fine restaurant. You're willing to use your brains to be even more beautiful. So, after studying them all, you'll probably choose the one that will help the most: Ulalume Eyeshadow.

8. The escort service provides very attractive partners for your night or weekend in London. They know the city well—its restaurants, clubs, and history. You can learn a lot from these knowledgeable and liberal-minded young people! Above all, they want you to have a good time! (Adv.)
9. We can't promise miracles, but that's exactly what seems to happen when you cook your dinner in an Instant-Magic oven.
10. "You are not only a brilliant teacher," said the student, "but a fair-minded one as well. Would you be kind enough, please, to have another look at my examination paper? I think your graduate assistant may have made a mistake."

Exercise 99

Critically discuss the following "arguments," identifying any fallacies present:

1. These pills must be safe and effective for reducing, for they have been endorsed by Miss Betty Shapely, star of stage, screen, and television.
2. Of course there's life on Mars. Scientists have not proved there isn't, have they?
3. Ann Landers has made a lot of money giving advice to people with marital difficulties. But I've just read that she was divorced after thirty-six years of marriage. Since she cannot solve her own problems, a person would be foolish to accept her advice.
4. You've studied long and worked hard for the position you hold today. But some day you may be an academic casualty, a victim of a myopic and arbitrary administrator. Who is looking after your rights? Who is protecting your claims to tenure and academic freedom? We are, the Association of Militant Professors. Join now—before it's too late.
5. You don't have to throw in the towel when you reach the age of 40. "Astounding Action" Cream not only makes you look younger—you feel younger too. It works on your skin as well as under it! It's simply amazing!
6. Someone near and dear to you is hoping for a Dingdong watch as a graduation present this year. Don't disappoint them! (Bad grammar in original.)

Exercise 100

Critically discuss the following "arguments," identifying any fallacies present:

1. Zen Buddhism must be a very rewarding form of religious worship. More and more people are engaged in it.
2. Bedsheets are for sharing—with that special one—for that special experience. Ecstasy Silken Sheets mark the climax of the textile-workers' art.
3. Some women are more exuberant than others. They bring enthusiasm and joie de vivre to everything they do. It is for such women as this, women like you, that Pansy's Pantyhose are designed.
4. She's only six years old, and other little girls are in school. But she is in

an iron lung. I know that you will want to help her. Contribute generously when a volunteer calls at your home.

5. "Of course my interpretation of Faulkner is correct," said the teacher. "You'd better believe it if you want to pass the next exam!"

6. Girls! If you want to lose weight, enroll at Camp Cinderella this summer. Lose up to fifty pounds. Results guaranteed. You'd better believe the boys will look at you differently when you go back to school in the fall!

7. Because you enjoy going first class, you will ask for the best when you order whisky: Transport Scotch.

Exercise 101

Critically discuss the following "arguments," identifying fallacies present:

1. "Are you a lyricist or a poet? We'd like to get you into the professional music business."

2. Babe Ruth, when asked to defend his salary which was greater than that of the president of the United States, said, "I had a better year than he did."

3. It is a well-known fact that George Washington threw, or tried to throw, a silver dollar across the Potomac River.

4. You'll love the Bahamas. You may even be loved in the Bahamas! Here the women, like the flowers, bloom and are beautiful. The Ace Travel Agency can get you there—the rest is up to you.

5. Yes, our shampoo contains beer—an active, bubbling ingredient. But please don't drink it! Use it on your hair!

6. Beautiful girl in TV commercial purrs: "All my men wear Belgian Leather— or they wear nothing at all!"

Exercise 102

Critically discuss the following "arguments," identifying the fallacies present:

1. I work hard and try to provide for my family. But medical expenses are ruining me. I had to see the doctor yesterday. He charged me $40 and told me to go home and take an aspirin. Then he drove off in a new Cadillac. I tell you, we've got to socialize medicine!

2. Churchill on bureaucracy: The trouble with our civil servants is that they are neither servants nor very civil.

3. "Yesterday, December 7, 1941—a date that will live in infamy—the United States of America was suddenly and deliberately attacked by naval and air forces of the Empire of Japan." (Franklin Roosevelt, War Message to Congress.)

4. Do you really want to give up the nicotine habit? We have a way, and it works. Send $1.98 to. . . .

5. "Continued dependence upon relief induces a spiritual and moral disintegration fundamentally destructive to the national fibre. To dole out relief in

this way is to administer a narcotic, a subtle destroyer of the human spirit.''
(Franklin Roosevelt, Message to Congress, 1935.)
6. So you are a self-made man? I believe it. And you worship your Creator.

Exercise 103

Critically discuss the following "arguments," identifying the fallacies present:

1. "On this tenth day of June, 1940, the hand that held the dagger has struck it into the back of its neighbor." (Franklin Roosevelt.)
2. We discussed religion for most of the trip, but he stubbornly resisted my arguments. When we parted I told him that we would have to go our own ways—"you to worship God in your way, I to worship Him in His."
3. "Demosthenes told Phocion, 'The Athenians will kill you some day when they once are in a rage.' 'And you,' said he, 'if they once are in their senses.' '' (Plutarch.)
4. As every schoolchild knows, the first battle between ironclad naval ships involved the *Monitor* and the *Merrimac*.
5. You may be right about ethnic jokes being in poor taste. But let me tell you about a bumper sticker I saw yesterday. It said, "Thank God, I'm Polish!" And the thing was on upside down.
6. Do you want to be a model—or just look like one? Write to The Grendel School and receive a free booklet by return mail.
7. The Missouri Auditor, Republican Margaret Kelly, stated in her audit that the office of the St. Louis License Collector had failed to collect almost $9 million in taxes and was the most poorly run public office she had ever audited. The License Collector, Democrat Billie A. Boykins, responded in her first press conference by saying: 'The Republicans want to get their grafty little hands on this city, and so they want to discredit all of us Democrats. . . . My personal belief is that Margaret Kelly and her merry little band of witch hunters are running a personal attack upon city Democrats." (See *St. Louis Post-Dispatch,* March 29, 1989, p. 3A.)

Chapter 12

The Uses of Logic

PREVIEW

This chapter is more concerned with techniques than with logical principles. It deals with the uses to which logical principles can be put. While the general purpose of logic is the attainment of truth, this purpose can additionally be broken down into at least four types. Each of these types is discussed in a section of this chapter. Master the following:

1. How to evaluate someone else's argument by exposing its structure. Every part of it is labelled as a premise, unstated assumption, subconclusion, conclusion—or simply as an irrelevance. Only when this has been completely done in detail are you in a position definitively to answer the question: WHAT DOES HE KNOW?

2. How to set up your own argument. Every part of it is labelled (as above). The truth of every premise and the soundness of every inference are established. Only when this is completely and correctly done are you in a position positively to answer the question: WHAT CAN I CLAIM?

3. How to solve problems and puzzles. Certain clues are presented in the premises or evidence offered to you. Only when you can exploit them logically and/ or intuitively are you in a position to answer the question: WHAT IS THE ANSWER?

4. How to think effectively about various courses of action. This requires the identification of means and ends, values and disvalues, desires and fears, prerequisites and consequences. Only when you have sorted all this out, can you confidently answer the question: WHAT SHOULD I DO?

Note: You will not be subjected to a ''diagnostic test'' for this chapter.

WHAT DOES HE KNOW?

Exposing the Structure

We learn a lot from what others say and write. Many of these oral and written expressions are testimonial—that is, they are reports of what has been seen, heard or felt. Whether we accept such expressions as true is based upon such considerations as: (1) Is the person generally truthful? (2) Is the person likely to be speaking truthfully now? (3) Is the person a good observer? (4) Does the person have a sound memory?

But many other things that we are asked to accept and believe are not reports of direct experience. They are conclusions of arguments. In these cases we are not concerned so much with reliability of testimony, but with the strength of the argument. When a person makes a claim, we want to know whether he has presented adequate grounds for that claim. Are his reasons true? Is his inference sound? In order to answer these questions we will have to *analyze* his argument.

In order to analyze an argument, we have to break it down into parts, ascertain the meaning of each part, and determine the relation of each part to the other parts. We must also eliminate irrelevancies and try to discern a structure for the whole argument. Our task is not simply the mechanical one of breaking the discourse into pieces and then putting the relevant ones back together again to make something that looks like an argument. From the beginning we look for relationships and try to discern the general structure of the argument. The process of analysis is an art. It is often tedious and replete with false starts. But it is an art the practice of which becomes more facile and accurate with experience.

What has been learned about meaning, deduction, and induction is indispensable in judging the strength of a claim, but these principles cannot profitably be applied until we have set out for ourselves the structure of the argument. It must be admitted that actual arguments do not usually come to us as neat little textbook exercises with listed premises and clearly indicated conclusions. The structure of an argument is seldom obvious. Analysis consists in the first place of making this structure explicit.

In order to do this, we must accurately distinguish reasons from conclusions and irrelevancies from both. We must be thorough—no element of the argument must escape our scrutiny. To do it graphically, we may want to label every part and draw boxes and arrows depicting relationships.

Let us examine an argument and make its structure explicit:

> Cable television should be brought into our county. It would bring us first-run movies, sports events, and other things which regular TV does not now provide. And it will be free of those endless commercials! Sure, it will cost us a little money, but think what we'll get for it!

We should first ask what the speaker is trying to prove. What claim is he making? It seems clear that the conclusion is contained in the first sentence. The other sentences in the paragraph express reasons for accepting the conclusion. We could diagram the argument in this way:

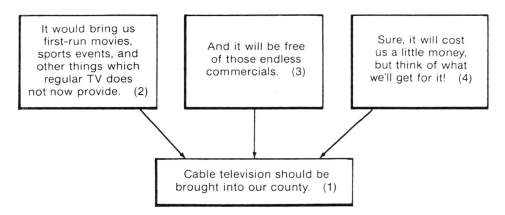

We could make the argument still clearer by rewriting some of its parts:

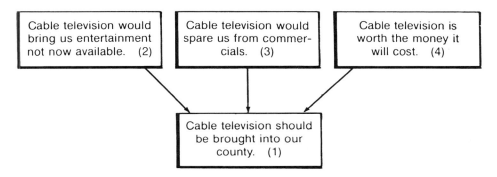

There are many questions we might want to raise about this argument, but its structure seems to be this:

However, although ④ is a reason for the conclusion, it does not seem to function in quite the same way that the other reasons do. Perhaps a more accurate view of the argument is to regard ④ as both a reason *and* a conclusion. If we view it as an intermediate conclusion following from ② and ③, as well as a reason for ①, the argument would look like this:

Consider this argument:

An applicant for a job should always dress appropriately. No one is going to hire a stylishly dressed lady in high heels to wait tables at a truck stop, and a girl in faded jeans will not get the job as receptionist at a medical center. You will enhance your chances if you dress in a way compatible with the work you hope to do.

What is the point of this argument? It seems to be expressed twice: in the first and last sentences. The second sentence gives two reasons for the conclusion. The structure of the argument is thus:

No one is going to hire a stylishly dressed lady in high heels to wait on tables at a truck stop. (2a)	A girl in faded jeans will not get the job as receptionist at a medical center. (2b)

An applicant for a job should always dress appropriately. You will enhance your chances if you dress in a way compatible with the work you hope to do. (1-3)

Once again, we will rewrite the parts in the interests of clarity:

Stylishly dressed ladies in high heels will not be hired for a waitress job at a truck stop. (2a)	Girls in faded jeans will not be hired for a receptionist job at a medical center. (2b)

Applicants increase their chances by dressing appropriately. (1-3)

The argument thus looks like this:

Here is another one:

In 1988, Charles Cochran of United Auto Workers argued on behalf of raising the minimum wage.[1] His argument contained these assertions in this order: [1] Annual earnings for a worker being paid the present minimum wage ($3.35) and putting in 40 hours a week would be $6968. This is significantly less than $8737, the poverty level for a family of three. [2] People working for the minimum wage are not simply teenagers earning pocket money. Seven out of 10 are adults (20 years or older); about three in 10 are heads of households; more than six in 10 are women. (Data from the Bureau of Labor Statistics.) [3] The minimum wage law was first enacted in 1938 to protect low-paid workers. The intention was that no worker should be paid less than half the average hourly wage of production workers. [4] The minimum wage has been raised several times to keep pace with inflation and the wages of production workers. [5] It was last raised in 1981 to its present $3.35. To equal the purchasing power of $3.35 in 1981, you would need to make $4.12 today. [6] The last time the minimum wage was half that of production workers was in 1968. "To equal the buying power of a minimum-wage paycheck in 1968, you would need to make $5.14 an hour today." [7] The purchasing power of the minimum wage, according to a study at George Washington University, is now at its lowest point since 1955. This, except for an *ad hominem* at the end, is the entire argument.

The conclusion is obvious: The minimum wage ought to be raised. The essay was written to counteract an argument against raising it that had been published a week before. The form of the argument is not as simple as it looks. We are given seven reasons for accepting the conclusion (which we will call [8]):

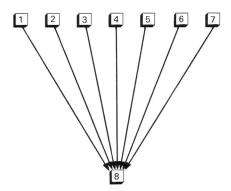

Just exactly how these premises support the conclusion will be discussed below.

Here is an argument from the writings of the free-love advocate, Emma Goldman:

If motherhood is the highest fulfillment of woman's nature, what other protection does it need, save love and freedom? Marriage but defiles, outrages, and corrupts

[1] See *St. Louis Post-Dispatch,* January 13, 1988, p. 2B.

her fulfillment. Does it not say to woman, Only when you follow me shall you bring forth life? Does it not condemn her to the block, does it not degrade and shame her if she refuses to buy her right to motherhood by selling herself? Does not marriage only sanction motherhood, even though conceived in hatred, in compulsion? Yet, if motherhood be of free choice, of love, of ecstasy, of defiant passion, does it not place a crown of thorns upon an innocent head and carve in letters of blood the hideous epithet, Bastard? Were marriage to contain all the virtues claimed for it, its crime against motherhood would exclude it forever from the realm of love.

Love, the strongest and deepest element in all life, the harbinger of hope, of joy, of ecstasy; love, the defier of all laws, of all conventions; love, the freest, the most powerful moulder of human destiny; how can such an all-compelling force be synonymous with that poor little State and Church-begotten weed, marriage?

Free love? As if love is anything but free! Man has bought brains, but all the millions in the world have failed to buy love. Man has subdued bodies, but all the power on earth has been unable to subdue love. Man has conquered whole nations, but all his armies could not conquer love. Man has chained and fettered the spirit, but he has been utterly helpless before love. High on a throne, with all the splendor and pomp his gold can command, man is yet poor and desolate, if love passes him by. And if it stays, the poorest hovel is radiant with warmth, with love and color. Thus love has the magic power to make of a beggar a king. Yes, love is free; it can dwell in no other atmosphere. In freedom it gives itself unreservedly, abundantly, completely. All the laws on the statutes, all the courts in the universe, cannot tear it from the soil, once love has taken root. If, however, the soil is sterile, how can marriage make it bear fruit? It is like the last desperate struggle of fleeting life against death.

Love needs no protection; it is its own protection. So long as love begets life no child is deserted, or hungry, or famished for the want of affection. I know this to be true. I know women who became mothers in freedom by the men they loved. Few children in wedlock enjoy the care, the protection, the devotion free motherhood is capable of bestowing.[2]

Because of the length of this argument, we will not take the space to number every sentence. Instead we will try to ascertain its components directly.

Goldman is evidently claiming that marriage is unnecessary, even for prospective mothers, and that everyone is better off when relations between the sexes are based on love. She holds that this is so because love and marriage are in conflict and love is superior to marriage. An acceptable structuring of the argument is:

---

[2] Emma Goldman, "Marriage and Love," *Anarchism and other Essays* (New York: Dover Publications, Inc., 1969), pp. 235–237.

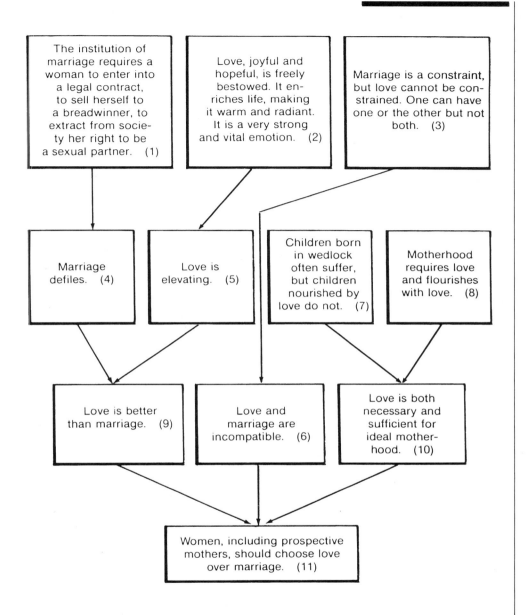

The institution of marriage requires a woman to enter into a legal contract, to sell herself to a breadwinner, to extract from society her right to be a sexual partner. (1)

Love, joyful and hopeful, is freely bestowed. It enriches life, making it warm and radiant. It is a very strong and vital emotion. (2)

Marriage is a constraint, but love cannot be constrained. One can have one or the other but not both. (3)

Marriage defiles. (4)

Love is elevating. (5)

Children born in wedlock often suffer, but children nourished by love do not. (7)

Motherhood requires love and flourishes with love. (8)

Love is better than marriage. (9)

Love and marriage are incompatible. (6)

Love is both necessary and sufficient for ideal motherhood. (10)

Women, including prospective mothers, should choose love over marriage. (11)

The form of the argument is thus:

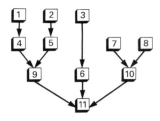

Let us examine one more argument:

Ladies and gentlemen of the jury, I will prove beyond a shadow of reasonable doubt that Joe Hill, with an accomplice, murdered the grocer, John Morrison, on the evening of January 10, 1914. The only witness to the murder, Merlin Morrison, has testified that the two assailants in his father's store wore bandanas and hats, but that the taller one resembled Hill's general appearance. Mrs. Seeley, who saw two men outside the store a few minutes before the shooting, testified that one of them had a thin face, sharp nose, large nostrils, light hair, and a scar on his face. Now while she declined to positively identify the defendant, her description certainly fits him. Merlin Morrison has also testified that his brother, Arlo, had gotten off a shot with his .38-caliber automatic before he too was gunned down. That his shot hit someone is established by Mrs. Hansen's testimony that she heard a man on the street near the store, wounded and stooped over, cry out, "Oh Bob." Miss Mahan testified that she saw a man, tall and thin, running from the store, and heard him cry out, "I'm shot!"

Now, what about Joe Hill? He was staying, along with his friend Otto Applequist, in the home of the Eselius brothers. It is admitted that he left the house between six and nine o'clock on the evening of January 10. Shortly before midnight he arrived on foot at the home of Dr. Frank McHugh, with a gunshot wound in his chest. While treating him, McHugh observed that he carried a gun in a shoulder holster. Dr. Bird then drove Hill to the Eselius house to recuperate, testifying that Hill threw a gun out of the window en route. The doctor also stated that Hill's wound could have been made by a .38-caliber automatic. Now, ladies and gentlemen, isn't this an interesting coincidence? Joe Hill wounded at just about the same time that the Morrison boy was trading shots with his assailant! And Hill almost identified as being near the store, and admittedly receiving medical treatment a few miles from the scene of the crime! And Hill's good friend, Applequist, disappears at the same time! No! These facts are not just a coincidence.

And this is the clincher. Hill has been asked to state his actions and whereabouts on that fateful evening. But he refuses! Dr. McHugh testified that Hill said something about a dispute with a man over a woman. That's how he got the wound! But who is that man? Who is that woman? Hill refuses to answer! Of course he does.

You, ladies and gentlemen of the jury, can draw but one conclusion. The defendant, Joe Hill, is guilty of first-degree murder!

The conclusion of the argument obviously is that Joe Hill murdered John Morrison. There appear to be three sets of facts to support this claim: Hill's presence in and near the store when the killings occurred, Hill's actions and condition after the murders, and Hill's refusal to provide an account of himself during the time the shooting took place. Let us take each in turn.

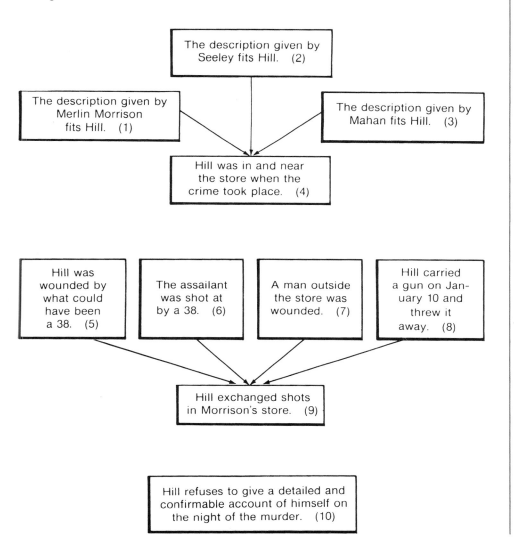

If we number the conclusion, that Hill murdered John Morrison, '11,' this would seem to be the structure of the prosecutor's argument:

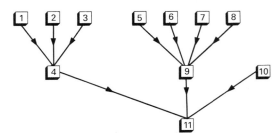

Concluding Summary: To answer the question, "what does he know?" we have to analyze his argument. This requires, first of all, exposing its structure. To do this we must identify premises, conclusion, and subconclusions, and discern the connections between them.

Evaluating the Argument

Once we think we have grasped the structure of an argument, we need to ask such questions as these: (1) Are the meanings of its key terms clear and consistent? (2) What unstated assumptions does it seem to contain, and are these assumptions true? (3) Is there good reason to believe that the premises are true? (4) How sound are the inferences? When these questions are answered, we should be ready to make a final determination of the strength of the argument.

With respect to the argument above, the one concerning cable television, we might want to question the truth of premises ② and ③ . Is it necessarily the case that entertainment over and above that which regular television provides would be made available? Program schedules of likely cable companies should be provided and consulted. And would the presence of additional programs really constitute additional *entertainment?* If a customer is assured of re-runs of "Petticoat Junction," he might not regard this as "entertainment." So we need to know what the speaker means by entertainment and whether it is the case that any cable company would provide it. The other premise should be scrutinized also. To what extent will cable television be free of commercials? Will the amount of commercial time vary from one company to another? It is quite possible that the speaker can answer our questions about his premises. He may have some particular companies in mind and be able to

---

His reasons are as two grains of wheat hid in two bushels of chaff; you shall seek all day ere you find them; and when you have them, they are not worth the search.

—*William Shakespeare,* The Merchant of Venice

show us from printed programs, brochures, and guarantees that our opportunities for entertainment are increased and that commercial messages are nonexistent. But we would have been foolish to accept his premises on faith.

Let us now look at the inference from ②︎ and ③︎ to ④︎. Does the conclusion that cable television is worth the money follow from the premises? Certainly, the benefits cited would be worth *some* amount of money. We would only have to make the assumption that anything that provides benefits is worth some amount of money. The argument would then be an enthymeme:

> [Whatever supplies benefits is worth some amount of money] UNSTATED ASSUMPTION
> Cable television supplies benefits (additional entertainment and freedom from commercials) ②︎ ③︎
> ∴ Cable television is worth some amount of money ④︎

This assumption is one we could probably go along with. The actual conclusion, however, is more vague than this. It states that the amount of money is "little." So the assumption we will need is somewhat different, and the argument will look like this:

> [Whatever supplies benefits is worth a little money] UNSTATED ASSUMPTION
> Cable television supplies benefits ②︎ ③︎
> ∴ Cable television is worth a little money ④︎

So now we have to examine the truth of the assumption. This is difficult to do because of the vagueness. Sixty dollars a month would not be "little." Sixty cents would be "little." But what about six dollars? Would this be "little?"

If the speaker had said that the cost would be eight dollars a month, his argument would be more straightforward and would look like this:

> [Whatever supplies benefits of a certain kind is worth eight dollars a month] UNSTATED ASSUMPTION
> Cable television supplies these benefits ②︎ ③︎
> ∴ Cable television is worth eight dollars a month ④︎

The vagueness has been eliminated in the conclusion and hence in the assumption. It now becomes possible to evaluate the acceptability of the assumption. But we have had to alter the argument significantly. As originally stated, the argument is seriously flawed by vagueness—and, as we have seen, by the ambiguity of its first premise and the lack of support for both of them.

Let us now examine the second part of the argument. Ignoring the vagueness of ④︎, we might want to question whether ①︎ follows from it. ①︎ follows from ④︎ only if we make explicit another assumption: whatever is worth the money should be brought in to the county. It is surely not self-evidently true that whatever is worth the money should be acquired. The county, as well as the household, may have more pressing needs for its money. A Stradivarius violin may well be worth $1000, but if one doesn't have enough money to handle his grocery bills, he would be foolish to buy it. That something is worth the price-tag attached to it does not mean that one should necessarily buy it. What is needed to support 1, in addition to the subconclusion that cable television is worth the money, is support for the view that this particular expenditure would be a wise one for the agencies and individuals who will pay for it.

When the assumptions are provided, the argument exhibits this structure:

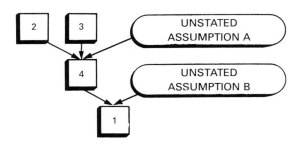

Our final judgment on the argument as a whole is that it is a very weak one. Its key terms are ambiguous and vague, and its inferences depend upon unstated assumptions that are far from being self-evidently true.

The second argument, the one about appropriate dress for job applicants, appears to be inductive. The conclusion is a generalization, although we are not certain whether it asserts that *all* applicants increase their chances or merely that *most* do. In any case, we must examine the sample on which it is based. The first element of the sample, 2, is the subclass of truck stop waitresses. The second element, 3, is the subclass of medical center receptionists. Are these premises true? They seem to be based on common sense rather than empirical study and are thus open to question. One would tend to accept them, but the argument would be stronger if these assertions had been based on interviews with representative groups, respectively, of waitress- and receptionist-hirers.

Even if we are satisfied with the truth of the premises, we should raise the question whether the sample offered is a fair sample. Does it accurately represent the entire class of occupations? Is it possible that there are occupations for which the dress of applicants would *not* affect their chances of getting the job? What about lifeguards, telephone canvassers, football players, seamstresses, musicians, nude models? The argument has offered some extreme and rather obvious cases and has gone too far in generalizing that all or most occupations are in a similar situation.

There is also the possibility in this argument that the speaker is begging the question. If, in the course of the conversation, it turns out that 'dressing appropriately' means 'dressing in a way that increases one's chances,' the "conclusion" is not an inductive conclusion at all, but simply a tautology.

The third argument, the one about the minimum wage, has a strong factual basis. But it is not obvious how the facts support the conclusion. The conclusion does not appear to be a generalization, a causal statement, or a hypothesis. Perhaps the argument is not an inductive one at all. If it is a deductive one, there are some missing premises. Not only is it possible to accept the truth of the premises while denying that of the conclusion, the premises are logically irrelevant to the conclusion. This is so because they state what *is* the case while the conclusion states what *ought* to be the case. Thus, in order to link the premises with the conclusion, we will have to supply some additional premises—including at least one that converts the factual to the normative. These would function in the argument as unstated assumptions.

These assumptions are that the intent of the original 1938 law was good, that this good should be sought today, and that an amendment of the law is the way to do it. These propositions or something similar to them must be added if the argument is to have any force at all. How can they be formulated and injected into a formal argument?

> [If low-paid workers were being protected, they would be receiving wages equal in purchasing power to those they received in 1938] UNSTATED ASSUMPTION A
> They are not receiving wages equal in purchasing power to those they received in 1938 $\boxed{1}$ $\boxed{5}$ $\boxed{6}$ $\boxed{7}$
> ∴ Low-paid workers are not being protected (SUBCONCLUSION B)
> Adults and heads of household are low-paid workers $\boxed{2}$
> ∴ Adults and heads of households are not being protected (SUBCONCLUSION C)
> If the minimum wage law were achieving its original goal, they would be protected $\boxed{3}$
> ∴ The minimum wage law is not achieving its original goal (SUBCONCLUSION D)
> The original goal of the law is right and proper (UNSTATED ASSUMPTION E)
> ∴ The minimum wage law is not achieving its original goal, which is right and proper (SUBCONCLUSION F)
> Any law that does not achieve its original goal (which is right and proper) should be amended so that it does produce that end (UNSTATED ASSUMPTION G)
> ∴ The minimum wage law should be amended so that it produces the right and proper end that it was designed to produce $\boxed{8}$

The argument now looks like this:

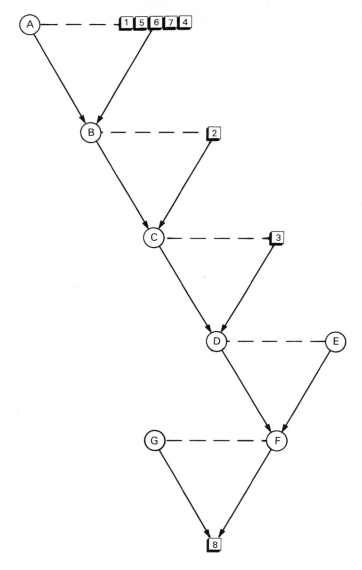

This is a valid deductive argument. If we can accept the factual premises as true, the argument is as strong as the unstated assumptions. Assumption A could be challenged by arguing that workers *are* being protected, although not as well as they were in 1938. Assumption E could be challenged by arguing that the goal is "socialistic" or "paternalistic," that workers should negotiate their own wages individually or through unions, that they should not rely on government statutes. Assumption G could be challenged by arguing that the situation in the country today is far different from what it was in 1938. The law that served a purpose then may be inappropriate today. It is not always wise to recycle old laws, because either their ends may no longer be legitimate or they may no longer be effective.

People may argue that the present law (as is) does serve a purpose (provides a cellar figure for wages), but that this is not the same as the original purpose (provide a breadwinner with a decent wage for his family). The critic will argue that the present law does not have to carry out the original intention (just as Social Security laws no longer carry out the original intentions of the program).

In summary, Cochran does give some facts in ② to show that we are still dealing with breadwinners and not casual or part-time workers. And he shows in ④ that some concern has been shown in minimum wage legislation over the years to provide a decent income for workers. The old purpose has *not* been lost sight of. But these considerations are not sufficient to establish the proposition that we have identified as the second assumption. It is this unstated assumption that is the most vulnerable part of the argument.

Emma Goldman's argument is very emotional. Its basic premises are presented in such a way as to win acceptance on the basis of feelings. Premise ① depends on the reader's sense of outrage; it is not a detached and balanced account of marriage. That marriage is sometimes felt to be a legal sale of sexual favors for economic security and respectability does not mean that this is its essential and common nature or that most women feel this way about it. Premise ② is perhaps acceptable, although its description of love is one-sided and calculated to contrast with that of marriage. Premise ③ explicitly brings out the opposite natures of marriage and love. But it is clearly false. Marriage is not always experienced as a constraint. It may freely be entered into. That the parties to the marriage have to get a license, fill out forms, and get lab tests is a nuisance, but lovers who decide to live together have certain nuisances to deal with also (and they are not solely results of society's attitude to their life style). That legal constraints are experienced in marriage does not necessarily destroy the feeling of love freely bestowed. The critic can thus maintain that the truth of ① and ③ is not self-evident and that ② is at best a half-truth.

If one grants the basic premises, however, subconclusions ④ , ⑤ , and ⑥ would seem to follow with the addition of rather obvious assumptions like:

> Anything which requires one to sell oneself or extract from society permission in order to have sexual relations is demeaning.

> Anything that is joyful and enriches life is elevating.

> When two relations cannot be experienced simultaneously, they are incompatible.

Having shown that marriage is bad and that love is good, Ms. Goldman can take the next step and conclude, ⑨ , that love is better than marriage. From ③ , she infers, ⑥ , that love and marriage are incompatible. This too is a sound inference, requiring only the assumption that relations generating opposite feelings are incompatible.

But before she can finally conclude that all women should choose love and reject marriage, she must face up to the special problem of motherhood. It turns out in 10 that love is both necessary and sufficient for ideal motherhood. One premise offered for this subconclusion is 7, which consists of pointing out that children born in wedlock often suffer, while those born out of wedlock to loving parents sometimes do not. The other premise, 8, points out the importance of love for motherhood. Though we may not want to question the truth of these premises, we would have to question their adequacy for the subconclusion 10. That some legitimate children are denied love and that some illegitimate children are not is a far cry from the position that love is the only requirement for successful motherhood and that it suffices for it. At most, 7 shows that *marriage* is neither necessary nor sufficient for ideal motherhood. It is pointless to try to formulate the many assumptions that would be needed to link 7 and 8 up with 10. It might be held that Ms. Goldman is simply arguing here that love is *more important* for successful motherhood than anything else, including marriage. But even so, the premises fall far short of providing sufficient support.

Finally, we may note the equivocation on the word 'love.' The term originally meant affection for the sexual partner. Now it means affection for the offspring. They are not quite the same. That love in the first sense inflames the heart of a woman is no assurance that love in the second sense will also.

Since Ms. Goldman does not explicitly state 11, it may be an implied conclusion. It does seem to be the point of her argument. This final conclusion, that women, even those desiring to have children, should choose love and reject marriage, does indeed follow from 9, 6, and 10. But, as shown above, there are good reasons for questioning at least one of these subconclusions.

The argument of the prosecutor in the trial of Joe Hill was deemed to be an excellent one by the jury. On June 27, 1914, he was found guilty and was sentenced two weeks later to be executed. Several months later he was killed by a firing squad. The jury had agreed with the judge that the circumstantial evidence was like a cable: strong, though some of its strands were weak.

The defense had chosen the analogy of a chain—which could be no stronger than its weakest link. And some of its links were indeed weak. That Hill was in and near the store, 4, was surely not established by the witnesses. The descriptions were general enough to apply to thousands of men. The witnesses, obviously led by the prosecutor, refused, despite strong urging, to make a positive identification.

That Hill exchanged shots with Arlo Morrison, 9, does not follow from the evidence. The other assailant may have fired at the Morrisons. Indeed, Hill might not have been in the store at all. He was not the only man wounded that night in Salt Lake City—some, in fact, were reported to have been in the same neighborhood. Hill, moreover, did not have a history of violent behavior. He was a friendly and easy-going man. That he possessed a gun is not strange in view of the need of I.W.W. organizers to protect themselves. What, exactly, could have been Hill's purpose in entering the store with a gun in his hand? To acquire a ''stake'' with which to get out of Utah? But Merlin Morrison had testified that the masked men had not asked for money (nor did they take any after the shooting). He said that one of the intruders had simply said to his father, ''We have got you now!'' Then the shooting began. This would indicate revenge as a motive, but there is no known evidence that Hill was even acquainted with the grocer. As a matter of police record, John Morrison had twice before (1903 and 1913) been attacked by masked assailants and had exchanged shots with them wounding at least one of them. All five of the men involved in the attacks escaped. *These* people may have had a motive, but what could Hill's motive have been? One other fact that would support an alternative hypothesis while calling into question ⑨ is that the bullet hole found in Hill's jacket was four inches lower than the hole in his chest. Did Hill have his hands in the air when he was shot? It is unlikely that he would have been in such a position while attacking the Morrisons.

It is possible to question the truth of one of the "facts" presented in support of ⑨. That the assailant was shot by a .38-caliber automatic, as asserted in ⑥, is not necessarily true. All Merlin, a lad of thirteen, could be sure of was that shots had been fired. Although the bullet that hit Hill went through his body, no spent cartridge was ever found in the store.

It may be argued, then, that subconclusion ⑨ is a hypothesis that is not a very good explanation of the facts, and that at least one of the "facts" is dubious. So this, the second link or strand, is weak. If Hill had not been wounded (or had successfully concealed his wound), he would not even have been arrested.

It was the third link or strand, ⑩, that was most damaging to Hill. If it is regarded as another fact, it does strongly support the final inductive hypothesis that Hill murdered Morrison. Clearly, however, one cannot *deduce* Hill's guilt from this statement unless he is willing to accept the assumption that suspects who refuse to explain their behavior at a time when a crime was committed are guilty of that crime. It is not an utterly unlikely alternative hypothesis that Hill, a romantic songwriter, did indeed wish to preserve the reputation of a woman. Why did she not come forward? She may have died. Perhaps she had been threatened. Or she may have placed her own welfare and reputation ahead of Hill's life. Another alternative hypothesis is that Hill maintained silence to protect his friend Applequist, who was in the store and did the shooting.

From the legal point of view, however, the prosecution should not have been permitted to identify Hill's refusal to testify with admission of guilt. The right not to testify was recognized even in the statutes of Utah. Whatever Hill's reason for silence may have been, his right to be silent should have been respected. It was the burden of the *state* to demonstrate that he had entered the grocery store and shot Morrison. Hill's refusal to take the stand and try to provide corroboration for his story should have had no bearing on the deliberations of the jury. The judge permitted the prosecution to place the burden on Hill to prove his innocence. The strength of the state's case thus loomed larger to the jury than it should have.

Joe Hill did not receive a fair trial, nor did the state prove beyond reasonable doubt that he had committed the crime. There may have been in the argument of the prosecution good evidence for the conclusion, but it fell far short of what is needed to send a prisoner to his death. This is a case in which acceptance of an argument depends on considerations beyond the theoretical question of what one reasonably should believe. The legal dictum that a man is presumed innocent until proved guilty requires stronger evidence than that which is perfectly adequate for an individual who merely wishes, for theoretical purposes, to incline his belief to the conclusion which is most probably true.

Concluding Summary: The second step in analyzing an argument is to examine the meaning of key terms, investigate the plausibility of assumptions and premises, and ascertain the soundness of all inferences. Finally, we are in position to evaluate the strength of the argument.

EXERCISES

Exercise 104

Analyze the following arguments and evaluate their strength:

1. Capital punishment should be handed out to all people convicted of first-degree murder. It is not only a just retribution for the criminal (''an eye for an eye''), but it also has beneficial consequences for society: It removes a dangerous person from our midst, it acts as a deterrent for all who are tempted to commit murder, and it spares taxpayers the expense of supporting murderers in prison.
2. I think I should take this summer off and go to Europe. I haven't had a vacation in six years, and I'm really getting stale. Sure, air flight is expensive, but next year the rates will be even higher. The American dollar is not so powerful over there, but it still does fairly well in Spain and Italy. The trip would be very educational: I could learn a lot about history, art, and what Europeans are like today. So I'd better start saving my money!

Exercise 105

Analyze the following argument and evaluate its strength:

''To defend the right of a lone, crazed American Nazi to grind out propaganda calling for the extermination of all Jews, as ACLU has done in the name of free speech, is, after all, a self-righteous and not particularly courageous stand, for American Jewry is not currently threatened by storm troopers, concentration camps and imminent extermination, but I wonder if the ACLU's position might change if, come tomorrow morning, the bookstores and movie theaters lining Forty-second Street in New York City were devoted not to the humiliation of women by rape and torture, as they currently are, but to a systematized, commercially successful propaganda machine depicting the sadistic pleasures of gassing Jews or lynching blacks?

''Is this analogy extreme? Not if you are a woman who is conscious of the ever-present threat of rape and the proliferation of a cultural ideology that makes it sound like ''liberated'' fun. The majority report of the President's Commission on Obscenity and Pornography tried to pooh-pooh the opinion of law enforcement agencies around the country that claimed their own concrete experience with offenders who were caught with the stuff led them to conclude that pornographic material is a causative factor in crimes of sexual violence. The commission maintained that it was not possible at this time to scientifically prove or disprove such a connection.

"But does one need scientific methodology in order to conclude that the anti-female propaganda that permeates our nation's cultural output promotes a climate in which acts of sexual hostility directed against women are not only tolerated but ideologically encouraged? A similar debate has raged for many years over whether or not the extensive glorification of violence (the gangster as hero; the loving treatment accorded bloody shoot-'em-ups in movies, books and on TV) has a causal effect, a direct relationship to the rising rate of crime, particularly among youth. Interestingly enough, in this area—nonsexual and not specifically related to abuses against women—public opinion seems to be swinging to the position that explicit violence in the entertainment media does have a deleterious effect; it makes violence commonplace, numbingly routine and no longer morally shocking.

"More to the point, those who call for a curtailment of scenes of violence in movies and on television in the name of sensitivity, good taste and what's best for our children are not accused of being pro-censorship or against freedom of speech. Similarly, minority group organizations, black, Hispanic, Japanese, Italian, Jewish, or American Indian, that campaign against ethnic slurs and demeaning portrayals in movies, on television shows and in commercials are perceived as waging a just political fight, for if a minority group claims to be offended by a specific portrayal, be it Little Black Sambo or the Frito Bandido, and relates it to a history of ridicule and oppression, few liberals would dare to trot out a Constitutional argument in theoretical opposition, not if they wish to maintain their liberal credentials. Yet when it comes to the treatment of women, the liberal consciousness remains fiercely obdurant, refusing to be budged, for the sin of appearing square or prissy in the age of the so-called sexual revolution has become the worst offense of all."[3]

WHAT CAN I CLAIM?

Finding the Premises

We can legitimately claim anything for which we have adequate grounds. Our claim is thus the conclusion of a deductive or inductive argument. How strongly we can press our claims depends upon the strength of that argument. It depends, therefore,

[3] Susan Brownmiller, *Against Our Will: Men, Women, and Rape* (New York: Simon and Schuster, 1975), pp. 395–6. Copyright © 1975 by Susan Brownmiller. Reprinted by permission of Simon & Schuster, a Division of Gulf & Western Corporation.

on the truth of the premises and the soundness of the inference. If the argument is deductive, we should make sure that the inference is valid. We will then be able to repose as much confidence in the conclusion as we have in the truth of the premises. If the argument is inductive, our confidence will be qualified by both the truth of the premises and the probability of the inference. Even if we are certain of the truth of the premises, we will avoid claiming certainty for the inductive conclusion.

Where do we get true premises?

One source for true premises is empirical. What have we in fact seen, heard, smelled, tasted, or felt? If we have seen a gun in the coat pocket of the butler, we may assert that a gun was in his coat pocket. If we have heard the howl of a hound on the moor, we may assert that such a sound occurred. If we have smelled the odor of cigarette smoke in the tool shed, we may assert that such an odor was present.

There are, however, obvious dangers here. Often people think they have experienced things which actually were inferences from what they in fact experienced. Was the object in the coat pocket really a gun or was it a wooden replica? Did the coat actually belong to the butler or was it merely hanging in his closet? Was the sound coming from the moor indeed the howl of a hound or could it have been a recorded scream of a clever mimic? Was the odor we experienced that of cigarette smoke or might it not have been a synthetic spray devised to smell like cigarette smoke? When one uses elements of his own experience as premises, he should guard against imparting more to them than what was actually experienced. There is no hard-and-fast line that can be drawn here. In all experience there is an element of inference. While we do not want to try to restrict ourselves to the sense data themselves, we do not want to go too far beyond them either. After having glimpsed a particular shape, we may draw back from asserting that it was a gun, but if we have had the opportunity to handle it, we may assert that it was a gun.

Another danger in utilizing our own experience springs from the fallibility of our own memory. How long ago did the experience occur? Did we write it down at the time or "fix it" in our memory in some way? Still another danger may exist if we ask ourselves whether we were reliable observers at the time the experience took place. Were we free from the distorting influence of alcohol or drugs? Were we wide awake? Were we tired? Were we, in short, in full possession of our faculties?

If we are putting forth a claim that we want others to accept, we also want them to accept our premises. Will they do so when we cite our own experience? This will depend upon our reputation for honesty and reliability. If they have no reason to believe that we are good witnesses, they will tend to doubt our experiential premises. It is advisable, then, that the facts we cite be not restricted to our own *private* experience. Did anyone *else* enter the garden and see the unicorn? Can some one verify or corroborate our report that Roger Rumpot was in the Stagger Inn last night? From the point of view of succeeding in getting our claim *accepted,* empirical evidence should be as public as possible.

This suggests another dimension for the class of observed facts as premises. We may rely on what *other* people have reported seeing, hearing, smelling, tasting, and feeling—so long as we (and the persons we hope to convince) are reasonably assured that they are good witnesses (honest and reliable). And here again, whether such reports can be corroborated or verified by others may be important for disarming critics who might wish to reject our claim.

A second general source for true premises lies in the field of science. Here we can rely on the authority of bona fide researchers in their appropriate fields. This is not a case of *argumentum ad verecundiam*, for these people are legitimate authorities and are vouched for by their colleagues. We can and must build our claims on the claims of others, since we have neither the time nor resources to establish these scientific truths ourselves.

Going to the legitimate authorities does not mean that we have to go *directly* to the individual himself (Archimedes, say, or Galileo). We may consult a book written by a person who is recognized by scientists in a particular field as a dependable expositor of the discoveries of others. This suggests a caution. Since scientific beliefs are constantly changing, we do better, other things being equal, in citing a recent work than an earlier one. We also should consult books published by established publishing houses of good reputation. Products of "vanity presses" should usually be avoided.

In addition to textbook accounts of scientific findings, one may also consult encyclopedias, almanacs, yearbooks, atlases, and the like, when, of course, they are products of reputable publishing houses.

The "findings" of science range from verifiable observations to highly speculative theories, from the color of rocks from the moon to the "big bang" theory of the origin of the universe. Some beliefs are regarded by scientists as virtually certain, while others are held to be only possibilities. In appealing to scientific findings as grounds for a claim, we should try to apportion our reliance on their truth to that degree of certainty felt by objective scientists in the field. That Caesar crossed the Rubicon is a hypothesis more confidently held by historians than the hypothesis that Leif Eriksson established a colony in "Vinland."

Some philosophers have held the view that certain sciences are inherently more certain or factual than others. Mathematics is most certain, with physics, astronomy, chemistry, and biology coming next. These are the "natural" sciences. Less dependable are the "social" sciences: psychology, political science, economics, and sociology. Without entering into a debate on which is most basic or reliable, one can assert that there is a great deal of interrelation between the sciences. It is seldom the case that a law in one science is held in total disregard of what is held in other sciences. There are no sharp lines demarcating and separating one science from the others. One can also assert that there are highly questionable theories in the "hard" (or "natural") sciences and that there are well-authenticated laws in the "soft" (or "social") sciences. There is, therefore, no escape from the task of determining the probable truth of the specific scientific findings we cite as grounds for our claims.

This is usually not difficult to do. A general reference book will, in most cases, report only views on which there is great agreement. A good textbook will usually label theories which are still in the speculative stage as such. Articles in scientific journals, however, present evidence for new "discoveries," but how compelling the evidence is is very difficult for a layman to ascertain.

A third source for premises consists of current newspapers and magazines. Here we must be very careful. We must first distinguish between "fact" and "opinion." A straight news report is generally more to be trusted than an editorial or signed column. But the line between fact and opinion is difficult to draw, and some publications are much less conscientious than others in attempting to distinguish what they report as fact and what they print as opinion. And among the more conscientious publications, an unconscious bias may operate to color their news reports, to slant their accounts, and to accept too readily (or too tardily) specific items submitted to them as news.

Even when bias does not operate, news reports themselves may be false. Reporters are fallible. Editors cannot "check out" every report. Communications often have to pass through several parties and through hundreds of miles before they finally reach the person who decides whether the story will be printed. Both writing and decision-making take place with an eye to the next deadline. And finally, errors may creep into the actual printing. If the printer chooses one wrong letter, a 'now' may become a 'not' and the whole sense of the statement reversed: "The rebels are not willing to lay down their arms."

The best one can do is to rely on the most respected of publications, *New York Times, Christian Science Monitor, Newsweek, Time,* and a few others, recognizing that even these have their own points of view and are subject to human error.

We have dealt here only with the "print media." What about radio and television? In the first place, there is much less news reported here than in newspapers and magazines, and it is often reported for its sensational or entertainment value. Moreover, it is difficult to evaluate, both with respect to what it asserts and what is its source. Unless one has tape-recorded the item, he can never be sure exactly what has been reported and where it originated. Radio and television reports are too evanescent.

Their great advantage is their timeliness. We find out immediately, for instance, that President Kennedy has been shot or that the New York Giants have won the Super Bowl. But these reports and others will be reported later and more fully in the print media. Ordinarily, then, we do better to draw our premises from newspapers and magazines than from the airwaves.

A fourth possible source for the grounds we appeal to in backing up a claim is "general knowledge." We don't always have to document or cite the source of a fact we present as a premise in an argument. Certain things are accepted as true by the educated public. We need not cite a particular historical writing to assert that Columbus visited the Caribbean in 1492, nor do we have to appeal to an astronomy book to assert that light travels at the speed of about 186,000 miles per second.

General knowledge, however, is the most treacherous source of information. All too often it has turned out to be the case that some "well-known fact" is completely erroneous. How many educated people still believe in the story of Washington and the cherry tree, the authenticity of the Piltdown man, the existence of the vaginal orgasm, and the therapeutic value of "bleeding?" We seem to be in a dilemma. We can't dispense with "general knowledge," but cannot fully trust it. A feeble

> *Whatever Sceptic could inquire for,*
> *For every why he had a wherefore.*
>
> —*Samuel Butler,* Hudibras

seizing of a horn is to say, yes, rely on general knowledge, but be wary and always on the lookout for possible challenges to it.

A fifth source of premises or grounds is quite different from the other four. It consists of statements that are part of an accepted code for behavior. These "codes" may be ethical systems, rules of etiquette, bylaws of organizations, contracts, statutes, state or national constitutions, as well as precedents in the interpretation of these various kinds of rules. We may rely on these codes or systems when we want to show that an action is unethical, impolite, unfeasible, unjust, illegal, unconstitutional, or otherwise forbidden. Or, of course, we may cite them to show that an action is acceptable. Generally, these rules which we select from codes are used as premises in deductive argument.

Are these premises *true?* Often, we need not know. They may be *taken* to be true by those who adhere to the systems or codes of which they are parts. Their truth, then, is relative to the acceptability of the whole from which they are cited. If parties to a dispute over the legality of an action done in the state of New York can agree that the legal code of that state is applicable, citation of its various statutes has the force of a true premise.

There are, however, certain problems in appealing to stipulative codes. One problem is that of knowing whether the particular code *is* applicable to the particular case in question. Is this law code the one presently in effect in the particular jurisdiction or is there a later revision? Is this system of etiquette (say, Amy Vanderbilt's) more appropriate than some other one (say, Emily Post's)? Does this system of ethics (say, Mill's) provide a more accurate set of norms than some other system (say, Kant's)?[4] We should, therefore, when we appeal to codes, appeal to those that are pertinent and whose pertinence is accepted by those we are arguing with.

A second problem is that caused by overlapping. A particular action may be impolite but moral. Another action could be legal but immoral. A contract can uphold an action which seems to violate the bylaws of an organization of which a party to the contract is a member. An action may be legal according to state law but conflict with "the law of the land." Here we can only make sure that what we are claiming clearly falls in one area. We openly declare that our conclusion is applicable merely to the field of ethics, or the field of etiquette, or whatever. If we want to claim any more than this, we will have to show that the particular code from which we select our rules takes precedence in some sense over the other codes.

A third problem in appeals to codes is interpretation. If we cite murder as an

---

[4] Ethics, when considered a rational enterprise, differs from the other codes. Its rules are established by thought rather than formal or informal stipulation. They make a claim to truth about the universe and may themselves, therefore, be argued about.

immoral act, we must be clear on what 'murder' means. Does it apply to war, self-defense, or abortion? If we cite the ''due process'' clause of the Constitution (or some precedent in its interpretation), we must make clear what the clause (or the judicial dictum) means. What does ''assault and battery'' mean in a law code? Does ''*ex officio*'' membership in committees specified in a set of bylaws mean ''nonvoting'' or does it leave the issue open?

Concluding Summary: Among the general sources for true premises are the following: direct experience by ourselves and others, the findings of science, current periodicals, ''general knowledge,'' and the stipulations contained in codes of conduct. Certain cautions, however, have to be borne in mind when seeking true premises in each of these general areas.

Formalizing the Argument

It is obvious that inferences from true premises must be sound if our claim is to be properly supported. Where these inferences are deductive, they should be valid; where they are inductive, they should have a high degree of probability.

It is useful in making a claim to go about it rather formally. Indicate which are the premises and which are the conclusions. Show what follows from what and the degree of soundness (from deductive validity to inductive probability) involved in each inference. State the assumptions, rather than leaving them unstated. Supply a source or warrant for all premises which are not intuitively self-evident. While not necessarily resorting to boxes, ovals, and arrows, as employed in the first section of this chapter, expose the structure of the argument as clearly as possible.

The usefulness of such a procedure is twofold: (1) It forces us to order our own thought. We can strengthen weak links, assure ourselves that we are operating on sound bases, avoid fallacies, and, finally, express the proper degree of confidence in the conclusion we draw or the claim that we state. (2) The procedure enhances the plausibility of our claim. It will be more persuasive to the reader or listener when he knows the links of the argument and the premises and inferences that make them up. It is true that presenting a clear picture of the course of our thought may make it easier for the critic to refute our argument. In exposing the structure of the argument, we at the same time tend to expose its weak points as well. But even this is helpful. The criticism will at least be directed at what is really our argument instead of what is *thought* to be our argument. We thus may be led to strengthen our argument, or at least to lessen our insistence that the conclusion or claim is true. To be freed from error is itself a step toward greater truth.

Let us look at an argument which presents its claims clearly and shows how it follows from grounds or premises.

I will try to show that American views toward sexual behavior have become increasingly permissive over the last thirty years or so, that a veritable ''sexual revolution'' has taken place. I will back up this claim by data in three broad categories: sexual behavior itself, social attitudes toward sexual behavior, and regulation of sexual behavior by legal statute.

If I can show that sexual activity outside marriage is more extensive, that society increasingly condones this behavior, and that laws are more tolerant regarding sexual behavior, I will have good grounds for my conclusion that a sexual revolution has taken place.

This conclusion is a deductive one. It follows from the three premises stated above, together with these two assumptions: (1) Behavior, attitudes, and laws constitute the indices for a society's view of sex. (2) If society's view of sex has undergone great change, then a revolution has taken place.

The first premise, that sexual behavior has increased in many areas outside marriage, is itself the conclusion of other premises. It must, of course, be an inductive conclusion, for it will rest on empirical studies, polls, and statistics which cannot claim with certainty to represent the population as a whole. But this inductive evidence is very convincing for each area for which it is cited.

According to the book, *Sexual Behavior in the Human Male* (1948), by Alfred C. Kinsey and others, 68 percent of non-college men engaged in premarital sex before the age of 17. A survey reported in *Playboy* magazine in January, 1974 gave the figure of 75 percent. In the case of college men, the figures were 23 percent in 1948 and over 50 percent in the *Playboy* survey. In the case of women, Kinsey's *Sexual Behavior in the Human Female* (1953) reported that 35 percent of single women had intercourse between the ages of 21 and 25. The *Playboy* survey reported that 75 percent of unmarried women had intercourse before age 25. A survey conducted by *Redbook* magazine (September, 1975) reported that 90 percent of unmarried women under 25 had had sexual intercourse.

The "Kinsey Report" shows that 24 percent of all husbands under 25 had extramarital relations, while the *Playboy* survey indicated that the figure is 32 percent. In the case of wives under 25, the figures are 8–9 percent in 1953 and 24 percent in 1973.

With respect to postmarital sexual activity, of males under age 56, 4 percent to 18 percent did not have coitus, according to Kinsey. According to the *Playboy* survey, the figure was zero. In the case of females, 33 percent to over 50 percent (mid-forties and above) did not have coitus. But according to the *Playboy* survey, the figure was only 10 percent.

One more set of figures is relevant. These figures come from the U.S. National Center for Health Statistics publication, the annual *Vital Statistics of the United States*. They show the percentage of illegitimate births. In 1940 the percentage was 3.5. In 1945, 4.1. In 1950, 3.9. In 1955, 4.5. In 1960, 5.3. In 1965, 7.7. In 1967, 9.0. In 1968, 9.7. In 1969, 10.0. And in 1970, the percentage was 10.7.

In view of these statistics, we have excellent reason for concluding that sexual behavior occurs much more often outside marriage than was the case a generation ago. And this conclusion serves as one of the major grounds for my contention that a sexual revolution has taken place.

The second major premise for this conclusion is that social attitudes have grown increasingly tolerant. This premise is itself the conclusion of empirical studies and generally known changes in customs over the last few decades. Although the evidence is overwhelming, I will only claim inductive probability, for there is an outside possibility that responders to questionnaries are not truly representative, and that the actual customs cited are not indicative of changing attitudes but represent the greater success and openness of individuals who have *always* been permissive in their attitudes.

Roper Polls, in 1937 and 1957, gave similar results to this question: "Do you think that it is all right for either or both parties to a marriage to have had previous sexual intercourse?" Over 50 percent of a national sample answered that it was wrong for both men and women. Twenty-two percent answered that it was all right for both men and women, and 8 percent indicated that it was all right for men only. The *Playboy* survey asked the question of married people. A large majority of men and women thought it was acceptable for males. Similar majorities of men and women also thought it was acceptable for females.

Changing customs can be cited without documentation, for they are generally known. One such custom is the degree of sexual explicitness in fiction and poetry published by reputable companies. The books of a generation ago, Lillian Smith's *Strange Fruit* and Norman Mailer's *The Naked and the Dead,* for instance, which were regarded as scandalous in their day ("banned in Boston" and elsewhere), are tame by today's standards. The skin-porn magazines, openly displayed today, have gone as far beyond the early *Playboy* as that magazine went beyond the old *Police Gazette*. There is no need any more for the furtive circulation of hard porn. Periodicals with no limit on subject matter, pictures, or language are easily available in every major city. Movies are now classified, but films receive the "PG" designation today that could not even have been publicly exhibited a few years ago. Movies with "R" designations would be considered only for private showing, and "X" and "Triple-X" would be restricted to stag parties. In our day, when a movie receives a "G" rating, it is the kiss of death. Television has not "progressed" so far, but it does bring actions and language into homes today that would not have been even considered for showing in the fifties and sixties.

The third major premise for the final conclusion that a sexual revolution has taken place is that laws at all levels have become increasingly permissive. Here again this premise is established as a conclusion from impressive evidence. Since I have neither the time nor space to compare the entire body of contemporary American law with the law that was in force a generation ago, I will claim only inductive probability for the conclusion.

In the publishing field, anything goes. It is no longer necessary to smuggle into this country copies of Joyce's *Ulysses* and Lawrence's *Lady Chatterley's Lover*. Pornographic books and magazines, hard as well as soft, encounter no legal disabilities in most cities and towns, and none whatever in the U.S. mail. "R"-rated movies are unmolested anywhere and "X" and "Triple-X" flourish in most large cities. Live nudity on the stage is legal in most cities and sex-shows in some.

Fornication, once interdicted, is accepted, so long as there is no public disturbance or "disorderly conduct." Individuals openly advertise for sexual partners in reputable periodicals (and some not so reputable).

Birth control equipment is openly sold, advertised, and displayed today, and available to all, while a generation ago it was difficult in some places for even married people to secure what they needed. According to Dr. Adele Hoffman, doctors may prescribe contraceptive devices to adolescents of any age with parental consent. Many states permit doctors to prescribe it *without* parental consent. Dr. Hoffman predicts, in her article in the December 1972 issue of *Medical Aspects of Human Sexuality,* that the number of such states will increase.

In January 1973 the Supreme Court ruled state statutes against abortion during the first two trimesters unconstitutional. A few years before this decision, legal abortion (except under very special circumstances) was nowhere in the country available. As things stand now, abortion can be barred only in the third trimester except when necessary to preserve the life or health of the mother.

Homosexual behavior, once universally legislated against, is legal now in most states between consenting adults.

Law respecting sexual behavior falls increasingly into the area of civil rights. The view today is that the individual must be the judge of his or her own

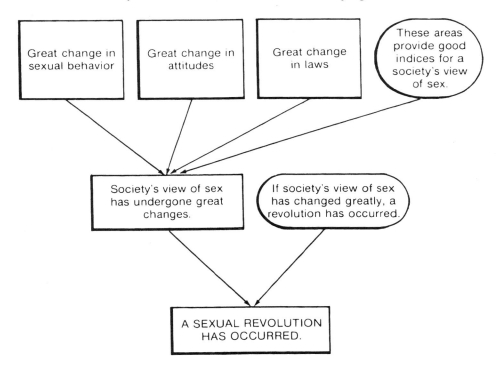

behavior, and the function of law is simply to prevent others from being harmed or wronged. Employers must now judge their workers on what they do on the job. Their sexual activity and sexual preferences are regarded as irrelevant. To view the situation in any other way is an invasion of privacy and/or a deprivation of civil rights.

Now, if it is the case that sexual behavior, attitudes, and laws are legitimate indications of how society views sex, that these indicators reveal a great change, and that a great change represents a revolution, then my conclusion follows.

Concluding Summary: One increases his or her chances of making a successful claim when he or she not only presents a strong argument but makes its structure explicit.

EXERCISE

Exercise 106

Present a formal argument for one of these conclusions:

1. Most voters are poorly prepared.
2. Intercollegiate athletics are corrupt and hypocritical.
3. The "Donation of Constantine" is a forgery.
4. _____ is a better novel than _____.
5. Sunspots affect weather on the earth.
6. Miracles have (have not) occurred.
7. A course in logic should (should not) be required for all baccalaureate degrees.
8. Abortion (except to save the mother) is wrong.
9. Wiretapping is legal (illegal).
10. The electoral college should be abolished.

WHAT IS THE ANSWER?

Problems

It must be said at the outset that no comprehensive account of problem-solving can be given here. Some suggestions, however, will be offered which may be of some use in seeking solutions for some kinds of problems.

Let us make a distinction between two kinds of problems. One kind of problem is theoretical; the other kind is practical. Examples of the first are: Who first set foot on the moon? When did Charlemagne die? What did Hamilton Jordan say to the wife of the diplomat? Is it true that Martin Luther married a nun? Why did Senator Kennedy decide to be a candidate for President in the 1980 election? Which native is telling the truth? How can we escape from the prison camp? Why does the

Cardinal football team usually lose? Examples of the second kind are: Should I propose marriage to Gwendolyn? Should I call the bet? Should I vote for Henry Kissinger? Should I drop this course? Should I change jobs next year? The first kind admittedly has practical implications, but the basic problem is to find an answer which is *true*. The second kind requires true data, but the basic problem is to make a wise decision, to choose a course of *action*. Theoretical problems will be discussed in this section (''What Is the Answer?''); practical problems will be dealt with in the last section of this chapter (''What Should I Do?'').

A further distinction in theoretical problems now has to be made: that between theoretical problems involving actual facts and theoretical problems that are contrived to test one's reasoning powers. The first we will simply call ''problems,'' and we will discuss them in this the first subsection of this section. The second we will call ''puzzles,'' and we will discuss them in the second subsection of this section.

Problems occur in a context. Our knowledge of that context will contribute to our formulating the problem precisely. It is because we already know that Jordan said something interesting to the lady on a specific occasion that we can ask the question about his exact words. It is because we already know something about the Cardinal football record that we can ask the question about its cause.

It is, however, not necessary always to formulate the problem precisely and perfectly at the beginning of an inquiry. The formulation may undergo revision and become more pointed as we proceed. We may first try to understand the ups-and-downs of the football team, then turn our attention to trying to understand why between the years of 1977 and 1990 it had a losing record. We may know something about medieval history and formulate the question, What was the Investiture Controversy? As we acquire more information about this exciting conflict between Gregory VII and Henry IV, we might want to change the question to one of these: What were the issues of the controversy? What arguments did Gregory rely on? What arguments did Henry rely on? Which side was the ultimate victor? Just as knowledge originally provided the setting for the problem, additional knowledge may refine it. Students who write a term paper or doctoral dissertation should not always be compelled to set out with a final version of their problem before them. Start with something, investigate, then restate the question.

This procedure has an additional advantage. One may, in his or her willingness to alter the formulation of the problem, be able in some cases to eliminate some false assumptions in the question itself. Perhaps Jordan did not even *meet* the woman in question. Perhaps there is *no* reasonably safe way to escape from the prison camp. Perhaps *neither* side emerged the winner in the Investiture Controversy.

Knowledge of the context of the problem will also help us come up with possible answers. Why is my roommate so sloppy? Knowledge of his character, his upbringing, his working schedule, his hobbies, and so on may suggest several possible answers. The more we know about Egypt, its weather patterns, the river banks, the drainage tendencies in the Nile valley, the better chance we will have of solving the problem of why the Nile River seasonably overflows its banks. The more we know about medieval European history and the nature of the ecclesiastical and secular authorities since the time of Charlemagne, the more equipped we will be to discover the real issues in the Investiture Controversy.

There is a danger, however, in this approach. The solution may lie outside the familiar and easily acquired knowledge of the problematic situation itself. We should be willing to think creatively, to formulate some answers that go beyond what an analysis of the situation itself might yield. We may try to explain the motion of Jupiter's moons on the basis of what is known about the celestial objects in their gravitational field, when in fact there is an *undiscovered* body that is exerting an influence. The key to solving the problem of the Nile may lie in what happens in the mountains hundreds of miles *south* of Egypt. Our sloppy roommate may be reacting against *our* compulsive tidiness. The best way to escape from the camp may be to *destroy* it, rather than flee from it. The real issue in the Investiture Controversy may be an utterly *new* one, rather than simply an intensification of the old and familiar church-state tensions. Knowledge of the problematic situation is indeed useful, indispensable in fact, but it should not close us off from innovative solutions that require the kind of knowledge that goes beyond a conventional and narrow analysis of the problematic situation itself.

Once the problem (question) has been formulated, we embark upon a search for its solution (answer).

Many problems can be solved by consulting books and periodicals in the library. Although few (if any) factual assertions can be accepted as absolutely true, we may accept most of what we read as factual assertions in textbooks and reference books published by reputable companies, as well as eyewitness accounts in reputable periodicals. Card catalogs by subject matter help us find what we are after. And so too will standard index works such as: *Readers' Guide to Periodical Literature, International Index to Periodicals, Social Science Index, Humanities Index, Bibliographic Index, Biographical Dictionaries Master Index, New York Times Index, The Times of London Index, Wall Street Journal Index,* and others. In addition, good libraries will contain such standard reference works as *Encyclopaedia Britannica, Encyclopedia Americana, Collier's Encyclopedia, Encyclopedia of Religion and Ethics, Encyclopedia of Philosophy, Encyclopedia of the Social Sciences, Encyclopedia of World Art, McGraw-Hill Encyclopedia of World Biography, Dictionary of International Biography, Dictionary of American Biography, Modern English Biography, Current Biography, Who's Who, Who's Who in America, International Who's Who, Contemporary Authors, Books in Print, Dictionary of American History, McGraw-Hill Dictionary of Art, Groves Dictionary of Music and Musicians, Library Journal Book Reviews, Congressional Quarterly Almanac,* and many more. Many problems, then, can be solved by following the injunction, "look it up." And the library supplies the resources.

Some problems can be solved by subsuming a particular instance under a general statement. What is Congressman Brown's salary? All we need to find out is the salary of all Congressmen, then deduce Brown's. Other problems require several premises and one or more subconclusions. Will Agnes meet me tonight at the Zebra Lounge in Knoxville? She said she would unless Clarence is in town—and she never lies. Helen (who is to be trusted) called me an hour ago from Billings and told me she had seen Clarence at a ski lodge. The happy answer to this problem, then, is that Agnes will be there.

A final example of deduction problem solving is this: A celestial navigator asks himself, "Where am I?" He may reason that the altitude at a specific time of a specific star, Arcturus, will by deduction place him somewhere on a "line of position." Determining the altitude of another star, Sirius, with his sextant will deductively establish him on another "LOP." So he shoots the stars and calculates his LOP's. He draws the two lines on his chart and concludes deductively that he is precisely at the point where the lines intersect. His confidence in his conclusion will be proportioned to the confidence he has in his chronometer, his sextant, and his own calculations.

Other problems, however, are not so easily solved. Some of them require causal analysis. We must conduct our own or evaluate analyses of others. "Why does the Cardinal football team usually lose?" Possible causal factors here would be inept coaching, poor organization above the coaching level, poor communication among the parts of the organization, unwise trades, low salaries and morale, poor draft choices. Comparisons of the Cardinal organization with successful organizations might, through the use of the method of difference, yield some answers. Use of the method of agreement in studying successful teams might suggest some more or confirm some that we have already formulated.

The problem of giving up smoking could also be approached as a causal one. How have other victims of the habit been able to break it? Gradual reduction? "Cold turkey"? Use of hypnosis? Use of pills? If we can find several instances of people like ourselves who have succeeded, we could try to discover one common factor in all the positive cases where success has resulted.

Use of Mill's methods is inductive, so any answer we arrive at is, in the broad sense, a hypothesis. It is, then, in principle, testable. Unless we own the Cardinal football team, we would not be able actually to test our solution to the team's poor showing, but we could test various theories for breaking the nicotine habit.

The problem of getting out of a prison camp could also be approached inductively, and any hypothesis we formulated could be tested. We would want to think deeply, however, before we put a plan to the test, for failure could be fraught with dire consequences. That we may not actually want to test a particular hypothesis does not mean, however, that we could not test it in our imagination. That is, we can draw out the implications or consequences of a hypothesis in our mind.

Certain hypotheses for getting out of Stalag-Luft III may occur to us. (1) Bribe the guards with currency and Red Cross packages. (2) Overpower the guards. (3) Dig a tunnel to a point in the forest beyond the fence. Which will work? The hypothesis that we can escape by bribing the guards does not seem promising, for the assumption that they will live up to their word and let us pass is questionable. They may accept our bribes then shoot us down when we tried to scale the fence. Knowing what we do about their character, this result is just as likely. The hypothesis that we can escape by overpowering the guards is also not promising, for one consequence of a physical attack on the alert and well-armed guards is death. So we think a bit more of the escape-by-tunnel hypothesis.

The guards realize that prisoners often try to escape through tunnels, and they are very watchful for signs of tunneling near and under the prisoners' building. If the way out is a tunnel, it will have to be a very unusual one. It will have to begin at a place not periodically checked, but one to which the prisoners have easy and unsuspicious access. The digging must take place under the very noses of the guards but at the same time be unseen.

This plan may occur to us: Start the tunnel at some point in the exercise area. Conceal its opening by a moveable structure of some kind. How about a vaulting horse? Build a wooden vaulting horse and carry it daily to the area. Hide a man inside it. While the other prisoners are vaulting, the man inside is working on the tunnel. When he finishes his day's work, he covers up the opening with boards and dirt while crouched inside the horse. Together with the dirt he has unearthed he is then carried back to the barracks. Set the horse down at the same point each day as the tunneling goes on.

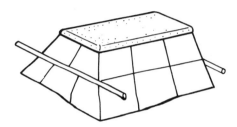

The plan must be refined and many other related problems solved, such as: How to get wood to build the horse, how to carry the dirt back to the barracks, how to dispose of the dirt, how to ventilate the tunnel, how to shore up its sides, how to know when it is long enough, and many more. But the basic solution to the problem of getting out of the prison centers on the use of a vaulting horse. Whether this hypothesis will be verified by success, lies in the future.[5]

About ten years ago, many Americans were confronted with the problem of the starving Cambodians. Why, despite the earnest efforts of many states and voluntary organizations, did the Cambodian people continue to die by the thousands? UNICEF, the Red Cross, and several religious groups tried to stem mass starvation. The United States appropriated $30 million for Cambodian famine relief, and on November 2, 1979, the Senate unanimously approved an additional $30 million. Yet the people continued to starve.

This problem, like many others, was a theoretical problem with practical ramifications. But to be able to answer the theoretical *why?* is not the same thing as to be able to succeed in the practical object of getting massive relief to these unfortunate

---

[5] In actual fact, the plan did prove to be a solution. Three prisoners escaped from Stalag-Luft III in 1943 and made it safely back to Britain. See Eric Williams, *The Wooden Horse* (New York: Abelard-Schuman, 1958).

people. Solution to the theoretical problem was, however, a necessary condition to solving the practical problem. Here we are concerned solely with the former.

On the basis of newspaper accounts, we may have felt that the solution to the problem lay in the understanding of certain political realities. In Cambodia itself there were at least three factions: (1) The followers of Prince Sihanouk (then exiled in North Korea), formerly backed by the United States. (2) The Khmer Rouge, followers of the fallen dictator Pol Pot, a group backed by China and seated in the United Nations. (3) The followers of Heng Samrin, backed by Vietnam and the USSR, installed in Phnom Penh and engaged in a civil war with the Khmer Rouge. How and to what extent did this internal situation frustrate efforts to deliver food? Did one faction seek to prevent relief that would strengthen a rival faction? Why had the Phnom Penh government refused to allow food to be trucked into Cambodia from Thailand (the "land bridge")? Was much of the food that did get through skimmed off by the soldiers of one of the warring factions? Senator John Danforth said after his return from Cambodia: "We cannot accept the possibility that a government or an alleged government is going to willfully consign hundreds of thousands of its own citizens to a needless death." But this may be exactly what was happening.

Troops and officials of Vietnam were also in Cambodia. How much of the relief supplies did they intercept for use in Vietnam (also in need of food and medicine)?

On the Cambodian border is Thailand, a nation concerned for its own survival and fearful of the Cambodians, Vietnamese, and Chinese. Thailand has been the intended destination of thousands of Cambodian refugees. In June 1979, it forced 42,000 of them to return to Cambodia. In the fall, however, the Thais were more receptive, reasoning perhaps that it is to their interest to preserve the existence of the Cambodian people (who will return home when the fighting stops) as a buffer against the Vietnamese. Meanwhile, many Khmer Rouge units were dug in near the Thailand border.

Then, too, we must try to understand American politics—international and domestic. The United States could support neither the stooges of Vietnam nor the unsavory Khmer Rouge. The reluctance of some American officials to expedite aid may have stemmed from unwillingness to strengthen either of these perhaps genocidal regimes. Domestically also, politics operated. Each party watched the actions of the other, making political capital whenever possible. Within the Democratic Party, Kennedy partisans attacked Carter for moving too slowly, while Carter partisans attacked Kennedy for oversimplifying the situation and advocating "grandstand" measures.

Political realities in both the United States and Cambodia have changed. The Vietnamese, for example, have moved out of Cambodia, and the Khmer Rouge and Sihanouk have made common cause. But starvation in Cambodia is still a problem in 1990—as it is in Ethiopia and elsewhere. People are in need, food is available, but thousands perish. *Why?* Before practical measures can be taken to relieve the

---

Man is a reed, the weakest in nature, but he is a thinking reed.
                    —*Blaise Pascal*, Pensées

situation, this theoretical question must be answered. A testable hypothesis that explains the facts must be formulated.

Concluding Summary: Solution of theoretical problems requires knowledge of facts relevant to the situation or context in which the problem arises. Some solutions can be found in reference books. Others are conclusions of deductive arguments. Others are inductive hypotheses, which are in principle testable.

Puzzles

There is an isolated village where all the people are named Jones or Smith. The Joneses always tell the truth and the Smiths always lie. A visitor to this village encountered three people on the street and asked them their names. The first villager answered, "Two of us are Joneses." The second answered, "Exactly one of us is a Jones." The third then said, "Yes, that is true." The problem is to determine the names of the three people.

We may solve this problem by examining possibilities and their consequences. The first possibility is that all three are named Jones. This is rejected, for if all are telling the truth there would be no inconsistency in their answers. The second possibility is that two are named Jones. But if this is so, the second and third villagers lied—which means that they are Smiths and only one, the first, is a Jones. So the second possibility, having led to its own contradiction, is rejected. The third possibility is that one is named Jones. But if this is so, the first villager lied and the other two told the truth. If this were the case, there would be two Joneses, not one. So the third possibility, having led to its own contradiction, is rejected. This leaves the possibility that none of the villagers is named Jones. That is, all are Smiths and liars. We encounter no difficulty in the implications of this view. The first villager lied when he claimed that two were Joneses. The second lied when he claimed that one was a Jones, and the third lied when he agreed with the second.

There are many popular puzzles based on truth-telling. The oldest is the one about the Cretan who maintained that all Cretans always lie. This cannot be true, for if 'all Cretans always lie' is true, then he has contradicted it in telling the truth. Thus it is false that all Cretans lie. If it is false that all Cretans lie, it is true that some of them do not. That some of them do not is consistent with the possibility that some do. So the speaker was one of those who lie, and his contention that all Cretans lie is simply an example of his proneness to lie.

This puzzle is similar to that involved in the statement:

All generalizations are false.

If it is true, then it must be false. If it is false, however, 'some generalizations are not false,' is true. Again, this leaves open the possibility that some *are* false. And that certainly is the case with respect to the original generalization. These two puzzles have often been called paradoxes, but they are really simply self-contradictions. A genuine paradox both cannot be true *and* cannot be false. For example:

> The sentence written in this box is false.

If it is true, it must be false. If it is false, it must be true. Unlike the others, it can be *neither* true *nor* false. There is no way to solve it without calling on the tools of advanced logical theory. The puzzles discussed in this section, however, are not paradoxes; they all have solutions based on ordinary logic.

The first puzzle requires rehearsing alternatives and their consequences. You are presented with three sealed boxes, all mislabled. Box (1) is labeled "Apples," Box (2) is labeled "Oranges," and Box (3) is labeled "Apples and Oranges." The labels, applied to different boxes, would be correct. The problem is to determine what each box contains after having selected *one fruit from one box.* Which box do you choose?

First alternative: Select from Box (1). If the fruit is an apple, you will know that it contains apples and oranges, for the box is mislabeled. But you will not be able to deduce anything about the other boxes. If the fruit is an orange, the box may be apples and oranges or simply oranges. So again you are stumped. Therefore, this alternative is rejected.

Second alternative: Select from Box (2). Similar reasoning applies. So this alternative is rejected.

Third alternative: Select from Box (3). If the fruit is an apple, you can be sure that the box contains nothing but apples, since the "Apples and Oranges" label is wrong. What about the other two boxes? One contains oranges and the other contains apples and oranges, but which is which? Box (2) cannot contain oranges, for that is what its label says. So it must contain apples and oranges. The contents of Box (1), mislabeled "Apples," must, therefore, be oranges, since that is the only remaining possibility. A similar line of conclusive reasoning would result if the fruit selected from Box (3) turned out to be an orange.

The third alternative gives us the solution, so it is from Box (3) that we should make our selection.

The next puzzle is about a bridge game involving people named Baker, Doctor, Shepherd, and Weaver. Their occupations are baker, doctor, shepherd, and weaver, but no occupation corresponds to a name. On the basis of these clues, we have to discover each man's occupation and where he sat at the bridge table:[6]

  1. Shepherd and the shepherd were partners.
  2. Baker and the weaver were partners.
  3. The doctor sat on Weaver's right.
  4. Baker sat South.

Our reasoning may proceed this way:

  5. Baker is not the weaver. /from (2)
  6. Baker is the doctor or the shepherd. /from (5)

[6] Adapted from Hubert Phillips, *My Best Puzzles in Logic and Reasoning* (New York: Dover Publications, 1961), p. 23 (38).

7. │⎯ Baker is the shepherd. /assumption
8. ┌ Baker's partner is Shepherd. /from (1) and (7)
9. │ Shepherd is the weaver. /from (8) and (2)
10. │ The other two players are Doctor and Weaver and they are partners.
   │ /from (8)
11. │ The other two players are the doctor and the baker. /from (7), (8), (9)
12. │ The doctor is either Weaver or sits across from him. /from (10) and (11)
13. │ The doctor is not on Weaver's right. /from (12)
14. │ The doctor sat on Weaver's right. /from (3)
15. Baker is not the shepherd. /from (7–14), *reductio ad absurdum*
16. Baker is the doctor. /from (6) and (15)
17. Baker the doctor sat South. /from (4) and (16)
18. Weaver sat West. /from (3) and (17)
19. The weaver sat North. /from (17) and (2)
20. The shepherd did not sit East. /from (18) and (1)
21. The shepherd did not sit North. /from (19)
22. The shepherd did not sit South. /from (17)
23. The shepherd sat West. /from (20), (21), (22)
24. Weaver the shepherd sat West. /from (18) and (23)
25. Shepherd sat East. /from (24) and (1)
26. Doctor sat North. /from (4), (18), (25)
27. Doctor the weaver sat North. /from (19) and (26)
28. The baker sat East. /from (17), (19), (22)
29. Shepherd the baker sat East. /from (25) and (28)

Our conclusion made up of (17), (24), (27), and (29), is that the places at the
card table were as follows:

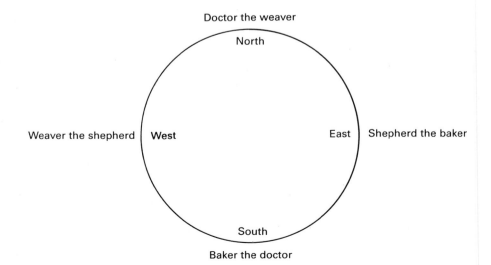

Doctor the weaver

North

Weaver the shepherd | **West** ⎯⎯ East | Shepherd the baker

South

Baker the doctor

Many puzzles do not lend themselves to the kind of patient, step-by-step reasoning illustrated above. They seem to require an intuitive approach, an ability to penetrate through to the heart of the matter. The conclusion comes to one as an inspiration or gestalt. Often this happy event is made possible by ability to grasp essential relationships while discarding conventional and distracting assumptions.

One famous puzzle is this: A man has a chance encounter with an old friend whom he has neither seen nor heard about for thirty years. The last time they had been together was as classmates in junior high school. The friend was accompanied by a young lady, who was introduced as the friend's daughter. "She was named after her mother," said the friend. "Ah!" answered the man, "your name must be Laverne!" HOW DID HE KNOW?

So long as we assume that the friend is a male, the solution remains impossible. But if we discard that assumption, the solution is easy. The friend is a woman. Knowing his friend's name, the man will of course know her daughter's name.

Another well-known puzzle is this: How many animals of each species did Moses take with him on the ark? In our eagerness to give the correct answer, "two," we fail to notice the false assumption in the utterance of the question itself. It was Noah, not Moses, who is supposed to have taken the animals on the ark.

Here is another one: You wish to get to a castle surrounded by a ten-foot moat. You have two planks, each nine-and-a-half feet long, but nothing with which to fasten them.

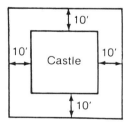

How can you use the planks to cross the moat?

It is perhaps when we realize that a corner may be used that we begin to see the solution:

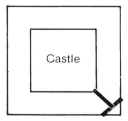

A mysterious object was found by archaeologists in the ruins of an ancient Roman city. An expression was engraved on one of its sides:

What does the expression mean and what was the object? If we get beyond the block of trying to decipher a "Latin" phrase, we immediately see the "translation" and the purpose of the object: TO TIE HORSES TO.

This next one is one of the many variations on the truth-teller/liar theme. A prisoner is confined in a cell with two doors. One leads to freedom, and one leads to the den of a large and hungry lion. The prisoner must open one of the doors. Outside the cell are two knowledgeable guards. The prisoner may ask one of them just one question requiring a yes-or-no answer before selecting the door. The trouble is that one of the guards always lies and the other always tells the truth, and the prisoner does not know which is which. WHOM DOES HE ASK AND WHAT IS HIS QUESTION?

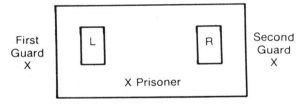

It obviously does no good to ask a guard whether one or other of the doors leads to freedom, for the prisoner will not know whether or not he is being told the truth. The breakthrough for this puzzle occurs when we realize that perhaps some information can be gained by asking a question *about* a question. Suppose the prisoner asked one of the guards (it is immaterial which one) this question:

> If I asked your mate whether the door on the left leads to freedom would he answer affirmatively?

There are four possibilities:

(1) The guard is a truth-teller and answers YES. If this is so, the other guard would indeed have answered "yes," but since he is a liar, the prisoner should not choose the door on the left.

(2) The guard is a truth-teller and answers NO. If this is so, the other guard would indeed have answered "no," but since he is a liar, the prisoner should choose the door on the left.

(3) The guard is a liar and answers YES. If this is so, the other guard would have answered "no," and since he is a truth-teller, the prisoner should not choose the door on the left.

(4) The guard is a liar and answers NO. If this is so, the other guard would have answered "yes," and since he is a truth-teller, the prisoner should choose the door on the left.

There is a fortuitous correspondence in all this. An affirmative answer from whichever guard he selects tells the prisoner to choose the door on the right. A negative answer tells him to choose the door on the left. The prisoner can save himself by his wits!

Finally, let us look at two types of problems that are found in most college and professional school aptitude tests.

The first is based on a letter or number series. One is required to predict what the next letter or number will be. To do this correctly, he has to discern a pattern in the series presented. In a sense, he is expected to formulate a hypothesis (the pattern) and make a prediction as to what will carry on the pattern. If there is no answer corresponding to his prediction among the set of answers from which he chooses, he has to formulate another "hypothesis."

In each of the letter series below, we have to predict the next two letters.

(1) A B C F E D G H I L K J M
(2) B A D C F E H G J I L

In the first, we proceed forward in the alphabet through three letters. Then we encounter a reverse direction for three letters. The forward-reverse sequences alternate. Is there any key determining the starting point for each three-letter sequence? Yes. Each sequence begins three letters after the previous sequence ends. That is, there is a two-letter gap between the last letter of each sequence and the first letter of the next. In extending the series we must retain the pattern. The last letter, 'M,' is the first of a three-letter sequence. This sequence must go forward, since the last one went backward. So the next two letters will be 'N' and 'O.' If 'N O' is not among the possible answers, we have to formulate another hypothesis, one that will be more complex. In the second series, we seem to have a series of two-letter sequences, and all go backward. What is the connection between the sequences? Each one begins three letters after the preceding one ends. The last letter is 'L,' the beginning of a new sequence. It will be followed by 'K.' The next letter will begin a new sequence, so it will be three beyond the 'K.' It must, therefore, be 'N.' So our answer is 'K N,' and if that is not among the suggested answers, we would have to formulate another hypothesis.

Here is a number series which we are asked to extend to the next number:

16   20   36   100

Do the numbers increase according to any pattern? The first increment is 4, the second is 16, and the third is 64. They are exponential. The first is 4 to the first power, the second is 4 to the second power (4 squared), and the third is 4 to the third power (4 cubed). The next number, then, should be the sum of 100 and 4 to the fourth power (256), namely, 356.

The last kind of puzzle we will look at is commonly called an exercise in analogical

> *He had been eight years upon a project for extracting sunbeams out of cucumbers, which were to be put in phials hermetically sealed, and let out to warm the air in raw, inclement summers.*
>
> —*Jonathan Swift*, Gulliver's Travels

reasoning. We may be given two series of figures with one figure missing in the second series. The problem is to supply the missing figure—or to select it from two or more possibilities. For example:

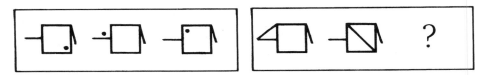

The choices are:

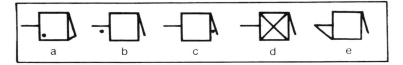

We have to discover what all in the first set have in common and discern a similar commonality in the second. But the second set, while preserving the basic commonality, does so with a difference. The missing figure will carry on the general resemblance of all five figures but will be consistent with the unique principle of the second set. In the first set, we find that each figure changes the location of one of the elements—the dot. The figures in the second set have no dots, but one element is moved around: the line that angles back to the box in the first figure and which is the diagonal of the box in the second figure. So the missing figure can be expected to contain a change in location of one element—the line, however, not the dot. Of the offered answers, we can reject 'a,' 'b,' and 'c,' for they contain dots. We reject 'd' because it contains an additional element. This leaves 'e.' It does conform to our requirements, so it must be correct.

Concluding Summary: Some puzzles can be solved by drawing deductive conclusions from given clues. Others require the mysterious ability to perceive the situation without blinders or stereotypes.

EXERCISES

Exercise 107

Solve these problems as adequately as time permits:

1. Whom did Hayes defeat in the election of 1876?
2. What happened to Amelia Earhart?

3. Which professional football teams still had a chance to make the playoffs last year when the regular season was 75% completed?
4. Why didn't your car start on _____?
5. Why does Edwin (or Edwina) not want to marry you?

Exercise 108

Solve these puzzles:

1. If a plane crashes directly on a line between two states, where should the survivors be buried?
2. Three intelligent women, Abigail, Bertha, and Clara, were candidates for a scholarship. Dean Keene decided to award the scholarship to the woman who could first solve a puzzle. The dean blindfolded the candidates and told them that she was placing hats on their heads. The hats may or may not have crosses on them. When the blindfolds were removed, each candidate was to raise her hand if she saw a cross. The one who could first state correctly whether her own hat had a cross would win the scholarship. When the blindfolds came off, all the hands went up. After a little while, Clara said, "Dean Keene, my hat has a cross." HOW DID SHE KNOW?
3. One afternoon Mrs. Marshall, Mrs. Price, Mrs. Torrey, and Mrs. Winters went shopping together, each with two errands to perform. One of the women had to visit the hardware store, two needed to go to the bank, two needed to go to the butcher shop and all but one needed to buy groceries. Their shopping was simplified quite a bit by the fact they lived in a small town which had only one store of each kind and only one bank. As a result they were soon done and on their way home. (1) Doris didn't go into the grocery store. (2) Both Ethel and Mrs. Winters bought meat. (3) Margaret came home with more money than she had when she started. (4) Mrs. Price didn't go into any of the places where Lucille or Mrs. Torrey went. WHAT WAS EACH WOMAN'S FULL NAME AND WHAT TWO PLACES DID EACH VISIT?[7]
4. Which hand is it more likely to draw in bridge? thirteen cards in the same suit or the thirteen highest cards?
5. The TV repairman has three sons, each studying at different universities. They are majoring in different subjects. One is named William; he is not at Yale. Wilbur is not at Harvard. The son at Yale is not studying philosophy. The son at Harvard is studying physics. Wilbur is not studying physiology. The third son is named Willis. One son attends Princeton. WHO IS STUDYING WHAT AND WHERE?[8]
6. What are the next two letters?

    A   D   F   I   K   N   P   S
7. What is the next number?

    1   2   4   8   1   3   9

---

[7] C. R. Wylie Jr., *Puzzles in Thought and Logic* (New York: Dover Publications, 1957).
[8] Adapted from Phillips, *op. cit.,* pp. 47–48 (90).

8. Which symbols should be substituted for the question mark?

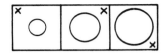   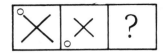

9. The university's football team won by a score of 17-0. It scored more points in each quarter than it had scored in the previous quarter. And there were no safeties. Fill in the quarter scores:

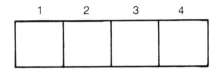

10. "Brothers and sisters have I none,
But this man's father is my father's son."
WHO IS "THIS MAN"?

WHICH SHOULD I DO?

Values

The connection that this section has with the previous one is obvious. In solving problems of what is the case, we move into position to make a good decision. Knowledge of the situation precedes intelligent choice of action. With respect to the starving Cambodians, we ask such questions as these: What is the political situation in Cambodia, Thailand, and Vietnam? Why have previous attempts to provide relief failed? What are our present resources in food, transportation, and communication? What diplomatic leverage do we have? What new plans for relief might work? These problems (theoretical with practical implications) must be solved before we can decide on what means, if any, we are to try next. The question of what I should *do* is best answered in the context of what I in fact *know*.

That knowledge is logically prior to decision-making does not mean that in actual practice problems of action always *come up* after problems of knowing have been solved. We do not ordinarily solve theoretical problems then proceed to put that knowledge to use. While theoretical problems are sometimes approached for the sake of the intrinsic knowledge their solution will yield, we usually seek truth that will aid us in achieving certain ends in life. Problem-solving, then, occurs not simply as an effort to find out what's what, but as an effort to act successfully. Problem-solving indeed is regarded by some as synonymous with making a sound decision. While this extreme is rejected, it must be conceded that the question of what action a person should take in a specific situation is itself a problem. And this kind of problem requires for its solution the kind of knowledge discussed in the previous section.

If we want to get out of the prison camp, we look for attractive hypotheses setting forth how this may be done. If we want to open the door to freedom, we will try to figure out which question will produce the information we need in order to make the right choice. If we don't want to waste our time, we will try to deduce whether Agnes will be in the Zebra Lounge. If we want to give up smoking, we will look for those methods that have worked for others. Our knowledge is now not simply "for its own sake," but for the sake of some values which we wish to promote.

In making wise decisions, we must take into account two general considerations: The first is the *values* that are important to us; the second is the *consequences* of alternative lines of conduct. The first is the subject of this subsection; the second is the subject of the next subsection.

Values are of two kinds: moral and nonmoral. The former are obligatory. Our moral code *requires* that we perform certain actions. The latter are optional. They are based on our desires. Certain ends are values simply because we value them. If one does not accept the notion of duty imposed by some objective code of morality, he or she merely has to work and act in the realm of desires. But if one does recognize moral obligations, the task is more complex. He or she will have to be sensitive to the possible conflict between duty and desire in his or her decision-making. Often, of course, there will be no conflict between what one ought to do and what one would like to do, but sometimes one will have to give up one or the other.

The values implicit in a code of morality fall into two or three categories: (1) Values for the self. Essentially these are virtue, good conscience, integrity—the state of moral existence itself. One is moral for the sake of morality. In addition there will be other things which one owes himself. What these are is dependent upon the particular ethical theory one espouses. They may be knowledge, self-realization, or other conditions of the person. (2) Values for others. These also will vary depending upon the particular morality. They may include justice, loyalty, generosity, trustworthiness, and other legitimate claims exerted on us by others. What we owe others may

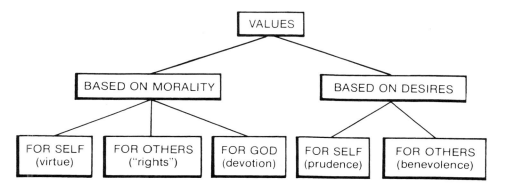

vary, depending upon whether the other is a member of the family, a friend, or a member of the community, nation, or the human race. (3) Values for God. A moral code does not have to be grounded in religious belief. An agnostic or atheistic moral standard is not only possible but may be very noble. Less likely, but still possible, is a religion with no ethical requirements beyond appeasing the deity. Often, however, ethics and religion go hand-in-hand. When this is the case, special duties may be owed to God. Examples are obedience, prayer, fellowship, faith, love, respect.

The values based on desires, ethical considerations aside, are those benefits sought for oneself and those sought for others. The first are called matters of *prudence,* the second are matters of *benevolence.* We desire things for ourselves and we desire things for others.

What are these values based on desires? Generally, they seem to be the components of happiness. They would include such things as health, wealth or security, personal development, status or respect or power, friendship, understanding, and various qualities of experience such as pleasures of food, drink, and sex, amusement, excitement, and enjoyment of beauty in nature and art. Each of these may be desired for the self or for others.[9]

Obviously some of these values which are widely *desired* by people may also be required as a matter of moral duty. Our moral code may, for example, *enjoin* us to seek the health and security of others or a state of understanding for ourself. And it may also occasionally be the case that what we *want* to do is what we *ought* to do. Saints Paul and Augustine, however, testify that this is not usually the case.

The essential fact of decision-making is that it must take place at the center of many conflicting claims. We may want to do X on behalf of ourself, but this conflicts with what we want to do on behalf of others. Or we want to do Y on behalf of others, but this conflicts with what morality requires that we do for them. Or we may want to do Z for ourself only to realize that this will conflict with something else we want to do for ourself.

Let us look at some examples. A talented young man wants to be a prize fighter. He also wants to be a violinist. Both require rigorous training. He cannot achieve excellence in both pursuits, so he must decide for one or the other. He will have to answer such questions as these: For which activity do I have the greater talent? Which kind of success do I prize more highly? What is the nature of the life of a professional fighter and how in attractiveness does it compare with the life of a professional musician? In view of the competition, in which area am I more likely to be successful? Are the means more attainable or less expensive for one goal than for the other? How much money and/or security can I expect to earn from each alternative? Should I choose a third goal which is perhaps more realistic? In order to make an intelligent decision, the young man will have to acquire a lot of knowledge about the fighting and music businesses, his own talent, and his own ability to work.

---

[9] Are there disinterested desires for *harm for others?* Are there interested desires for *harm for the self?* Yes, unfortunately, malice and masochism do exist. But I choose not to call their results *values,* even in the subjective sense of the term.

He will have to determine the fullest extent possible the consequences of various lines of action.

But the problem is oversimplified. The analysis is still within the area of prudence. What about his desires for the good of others? Which course of action will make his family happiest? Which course of action will lead to a greater good for people he cares for?

But this is still incomplete, for the moral question has not been raised. What are his moral standards, his ethical norms? Does he have pressing obligations to dependents that would rule out both endeavors? Is one kind of activity more noble or "human" than the other? Is he bound by promises that he may have made? How would his contribution to society as an exciting boxer compare with his contribution as a sensitive musician?

A young woman must decide whether to move from home and get an apartment of her own. In this case, we will start with the moral side—although it makes no difference where one starts, so long as one includes all three of the relevant concerns (morality, prudence, and benevolence) in her or his analysis. She might ask herself such questions as these: Do I have obligations to my parents that can only be fulfilled if I live with them? Do I have obligations to myself that can be fulfilled only by "going on my own"? If these sets of obligations conflict, which should take precedence? Will my attempt to lead a moral life be more likely to succeed if I stayed home rather than moved away?

Then she must ask herself what she *wants* to do and whether what she wants to do is consistent or reconcilable with what she ought to do. Suppose she finds the idea of her greater freedom very attractive. She will be able to come and go as she pleases, without questions or "dirty looks." She will be able to decorate the apartment according to her own tastes. She will be closer to her place of employment. And she will have a lot more space. Moreover, she will please many other people: her friends, who can visit her more often, stay longer, and play the kind of music they like. She will also please her boyfriend, who is under some constraint in her parents' home. At the same time, there are advantages in staying where she is. In the first place, it is much less expensive. She also is relieved of many of the housekeeping chores. Her parents' home is also considered safer than the downtown apartment she has her eye on. And as far as making other people happy, her decision to remain would make her parents, whom she loves, far happier than should she leave.

Perhaps she should remain at home for a few more years. She would be more mature and her parents more understanding. She would be in better financial shape. But to delay would be to lose the apartment she has found. And it would be more difficult to leave if her parents became more dependent on her in the course of time. And her sense of being stifled under her parents' roof would grow more intense.

Our heroine will have to gather all the relevant facts of her situation and study them carefully. She will have to weigh and compare the likely consequences of each available course of action.

Some problems in decision-making are joint problems—what should *we* do? Consider the case of a married couple, perhaps consisting of the protagonists of the first two examples. The husband is about to graduate from the music conservatory and the wife is still working at the office of an insurance company. They are in their mid-twenties and have been married for two years. They now ask themselves: Should we have a child?

In discussing the problem, they may raise certain moral issues. Are they being consistent with their moral convictions in continuing to use contraception? Will they be able to support a child properly? Will they be able to give adequate time to the rearing of a child? Will one of the parents have to give up his/her job, and, if so, which one ought to do it? In consulting their desires, they find strong reasons for having a child. They both like children and want to have some of their own while they are young enough to enjoy them. They know they would be intelligent and loving parents. They are both healthy and the genetic outlook for conceiving and bearing a baby at this time is favorable.

On the other hand, there are serious financial and professional factors militating against having children. The man, as a music student, has expenses that exceed his occasional earnings. The couple would have to move from their downtown apartment to a house or large apartment. There is even a question whether the husband could stay in school. Surely the wife would have to continue to work. Baby-sitters and child-care centers cost money, and so do all the baby paraphernalia, to say nothing of the medical costs of pregnancy and delivery. The wife's professional development will also be threatened by pregnancy and motherhood, and she has always wanted a career of her own.

If the couple can come to terms with these moral and prudential issues, they may see their way clear to have a baby and be ready to indulge their strong desire for one. But they will still have to answer in a cold and calculating way this question: Would a child at this time be sufficient compensation for all that we will have to give up?

Finally, let us consider the case of Abraham, whose story is related in the book of Genesis. God told him to sacrifice his son Isaac as a burnt offering. Abraham evidently had some agonizing thinking to do before he could come to a decision. Was it truly the voice of the Lord ordering him to do this thing? He believed that it was. Was his moral duty to obey God greater than his moral opposition to human sacrifice? It was. Was it greater than his paternal duty to Isaac? He believed that it was. Now Abraham had to decide whether to follow his conception of moral duty or to heed the dictates of his own heart. This could not have been an easy decision, but he chose the former. As we all know, God was just testing Abraham, and Isaac was spared at the last instant. But Abraham did not know this, for if he had, it would not have been a test.

Not all decisions, happily, are as grim as this. But many of them require a choice from among two or more sets of evils. To choose the better is in effect at

---

Be ye therefore wise as serpents, and harmless as doves.

—Matthew 10:16

the same time to choose the lesser of two evils. Decisions are often made in the situation of a dilemma (or trilemma) where each choice brings with it a set of consequences productive of pain as well as pleasure. It is rarely the case that we can "eat our cake and have it too." To choose the greater good is to give up the lesser good, and the latter may be highly prized. To avoid the greater evil is to take on a lesser evil, and the latter may be a bitter pill itself. But the greater the knowledge the agent has of the situation, the competing claims and wants, and the probable consequences of alternative actions, the better the chance he will have of producing, "all things considered," the best results.

Concluding Summary: To make intelligent decisions, a person should get clear on the various values attached to alternative ways of acting. He or she will then have to judge their relative strength and determine on the basis of available knowledge which course of action will most likely tend to produce the most desirable set of consequences.

Means and Ends

It is obvious that knowledge of means and ends is crucial in decision-making. What will be the consequences of this act? What will I have to do to *bring about* this goal? We must know the results of intended action and the means of intended results.

Many problems in decision-making arise simply because we do not have very dependable knowledge of the causal connections between our actions and other events. The decisions implied in the puzzle-discussion above are comparatively easy. The prisoner can be sure, if he thinks well, that he can find the door to freedom; and the person confronted by the boxes of fruit can with certainty accurately label them. And in the problem-discussion above, the lover can confidently decide whether to keep his tryst at the Zebra Lounge, just as the navigator can with full assurance decide what heading to take.

Often, however, we have to act on insufficient knowledge: we have to rely on inductive or deductive probability. The individual who decides to take another job with another company may believe that he will have a better chance for advancement, but he cannot be sure. The best he can do is find out all he can about the two companies and his prospects, getting what assurances from them that he can. The golfer who must select a club for his next shot will examine his lie closely, check the wind, study the distance to the green, and recall how firmly he has been hitting the ball with each of the clubs in question. The club he selects may or may not be the right one. The dutiful daughter who is trying to select a Christmas present will review in her mind her mother's desires, needs, and possessions and hope that her decision to get her a cashmere sweater will produce the desired end. The director of the relief agency which is trying to get food into Cambodia will act in as knowledgeable a way as he can, but can never be sure that the shipment will get to the starving

> *There is a tide in the affairs of men,*
> *Which, taken at the flood, leads on to fortune.*
> —*William Shakespeare,* Julius Caesar

civilians he hopes to serve. Where the chance for success is less than perfect, there must be risk of failure.

There is no escape from decision-making in inaction. To decide to do nothing is, of course, itself a decision, and one that is fraught with consequences. Which company shall I choose with which to insure my car? The decision not to choose a company is a decision to be uninsured. Should I major in government or biology? The decision not to choose a major before next registration is in effect a decision to postpone receiving a degree. Should I spend my vacation at a ski lodge in Colorado or at a lake in Minnesota? Or somewhere else? If I don't make up my mind, I'll end up at home; and if I delay too long, reservations for the lodge and the lake will be unavailable. This is not to say that one should always seize one of two or three obvious options or that he should never postpone making his decision. But he should be aware that dilatory tactics are themselves followed by consequences that should be taken into account. What he may gain in knowledge by protracted thought may be paid for dearly in loss of benefits. Timeliness is itself a factor.

It is sometimes wise to act in a way that is at least as likely to produce failure as it is to produce success. If one has the choice between doing nothing and taking a chance, he may opt for the latter when the benefits of the latter greatly exceed the known benefits of the former. Neil Armstrong could have remained a successful officer in the armed forces, leading a fairly safe life, but he opted for the role of the astronaut and became the first man to walk on the moon. Christopher Columbus could have remained an obscure ship captain, but he set out to sail to the Indies. The prisoners at Stalag-Luft III could have remained in the camp until the end of the war, but they chose the risky option of building the "wooden horse" and tunneling to freedom. The poker player, eyeing the enormous pot, throws in his last pile of chips to call the bet, although his mathematical probability of winning is less than fifty percent. Where the payoff on a sure thing is much less than the payoff on a questionable one, the decision-maker may opt for the latter. Taking a "calculated risk" requires one to evaluate the importance to him of the possible outcomes, their probabilities, and his willingness to pay the price of failure. The dreamer, however, who foolishly, frantically, and habitually seeks the "big score" without careful thought and planning is doomed to disappointment. A *calculated* risk is one that is deliberate and knowledgeable.

> *True wisdom consists not in seeing what is immediately before our eyes, but in foreseeing what is to come.*
> —*Terence,* Adelphi

Suppose that we have discovered efficacious means for the end we wish to produce. Should we forthwith put our plan into action? Not necessarily. We should ask this question: What *other* ends will my actions produce and can I "live with them?" We should make sure that we have anticipated *all* the consequences, not simply those we are seeking to produce. Our means have other ends (or results) and the anticipated result will itself be a means for additional ends or results. It has been observed that there is really no *final* end but death, but this is a mistake. Not even my death is a final end, for it will have consequences for those who survive me.

Many examples can be given of winning the battle but losing the war. In World War I, Germany successfully invaded Belgium in a plan to envelop France from the north, but in violating Belgian neutrality, which Germany was pledged to uphold, Germany aroused world opinion against herself and brought Britain into the war. In a less serious area, we may note the case of a baseball manager who achieved his goal of sweeping an important four-game series by using his two best pitchers. He swept the series, but the pitchers developed sore arms from being overworked and were not much use the rest of the season. A specific drug may successfully cope with an illness, but have unfortunate side effects. A chemical may successfully destroy a bacillus only to produce a more virulent strain.

Finally, the decision-maker must ask himself the question, does the end justify the means? The end does indeed sometimes justify the means—that is the only thing that *can* justify it. Painful means sometimes must be adopted to produce a worthwhile end. We go to the dentist and to surgeons for the sake of our health. We read dull textbooks for the sake of our grade point average. We turn down rich desserts for the sake of our waistline. We engage in wars in order to protect our national interest or to survive. We send criminals to prison in order to protect the public safety. None of these things is justified in itself. They are done for the sake of the ends they promote. But not all means are justified by a particular end. The means may be efficacious and the end may be worthwhile, but a disproportion may exist. Sometimes the price is too high.

It may have been a legitimate end conceived by Presidents Johnson and Nixon to preserve the friendly and non-communist regime of South Vietnam against the Viet Cong and the forces of North Vietnam. But eventually it became apparent to most Americans that the price in American and Vietnamese casualties and the destruction of the Indochinese landscape was too great to pay. So instead of further escalating our military efforts and perhaps resorting to nuclear warfare, our government decided to abandon the end and pull out. It is quite likely that this decision was much too late in coming.

It would be possible to greatly curtail illegal parking and speeding if offenders were given twenty years of hard labor, but this, in the light of the intended end, seems excessive.

The workaholic who ignores his family and friends in pursuit of legitimate ends is paying too great a price. Unless he is solving the fuel problem, writing another *Divine Comedy,* or some such grand achievement, he has chosen an end that does not justify his means. As John Dewey said, "We only live at the time that we live.'' Life consists of present moments, and a life where the present is nothing and the future is everything is a life of bad decisions.

Examples of an achieved end itself serving as a means for an undesirable end are easy to imagine. Our prisoners of war may achieve their end of gaining freedom from the camp, but their freedom in enemy territory may subject them to great danger. They may even make it back to their own lines only to find that they are thrust back into combat and assigned a perilous mission. For these reasons some prisoners refused to embark on an escape attempt even when its chance of success was good. Another example is this: Naturalists may succeed in destroying a particular species which is considered a pest, only to see the rapid multiplication of a more harmful species hitherto controlled by the first. One problem was solved only to produce a greater one. A final example: A husband was concerned about his wife's timidity. He wanted her to be more assertive and independent. He studied the problem and discovered the right means for altering her personality. The counseling sessions worked, and the end was attained. But the wife used her new independence to leave her husband. She had not cared for him for years, but had lacked the courage to do anything about it. In decision-making, one must foresee the ends of ends—that is, how the desired result may itself function as a cause.

A similar and related consideration is the effect a projected series of actions will have on the agent himself. The actions that he takes make a difference in his own nature, both at the beginning and during the course of events that lead to the achieved end. The decision-maker must ask himself what alteration *he* will undergo in each option he considers. Will he lose his integrity or self-respect? Will he set up habits of behavior that he deplores? Will he be the kind of person, once the end is attained, who will be able to enjoy that end?

Let us look at some examples. An individual has the chance to steal some money without being caught. But in gaining the money he has lost his honesty. He has by his action transformed not only his bank account but his character as well. A student who chooses easy courses or who gets by with as little work as possible fails to develop the industry and patience that would serve him well in other walks of life. He will lack both confidence and study skills when the exigencies of life force him to master an unfamiliar body of knowledge. An individual who capitulates to the allure of rich food, drink, tobacco, or drugs may create a need in himself for these things. He enjoyed the pleasures and then found to his sorrow that he was addicted to them. The businessman who works hard for years in order to pile up wealth may look forward to a time of joyous retirement. He will have the time and money at last to taste all those delights he denied himself. But his time of self-indulgence may never come. His health may be ruined by his labors. Or his vitality may have been so sapped that a trip around the world or a vacation in the Bahamas is a chore instead of a reward. Having ignored the satisfaction of art, sport, and play for many

---

Our deeds determine us, as much as we determine our deeds.
                                                            —George Eliot, Adam Bede

years, he may find himself the kind of being in whom all sensibilities for such pleasures have completely atrophied. He has worked for the future, but when it comes he is a different man.

The most obvious kind of questionable subjection of means to an end is the willingness to choose immoral means for the sake of some professedly greater good. As Creon told Antigone, "Someone has to do the dirty work." Nixon defended himself in similar terms when he appealed to "national security" to excuse his breaking of the law and his lies. But it must be said that sometimes unsavory things *do* have to be done in order to produce a greater end. The man who steals to prevent his children from starving is not a scoundrel. The citizen who does violence to a mugger who attacks him is within his rights. The soldier who kills in defense of his country is not a murderer. We should not oversimplify and condemn actions without examining the context in which they occur.

At the same time, however, there are many dangers one must be aware of before he decides to do a wrong for the sake of a greater right. (1) Is his decision to do the deed perhaps only a rationalization to support an end that is only a good to himself? Is his purpose to benefit society or himself? (2) Is there a way to achieve the end, even if it is more difficult, that does not require questionable means? (3) Does he brutalize himself or compromise his integrity when he relies on dubious means? (4) Does he foster dangerous personal habits in his own person in being willing to "rise above principle" in his concern for the expeditious? One case of doing this, even when justifiable, may make it easier to compromise his principles the next time—when the end is not so noble.

It should by now be obvious that the question of values is not merely the simple one of identifying and sorting out the things that we value. As we have seen, many values have a "price" and valuable experiences have consequences. Values frequently conflict with one another. Some values take precedence over others. If we wish to act with deliberation and responsibility, we must think through some rather difficult problems. These involve more than concern for factual means and ends. They also involve concern for what is really worthwhile or estimable, our ultimate commitments. Just as the individual reasons with himself in seeking to determine and defend his best action, so too he can be subjected to criticism by others for his choice. Did he inaccurately ascertain the various means/end relationships? Did he fail to take into account certain relevant moral claims? Did he properly judge the degree of desirability of a particular value? Does he really know the nature or quality of the thing he professes to value? These and many other considerations show that concern for values in choosing actions requires more than consulting our feelings and inclinations. That value judgments are involved in an argument about what action should be taken does not mean that there is really nothing to argue about. The answer to the question, *what should I do?*, must be defended by the agent to himself, and in principle to others as well.

Concluding Summary: It is often the case that one has to decide on a course of action without full knowledge of the means or the ends. He must act with the probable knowledge he has and may even opt for a course of action where the result is improbable if there is much to be won. But even when his knowledge of means/end connections is adequate, he should alert himself to the possibility of unforeseen ends, ends that themselves produce undesirable results, and means that may not be justified by the end in view.

EXERCISES

Exercise 109

State the kind of information you would seek if you had to make a decision on:

1. Whether to buy a new car.
2. Whether to enlist in the armed services.
3. Whether to live in a coeducational dormitory.
4. Whether to try cocaine.
5. Whether to contribute money to the United Fund.

Exercise 110

Indicate the conflicts of ends that arise when you are trying to decide:

1. Whether to buy a new car.
2. Whether to enlist in the armed services.
3. Whether to live in a coeducational dormitory.
4. Whether to try cocaine.
5. Whether to contribute money to the United Fund.

Exercise 111

Criticize a recent decision made by:

1. The President of the United States.
2. The Congress of the United States.
3. Yourself.

Exercise 112

Defend a recent decision made by:

1. The President of the United States.
2. Your instructor.
3. Yourself.

Exercise 113

Your child, spouse, roommate (choose one) is very messy. Clothes are strewn around, food is not put away, books are on the floor, etc. You are very upset and want to induce this person to be neater. What do you do?

Chapter 13

Appendix: Venn Diagrams

CATEGORICAL STATEMENTS

Diagramming Categorical Statements

Categorical statements may be portrayed by means of Venn diagrams. To make a Venn diagram we first draw overlapping circles within a box. If the particular statement we are diagramming is about the classes denoted by '*S*' and '*P,*' we label the circles accordingly. The circled area labeled '*S*' may be thought to contain all members of the class of things denoted by '*S.*' The circled area labeled '*P*' contains all the members of the class denoted by '*P.*' The box itself represents the universe of discourse; it contains all members of the two classes, as well as things which are neither *S* nor *P*. The basic diagram will look like this:

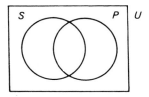

The basic diagram contains four areas:

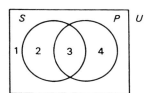

Area 1 contains things which are neither *S* nor *P*.

Area 2 contains things which are *S* but not *P*.

Area 3 contains things which are both *S* and *P*.

Area 4 contains things which are *P* but not *S*.

Areas are provided for all possible combinations of the subject and predicate classes and their negatives (or complements).

We may express any categorical statement by shading an appropriate area or by placing an asterisk in an appropriate area. Shading stands for *does not exist*. Non-existence will also be expressed as '$=O$.' The asterisk stands for *at least one exists*. Existence will also be expressed as '$\neq O$.'

The *A* statement 'all stones are pebbles' can be diagrammed by showing that there are not any stones that are not pebbles. That is, stones that are not pebbles do not exist. So area 2 must be shaded out:

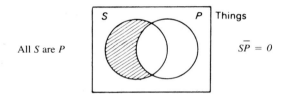

We diagram the *E* statement 'no stones are pebbles' by showing that there is nothing in the universe of discourse that is both a pebble and a stone. That is, stones that are pebbles do not exist. So area 3 must be shaded out:

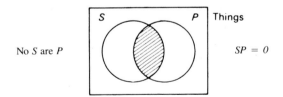

We can diagram the *I* statement 'some stones are pebbles' by showing that there is at least one stone that is a pebble. That is, at least one thing exists that is both a stone and a pebble. So we place an asterisk in area 3:

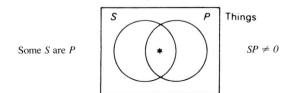

We can diagram the O statement 'some stones are not pebbles' by showing that there is at least one stone that is not a pebble. That is, at least one thing exists that is a stone but not a pebble. So we place an asterisk in area 2:

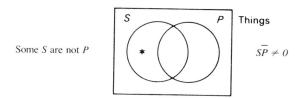

Some S are not P

We can also diagram statements about the negatives (or complements) of the two classes:

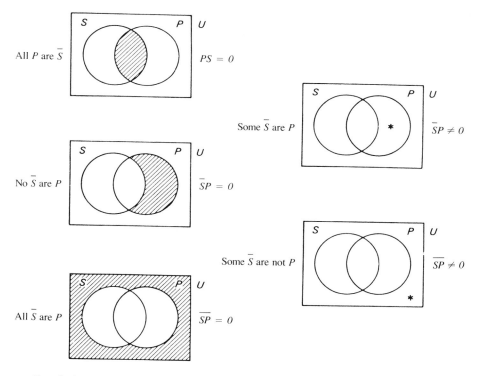

Concluding Summary: Anything that can be asserted in a categorical statement can be represented in a Venn diagram.

The Square of Opposition

These diagrams confirm some of the things we learned from the traditional Square of Opposition: A's and O's are contradictory. They cannot both be true and they cannot both be false. This is so because they say conflicting things about the same area. The *A* says there is no existence in area 2, while *O* says there *is* existence there:

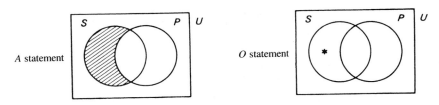

They also confirm the fact that *E*'s and *I*'s are contradictory. Here, too, mutually exclusive claims are made for the same area. The *E* asserts non-existence; the *I* asserts existence:

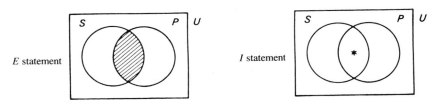

The diagrams do not, however, confirm other things we learned from the traditional square. It does not confirm that the contraries, *A*'s and *E*'s, cannot both be true. No conflict is apparent in these two diagrams:

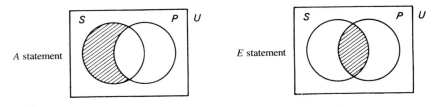

Indeed, the two statements could be portrayed on the diagram:

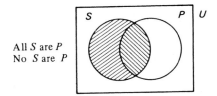

But consider what this means in terms of our original example: Things that are stones do not exist! If we are willing to assume that stones do exist, the traditional square is correct, for the *A* and *E* cannot both be true:

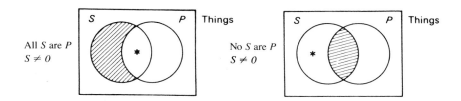

If we are not willing to make the assumption, the *A* and *E* are compatible; they may both be true.

Whether we make the assumption or not, they could both be false. They *are* both false if some stones are pebbles and some are not:

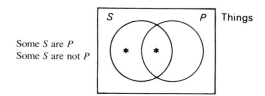

The traditional Square of Opposition also told us that we can infer the truth of particulars from the truth of universals: If an *A* statement is true, then its subaltern, an *I* statement, is also true; if an *E* statement is true, then its subaltern, an *O* statement, is also true. But the *A* and *E* do not provide the guaranteed existence that the *I* and *O* require. So once again, the inference from universals to their subalterns is valid only if we assume existence in the subject classes:

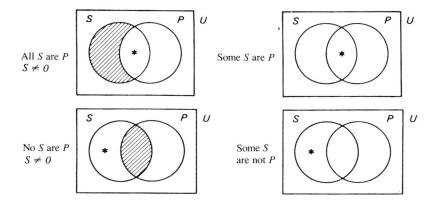

According to the traditional Square of Opposition, subcontraries may not both be false. But if existence is not assumed, they *could* both be false. And they *would* both be false if the actual situation were this:

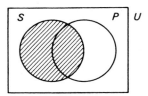

Finally, it may be recalled that it was said that the falsity of the universals could be inferred from the falsity of their subalterns. But the falsity of the *I* simply means that non-existence characterizes area 3:

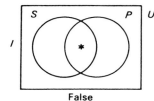

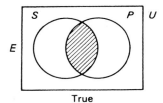

Such a situation does not conflict with the *A* statement. Perhaps there is nothing at all in the class denoted by '*S*.' So, unless we are willing to assume that there is existence somewhere in the subject class, we will not be able to infer anything about its superaltern from the falsity of the *I* statement. The same course of thought is applicable to the *O* statement and its superaltern.

Concluding Summary: The traditional Square of Opposition holds only if we are willing to assume that universal statements have *existential import.* If we do not make this assumption, the following principles hold:

A and *E* statements may both be true and may both be false.

I and *O* statements may both be false and may both be true.

If an *A* statement is true, nothing can be known about the *I;* if an *E* statement is true, nothing can be known about the *O.*

If an *I* statement is false, nothing can be known about the *A;* if an *O* statement is false, nothing can be known about the *E.*

The principles that both the traditional and the "existential" Square of Opposition have in common are:

Contradictories always have opposite truth-values.

If the *A* statement is false, nothing can be known about the *I;* if the *E* statement is false, nothing can be known about the *O.*

If the *I* statement is true, nothing can be known about the *A;* if the *O* statement is true, nothing can be known about the *E.*

Singular Statements

What about singular statements? In earlier chapters we have treated them as universal statements. But singular statements, unlike universal statements, seem to assert existence. So we will use shading *and* the asterisk to express them on a Venn diagram. For example:

Jimmy Carter is a Democrat

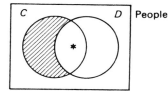

Jimmy Carter is not a Democrat

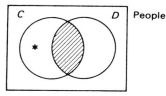

These appear to be contradictory. They certainly cannot both be true at the same time, since they make conflicting claims for the same areas. And, if we are willing to assume that Jimmy Carter exists, they cannot both be false. He must be a Democrat or not a Democrat. Since the two statements always have opposite truth-values; they are contradictories.

But we cannot *always* assume that the subjects of singular statements exist. Consider these singular statements:

Algernon W. Snerd is a Democrat.

The present king of France is bald.

If these statements are known to be true, there is no problem. The subject exists. But if they are false, the question of existence is open. The first statement could be false because Snerd, while existent, is a Republican; but it may be false because no one by that name exists. The second statement may be false because the king is not bald, but it may be false because there is no king of France. From the falsity of the first, it does not necessarily follow that Snerd is not a Democrat, for he may not exist at all. From the falsity of the second, it does not necessarily follow that the king of France is not bald, for there may not be a king of France.

'Algernon W. Snerd is a Democrat' and 'Algernon W. Snerd is not a Democrat' could both be false. And 'The present king of France is bald' and 'The present king of France is not bald' could both be false. Without the existential assumption, singular statements and their negatives behave like contraries; they can both be false.

Concluding Summary: Singular *A* and *E* statements are contradictories, strictly speaking, only if we are willing to assume that the subject exists. In that case they always have opposite truth-values. But if we do not make that assumption, they are contraries, for they could both be false.[1]

---

[1] The whole problem of singular statements and "definite description" is handled much better by the tools of modern symbolic logic than in the context of categorical statements.

Equivalence and Compatibility

Venn diagrams may be used to determine whether pairs of statements are equivalent. They are equivalent if and only if the diagrams for them are identical. For example:

(1) 'All S are P' and 'No S are $\overline{P}$'

The first tells us: $S\overline{P} = O$. The second tells us: $S\overline{P} = O$. In both cases we shade out area 2, getting identical diagrams. So the statements are equivalent.

(2) 'All S are P' and 'All $\overline{P}$ are $\overline{S}$'

The first tells us: $S\overline{P} = O$. The second tells us: $\overline{P}\,\overline{\overline{S}} = O$ or $\overline{P}S = O$. In both cases we shade out area 2, getting identical diagrams. So the statements are equivalent.

(3) 'Some S are P' and 'Some P are S'

The first tells us: $SP \neq O$. The second tells us the same thing, so the statements are equivalent.

(4) 'No S are P' and 'All P are $\overline{S}$'

The first tells us: $SP = O$. The second tells us: $P\overline{\overline{S}} = O$ or $PS = O$. In both cases we shade out area 3, getting identical diagrams. So the statements are equivalent.

(5) 'All S are P' and 'All P are S'

The first tells us: $S\overline{P} = O$. The second tells us: $P\overline{S} = O$. The resulting diagrams are different:

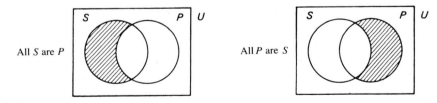

All S are P All P are S

So the statements are not equivalent. Since they do not claim conflicting things for the same area, they are compatible.

(6) 'No S are P' and 'No $\overline{S}$ are $\overline{P}$'

The first tells us: $SP = O$. The second tells us: $\overline{S}\,\overline{P} = O$. The resulting diagrams are different:

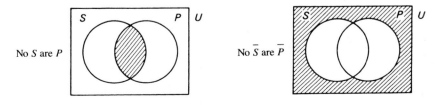

No S are P No $\overline{S}$ are $\overline{P}$

So, while the statements are compatible, they are not equivalent.

(7) 'Some S are not P' and 'No $\overline{P}$ are S'

The first tells us: $S\overline{P} \neq O$. The second tells us: $\overline{P}S = O$. The resulting diagrams are different:

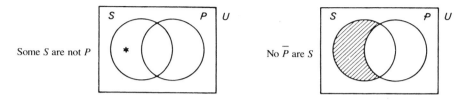

So the statements are not equivalent. The diagrams also tell us that they are incompatible because they cannot both be true at the same time. Because they cannot both be false at the same time, they are contradictory as well.

(8) 'All $\overline{P}$ are $\overline{S}$' and 'No S are P'

The first tells us: $\overline{P}\,\overline{\overline{S}} = O$ or $\overline{P}S = O$. The second tells us: $SP = O$. The resulting diagrams are different:

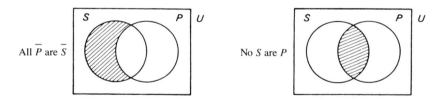

So they are not equivalent. If we decline to make an existential assumption, they are compatible. If we assume that there exists at least one thing in the class denoted by 'S,' then the statements are incompatible. They are not contradictory, for they could both be false.[2]

When may we assume existence? When we have good reason to do so. We can assume that stones and pebbles exist, but should be wary of claiming existence for Martians, Goldilocks, perfect golf shots, or emperors of Chicago. We could get into trouble if we do. For example:

(1) All Martians are living beings.
(2) Therefore, some Martians are living beings.
(3) Therefore, some living beings are Martians.

(1) is plausible. (2) is the valid subaltern, if we assume that Martians exist. But (3), although it is the valid converse of (2), is dubious.

---

[2] A contradiction can be deduced, since the subaltern of 'No S are P' is contradictory to 'All $\overline{P}$ are $\overline{S}$'.

The question of existence is relative to the universe of discourse. If our universe of discourse is *physical things,* we should be reluctant to grant existence to unicorns. But if our universe of discourse is *mythical beings,* we can quite safely assume existence and argue that, since all unicorns are four-footed creatures, some four-footed creatures are unicorns. But this conclusion would have to be understood only in the realm of mythical beings!

Concluding Summary: The Venn diagram method can be used for determining whether statement-pairs are compatible, equivalent, or contradictory.

EXERCISES

Exercise 114

Using the method of Venn diagrams, determine whether the following are compatible or incompatible. Where the former, state whether equivalent or non-equivalent; where the latter, state whether contradictory or non-contradictory. Make no existential assumptions.

1. All angels are happy.
   No happy people are non-angels.
2. No birds are reptiles.
   No non-birds are non-reptiles.
3. Some pets are not rabbits.
   Some non-rabbits are not non-pets.
4. Some non-chairs are not soft.
   All non-chairs are soft.
5. The President of the United States is a southerner.
   The President of the United States is not a southerner.
6. All perfect fluids are non-abrasive.
   All abrasive things are non-perfect fluids.

Exercise 115

Using the method of Venn diagrams, determine whether the following are compatible or incompatible. Where the former, state whether equivalent or non-equivalent; where the latter, state whether contradictory or non-contradictory. Choose a universe of discourse such that existential assumptions can plausibly be made.

1. All devils are tormented.
   No devils are tormented.
2. Some jokes are funny.
   Some non-funny stories are not non-jokes.
3. All centaurs are fierce.
   Some centaurs are fierce.
4. Some cameras are expensive.
   No expensive things are cameras.

5. All zebras are mammals.
   No mammals are zebras.
6. Hamlet is a Dane.
   Hamlet is not a Dane.

SYLLOGISMS

Diagramming Syllogisms

Venn diagrams can be used to test the validity of syllogisms. Their use for this purpose is based on the principle of deductive validity itself: the conclusion is "contained in" the premises. If and only if the syllogism is valid, we will find that in diagramming the premises we have also diagrammed the conclusion.

The diagram for syllogisms employs circles for three classes. These circles overlap in such a way that eight areas are produced:

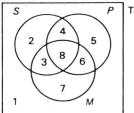

Area 1 contains things that are neither S, P, nor M ($\overline{SPM}$).

Area 2 contains things that are S but not P or M ($S\overline{PM}$).

Area 3 contains things that are S and M but not P ($SM\overline{P}$).

Area 4 contains things that are S and P but not M ($SP\overline{M}$).

Area 5 contains things that are P but not S or M ($P\overline{SM}$).

Area 6 contains things that are P and M but not S ($PM\overline{S}$).

Area 7 contains things that are M but not S or P ($M\overline{SP}$).

Area 8 contains things that are S, P, and M (SPM).

Let us diagram the premises of this syllogistic form:

All P are M
No S are M
∴ No S are P

First, we must diagram one of the premises. Selecting the major premise, we deal only with the circles for P and M, ignoring the circle representing S:

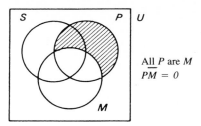

All P are M
$\overline{PM} = 0$

Next, on the same figure, we diagram the minor premise, dealing only with S and M while ignoring P:

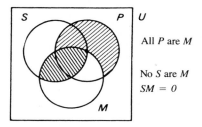

All P are M

No S are M
$SM = 0$

The syllogism is valid if and only if we find the conclusion is fully and unequivocally expressed on the diagram. This indeed is the case. Areas 4 and 8 are shaded out, which is what the statement, 'No S are P,' says is the case.

We will do another one:

> All P are M
> All S are M
> ∴   All S are P

Diagramming the first premise gives us:

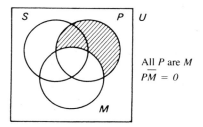

All P are M
$\overline{PM} = 0$

Adding the minor premise gives us:

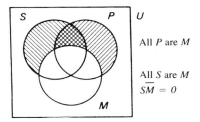

All P are M

All S are M
$\overline{SM} = 0$

Do we find that the conclusion has been expressed as the result of expressing the premise? We do not. Areas 2 and 3 would have to be shaded out for the statement 'All S are P' to be expressed in the diagram, but 3 is unshaded. There is thus a possibility that something could be in the S class and not in the P class—a possibility the conclusion rules out. So the argument is invalid.

Let us diagram this syllogistic form:

>   Some P are M
>   All M are S
> ∴ Some S are P

When one premise is particular, it should be diagrammed last. Diagramming the minor premise will give us:

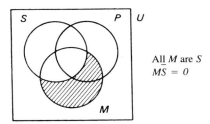

All M are S
$\overline{MS} = 0$

Now we add the particular premise. The asterisk expressing existence can only go in area 8:

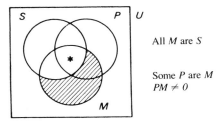

All M are S

Some P are M
$PM \neq 0$

Can we read off the conclusion from the completed diagram? Yes, we can. Existence is guaranteed in an area common to S and P—which is what the conclusion asserts.

Here is another syllogistic form:

> Some *M* are *P*
> No *S* are *M*
> ∴ Some *S* are not *P*

Doing the universal premise first, then adding the asterisk, we get:

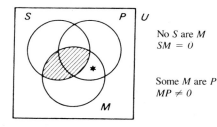

No *S* are *M*
$SM = 0$

Some *M* are *P*
$MP \neq 0$

For the conclusion to have been validly drawn from the premises, there should be an asterisk in area 2. But there is not. So the syllogism is invalid.

Another syllogistic form:

> All *P* are *M*
> Some *S* are *M*
> ∴ Some *S* are *P*

Doing the universal premise first, we get:

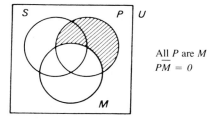

All *P* are *M*
$\overline{PM} = 0$

Now we have to add an asterisk in order to express the minor premise. Where do we put it? It could be in area 3, and it could be in area 8. Since the premise simply guarantees the existence of "at least one," we cannot be sure that it is in one place to the exclusion of the other. So we will put it on the border line:

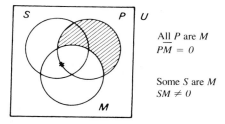

All *P* are *M*
$\overline{PM} = 0$

Some *S* are *M*
$SM \neq 0$

The conclusion claims that there is existence in an area common to *S* and *P*. But this is not necessarily true. The existence *could* be in area 3 instead. Since the conclusion does not necessarily follow, the syllogism is invalid.

Any syllogism violating Rule 5 will obviously be invalid by the Venn method, because if there are no asterisks in the diagram, a particular conclusion could not possibly be read from it.

If, however, existential assumptions are made *along with* the premises of a syllogism containing two universal premises, the strictures of Rule 5 are evaded. Consider this syllogistic form:

> All *M* are *P*
> <u>All *S* are *M*</u> $S \neq O$
> ∴ <u>Some *S* are *P*</u>

After diagramming the categorical premises, we have:

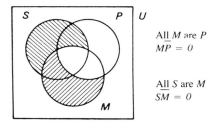

All *M* are *P*
$M\overline{P} = 0$

All *S* are *M*
$S\overline{M} = 0$

Expressing the existential assumption in the only area left for it, we get:

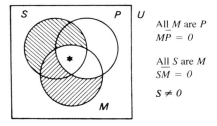

All *M* are *P*
$M\overline{P} = 0$

All *S* are *M*
$S\overline{M} = 0$

$S \neq 0$

The completed diagram does indeed contain the conclusion: Something exists in the area common to *S* and *P*.

Concluding Summary: Every syllogism invalidated by the five rules given earlier is invalidated by the Venn method. And every syllogism validated by the rules is validated by the Venn method. The Venn method is not only an alternative method to the rules method, it proves graphically the legitimacy of the rules.

Diagramming Arguments Equivalent to Syllogisms

We have called arguments containing more than three terms equivalent to syllogisms when the statements making them up can be changed to equivalent statements in such a way that the argument has been reduced to three terms. When the excess terms are negatives of one another, this reduction can always be performed. The Venn method can be used to test arguments equivalent to syllogisms *directly*. That is, the statements can be diagrammed as they stand without manipulation.

Some examples:

(1) All M are $\overline{P}$ $M\overline{P} = O$
     No S are $\overline{M}$ $S\overline{M} = O$
$\therefore$ All $\overline{P}$ are $\overline{S}$

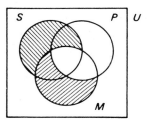

This is valid, because the conclusion, 'All $\overline{P}$ are $\overline{S}$' $(\overline{P}\overline{S} = O)$, can be read from the diagram.

(2) All $\overline{M}$ are P $\overline{M}\overline{P} = O$
     All $\overline{M}$ are S $\overline{M}\overline{S} = O$
$\therefore$ No $\overline{S}$ are $\overline{P}$

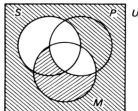

This is valid, because the conclusion, No $\overline{S}$ are $\overline{P}$ $(\overline{S}\overline{P} = O)$, can be read from the diagram.

(3) Some M are P $MP \neq O$
     All M are $\overline{S}$ $M\overline{S} = O$
$\therefore$ Some S are not P

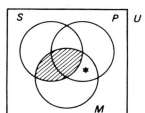

This is invalid, because the conclusion, 'Some S are not P' $(S\overline{P} \neq O)$, cannot be read from the diagram.

(4) All $\overline{M}$ are $\overline{P}$ $\overline{M}P = O$
    Some M are S $MS \neq O$
$\therefore$ Some S are P

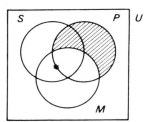

---

*Mr. Venn's Method of Diagrams is a great advance on [Euler's] Method.
. . . [But Venn's approach] would involve us in very serious trouble, if we
ever attempted to represent No $\overline{X}$ are $\overline{Y}$.' Mr. Venn once encounters this
awful task; but evades it, in a quite masterly fashion, by the simple foot-note
'We have not troubled to shade the outside of this diagram'! . . .*

*'With four terms in request,' Mr. Venn says, 'The most simple and symmetrical
diagram seems to me that produced by making four ellipses intersect one
another in the desired manner.'*

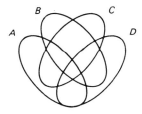

For five *letters, 'the simplest diagram I can suggest,' Mr. Venn says. . . .*

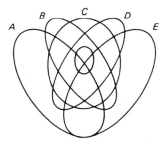

Beyond six *letters Mr. Venn does not go.*

—Lewis Carroll, Symbolic Logic

This is invalid, because the conclusion, 'Some S are P' ($SP \neq O$), cannot be read from the diagram.

(5) All M are $\overline{P}$ $MP = O$
     Some S are not $\overline{M}$ $SM \neq O$
∴ Some S are not P

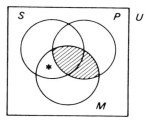

This is valid, because the conclusion, 'Some S are not P' ($S\overline{P} \neq O$), can be read from the diagram.

Concluding Summary: When extra terms in a syllogistic argument are negatives (or complements) of the other terms, the argument can be diagrammed as it stands and its validity tested by the Venn method.

EXERCISES

Exercise 116

Determine the validity of the following syllogisms by means of Venn diagrams:

1. No people who succeed are contemptible
    No patient people succeed
∴ All patient people are contemptible

2. Some conceited people are disliked
    Some athletes are conceited
∴ Some athletes are disliked

3. No people who assign work are lovable
    All teachers assign work
∴ No teachers are lovable

4. All doctors who possess magical healing powers are people with magical
      healing powers
    All doctors who possess magical healing powers are doctors
∴ Some doctors are people with magical healing powers

5. All things that are earned are precious
    Some pennies are not precious
∴ Some pennies are not earned

6. The present king of France is hairy
    Harry is the present king of France
∴ Harry is hairy

Exercise 117

Determine the validity of the following syllogistic arguments by means of Venn diagrams:

1. All persuasive things are misleading
   All ads are persuasive (assume that ads exist)
   ∴ Some ads are misleading
2. All cigarettes are dangerous
   Some cigarettes are beautifully packaged
   ∴ Some things that are beautifully packaged are dangerous
3. All poodles are mammals
   All dogs are mammals (assume that dogs exist)
   ∴ Some dogs are poodles
4. All trained people are prepared
   No scouts are untrained
   ∴ No scouts are unprepared
5. All arduous things are challenging
   All challenging things are worthwhile
   ∴ All worthwhile things are arduous
6. All men are mortal
   Socrates is a man
   ∴ Socrates is mortal

Answers to Preview Questions

CHAPTER 2

1. Slender.
2. No.
3. He had written out his speech and left it on the desk. OR He had written out his mailing address and left it on the desk.
4. The newscaster will be back tomorrow with news that is more important. AND The newscaster will be back tomorrow with more news that is important.
5. No.
6. No.
7. No.
8. Bring home a loaf of fresh bread—and by 'fresh' I mean a loaf that has been baked in the last twelve hours.
9. False.
10. False.

CHAPTER 3

1. No.
2. No.
3. William is tall.
4. No.
5. Yes.
6. True.
7. False.
8. No.

9. No.
10. True.

CHAPTER 4

1. Yes.
2. No.
3. Yes.
4. No.
5. No.
6. Yes.
7. Yes.
8. Yes.
9. Yes.
10. No.

CHAPTER 5

1. (a) Valid.
   (b) Invalid.
   (c) Valid.
   (d) Invalid.
   (e) Invalid.
2. (a) Socrates is mortal.
   (b) Some mammals are poodles.
   (c) IMPOSSIBLE.
   (d) No wormy things are delicious.
   (e) Some Frenchmen are Christians.

CHAPTER 6

1. She works hard.
2. NOTHING.
3. NOTHING.
4. Some tests are not positive.
5. NOTHING.
6. Throwing a seven.
7. Surviving a domestic flight on an airline.
8. .25.
9. No.
10. 9 to 1.

CHAPTER 7

1. True.
2. True.
3. $p \rightarrow (q \ \& \ r)$.
4. Particular, universal, singular.
5. No; no.
6. Yes.
7. Yes.
8. Agnes is richer than Robert.
9. NOTHING.
10. Yes.

CHAPTER 8

1. No.
2. No.
3. No.
4. No.
5. No.
6. Inductive generalizations and generalized descriptions.
7. No.
8. No.

CHAPTER 9

1. Tension, pain, noise, and a recent nap are examples.
2. No.
3. Yes.
4. No.
5. He has ignored other differences.
6. No.
7. No.
8. Yes.

CHAPTER 10

1. No.
2. No.
3. Profit taking, adverse report on trade imbalance, and jump in rate of inflation are examples.

4. No.
5. The student skipped the exam because he was unprepared.
6. The very simple account.
7. She is selling cookies.
8. True.

CHAPTER 11

1. No.
2. No.
3. When you want to know whether or not to believe him/her, when you are considering marrying him/her, or when you are deciding whether or not to lend him/her money are examples.
4. No.
5. Yes.
6. Yes.
7. When it is dispassionate.
8. Vacation and travel brochures, movies, books, and cosmetics are examples.
9. Yes.
10. It is false.

Answers to Exercises (Odd-Numbered Problems)

ANSWERS TO EXERCISE 1

1. False.
3. False.
5. False.
7. False.
9. False.
11. True.
13. True.
15. False.

ANSWERS TO EXERCISE 2

1. 'Penelope' is Greek but Penelope is English.
3. 'Sam' is the name of my uncle, but "Sam" is the name for that name.
5. "Pronounce 'Roosevelt' correctly," she said.
7. He is a competent performer, but something of a "hot dog."
9. Always capitalize 'Budweiser.'
11. If you add an 's' to 'cares,' which is plural, you get 'caress,' which is singular.
13. 'Able was I ere I saw Elba' is a palindrome.
15. 'Ave Maria' is a Latin expression.
17. 'Small' is smaller than 'smaller.'
19. His "term paper" consisted of a page of hastily scrawled notes.

ANSWERS TO EXERCISE 3

1. No.
3. Yes.
5. Yes.
7. No.
9. No.

ANSWERS TO EXERCISE 4

1. Extension.
3. Neither.
5. Extension.
7. Intension.
9. Intension.

ANSWERS TO EXERCISE 5

1. Extension: different.   Intension: different.
3. Extension: same.   Intension: same.
5. Extension: different.   Intension: different.
7. Extension: same.   Intension: same.
9. Extension: unknowable.   Intension: unknowable.

ANSWERS TO EXERCISE 6

1. A trifle off pitch
3. Proud, proud
5. Show signs of injury
7. Still needs work OR does not suit our publication policy OR is not the sort of thing we publish
9. Financially strapped OR in need of money

ANSWERS TO EXERCISE 7

There is room for legitimate disagreement in each of these.

1. assumes the inequality of the sexes
   prejudiced against women

male chauvinist
sexist pig
3. realistic
sexually explicit
pornographic
obscene
5. sensational
beautiful
pretty
attractive

ANSWERS TO EXERCISE 8

1. *mad*—semantical
3. *he*—syntactical (what is its antecedent?)
5. *may*—semantical
7. *shot*—semantical and syntactical (is its subject 'film' or 'Serpico'?)
9. 'WASTE'—syntactical (is it a verb or adjective?)

ANSWERS TO EXERCISE 9

1. Wife, in her fifth marriage, charged with poisoning her husband. OR Wife charged with poisoning all five of her husbands.
3. The Democratic Party opposes quotas; they are inconsistent with the principles of our country. OR The Democratic Party opposes those quotas that are inconsistent with the principles of our country.
5. Buy these dresses for a ridiculous price. OR Buy these dresses for a ridiculous shape.
7. Employees are the only people permitted to eat in the cafeteria. OR Employees may eat in the cafeteria and nowhere else.
9. If I wanted to, I could write like Shakespeare. OR If I had the brains, I could write like Shakespeare.

ANSWERS TO EXERCISE 10

1. Equivocation.
3. Division.
5. Division.
7. Equivocation.
9. Composition.

ANSWERS TO EXERCISE 11

1. Composition.
3. Division.
5. Amphiboly.
7. Equivocation.
9. Composition.

ANSWERS TO EXERCISE 12

1. Equivocation on relative term: 'old.'
3. Equivocation on relative term: 'successful.'
5. Equivocation on relative term: 'mother.'

ANSWERS TO EXERCISE 13

1. *long lasting*—sixty months.
3. *good*—proved by the Q-test to be able to do the job it was designed to do.
5. *great*—awarded five stars in *Gulliver's Gourmet Guide.*
7. *big*—40 percent.
9. *new play*—play written for the 1990 season.

ANSWERS TO EXERCISE 14

1. Too vague.
3. Not too vague.
5. Not too vague.
7. Not too vague.
9. Too vague.

ANSWERS TO EXERCISE 15.

1. Extensional: by example.
3. Intensional: operational.
5. Extensional: ostensive.
7. Intensional: genus/differentia.
9. Extensional: enumerative.

ANSWERS TO EXERCISE 16

1. Figurative language.
3. Seeks to produce an emotional reaction.
5. Describes instead of defining.
7. Obscure language.
9. Circular.
11. Too narrow.

ANSWERS TO EXERCISE 17

1. Af
3. Ah
5. Bc
7. Be
9. Bi

ANSWERS TO EXERCISE 18

3. 'X is the parent of Y and X is female.'
5. 'X is the child of Y and X is female.'
7. 'X is the grandparent of Y, and X is male.'
9. 'X is the sibling of Y, and X is female.'
11. 'There is a Z such that Z is the grandparent of Y, and X is the sister of Z.'

ANSWERS TO EXERCISE 19

1. D
3. B
5. A
7. B
9. C
11. A

ANSWERS TO EXERCISE 20

1. C
3. B
5. B
7. C
9. B

ANSWERS TO EXERCISE 21

1. B—Persuasive definition of 'pornography.'
3. A—Question-begging definition of 'fetus.'
5. A—Question-begging definition of 'person of discerning taste.'

ANSWERS TO EXERCISE 22

1. Directive.
3. Expressive.
5. Expressive.
7. Informative.
9. Informative.
11. Directive.
13. Directive.
15. Directive.
17. Informative.
19. Expressive.

ANSWERS TO EXERCISE 23

1. Verbal.
3. Belief.
5. Belief.
7. Attitude and belief.

ANSWERS TO EXERCISE 24

1. He didn't do any good.
3. People who play golf are crazy.
5. You have not been calling out distinctly in the past.
7. No one cares.
9. She was good-looking.

ANSWERS TO EXERCISE 25

1. Accent.
3. Complex question.
5. Accent.

ANSWERS TO EXERCISE 26

  1. Some / animals / are / dangerous beings /
  3. No / cheaters / are / winners /
  5. Some / shortstops in the Brooklyn organization / are / left-handers /
  7. Some / women / are not / dependent beings /
  9. Some / students / are / industrious people /

ANSWERS TO EXERCISE 27

  1. All / traits that make men good Christians / are / traits that make them good citizens /
  3. All / people who love best all things both great and small / are / people who pray best /
  5. All / houses that shelter a friend / are / happy houses /
  7. No / things that are great / are / things that were achieved without enthusiasm /
  9. Some / fruits / are / things that ripen after picking /

ANSWERS TO EXERCISE 28

  1. All / times when the going gets tough / are / times when the tough get going /
  3. All / people who wait / are / people to whom all things come /
  5. All / people who are great / are / people who are misunderstood /
  7. All / students who hate to do homework / are / students who should do homework / AND All / students who should do homework / are / students who hate to do homework /
  9. All / young men / are / people who think old men are fools / AND All / old men / are / people who know young men are fools /
11. All / people who are not the cobbler's child / are / people who are well shod /
13. Some / TV programs / are / educational programs /
15. Some / people who bet on that game / are / people who will be disappointed /

ANSWERS TO EXERCISE 29

  1. Conditional.
  3. Strong disjunction.
  5. Disjunction.

7. Conditional.
9. Strong disjunction.

ANSWERS TO EXERCISE 30

1. $s \rightarrow q$
3. $\sim r \rightarrow \sim a$
5. $b \vee\!\!\!\vee p$
7. $p \vee\!\!\!\vee h$
9. $e \,\&\, t$

ANSWERS TO EXERCISE 31

1. b = one goes to bed early
   r = one rises early
   h = one will be healthy
   w = one will be wealthy
   i = one will be wise

   $(b \,\&\, r) \rightarrow (h \,\&\, w \,\&\, i)$

3. m = I can raise the money
   b = I'll buy the house
   r = they raise the price

   $\sim r \rightarrow (m \rightarrow b)$

5. t = the market takes a plunge
   g = interest rates go up
   s = I'll consider selling out
   i = I'll invest in treasury notes

   $\sim (t \vee g) \rightarrow \sim (s \,\&\, i)$

ANSWERS TO EXERCISE 32

1. Tautologous.
3. Synthetic.
5. Tautologous.
7. Tautologous.
9. Self-contradictory.
11. Synthetic.

13. Synthetic. At the time Henry's story was written (1906), 2 cent and 3 cent pieces were in circulation.
15. Self-contradictory.

ANSWERS TO EXERCISE 33

1.

m	e	~m	m & e	(m & e) & ~m
T	T	F	T	F
F	T	T	F	F
T	F	F	F	F
F	F	T	F	F

Self-contradictory

3.

m	e	m & e	(m & e)→m
T	T	T	T
F	T	F	T
T	F	F	T
F	F	F	T

Tautologous

5.

e	a	~e	~a	e→a	~e v ~a	(e→a) & (~e v ~a)
T	T	F	F	T	F	F
F	T	T	F	T	T	T
T	F	F	T	F	T	F
F	F	T	T	T	T	T

Synthetic

ANSWERS TO EXERCISE 34

1.

p	q	~p	p→q	~p→q	(p→q) & (~p→q)
T	T	F	T	T	T
F	T	T	T	T	T
T	F	F	F	T	F
F	F	T	T	F	F

Synthetic

3.

p	q	~p	p v q	(p v q) & ~p	[(p v q) & ~p]→q
T	T	F	T	F	T
F	T	T	T	T	T
T	F	F	T	F	T
F	F	T	F	F	T

Tautologous

5.

p	q	~q	p v ~q	p→(p v ~q)
T	T	F	T	T
F	T	F	F	T
T	F	T	T	T
F	F	T	T	T

Tautologous

ANSWERS TO EXERCISE 35

1. No athletes are rich.
3. All vegetables are nutritious.
5. All ministers are virtuous.
7. Some things that expand when heated are not metals.
9. Santa Claus does not have a white beard.

ANSWERS TO EXERCISE 36

1. He reported on time and there was a penalty.
3. Gephardt is not President and this newspaper is not wrong.
5. The gate is not up or a train is not coming.
7. Wishes are horses and beggars do not ride.
9. The Soviet Union does not walk out and the summit will be a failure.
11. Stella is not good-looking or she has a pleasant personality.
13. No space shuttles are dangerous and I have not been misinformed.

ANSWERS TO EXERCISE 37

1. No juicy things are grapes.
3. Some non-taxpayers are not non-bums.
5. All non-good drivers are non–men.

7. Some robins are birds.
9. Some non-good sports are winners.

ANSWERS TO EXERCISE 38

1. Compatible, equivalent.
3. Incompatible, non-contradictory.
5. Incompatible, non-contradictory.
7. Incompatible, contradictory.
9. Incompatible, non-contradictory.

ANSWERS TO EXERCISE 39

5.

p	~p	~(~p)
T	F	T
F	T	F

7.

p	q	p v q	q v p
T	T	T	T
F	T	T	T
T	F	T	T
F	F	F	F

9.

p	q	r	q & r	p v q	p v r	p v (q & r)	(p v q) & (p v r)
T	T	T	T	T	T	T	T
F	T	T	T	T	T	T	T
T	F	T	F	T	T	T	T
F	F	T	F	F	T	F	F
T	T	F	F	T	T	T	T
F	T	F	F	T	F	F	F
T	F	F	F	T	T	T	T
F	F	F	F	F	F	F	F

ANSWERS TO EXERCISE 40

1. Compatible, non-equivalent.
3. Incompatible, contradictory.

5. Compatible, non-equivalent.
7. Incompatible, contradictory.
9. Compatible, equivalent.

ANSWERS TO EXERCISE 41

1. Compatible, non-equivalent.
3. Incompatible, non-contradictory.
5. Incompatible, contradictory.
7. Compatible, non-equivalent.
9. Compatible, equivalent.

ANSWERS TO EXERCISE 42

1. (a) False.
   (b) True.
   (c) Unknown.
   (d) True.
   (e) True.
   (f) False.
   (g) False.

3. (a) True.
   (b) True.
   (c) Unknown.
   (d) False.
   (e) True.
   (f) True.
   (g) False.

5. (a) False.
   (b) False.
   (c) Unknown.
   (d) True.
   (e) Unknown.
   (f) Unknown.
   (g) Unknown.

ANSWERS TO EXERCISE 43

1. (a) True.
   (b) True.

(c) False.
(d) Unknown.

3. (a) True.
   (b) True.
   (c) True.
   (d) False.

5. (a) Unknown.
   (b) True.
   (c) True.
   (d) Unknown.

ANSWERS TO EXERCISE 44

1.

			Prem.	*Concl.*	
p	*q*		$p \leftrightarrow q$	$q \rightarrow p$	
T	T		T	T	√
F	T		F	F	
T	F		F	T	
F	F		T	T	√ *Valid*

3.

			Prem.	*Concl.*	
p	*q*		$\sim q$	$p \rightarrow q$	$p \vee \sim q$	
T	T		F	T	T	√
F	T		F	T	F	√ !
T	F		T	F	T	
F	F		T	T	T	√ *Invalid*

5.

			Concl.	*Prem.*	
p	*q*		$p \rightarrow q$	$\sim(p \rightarrow q)$	
T	T		T	F	
F	T		T	F	
T	F		F	T	√ !
F	F		T	F	*Invalid*

ANSWERS TO EXERCISE 45

1. Inductive.
3. Deductive.
5. Deductive.
7. Deductive.
9. Deductive.

ANSWERS TO EXERCISE 47

1. Invalid . . . 4
3. Invalid . . . 3
5. Valid.
7. Invalid . . . 3
9. Valid.

ANSWERS TO EXERCISE 48

1. Barbara, Celarent, Darii, Ferio.
3. Darapti, Disamis, Datisi, Felapton, Bocardo, Ferison.

ANSWERS TO EXERCISE 49

1. Invalid . . . 2
3. Not a syllogism.
5. Invalid . . . 3
7. Valid.
9. Invalid . . . 4
11. Valid.

ANSWERS TO EXERCISE 50

1. All times when it is cold are times when she wears her blue coat
   No times that are today are times when she wears her blue coat
∴. No times that are today are times when it is cold

   Valid

3. All people who deserve the fair are brave
   Clifford is brave
∴. Clifford is a person who deserves the fair

   Invalid: Rule #3

5. All people who laugh at that joke are morons
   All the present company are people who laugh at that joke
∴ All the present company are morons

   Valid

7. All good songs are old songs
   Some hymns are old songs
∴ Some hymns are good songs

   Invalid: Rule #3

ANSWERS TO EXERCISE 51

1. All successful men are people who give credit to their mother
   Roger is a person who gives credit to his mother
∴ Roger is a successful man

   Invalid (Rule #3)

3. All reports of miracles are reports that conflict with universal human experience
   All reports that conflict with universal human experience are reports that should be doubted
∴ All reports of miracles are reports that should be doubted

   Valid

5. All people who should take a course in logic are people who wish to improve their powers of reasoning
   All college students are people who wish to improve their powers of reasoning
∴ All college students are people who should take a course in logic

   Invalid (Rule #3)

ANSWERS TO EXERCISE 52

1. No drinkers are men in perfect condition
   Some men in perfect physical condition are athletes
∴ Some athletes are not drinkers

   Valid

3. All worldly goods are material
   All material things are changeable
∴ All changeable things are worldly goods

   Invalid (Rule #4)

5. No ambiguous arguments are reasonable
    All reasonable arguments are valid

∴ No valid arguments are ambiguous

   Invalid (Rule #4)

7. All non-dancers are non-singers
    All non-singers are actors

∴ All actors are non-dancers

   Invalid (Rule #4)

9. All writers are literate
    Some writers are not intelligent

∴ Some literate people are not intelligent

   Valid

ANSWERS TO EXERCISE 53

1. All people with red hair have a temper.
3. Some music is not noise.
5. Impossible.
7. All cedars are fragrant.
9. All cities are crowded.

ANSWERS TO EXERCISE 54

1. (1) All things that I have that are made of tin are saucepans of mine
    (3) No saucepans of mine are useful

    ∴ [No things that I have that are made of tin are useful]
    (2) All presents of yours are useful

    ∴ No presents of yours are things that I have that are made of tin

   Valid
   OR

    (2) All presents of yours are useful
    (3) No saucepans of mine are useful

    ∴ [No saucepans of mine are presents of yours]
    (1) All things that I have that are made of tin are saucepans of mine

    ∴ No presents of yours are things that I have that are made of tin

   Valid

3. (1) No articles of food allowed by my doctor are very rich
   (3) All wedding cakes are very rich
   ───
   ∴ [No wedding cakes are articles of food allowed by my doctor
   (4) All articles of food that are suitable for supper are articles of food
        allowed by my doctor
   ───
   ∴ [No wedding cakes are articles of food that are suitable for supper]
   (2) All articles of food that are suitable for supper are things that agree
        with me
   ───
   NOTHING FOLLOWS IF WE INVOKE RULE #5.

   But if we do not, we can conclude:

   Some articles of food that agree with me are not wedding cakes

   NOTE: We may also begin with (1) and (4) or with (2) and (4), but in
   both cases we encounter a link in the chain where the applicability of Rule
   #5 becomes pertinent. If we ignore the rule, the same final conclusion
   emerges.

ANSWER TO EXERCISE 55

1. (1) All interesting poems are poems popular among people of real taste
   (4) No affected poems are poems popular among people of real taste
   ───
   ∴ [No affected poems are interesting poems]
   (2) All modern poems are affected poems
   ───
   ∴ [No modern poems are interesting poems]
   (5) All poems on the subject of soap bubbles are modern poems
   ───
   ∴ [No poems on the subject of soap bubbles are interesting poems]
   (3) All poems of yours are poems on the subject of soap bubbles
   ───
   ∴ [No poems of yours are interesting poems]

   Valid (if we assume that 'modern' and 'ancient' are contradictories)

NOTE: Other sequences that validly yield the same conclusion are:

(3)	(2)	(2)	(2)	(2)	(2)
(5)	(4)	(4)	(5)	(5)	(5)
(2)	(1)	(5)	(3)	(4)	(4)
(4)	(5)	(3)	(4)	(1)	(3)
(1)	(3)	(1)	(1)	(3)	(1)

ANSWERS TO EXERCISE 56

1.

		Concl.	Prem.	Prem.
p	q		~p	~p v q
T	T		F	T
F	T		T	T
T	F		F	F
F	F		T	T

√

√ ! *Invalid*

3.

		Prem.	Concl.	Prem.
p	q		~p	~q	p→q
T	T		F	F	T
F	T		T	F	T
T	F		F	T	F
F	F		T	T	T

√ !

√ *Invalid*

5.

			Prem.	Concl.		Prem.
p	q	r		~q	p→q	(p→q) ⩔ r
T	T	T		F	T	F
F	T	T		F	T	F
T	F	T		T	F	T
F	F	T		T	T	F
T	T	F		F	T	T
F	T	F		F	T	T
T	F	F		T	F	F
F	F	F		T	T	T

√

Valid

7.

			Prem.	Prem.	Concl.
p	q	r		~p	p v q v r	q v r
T	T	T		F	T	T
F	T	T		T	T	T
T	F	T		F	T	T
F	F	T		T	T	T
T	T	F		F	T	T
F	T	F		T	T	T
T	F	F		F	T	F
F	F	F		T	F	F

√
√
√

Valid

ANSWERS TO EXERCISE 57

1. $p \vee w$
   $\dfrac{\sim p}{}$

   $\therefore$ w *Valid*

3. $\sim h \rightarrow 1$
   $\dfrac{1}{}$

   $\therefore$ $\sim h$ *Invalid*

5. $i \rightarrow h$
   $\dfrac{\sim i}{}$

   $\therefore$ $\sim h$ *Invalid*

7. g
   $\overline{}$
   $\therefore$ $b \vee g$ *Valid*

9. $\sim m \rightarrow \sim b$
   $\dfrac{\sim m}{}$

   $\therefore$ $\sim b$ *Valid*

ANSWERS TO EXERCISE 58

1. $p \rightarrow v$
   $\dfrac{\sim v}{}$

   $\therefore$ x *Invalid*

3. $s \rightarrow \sim k$
   $\dfrac{k}{}$

   $\therefore$ $\sim s$ *Valid*

5. $\sim w \rightarrow \sim h$
   $\dfrac{\sim w}{}$

   $\therefore$ x *Invalid*

7. $m \rightarrow c$

   $\therefore$ $\dfrac{c \rightarrow h}{\sim m \rightarrow \sim h}$ *Invalid*

9. $\sim s \rightarrow \sim a$
   $\dfrac{\sim a}{}$

   $\therefore$ $\sim s$ *Invalid*

ANSWERS TO EXERCISE 59

1. $g \rightarrow l$
   $\sim m \rightarrow d$
   $\underline{g \lor \sim m}$
   $\therefore \ l \lor d$

   Slip between the horns: Argue that Soviet leadership could pursue a middle course by granting some political autonomy to the nationalities while imposing a general economic plan. *Grasp the second horn:* Argue that it can refuse to make concession, but outbreaks will not continue—because repression will be strict and vigorous enough to deter them.

3. $h \rightarrow s$
   $g \rightarrow d$
   $\underline{\sim s \lor \sim d}$
   $\therefore \ \sim h \lor \sim g$

   Grasp the first horn: His failure to score was an "off-night" and did not follow from not being permitted to shoot. He was permitted to shoot and he did not score well from the field. *Grasp the second horn:* His failure to draw fouls was not caused by not being guarded closely, but by the careless work of the officials. He was guarded closely and did not draw many fouls.

5. $x \rightarrow m$
   $y \rightarrow g$
   $\underline{x \lor y}$
   $\therefore \ m \lor g$

   Slip between the horns: If you call the antecedents 'j' and '$\sim$j,' there is no way to slip between the horns. But if 'x' is taken to mean 'say what is just' and 'y' is taken to mean 'say what is unjust,' there is obviously a way to avoid both: by not saying anything at all. *Grasp the first horn:* Argue that men will not necessarily hate you. They will respect you for your honesty. *Grasp the second horn:* Argue that the gods will not hate you. They will forgive your mortal weakness.

7. $s \rightarrow l$
   $\sim s \rightarrow p$
   $\underline{s \lor \sim s}$
   $\therefore \ l \lor p$

   Since the third premise is a tautology, the only way to refute the dilemma is to *grasp a horn.* The first conditional can be challenged by arguing that a loss is not inevitable. You will make some improvements in the property and find a hot-shot real estate agent.

ANSWERS TO EXERCISE 60

1. $(t \ \& \ m) \rightarrow c$
   $\sim c$
   ∴ $\overline{\sim m \ v \sim t}$ *Valid*

3. $s \rightarrow (b \ v \ h)$
   $\sim h$
   ∴ $\sim s$ *Invalid*

5. $b \ v \ (i \ \& \ t)$
   $\sim i$
   ∴ $\sim b$ *Valid*

7. $c \ \underline{v} \ (d \ \& \ g)$
   c
   ∴ $\sim g$ *Invalid*

9. $u \rightarrow (h \ \& \ g)$
   u
   ∴ x *Invalid*

ANSWERS TO EXERCISE 61

1. $[(p \rightarrow \sim q) \ \& \ q] \rightarrow \sim p$

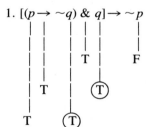

        T   (T)   *Valid*

3. $\{[(p \ \& \ q) \rightarrow r] \ \& \ q\} \rightarrow r$

        F   *Invalid*

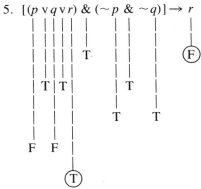

5. $[(p \lor q \lor r) \& (\sim p \& \sim q)] \to r$

         T-   ⒡

   T | T | | T

           T   T

  F F

    ⒯   *Valid*

7. $\{[(p \lor q) \to (r \& s)] \& q\} \to s$

               T | F

               ⒯

        T

              F

           F

    F

  F ⒡   *Valid*

9. $[(p \lor q \lor r) \& \quad p \& q] \to \sim r$

                | T   F

       T   T T

  T T T   *Invalid*

11. $\{[p \lor (q \& r)] \& \sim r\} \to p$

              T | F

              ⒯

   | T | | |

  F | T |

      T ⒯   *Valid*

13. $\{[(p \lor q) \veebar r] \& p\} \rightarrow \sim r$

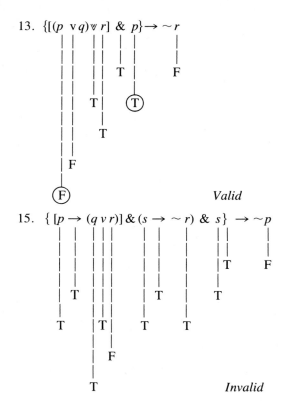

Valid

15. $\{[p \rightarrow (q \lor r)] \& (s \rightarrow \sim r) \& s\} \rightarrow \sim p$

Invalid

ANSWERS TO EXERCISE 62

1. $2/52 = .038$.
3. $18/38 = .474$ (assuming that the wheel has a zero and a double zero, both green).
5. $1/10 = .1$.
7. $1 - .677 = .323$.
9. $1/7 = .143$.

ANSWERS TO EXERCISE 63

1. $4/52 + 2/52 = 6/52 = .115$.
3. $1/2 \times 1/2 \times 1/2 = 1/8 = .125$.
5. $36/38 = .947$.
7. $1 - (3/4 \times 3/4 \times 3/4) = 1 - 27/64 = 1 - .422 = .578$.
9. $.312 + 13/242 = .312 + .054 = .366$.

ANSWERS TO EXERCISE 64

1. .25 (1 + 4) = $1.25 (expected value for every dollar bet).
3. .5 (1 + 1) = $1.00 (expected value for every dollar bet).
5. 1/6 (1 + 5) = $1.00 (expected value for every dollar bet).
7. .76 (1 + 1) = $1.52 (expected value for every dollar bet).
9. 0 × (1 + 10,000) = 0 (expected value for every dollar bet).

ANSWERS TO EXERCISE 65

1.
1. p→q	*premise*
2. p v r	*premise* /∴ ~r→q
3. r v p	*2 (Comm.)*
4. ~r→p	*3 (M.I.)*
5. ~r→q	*4, 1 (C.S.)*

3.
1. p & q	*premise*
2. p→(r v s)	*premise*
3. ~s	*premise* /∴ q & r
4. p	*1 (Simp.)*
5. r v s	*2, 4 (M.P.)*
6. r	*5, 3 (D.A.)*
7. q	*1 (Simp.)*
8. q & r	*6, 7 (C.A.)*

5.
1. p ⩛ q	*premise*
2. p	*premise* /∴ r v ~q
3. (p & ~q) v (~p & q)	*1 (S.D.)*
4. (~p & q) v (p & ~q)	*3 (Comm.)*
5. ~(~p & q)→(p & ~q)	*4 (M.I.)*
6. (p v ~q)→(p & ~q)	*5 (D.M., D.N.)*
7. p v ~q	*2 (Add.)*
8. p & ~q	*6, 7 (M.P.)*
9. ~q	*8 (Simp.)*
10. ~q v r	*9 (Add.)*
11. r v ~q	*10 (Comm.)*

7.
1. r v (w & l)	*premise*
2. r→s	*premise*
3. ~s	*premise* /∴ l
4. ~r	*2, 3 (M.T.)*
5. w & l	*1, 4 (D.A.)*
6. l	*5 (Simp.)*

9. *1.* **c v ~ i**   *premise*
    2. **~(c & ~ s)**   *premise*   /∴ i→s
    3. **~ c v s**   *2 (D.M.)*
    4. **c→s**   *3 (M.I.)*
    5. **~ i v c**   *1 (Comm.)*
    6. **i→c**   *5 (M.I.)*
    7. **i→s**   *6, 4 (C.S.)*

11. *1.* **r & g**   *premise*
    2. **~w→~r**   *premise*
    3. **w→d**   *premise* /∴ g & d
    4. **r**   *1 (Simp.)*
    5. **~~r**   *4 (D.N.)*
    6. **~~w**   *2, 5 (M.T.)*
    7. **w**   *6 (D.N.)*
    8. **d**   *3, 7 (M.P.)*
    9. **g**   *1 (Simp.)*
    10. **g & d**   *9, 8 (C.A.)*

13. *1.* **g→n**   *premise*
    2. **n→t**   *premise*
    3. **g v k**   *premise*
    4. **k→d**   *premise* /∴ ~ d→t
    5. **~d→~k**   *4 (Contrap.)*
    6. **~g→k**   *3 (M.I.)*
    7. **~k→g**   *6 (Contrap.)*
    8. **~d→g**   *5, 7 (C.S.)*
    9. **~d→n**   *8, 1 (C.S.)*
    10. **~d→t**   *9, 2 (C.S.)*

15. *1.* **s→b**   *premise*
    2. **b→~p**   *premise*
    3. **~s→e**   *premise*
    4. **e→p**   *premise* /∴ ~ s↔p
    5. **s→~p**   *1, 2 (C.S.)*
    6. **~s→p**   *3, 4 (C.S.)*
    7. **p→~s**   *5 (Contrap.)*
    8. **(~s→p) & (p→~s)**   *6, 7 (C.A.)*
    9. **~s↔p**   *8 (Bic.)*

ANSWERS TO EXERCISE 66

1.　　*1.* (a & b) v c　　　　　　*premise*　　　　　*1.∴ ~b→c*
　　　2. ⎸　~b　　　　　　　*assumption*
　　　3. ⎹　~b v ~a　　　　　*2 (Add.)*
　　　4. ⎹　~a v ~b　　　　　*3 (Comm.)*
　　　5. ⎹　~(a & b)　　　　*4 (D.M.)*
　　　6. ⎹　(a & b) v c　　　*1 (Reit.)*
　　　7. ⎹　c　　　　　　　*6, 5 (D.A.)*
　　　8. ~b→c　　　　　　*2–7 (C.P.)*

3.　　*1.* ~p v ~s　　　　　　　*premise*
　　　2. (q v t)→r　　　　　*premise*　　　*/∴ p→[q→(r & ~s)]*
　　　3. ⎸p　　　　　　　　*assumption*
　　　4. ⎹　⎸q　　　　　　*assumption*
　　　5. ⎹　⎹　(q v t)→r　　*2 (Reit.)*
　　　6. ⎹　⎹　q v t　　　　*4 (Add.)*
　　　7. ⎹　⎹　r　　　　　　*5,6 (M.P.)*
　　　8. ⎹　⎹　~p v ~s　　　*1 (Reit.)*
　　　9. ⎹　⎹　p　　　　　　*3 (Reit.)*
　　　10. ⎹　⎹　~s　　　　　*8, 9 (D.A.)*
　　　11. ⎹　⎹　r & ~s　　　*7, 10 (C.A.)*
　　　12. ⎹　q→(r & ~s)　　*4, 11 (C.P.)*
　　　13. p→[q→(r & ~s)]　*3, 12 (C.P.)*

5.　　*1.* t　　　　　　　　　*premise*　　　*/∴p→{q→[r→(s→t)]}*
　　　2. ⎸p　　　　　　　　*assumption*
　　　3. ⎹　⎸q　　　　　　*assumption*
　　　4. ⎹　⎹　⎸r　　　　*assumption*
　　　5. ⎹　⎹　⎹　⎸s　　*assumption*
　　　6. ⎹　⎹　⎹　⎹　t　*1 (Reit.)*
　　　7. ⎹　⎹　⎹　s→t　*5–6 (C.P.)*
　　　8. ⎹　⎹　r→(s→t)　*4–7 (C.P.)*
　　　9. ⎹　q→[r→(s→t)]　*3–8 (C.P.)*
　　　10. p→{q→[r→(s→t)]}　*2–9 (C.P.)*

ANSWERS TO EXERCISE 67

1.　　*1.* ⎸(p v q)→r　　　　　　　　*assumption*
　　　2. ⎹　~r→~(p v q)　　　　　*1 (Contrap.)*
　　　3. ⎹　~r→(~p & ~q)　　　　*3 (D.M.)*
　　　4. [(p v q)→r]→[~r→(~p & ~q)]　*1–3 (C.P.)*

5.	$\llcorner \sim r \rightarrow (\sim p \ \& \ \sim q)$	*assumption*
6.	$\sim(\sim p \ \& \ \sim q) \rightarrow r$	*5 (Contrap., D.N.)*
7.	$(p \lor q) \rightarrow r$	*6 (D.M., D.N.)*
8.	$[\sim r \rightarrow (\sim p \ \& \ \sim q)] \rightarrow [(p \lor q) \rightarrow r]$	*5–7 (C.P.)*
9.	$\{[(p \lor q) \rightarrow r] \rightarrow [\sim r \rightarrow (\sim p \ \& \ \sim q)]\} \ \&$ $\{[\sim r \rightarrow (\sim p \ \& \ \sim q)] \rightarrow [(p \lor q) \rightarrow r]\}$	*4, 8 (C.A.)*
10.	$[(p \lor q) \rightarrow r] \leftrightarrow [\sim r \rightarrow (\sim p \ \& \ \sim q)]$	*9 (Bic.)*

3.	**1.**	$\llcorner \sim(p \rightarrow q)$	*assumption*
	2.	$\sim(\sim p \lor q)$	*1 (M.I.)*
	3.	$\sim p \ \& \ \sim q$	*2 (D.M.)*
	4.	$p \ \& \ \sim q$	*3 (D.N.)*
	5.	$\sim(p \rightarrow q) \rightarrow (p \ \& \ \sim q)$	*1–4 (C.P.)*
	6.	$\llcorner p \ \& \ \sim q$	*assumption*
	7.	$\sim(p \ \& \ \sim q)$	*6 (D.N.)*
	8.	$\sim(\sim p \lor q)$	*7 (D.M.)*
	9.	$\sim(p \rightarrow q)$	*8 (M.I.)*
	10.	$(p \ \& \ \sim q) \rightarrow \sim(p \rightarrow q)$	*6–9 (C.P.)*
	11.	$[\sim(p \rightarrow q) \rightarrow (p \ \& \ \sim q)] \ \& \ [(p \ \& \ \sim q) \rightarrow \sim(p \rightarrow q)]$	*5, 10 (C.A.)*
	12.	$\sim(p \rightarrow q) \leftrightarrow (p \ \& \ \sim q)$	*11 (Bic.)*

5.	**1.**	$\llcorner p \ \& \ (q \ \& \ r)$	*assumption*
	2.	$q \ \& \ r$	*1 (Simp.)*
	3.	q	*2 (Simp.)*
	4.	p	*1 (Simp.)*
	5.	$p \ \& \ q$	*4, 3 (C.A.)*
	6.	r	*2 (Simp.)*
	7.	$(p \ \& \ q) \ \& \ r$	*5, 6 (C.A.)*
	8.	$[p \ \& \ (q \ \& \ r)] \rightarrow [(p \ \& \ q) \ \& \ r]$	*1, 7 (C.P.)*
	9.	$\llcorner (p \ \& \ q) \ \& \ r$	*assumption*
	10.	$p \ \& \ q$	*9 (Simp.)*
	11.	p	*10 (Simp.)*
	12.	q	*10 (Simp.)*
	13.	r	*9 (Simp.)*
	14.	$q \ \& \ r$	*12, 13 (C.A.)*
	15.	$p \ \& \ (q \ \& \ r)$	*11, 14 (C.A.)*
	16.	$[(p \ \& \ q) \ \& \ r] \rightarrow [p \ \& \ (q \ \& \ r)]$	*9, 15 (C.P.)*
	17.	$\{[p \ \& \ (q \ \& \ r)] \rightarrow [(p \ \& \ q) \ \& \ r]\} \ \&$ $\{[(p \ \& \ q) \ \& \ r] \rightarrow [p \ \& \ (q \ \& \ r)]\}$	*8, 16 (C.A.)*
	18.	$[p \ \& \ (q \ \& \ r)] \leftrightarrow [(p \ \& \ q) \ \& \ r]$	*17 (Bic.)*

ANSWERS TO EXERCISE 68

1.   *1.* p→~q   *premise*
     2. p→(p & q)   *premise*   /∴ ~p
     3. | p   *assumption*
     4. | p→~q   *1 (Reit.)*
     5. | ~q   *4, 3 (M.P.)*
     6. | p→(p & q)   *2 (Reit.)*
     7. | p & q   *6, 3 (M.P.)*
     8. | q   *7 (Simp.)*
     9. | q & ~q   *8, 5 (C.A.)*
    10. p→(q & ~q)   *3–9 (C.P.)*
    11. ~p   *10 (R.A.)*

3.   *1.* r v g   *premise*
     2. (r v i)→(p & w)   *premise*
     3. ~p   *premise*   /∴ g
     4. | ~g   *assumption*
     5. | r v g   *1 (Reit.)*
     6. | r   *5 (D.A.)*
     7. | (r v i)→(p & w)   *2 (Reit.)*
     8. | ~p   *3 (Reit.)*
     9. | ~p v ~w   *8 (Add.)*
    10. | ~(p & w)   *9 (D.M.)*
    11. | ~(r v i)   *7–10 (C.P.)*
    12. | ~r & ~i   *11 (D.M.)*
    13. | ~r   *12 (Simp.)*
    14. | r & ~r   *6, 13 (C.A.)*
    15. ~g→(r & ~r)   *4–14 (C.P.)*
    16. ~~g   *15 (R.A.)*
    17. g   *16 (D.N.)*

5.   *1.* u→w   *premise*
     2. ~u→h   *premise*
     3. ~h   *premise*   /∴ w
     4. | ~w   *assumption*
     5. | u→w   *1 (Reit.)*
     6. | ~u   *5, 4 (M.T.)*
     7. | ~u→h   *2 (Reit.)*
     8. | h   *7, 6 (M.P.)*
     9. | ~h   *3 (Reit.)*
    10. | h & ~h   *8, 9 (C.A.)*
    11. ~w→(h & ~h)   *4–10 (C.P.)*
    12. ~~w   *11 (R.A.)*
    13. w   *12 (D.N.)*

ANSWERS TO EXERCISE 69

1. (∃x)(Sx & ~Wx)
3. (∃x)[Mx & (~Lx & ~Hx)]
5. (x)~(Fx & Ix) OR ~(∃x)(Fx & Ix)
7. (∃x)(Px & Tx)→(y)(Py→Ky)
9. (x)[(Rx & Wx)→(Ux & Ix)]

ANSWERS TO EXERCISE 70

1. | | | |
   |---|---|---|
   | *1.* **(x)(Lx→Ox)** | *premise* | |
   | *2.* **(x)(Ox→Gx)** | *premise* | /∴ **(x)(~Gx→~Lx)** |
   | *3.* **La→Oa** | *1 (UI)* | |
   | *4.* **Oa→Ga** | *2 (UI)* | |
   | *5.* **La→Ga** | *3, 4 (C.S.)* | |
   | *6.* **~Ga→~La** | *5 (Contrap.)* | |
   | *7.* **(x)(~Gx→~Lx)** | *6 (UG)* | |

3. | | | |
   |---|---|---|
   | *1.* **(∃x)(Px & Wx)→(∃y)(Py & Ly)** | *premise* | |
   | *2.* **Ps & Ws** | *premise* | /∴ **~(x)(Px→~Lx)** |
   | *3.* **(∃x)(Px & Wx)** | *2 (EG)* | |
   | *4.* **(∃y)(Py & Ly)** | *1, 3 (M.P.)* | |
   | *5.* **Py & Ly** | *4 (EI)* | |
   | *6.* **~~(Py & Ly)** | *5 (D.N.)* | |
   | *7.* **~(~Py v ~Ly)** | *6 (D.M.)* | |
   | *8.* **~(Py→~Ly)** | *7 (M.I.)* | |
   | *9.* **(∃x)~(Px→~Lx)** | *8 (EG)* | |
   | *10.* **~(x)~~(Px→~Lx)** | *9 (QN)* | |
   | *11.* **~(x)(Px→~Lx)** | *10 (D.N.)* | |

5. | | | |
   |---|---|---|
   | *1.* **Hc→Cc** | *premise* | |
   | *2.* **Cc→(x)(Px→Kx)** | *premise* | |
   | *3.* **Pj & ~Kj** | *premise* | /∴ **~Hc** |
   | *4.* **~~(Pj & ~Kj)** | *3 (D.N.)* | |
   | *5.* **~(~Pj v Kj)** | *4 (D.M., D.N.)* | |
   | *6.* **~(Pj→Kj)** | *5 (M.I.)* | |
   | *7.* **(∃x)~(Px→Kx)** | *6 (EG)* | |
   | *8.* **~(x)~~(Px→Kx)** | *7 (QN)* | |
   | *9.* **~(x)(Px→Kx)** | *8 (D.N.)* | |
   | *10.* **~Cc** | *2, 9 (M.T.)* | |
   | *11.* **~Hc** | *1, 10 (M.T.)* | |

7. | | | |
   |---|---|---|
   | *1.* **(∃x)(Px & Wx)→(y)(By→Ly)** | *premise* | |
   | *2.* **(y)[(By→Ly)→(By→~Hy)]** | *premise* | ∴(∃x)(Px & Wx)→(y)(By→ ~ |

3.	$\lfloor$ ∃x(Px & Wx)	*assumption*
4.	(∃x)(Px & Wx)→(y)(By→Ly)	*1 (Reit.)*
5.	(y)(By→Ly)	*4, 3 (M.P.)*
6.	(y)[By→Ly]→(By→ ~Hy)]	*2 (Reit.)*
7.	By→Ly	*5 (U.I.)*
8.	(By→Ly)→(By→ ~Hy)	*6 (U.I)*
9.	By→ ~Hy	*8, 7 (M.P.)*
10.	(y)(By→ ~Hy)	*9 (U.G.)*
11.	(∃x)(Px & Wx)→(y)(By→ ~Hy)	*3–10 (C.P.)*

ANSWERS TO EXERCISE 71

1. Ear
3. (x)Rrx
5. (x)(y)[(Cxy & Eyx)→Pxy]
7. ~(∃x)[(y)Lxy]
9. (x)[(Sx & Mx)→ ~(∃y)Ixy]

ANSWERS TO EXERCISE 72

1. Asymmetrical, irreflexive, transitive.
3. Symmetrical, irreflexive, non-transitive.
5. Non-symmetrical, irreflexive, transitive.
7. Asymmetrical, irreflexive, intransitive.
9. Non-symmetrical, non-reflexive, non-transitive.

ANSWERS TO EXERCISE 73

1.

1. (x)(y)[(Rx & Ly)→Dxy]	*premise*	
2. Rb	*premise*	
3. La	*premise*	/∴ **Dba**
4. (y)[(Rb & Ly)→Dby]	*1 (UI)*	
5. (Rb & La)→Dba	*4 (UI)*	
6. Rb & La	*2, 3 (C.A.)*	
7. Dba	*5, 6 (M.P.)*	

3.

1. Tfd v Hfd	*premise*	
2. (x)(Txd→Sx)	*premise*	
3. ~Sf	*premise*	/∴ **Hfd**
4. Tfd→Sf	*2 (UI)*	
5. ~Tfd	*4, 3 (M.T.)*	
6. Hfd	*1, 5 (D.A.)*	

5. *1.* (x)(y)(Cxy→Sx)   *premise*
    2. (x)(y)(Oxy→Cxy)   *premise*   /∴ Obs→Sb
    3. | Obs   *assumption*
    4. | (x)(y)(Oxy→Cxy)   *2 (Reit.)*
    5. | (y)(Oby→Cby)   *4 (UI)*
    6. | Obs→Cbs   *5 (UI)*
    7. | (x)(y)(Cxy→Sx)   *1 (Reit.)*
    8. | (y)(Cby→Sb)   *7 (UI)*
    9. | Cbs→Sb   *8 (UI)*
    10. | Cbs   *6, 3 (M.P.)*
    11. | Sb   *9, 10 (M.P.)*
    12. Obs→Sb   *3–11 (C.P.)*

ANSWERS TO EXERCISE 74

1. *1.* (x)[(Fx & Lx)→Phx]   *premise*
    2. Lh   *premise*   /∴ ~Fh
    3. (x)~Pxx   *premise (the relation is irreflexive)*
    4. (Fh & Lh)→Phh   *1 (UI)*
    5. ~Phh   *3 (UI)*
    6. ~(Fh & Lh)   *4, 5 (M.T.)*
    7. ~Fh v ~Lh   *6 (D.M.)*
    8. ~Fh   *7, 2 (D.A.)*

3. *1.* (x)(Lx→Nxa)   *premise*
    2. Lc   *premise*   /∴ ~Nac
    3. (x)(y)(Nxy→~Nyx)   *premise (the relation is*
                                        asymmetrical)
    4. Lc→Nca   *1 (UI)*
    5. Nca   *1, 2 (M.P.)*
    6. (y)(Ncy→~Nyc)   *3 (UI)*
    7. Nca→~Nac   *6 (UI)*
    8. ~Nac   *7, 5 (M.P.)*

5. *1.* Gga   *premise*
    2. Gar   *premise*
    3. (x)(~Gxr→Dx)   *premise*   /∴ Dg
    4. (x)(y)(z)[(Gxy & Gys)→~Gxz] *premise (the relation is intransitive)*
    5. (y)(z)[(Ggy & Gyz)→~Ggz]   *4 (UI)*
    6. (z)[Gga & Gaz)→~Ggz]   *5 (UI)*
    7. (Gga & Gar)→~Ggr   *6 (UI)*
    8. Gga & Gar   *1, 2 (C.A.)*
    9. ~Ggr   *7, 7 (M.P.)*

| 10. ~Ggr→Dg | 3 (*UI*) |
| 11. Dg | 10, 9 (*M.P.*) |

ANSWERS TO EXERCISE 75

1. Illuminates a concept.
3. Illuminates a concept.
5. Serves as the basis of an argument.

ANSWERS TO EXERCISE 76

1. Illuminates a concept.
3. Illuminates a concept.
5. Illuminates a concept.

ANSWERS TO EXERCISE 77

1. *Question the assumed resemblances* by pointing out: Dogs are property, while humans are not; dogs are not subject to religious or moral laws; dogs do not spiritualize the sexual act as humans sometimes do; dogs are not involved in family life in the same way humans are; dogs are not accorded constitutional rights as people are; and so on. *Extend the analogy* by arguing that humans, just as dogs, should be bought and sold, should be destroyed at birth if defective, should be used as pets, and so on.

3. *Question the assumed resemblances* by pointing out: The players, unlike slaves, can resign from the system at any time; the players receive very good salaries and live very well during the season; the players, unlike slaves, are accountable to their employers in only a small part of their lives, and so on. *Extend the analogy* by arguing that: "Freed" players should seek full rights in the North (or in Liberia); emancipation can be achieved only by violence, and so on.

5. *Question the assumed resemblances* by pointing out: Animals, unlike humans, possess little if any property; animal behavior is determined by instinct, while human conduct may result from thought and deliberation; an animal species is restricted to one form of social life while many possibilities exist for human groups; humans are more predatory toward their own species than animals are, and so on. *Extend the analogy* by arguing: We will seek the same standard of life as the animals, namely, bare subsistence; we will not educate our offspring in any formal or institutional way; since animals' "socialism" does not require a political framework, neither will humans'.

ANSWERS TO EXERCISE 78

1. All primates subsist largely on fruit and vegetables.
3. All groups of individuals related by blood or interest should have elected rulers.
5. All Cole Porter songs have clever lyrics.

ANSWERS TO EXERCISE 79

1. (a) Strengthens . . . #2
   (b) Weakens . . . #1
   (c) Strengthens . . . #4
   (d) Strengthens . . . #3
3. (a) Weakens . . . #1
   (b) Strengthens . . . #2 and #3
   (c) Weakens . . . #1
   (d) Strengthens . . . #1

ANSWERS TO EXERCISE 80

1. (a) Huey quacks.
   (b) Most ducks quack.
3. (a) 60 percent of all Cuyahoga County high school graduates go on to college.
   (b) A majority of all Ohio county high school graduates go on to college.
5. (a) No Asian camels have two humps.
   (b) Most camels do not have two humps.

ANSWERS TO EXERCISE 81

1. C
3. A
5. B or D

ANSWERS TO EXERCISE 82

1. These professors are active professionally and can afford to go to meetings. It may be the case that these qualities are more associated with those who possess a doctorate than with those who do not.
3. These drivers, who work in a fashionable area of London, one frequented by tourists and shoppers, could be expected to be more favorable to royalty

and aristocracy in general than those who operate in less pretentious areas. Their livelihood depends in part on the preservation of the old society and its symbols.
5. These women would be older, more settled, and more conservative than most California women, all qualities that might affect their views on trial marriage.

ANSWERS TO EXERCISE 83

1. Students from private and public institutions.
   Students from all geographic areas.
   Students with various religious preferences.
3. Male and female students.
   Students with various majors.
   Students from each of the courses taught by Mr. Pelf.
5. Poems from different periods of time.
   Poems of various poetic forms.
   Poems written by major and minor poets.

ANSWERS TO EXERCISE 84

1. There is a Disney "formula" which, when carried out in a movie, causes enjoyment for a great many movie goers.
3. Drunkenness causes lack of control and poor judgment on the part of drivers.
5. The genes that produce red hair also cause, or are associated with, genes that cause violent tempers.
7. Among the causes for the development of a great city is location on a waterway.
9. Being left-handed causes bowlers to have an advantage on many lanes—perhaps because the side they come in from is less worn.

ANSWERS TO EXERCISE 85

1. Sufficient.
3. Necessary.
5. Sufficient.
7. Necessary.
9. Necessary.

NOTE: Many of these are debatable.

ANSWERS TO EXERCISE 86

1. Is contributing to the shrine the only factor the three safe trips have in common? If not, then it need not be the cause or a part of the cause.
3. Since these three cases are so diverse (and thus unlikely to have another factor in common), this is a convincing use of the Method of Agreement.
5. This is a convincing argument, but other factors which the instances may have had in common should not be overlooked: proper rest and same subject matter. Studying may be an important element in the cause of the student's success, but there are probably other elements at work as well.

ANSWERS TO EXERCISE 87

1. The brand of paint was not the only difference. Another obvious difference, which the commissioners overlooked, was that traffic near Wilma's was much heavier than near the library.
3. There are surely other differences. The weather? The skill of the pilots? The conditions of the airplanes?
5. There *must* be another difference! Perhaps one plant had a disease not discernible two weeks ago. Perhaps one plant was from better stock.
7. This is, as it stands, a poor use of the Method of Difference. Only if it could be shown that the decision to indict was the only difference in the United States' bargaining stance could the argument have any force. It is quite possible that the decision was a causal factor, but much more evidence is required to make it plausible.

ANSWERS TO EXERCISE 88

1. The increase in crime in past years may have caused an increase in the amount of money appropriated to combat it. The city may be confusing the effect with the cause. In any case, further study would probably disclose *other things* covarying with the crime statistics.
3. This is quite convincing.

ANSWERS TO EXERCISE 89

1. I would use the method of agreement in order to discover whether there was one factor which preceded all my headaches. I would then test this factor by means of the method of difference or the method of covariation.
3. I would use the methods of difference and covariation, taking every precaution to ensure that the smoking of marijuana is the only difference. In the case of

one individual, such factors as these would be kept the same from one sexual performance to another: time elapsed since previous sexual experience, the kind and degree of sexual stimulation, and intake of food and alcohol. If two groups are tested, one receiving marijuana and the other not, both groups should be of same age and background, similar interest in sex, and subjected to the same conditions.

5. The method of difference would yield good results here. Care would have to be taken that the induced weightlessness was indeed the only difference in the condition of the person or persons tested. An individual might have strange experiences simply because he knows he is being tested or because he *thinks* he is weightless.

ANSWERS TO EXERCISE 90

1. Herbert has been jilted by Helen.
3. Giles is in prison.
5. The crew found an island paradise and abandoned ship.

ANSWERS TO EXERCISE 92

1. Look for pieces of abandoned railway ties—and expect to find them. AA: Interurban lines were constructed on railway ties.
3. Check the surviving documents of the Gestapo—and expect to find some mention of Helmut. AA: The names of all Gestapo agents appear somewhere in the records of the Third Reich.
5. Find out whether Jones is at home or at school or on the golf course—and expect to find that he is at none of these places. AA: People who are interviewed for important jobs are willing to alter their normal routines.

ANSWERS TO EXERCISE 93

1. False.
3. False.
5. True.
7. False.
9. True.

ANSWERS TO EXERCISE 94

1. C
3. A

5. A
7. C (or B)
9. B
11. A

ANSWER TO EXERCISE 95

1. Hypothesis: I have anemia.
   Test: Schedule a laboratory blood test.
   Prediction: Deficiency of red blood cells.
2. Hypothesis: I have spring fever.
   Test: Engage in many vigorous outdoor activities.
   Prediction: Symptoms will disappear in a few days.
3. Hypothesis: I am in love with a person who hardly knows me.
   Test: Try to get better acquainted with this person.
   Prediction: Symptoms will disappear in a few weeks—although I may be angry or miserable instead of listless.

NOTE: There are many other possible hypotheses.

ANSWERS TO EXERCISE 96

1. Argumentum ad hominem.
3. Appeal to hope.
5. Argumentum ad ignorantiam.
7. Argumentum ad verecundiam.
9. Appeal to flattery.

ANSWERS TO EXERCISE 97

1. Appeal to fear.
3. Argumentum ad hominem.
5. Argumentum ad baculum.
7. Appeal to hope.
9. Argumentum ad hominem.

ANSWERS TO EXERCISE 98

1. Argumentum ad misericordiam.
3. Appeal to hope.
5. Appeal to fear.

7. Appeal to hope and to flattery.
9. Appeal to hope.

ANSWERS TO EXERCISE 99

1. Ad verecundiam. Miss Shapely is not a legitimate authority on reducing pills, so her testimonial is irrelevant and should be ignored.
3. Ad hominem. Her own marital experiences are irrelevant to the quality of her advice. The advice should be evaluated on its own merits.
5. Appeal to hope. The extravagant claims are not documented in any way. The consumer is moved to try the cream simply on the *chance* that it may be somewhat effective.

ANSWERS TO EXERCISE 100

1. Ad populum. That many people engage in this kind of worship (or any other) does not mean that it is rewarding. People may worship in order to avoid being thought eccentric—or in order to be thought eccentric. Others may be seeking an elusive peace of mind. Others may be motivated by fear. And some may just be taking up a fad.
3. Appeal to flattery. The reader is expected to identify herself with these stimulating women. Since the pantyhose are suitable for such women, they will be suitable for her also.
5. Ad baculum. The threat has nothing to do with the soundness of the teacher's interpretation. The student may, as an act of prudence, restate the teacher's interpretation on the next exam, but no reason has been presented to believe that the interpretation is sound.
7. Appeal to flattery. The reader is flattered for his supposedly high standards, but no evidence is provided that the scotch will meet these standards.

ANSWERS TO EXERCISE 101

1. Appeal to hope. This appeal exploits those people (especially the young) who have dreams of success in the world of music and are willing to .pay money to indulge in their hope. In their emotional state they will not rationally evaluate the claims of the company that holds out the hope to them.
3. Appeal to authority (tradition). There is not one shred of evidence that Washington ever did this. That a story has been repeated for generations (like the one about the cherry tree) simply means that it is ''well-known''; it does not mean that the events it relates are ''facts.''

5. Appeal to humor. Amused by the thought of drinking shampoo, we are expected to be receptive to the brand offered and buy it uncritically.

ANSWERS TO EXERCISE 102

1. Appeal to indignation. The discrepancy between the ability to pay and the high fees demanded by doctors is used to persuade us to embrace socialized medicine without a careful examination of the problem. Caught in the grip of the emotion of indignation, we are expected to hastily accept what may be an oversimplification.
3. Appeal to hate. Hating the Japanese and their allies so deeply, Americans will not need any additional reasons for immediately committing themselves to declaring an all-out war against Japan or Germany.
5. Appeal to fear. Roosevelt paints a horrible picture of people on relief in order to get Congressional approval of alternative ways of dealing with the problem of need. His strategy is to oversimplify: Choose either destructive relief programs or *my* program.

ANSWERS TO EXERCISE 103

1. Appeal to hate and indignation. This view of Italy's (dastardly) attack on France will inflame Americans' emotions against the Axis powers and deflect criticism of Roosevelt's program of assistance for the western democracies.
3. Appeal to humor (ridicule). Phocion distracts Demosthenes from his attack by turning the tables. If Demosthenes now begins to defend himself instead of pressing his attack on Phocion, Phocion has succeeded.
5. Appeal to humor. The speaker appears to agree with his opponent about ethnic jokes being in poor taste, but he tells one that is so funny that he believes that the question of its poor taste will be overlooked.
7. Ad hominem. Instead of answering the auditor's charges, Ms. Boykins attacks the motives of the auditor and her party. The motives are irrelevant. The auditor's criticisms were substantiated. Ms. Boykins should accept them or refute them—instead of accusing the Republicans of committing the ad hominem fallacy.

ANSWER TO EXERCISE 104

The answer might take some such a form as this:

1.

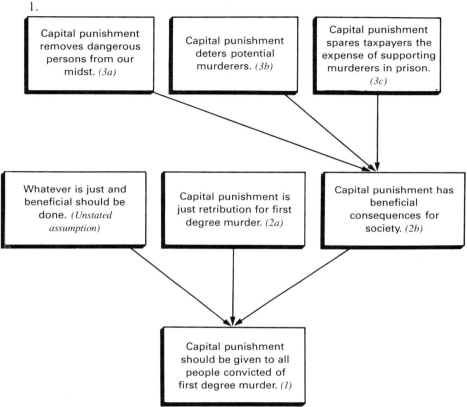

This is a straightforward and plausible argument. An assumption is needed, however, to derive the final conclusion: Whatever is just and beneficial should be done. The subconclusion 2*b* does follow from premises 3*a*, 3*b*, 3*c*, but it is one-sided, ignoring the possible unfavorable consequences of capital punishment. The weakest part of the argument lies in its premises. Are they true? 2*a* could be challenged by asking whether retribution *ever* is just, and whether capital punishment is appropriate for murder. 3*a* could be challenged by asking whether judicial errors might cause undangerous (or innocent) people to be removed; moreover life imprisonment with no parole would remove persons just as effectively. 3*b* could be challenged by asking for evidence that capital punishment does indeed deter. 3*c* could be challenged by showing the great expense incurred in appeal procedures and actual executions. In short, because of the dubious premises, the argument is quite weak, despite its formal validity.

ANSWER TO EXERCISE 106

It is impossible to anticipate all the approaches to any one of these theses.

ANSWERS TO EXERCISE 107

1. A book on American history will provide the information needed for a quick solution to this problem. So will an almanac, encyclopedia, or Hayes biography.
3. Newspapers and sports magazines will provide the data needed to solve this problem: the regulations for participating in the playoffs, the standings of the teams when the season was 75 percent completed, and the remaining schedule. This will be an exercise in deductive logic.
5. Here, the individual will formulate hypotheses and seek confirmation and disconfirmation.

ANSWERS TO EXERCISE 108

1. The survivors will not be buried anywhere, for they are not dead.
3.
1. The women's last names are Marshall, Price, Torrey, and Winters	/premise
2. Each woman performs two errands	/premise
3. One woman visited the hardware store	/premise
4. Two women visited the bank	/premise
5. Two women visited the butcher shop	/premise
6. Three women visited the grocery store	/premise
7. Doris did not visit the grocery store	/premise
8. Ethel and Mrs. Winters visited the butcher shop	/premise
9. Margaret visited the bank	/premise
10. Mrs. Price did not go to any place that Lucille or Mrs. Torrey visited	/premise
11. Mrs. Price is not Lucille	/from #10
12. Mrs. Torrey is not Lucille	/from #10
13. Mrs. Price did not visit the grocery store	/from #10, #6
14. Lucille visited the grocery store	/from #11, #13, #6
15. Mrs. Marshall visited the grocery store	/from #6, #13
16. Mrs. Torrey visited the grocery store	/from #6, #13
17. Mrs. Winters visited the grocery store	/from #6, #13
18. Mrs. Winters is not Ethel	/from #8
19. Mrs. Price is Doris	/from #13, #7, #6
20. Doris Price did not visit the butcher shop	/from #19, #5, #8
21. Doris Price visited the hardware store and the bank	/from #1–#6, #13, #20

22.	Mrs. Torrey did not visit the bank	/from #21, #10
23.	Mrs. Torrey did not visit the hardware store	/from #3, #21
24.	Mrs. Torrey visited the butcher shop	/from #22, #23
25.	Mrs. Torrey is Ethel	/from #8, #24
26.	Mrs. Winters did not visit the bank	/from #8, #17
27.	Mrs. Marshall visited the bank	/from #26, #22
28.	Mrs. Marshall is Margaret	/from #9, #21, #27
29.	Mrs. Winters is Lucille	/from #19, #25, #28
30.	Lucille Winters visited the butcher shop	/from #8, #29

Summary: Margaret Marshall visited the grocery store (#17, #28) and the bank (#27, #28). Ethel Torrey visited the grocery store (#16, #25) and the butcher shop (#24, #25). Lucille Winters visited the grocery store (#17, #29) and the butcher shop (#30). Doris Price visited the hardware store (#21) and the bank (#21).

5.

1.	There are three sons at three different universities	/premise
2.	Each son is majoring in a different subject	/premise
3.	William is not at Yale	/premise
4.	Wilbur is not at Harvard	/premise
5.	The son at Yale is not studying philosophy	/premise
6.	The son at Harvard is studying physics	/premise
7.	Wilbur is not studying physiology	/premise
8.	One son is named Willis	/premise
9.	One son attends Princeton	/premise
10.	The three sons are William, Wilbur, and Willis	/from #3, #4, #8
11.	The three universities are Yale, Harvard, and Princeton	/from #5, #6, #9
12.	The three subjects are philosophy, physics, and physiology	/from #5, #6, #7
13.	The son at Yale is not studying physics	/from #6
14.	The son at Yale is studying physiology	/from #5, #11, #12, #13
15.	Wilbur is not at Yale	/from #14, #7
16.	Willis is at Yale	/from #10, #3, #15
17.	Philosophy is being studied at Princeton	/from #6, #11, #12, #14
18.	Wilbur is not at Yale	/from #16
19.	Wilbur is at Princeton	/from #4, #18
20.	Wilbur is studying philosophy	/from #17, #19
21.	William is not at Princeton	/from #19
22.	William is at Harvard	/from #3, #21
23.	William is studying physics	/from #6, #22

Summary: William studies physics at Harvard (#22, #23). Wilbur studies philosophy at Princeton (#19, #20). Willis studies physiology at Yale (#14, #16).

7. 27. The first sequence consists of doubling the preceding number: 2 is twice 1; 4 is twice 2; 8 is twice 4. Then the series reverts to 1, which begins a new sequence. Each number is tripled: 3 is thrice 1; 9 is thrice 3. The next number should be thrice 9: 27.

9.

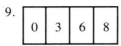

| 0 | 3 | 6 | 8 |

A field goal was scored in the second quarter, a touchdown in the third, and a touchdown with a two-point conversion in the fourth.

ANSWERS TO EXERCISE 109

The answers will vary with the individual, so the following answers are only examples and are not exhaustive:

1. Its price, the availability of other transportation, condition of savings, income, financial obligations, condition of present car (if any), overall transportation needs, and so on.
3. Conditions for study, opportunities for enhanced social life, nearness to library and classroom buildings, relative expense, maturity of self and dormmates, and so on.
5. The agencies that the fund supports, the amount that is taken out for administration, the possibility of other charities with greater need, my financial situation, and so on.

ANSWERS TO EXERCISE 110

Many answers, of course, are possible here. One conflict in each case will be cited.

1. Greater mobility versus savings that will barely pay for educational expenses.
3. Desire to meet and interact with members of opposite sex versus the need to study hard and long hours.
5. Concern for the Girl Scout movement versus concern for research for muscular dystrophy.

ANSWER TO EXERCISE 111

There are many possible decisions here and many ways to criticize them.

ANSWER TO EXERCISE 112

There are many possible decisions here and many ways to defend them.

ANSWERS TO EXERCISE 114

1. All A are H $\qquad$ No H are $\overline{A}$

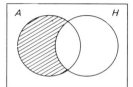 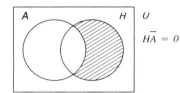

Compatible, non-equivalent

3. Some P are not R $\qquad$ Some $\overline{R}$ are not $\overline{P}$

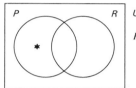 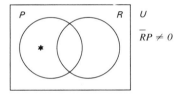

Compatible, equivalent

5. P is an S $\qquad$ P is not an S

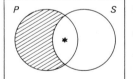 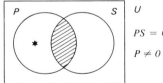

Incompatible, non-contradictory

NOTE: If we assume that it is true that there is one and only one President of the United States, then the statements are incompatible and contradictory (since they cannot both be false).

ANSWERS TO EXERCISE 115

1. All D are T   No D are T

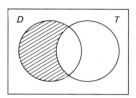   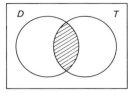

Compatible, non-equivalent

NOTE: If we assume that devils exist, the statements cannot both be true. They would be incompatible and non-contradictory.

3. All C are F   Some C are F

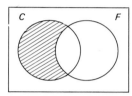   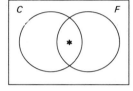

Compatible, non-equivalent

5. All Z are M   No M are Z

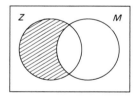   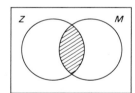

Compatible, non-equivalent

NOTE: If we assume that zebras exist, the statements cannot both be true. They would be incompatible and non-contradictory.

ANSWERS TO EXERCISE 116

1. No S are C $\quad\overline{SC} = 0$
   No P are S $\quad P\overline{S} = 0$
   All P are C

   The conclusion, $P\overline{C} = 0$, cannot be read from the diagram, so the syllogism is *invalid*.

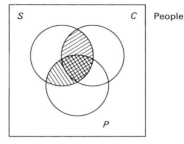

3. No A are L $\quad\overline{AL} = 0$
   All T are A $\quad T\overline{A} = 0$
   No T are L

   The conclusion, $\overline{TL} = 0$, can be read from the diagram, so the syllogism is *valid*.

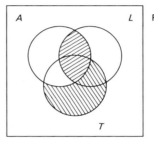

5. All E are P $\quad E\overline{P} = 0$
   Some N are not P $\quad N\overline{P} \neq 0$
   Some N are not E

   The conclusion, $N\overline{E} \neq 0$, can be read from the diagram, so the syllogism is *valid*.

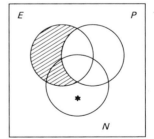

ANSWERS TO EXERCISE 117

1. All P are M $\quad P\overline{M} = 0$
   All A are P $\quad A\overline{P} = 0, A \neq 0$
   Some A are M

   The conclusion, $AM \neq 0$, can be read from the diagram, so the syllogism is *valid*.

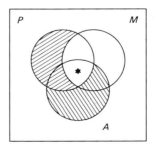

3. All P are M $P\overline{M} = 0$
   All D are M $D\overline{M} = 0,\ D \neq 0$
   Some D are P

   The conclusion, $DP \neq 0$,
   cannot be read from the
   diagram, so the syllogism
   is *invalid*.

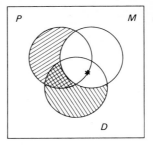

Animals

5. All A are C $A\overline{C} = 0$
   All C are W $C\overline{W} = 0$
   All W are A

   The conclusion, $W\overline{A} = 0$,
   cannot be read from the
   diagram, so the syllogism
   is *invalid*.

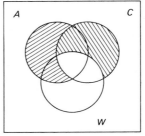

Things

Index

Q

R